D0710751

BURNING DOWN THE HOUSE

W·W·NORTON & COMPANY

NEW YORK   LONDON

BURNING DOWN THE HOUSE

MOVE and the Tragedy of Philadelphia

**JOHN ANDERSON
and HILARY HEVENOR**

Published simultaneously in Canada by Penguin Books Canada Ltd.,
2801 John Street, Markham, Ontario L3R 1B4
Printed in the United States of America.

The text of this book is composed in Avanta, with display type set in Helvetica
Compressed. Composition and manufacturing by the Haddon Craftsmen, Inc.
Book design by Jacques Chazaud

First Edition

Library of Congress Cataloging-in-Publication Data

Anderson, John, 1954 Mar. 27–
    Burning down the house.

    Includes index.
    1. MOVE (Organization) 2. Black nationalism—
Pennsylvania—Philadelphia. 3. Afro-Americans—
Pennsylvania—Philadelphia. 4. Philadelphia (Pa.)—
Race relations. 5. Public relations—Pennsylvania—
Police. I. Hevenor, Hilary, 1957–   . II. Title.
F158.9.N4A53 1987   974.8′11043   87-5482

ISBN 0-393-02460-1

W. W. Norton & Company, Inc., 500 Fifth Avenue, New York, N. Y. 10110
W. W. Norton & Company Ltd., 37 Great Russell Street, London WC1B 3NU

1 2 3 4 5 6 7 8 9 0

For our families

Contents

Part II

Preface

This book began with the shared horror of Monday, May 13, 1985, when we, like so many Philadelphians, sat transfixed before a television set and watched the events at the MOVE house on Osage Avenue unfold before our eyes. By early evening, we knew that a tragedy had taken place and that we had in some very real sense participated in it.

Was what had happened in Philadelphia merely a quirk of that city? Or was it metaphor for something else? Might it not have been, in the fullest sense of the words, an American Tragedy?

We knew that what we had witnessed was part of a great story, a story that touched on questions of terrorism, of police brutality, of political chicanery, of race and the meaning of being black in America, of the frightful realities of "management decision-making" when applied to the governing of our cities.

When, in the fall of 1985, the Philadelphia Special Investigation Commission, the so-called "MOVE Commission," began its daily, public hearings, we were there as we were every day to hear every witness until the last pounding of the gavel.

In the winter of 1985, our life revolved around libraries and microfilm readers. Newspaper accounts from the early 1970s on had to be read, copied, and filed. The history of MOVE had to be learned by heart, until it had become ingrained. No aspect of MOVE's story was too small to be left unstudied. In the process, we learned more than a little about Philadelphia itself.

With the new year came the trial of Ramona Africa, the only adult MOVE member to survive the May conflagration. Again, we were present every day for over a month, this time in Room 253 of City Hall, from *voir dire* (the selection of jurors) until the verdict was announced in February. Months later, we returned to the same place for sentencing.

The late winter was spent reading through the thousands of pages of transcripts from that trial. There was yet more reading to do though, reading that would inform the whole of this book. Beginning in the fall and continuing over a period of months, we pored through the thousands upon thousands of pages of unpublished documents gathered by the MOVE Commission.

The MOVE Commission files were invaluable; they formed the backbone of this book. They consist of the hundreds of original interviews conducted by Philadelphia homicide detectives in the days following May 13, frequently cursory, but not unrevealing; the critical, detailed interviews (the so-called "302s") carried out by MOVE Commission investigators in the late summer of 1985; the various fire marshals' reports; the transcripts of the MOVE Commission hearings; internal MOVE Commission position papers (summaries such as "The Alley," "A Team," "B Team," and the like); and a wealth of related documents, including copies of Detective William Stephenson's log of May 13, arrest warrants for Frank James Africa and others, a carbon copy of an application for the storage of explosives (including the military explosive C-4) signed for by Lt. Frank Powell, the man who dropped the bomb from the helicopter. There were photographs, diagrams, maps, and sections of the relevant law codes.

Finally, and above all, there were the interviews, the conflicting, damning, damnable interviews in the written and transcribed words of the participants. The whole, bitter history of MOVE was alive in every interview. No writer could have had a better source about what happened on May 13, 1985.

Burning Down the House is neither an apology for MOVE, nor an apology for Philadelphia politicians or for Philadelphia policemen. On this score we have been adamant from beginning to end. Our only prejudice, if that is the word for it, is for the victims and the innocents, for MOVE's children and for its neighbors.

Acknowledgments

In the course of researching and writing this book the authors have received timely, thoughtful, and generous assistance from many quarters.

Our families, as always, have supported us in ways too numerous to elaborate. We can only express our thanks and our love to each and all.

Friends at the University of Pennsylvania helped in various kind ways. To David J. DeLaura, Chairman of the University of Pennsylvania English Department, who arranged leave time, we owe heartfelt thanks for long years of support.

Peshe Kuriloff and Neal Hébert of the Writing Across the University Program provided the word processing facilities and a congenial atmosphere for the writing the book. To them and to the faculty and staff of the department of english at the University of Pennsylvania, we say thank you.

The authors wish also to acknowledge a generous grant from the University of Pennsylvania Research Foundation which did much to facilitate the preparation of this book.

Three principals in the trial of Ramona Johnson Africa—Daniel Stevenson of the Philadelphia Public Defender's Association, former Assistant District Attorney Joseph J. McGill, and the Hon. Michael R. Stiles of the Common Pleas Court of Pennsylvania—gave generously of their time in granting us many a long interview in the course of their very busy schedules.

Two transplanted Philadelphia newsmen, F. Gillman Spencer and

Michael Pakenham, both of the New York *Daily News,* provided us with a wealth of good stories and background information.

Donald R. Cutler of the Sterling Lord Agency and his assistant Ruthanne Sutor have been angels. Don, in particular, was the source of much wise advice and counsel; and it was always comforting to know that we were in such good hands.

Our friends Charity Hume and Christopher Lewis first introduced us to Donald Cutler, and they have been both strong allies and good counselors.

Finally, we should like to thank the staff at W.W. Norton & Company. Donald Lamm, James Mairs, and Ed Barber lent their support to this project at a very early date. For that act of faith, we shall always be grateful. Our copy editor, Jeremy Townsend, has done yeoman work with intelligence and grace. Dean Siegel and Amy Silin helped in many and sundry ways in the latter stages of our work, and we thank them both.

Above all, though, our thanks are owed to James Mairs, our editor extraordinaire. At once wise and supportive beyond measure, he has driven us always to do our best. In doing so, Jim has been everything a writer could want in an editor—and more.

Philadelphia, Pennsylvania
February 26, 1987

Introduction

On May 13, 1985, a bomb containing as much as three and a half pounds of a high-grade military explosive was dropped from a state police helicopter onto the roof of a row house in a middle-class black residential neighborhood of Philadelphia. The house itself was heavily fortified: its windows barred and covered with wooden slats, its doors barricaded, the interiors reinforced by movable, fortress-like devices made of railroad beams and mortar. On the rooftop of the house were two "bunkers," one at the front overlooking a narrow, tree-lined street and one at the rear overlooking a much narrower alleyway. The bunkers were made of plywood and reinforced with sheetmetal and heavy wooden beams. Steel plates with holes bored into the steel covered the windows of the bunkers. These were the "shooting holes," large enough to accommodate the bores of rifles and shotguns. Drums of gasoline, clearly marked, clearly visible, stood near the bunkers even as the bomb fell.

Thirteen people were inside that house, six of them children. They were members of MOVE—followers of an enigmatic black man who called himself John Africa—and their children. There were arrest warrants for some of the adults and a search warrant for the house. The children were to be placed in "protective custody."

Outside the house, on nearby rooftops and inside other houses—"fire posts," the commissioner of police called them—stood or else squatted a hundred or so heavily armed, flak-jacketed Philadelphia cops. For most of a long night and a longer day they had exchanged gunfire with the people inside the fortified house at 6221 Osage Avenue. They had been treated, via a loudspeaker, to bloodcurdling accounts of what John Africa and MOVE would do to them, how they would choke in their own blood, how their widows and children would use their life insurance policies, how their women would be in bed with other men even before the dead husbands were safely in the grave. Now, with the dropping of the bomb, some of the police were laughing. "That's the last time they'll call the [police] commissioner a motherfucker," one of them said. The men he was with laughed heartily.

The bomb that fell from the helicopter exploded with devastating impact. A large bright ball of orange fire rose from the bomb's point of impact and began to spread.

The mayor told his managing director, a retired army general, to put out the fire. The managing director has testified that he told the police commissioner to put the fire out. The fire commissioner and the police commissioner discussed the situation among themselves. They decided to let the bunker burn.

Giant "squrt" guns manned by waiting firemen were turned on and off. Mostly, the squrts stayed off. The bunker continued to burn. The flames spread further. Neighboring houses began to catch fire.

Back in the alley, MOVE's children began coming out of the fiery house at 6221. "Here come the kids! Here come the kids!" the children shouted as they were told to by the adults. "They're coming out, they're coming out!" the police walky-talkies crackled. There was gunfire, and the children retreated back into the house or were shot down in the alley. The fire continued to spread into the humid spring night.

When counting time came, eleven people—five of them children—were found dead in that house, two hundred fifty-three people were homeless, and sixty-one houses were no more.

A woman and a child survived the holocaust. The woman, Ramona Johnson Africa, belonged to MOVE and would one day be tried and convicted for her part in the May 13 confrontation. The child, a boy of thirteen known then as Birdie Africa, escaped the flames that took his mother's life. She had kept her faith in John Africa and perished in the fire.

Today, Birdie's father, a retired Airman long separated from the mother, has custody of the boy, now known as Michael Moses Ward. His son, Andino Ward says, is still haunted by nightmares. In Michael's dreams, the two of them, father and son, run into the burning MOVE house only to discover that it is full of monsters. In another of the nightmares, Michael finds that the whole world is on fire.

This is a story as simple and as complicated as hatred. It is a story of the atrocities of war with none of war's heroics. It is a story of fools and knaves—and of innocent children who suffered and died that the will of adults might be acted out.

It is a bad story.

PART I

It's just incredible. It just does not explain. Or perhaps that's it: they don't explain and we are not supposed to know. . . . You re-read, tedious and intent, poring, making sure that you have forgotten nothing, made no miscalculation; you bring them together again and again nothing happens: just the words, the symbols, the shapes themselves, shadowy inscrutable and serene, against that turgid background of a horrible and bloody mischancing of human affairs.

—WILLIAM FAULKNER, *Absalom, Absalom!*

1

John Africa's Revolution

It was 1931. Herbert Hoover was president, and America was fighting its way out of a depression. The place was West Philadelphia, where the people were mostly black and where the Depression had hit hard.

The date was July 26, and the occasion was the birth of a baby boy at the old Philadelphia General Hospital, the city's charity hospital. The baby's name, Vincent Lopez Leaphart.

"Long live John Africa!" MOVE's accolytes would one day shout at the very sight of Vince Leaphart. But that lay far ahead in the hazy future.

Vincent Leaphart grew up in a West Philadelphia neighborhood called Mantua, close to the Philadelphia Zoo. The neighborhood was and still is mostly black.

At home in Mantua, Vince's mother Lennie May had her hands full raising ten children. Vince's father, Frederick Leaphart, eked out a modest living for the family as a local handyman. They had both immigrated from the South and were Baptists, and the children were raised in that faith.

Little is known about the early life of Vincent Leaphart. His schooling was meagre, and he was considered a "slow learner." At age seven, he was given an IQ test at school; his score a paltry 84. Aged nine, he was classified as being "orthogenetically backward"—mildly retarded; aged fifteen, his IQ stood at 79 and he was transferred to a school for students with learning disabilities. At age sixteen, Vince dropped out of school for good. A year later, he was arrested for armed holdup and for automobile theft. (The disposition of the case is unclear, for the court records no longer exist.)*

Drafted in 1952, Vince Leaphart served two years in the army, including a year at the Korean front. Home again, he began dating a young neighborhood girl, Dorothy Clark, in October of 1954. Leaphart listed his occupation as that of "interior designer." He helped arrange shop displays.

Vincent and Dorothy were married on March 12, 1961, in the home of a local minister. Almost from the start, there were more than the usual tensions in the marriage. Dorothy discovered that she was unable to conceive, and this seems to have figured prominently in the domestic travails of the young couple. Leaphart, meanwhile, began commuting between the Chelsea section of New York, where he was said to have studied "interior design," and their home in West Philadelphia.

In 1965, Dorothy joined the Kingdom of Yahweh, a religious sect whose members were required to maintain a vegetarian diet. The Kingdom's dietary rules were strict; she and her fellow sectarians, she said, were following the "principles of natural law."

Without accepting Dorothy's religion, Vince Leaphart was nevertheless absorbing its language. At the time, he told Dorothy that he neither understood her dietary regimen nor the principles behind it. Later, in the guise of John Africa, he would adopt both the regimen and some of the rhetoric of the Kingdom of Yahweh.

Early in 1966, at a time when the the couple was living in a second floor apartment at Fifty-fifth and Walnut Streets in West Philadelphia, Dorothy brought charges against Vince. She told a magistrate that her husband had struck her. The case was eventually dismissed.

In 1967, Vincent and Dorothy Leaphart separated.

Sometime around 1971, Leaphart moved into the Powelton Village section of West Philadelphia. Powelton, which borders Mantua on one side and the Drexel University campus on the other, was in those days a haven for what were then considered "free-thinkers": drop-outs, drug experimenters, and sixties-style radicals. Powelton Village encompassed a varied lot, including undergraduates, graduate students, and faculty from the nearby universities—the Ivy League's University of Pennsylvania and the technically oriented Drexel University.

In this hodgepodge of blacks and whites, students and professors, gays and straights, hippies and young professionals, Leaphart, made his living in carpentry and repairs—a "handyman," as his father had once been—

*Craig R. McCoy's article in the Philadelphia *Inquirer Sunday Magazine,* entitled "Who Was John Africa," was one source of information concerning Vincent Leaphart's childhood.

or else walking dogs for hire. He was said to have a wonderful feel for animals.

In the laid-back and radical milieu of Powelton Village, there would always be plenty of talk and plenty of talkers, the common language idealistic to the point of being fantastic. Vince Leaphart excelled both at talking and at spinning fantastic webs of "philosophy." In no time at all, he found himself with an audience, at first composed of interested listeners, then of followers.

One former disciple in those early days in Powelton says of Leaphart, "He talked to people who were reading all kinds of books, people who had Ph.D.'s and radical ideas. He picked their brains. That's how he did it, because he could barely read or write. When he put their ideas into his own language, it was very poetic. That was what attracted a lot of people. He sounded so good."

One of the Villagers who was attracted to Leaphart was Donald Glassey, then in his early twenties, his recent master's degree earned at the School of Social Work at Penn. The idealistic child of middle-class white parents, Glassey was ripe for an alliance with this friendly, older, uneducated black man, who like Glassey was interested in discussing "philosophy." The two quickly became close friends and before long Glassey had introduced Leaphart to his fellow residents at the Powelton Community Housing Project, better known simply as "The Co-Op."

A fateful alliance was in the making. As early as 1971, a statement of the "Collective Principles of Community Housing Inc." bears the signatures of both Donald J. Glassey and Vincent Leaphart. The manifesto begins, "All decision-making is non-hierarchical, non-authoritarian and open to the entire membership."

Years later, Glassey, long estranged from Vincent Leaphart, explained to a local reporter how their friendship had spawned "The Movement." Leaphart, Glassey said, "was very gentle and seemed to be a warm, loving-type person. I said, 'You have some fascinating ideas here, you should write them down.' And he said, 'That's a great idea, but I can't write very well.' I said, 'I can take care of that for you.' And we started."

Leaphart dictated as Glassey typed and edited what was known at first as the *The Book of Guidelines* or simply *The Book* or *The Guidelines*, and later as *The Teachings of John Africa*. This consisted of some three hundred typewritten pages in which was spelled out Leaphart's "naturalistic" philosophy.

"I took it down," Glassey now says rather disingenuously, "and I organized it—put sections together—but it was totally, one hundred percent his words." *The Book* took a year to complete. Later, there would be other versions, other disciples. Donald Glassey, though, was the enabler without whom there would have been no *Teachings* and no John Africa. For that alone, his is a heavy burden in the history that follows.

In the winter of 1973, the Co-Op began eviction proceedings against Leaphart. Consistent with his teachings in *The Guidelines,* Leaphart refused to fumigate his Co-Op-owned apartment at 3207 Pearl Street. He explained, sometimes angrily, that roaches were the same as people, they were all God's children. Other members of the Co-Op did not see it the same way. Even the most radical of the Co-Op members were appalled at the reality of Leaphart's "naturalist" philosophy, for, predictably, an infestation of roaches was spreading throughout their neighborhood.

Meanwhile, Glassey had in May of 1973 purchased half—Number 309—of a rambling, three-story Victorian home at 307–309 North Thirty-third Street for $7,800. Into this old mansion reminiscent of something from a Charles Addams cartoon, Leaphart moved his belongings, his animals—numbering thirty or more dogs and cats—and the rest of his "family." Together, they called themselves the American Christian Movement for Life, or else the Christian Life Movement. Eventually, the name would be shortened to "MOVE"; the reference points "Christian" and "American" eliminated, and the name capitalized. In later years, when asked what the name meant, MOVE people would shrug their shoulders and look unblinking at their interrogators and say, "Means MOVE."

The name "John Africa" was taken by Leaphart perhaps as early as 1972. Glassey said, it was chosen not out of racial solidarity but by way of paying hommage to "the continent where all life began." No one seems to know why Leaphart chose the first name "John."

Among the earliest members of the Movement were Leaphart's sisters, Louise James and LaVerne Sims, and their children. Both of the sisters had been taking sociology classes from Glassey at the Community College of Philadelphia. LaVerne Sims recalled in October of 1985, "Oh, it was in the early seventies, and I had talked to Louise. She had been to —she had talked to someone that was talking about the MOVE principle. We went to Community College, and this is where it all started, the beginning for us. Donald Glassey was the professor, he was teaching the principles of John Africa at that point. It was called *The Book.* And we got involved."

Louise James remembered how she, her only child, Frank James, Jr., then a teenager, and LaVerne had attended "study sessions" with "Professor" Glassey. Eventually, these study sessions would be held at 309 North

Thirty-third Street, Powelton Village, now designated "MOVE Headquarters."

In September 1985, James was asked why she and her sister would go to the Community College and "hear from a third party person, Professor Glassey, the teachings of John Africa, which are the beliefs of her brother, Vincent Leaphart. Why did her brother not inform James and her sister of the teachings of John Africa when there were family meetings, over dinner, and social functions? She replied that he did make several statements in their presence concerning such things as life in general and the back-to-nature concept, but they paid no particular attention to his philosophy of life. However, when they heard these same teachings and philosophy from Glassey, they became extremely interested and so joined the MOVE organization.

"When asked who John Africa was, Mrs. James advised that John Africa is the truth, that there is no other person on earth like John Africa. She said that Vincent Leaphart and John Africa are two different people. 'My blood brother, Vincent Leaphart, became John Africa, and he no longer exists.' She says she reveres and honors John Africa, who will never die but will live on as the truth. . . .

"John Africa is the founder of the MOVE organization and . . . succeeded her brother, Vincent Leaphart, who is a person of limited educational abilities. However, he became involved with Professor Glassey and through their involvement, Professor Glassey wrote the concepts and beliefs of John Africa as he obtained them from Vincent Leaphart."

Asked what Glassey and Leaphart had taught in those early days, James replied, "The absolute truth. Basically, mainly, we were being taught about the system, the corruption of this system, the corruption in politics. We were being taught family. We were being taught health. We were being taught how to sustain ourselves physically, mentally, but mainly it was just the absolute truth. That's what we were taught."

All the members of the MOVE family took the same surname, at first "Life" then "Africa," and all shared the same age, one. A contemporaneous sample of what John Africa was teaching his followers exists in a composition book taken from MOVE's headquarters in August 1978, following the organization's first major "confrontation with the System." On the cover of the notebook is the title, "Wisdom of Mama," and next to that, "Name Disciple Beawolf Africa," also known as Charles Sutton Morris, Jr. According to a former MOVE member, Beawolf was one of the "twelve disciples" to whom Leaphart (with Glassey's help) dictated his thoughts. "Mama," the former MOVE member explained, stood for "Mother Nature."

These are the words of John Africa, as recorded by Disciple Beawolf Africa:

"A baby cries when there is something missin' in its balance, when it crys, the parents will give the baby milk, if they don't stop the cryin', then they'll give it candy. When the baby cries again, you'll give it somethin' else, because you don't recognize what's causin' the baby to cry, and so it is with a scientist.

"Each time the baby cries you add more addictions in an attempt to cool it out. And when the baby cries you don't know which addiction, science, which pacifier, the baby is cryin' for, the plastic nipple, the candy, the boy, which color, all distortions, even the pickin' the baby up, holdin' it, rockin' it, singin' out to it, etc.

". . . .Science is a trick. Man will see the air and build a fan, see the sun and invent a light bulb, see a bird and build a plane. He will duplicate, copy the principle of life rather than DO AS, be like the principle of life. . . . The trick is man's only so-called protection, if you can get a cop's pistol, take it from him, he ain't protected no more. MOVE people have got to take science and turn it on 'em. We got the power, they got the science, and we are aware of both. . . .

"Use one pattern, hit where it's open, vital, wait until you know you gone hit it, put your fist out there with the intentions of him hittin' back so you can get an openin.' Hit him knowin' he's gone come back, so wait and get your mark, a lot of punches aren't necessary, as soon as you see you ain't gettin' in, stop. . . . Counterpunch. MOVE are counterpunchers."

Preparatory to counterpunching the System, Leaphart was still gathering followers. Louise James and LaVerne Sims, Frank James, Jr., Debbie Sims, Dennis Sims, and Chuckie Sims were in and out of the house at Powelton. Soon there were others: Beawolf, Jeanne, Ishongo, Sue, Alberta, Phil, Mo, Mary, Gerry, Janet, as many as thirty or forty by the mid-1970s. A few were white, most were black, many had problems with drugs, some with their parents or with "the System," some with the law.

Louise James later told investigators that, "The MOVE organization helped the community by assisting drunks, addicts, and gang problems of the community. She recalled that many MOVE members who were former addicts and drunks had their lives straightened out through following the guidelines of John Africa."

Jeanne Africa, a young white woman from New England, was in her late teens when she joined the organization. MOVE she says, "gave me a solid, secure family."

What John Africa "was trying to do," she has said, "was get back" to nature. John Africa taught her that the system "gave you color as separation. They gave you names for separation. They gave us gender for separation. We were always taught" by John Africa "to look at lower life forms. Dogs and cats don't know they're dogs and cats; they just know they're life."

John Africa, Jeanne says, "gave us a lot of solutions to problems we had in The Lifestyle. We had people who were on drugs, he got them off drugs. He was like a messiah."

Beawolf Africa echoed Jeanne's sentiments in his notebook: "The reason why it has not been confirmed or denyied [sic] as to whether or not your founder of MOVE, John Africa is the messiah, is so that MOVE members can feel comfortable, even though it been clearly spelled out. . . . It don't have to be said, just look at the accomplishments that has been made, the miracles (women who were condemned barren by scientists gave natural childbirth without any assistance, five of our women at this point, childrens eyes clear, addicts runnin' clear, retards runnin' again; obese people become firm and strong, anemic people gain weight, blood, get richer; sick animals nursed back to healthy, strong animals, intimidation or oppression limited)."

A white follower, currently serving time in state prison, is the former Sue Levino. A 1966 graduate of Lower Moreland High School in suburban Montgomery County, Levino Africa describes herself as a typical child of the white middle class. Her life story though is hardly "typical." She dropped out of school three times, worked as a waitress, and by her own reckoning was heavily addicted to drugs when Vince Leaphart came to her rescue. She joined MOVE at a time when she was ill with hepatitis. John Africa, she says, "ministered to her" and cured her both of hepatitis and drugs.

Jeanne Africa says now that John Africa "was teaching us how drugs came into society." John Africa would explain that, "Drugs were in the black community for a long time, but they didn't have [drug rehabilitation] programs until it got into the white community. . . . The hierarchy would give you drugs to control you."

Leaphart, Don Glassey says, "fed you things selectively and told you only that which he felt you could handle."

Jeanne recounts how John Africa would cease lecturing to his followers when he sensed them growing tired. "That's enough for today. You'll get sick." Occasionally, he would reward the faithful with "distortion days" when they could indulge in as much junk food as they wished.

Jeanne Africa: "He was very clever. It was magic. John Africa had many tricks, many illusions." By now, as Glassey has said, Leaphart had "total control" over his followers. He was, Glassey says, the absolute "leader" of this movement that lay outside the "authoritarian system."

Probably by 1972, certainly by 1973, John Africa and MOVE were beginning to make their presence known to a wider audience than the neighbors in Powelton. MOVE people had begun to protest against the "System," defined in the very broadest terms. MOVE picketers, often equipped with bullhorns, began to show up at the Philadelphia Zoo, at political rallies, on university campuses, at nearby medical and veterinary schools, and at area hospitals.

Inquirer reporter Frank Heick was present in mid-August 1974 at a meeting of the Southern Christian Leadership Conference held at the Mt. Olivet Tabernacle Baptist Church. The keynote speakers were those two well-known symbols of "the System" in America, Rev. Ralph David Abernathy, the head of the Southern Christian Leadership Conference, and Angela Davis, the sometime national political candidate of the Communist Party U.S.A.

As he took his seat in the church, the *Inquirer* reporter noticed a little group of men and women, about eight in number, who seemed "to have a pew to themselves." The members of this group, Heick wrote, stood out "because in the predominantly well-dressed crowd they [were] among the few in blue jeans and they [were] all wearing blue denim jackets. They also [were] the only ones in the church eating Gino's fried chicken and throwing the bones on the floor. They [were] passing cans of Seven-Up back and forth, and except for the sound of an occasional chicken bone hitting the floor, they [were] silent. This was my first encounter with MOVE."

It was not to be Heick's last encounter though. In early September 1974, he found himself covering a dinner given by Governor Milton Shapp for the governors of the original thirteen states at Bookbinder's Restaurant. "As was the case at most of the events of that week, MOVE was there. It was this night that MOVE members demonstrated their most baffling ability: How can they talk continuously, punctuating each phrase with an obscenity, without ever saying anything comprehensible? And how can they pass the microphone from one to another and never miss a syllable or obscene adjective? That night also was an early encounter with another MOVE trademark: The portable, battery-operated bullhorn."

There would be other demonstrations that year, most prominently against President Gerald R. Ford and at the old Philadelphia General Hospital, where Heick noted that the seven or eight MOVE demonstrators were "mostly women and very young children." What struck the *Inquirer* reporter most about the demonstration was the cold weather and the fact that the MOVE children were stark naked. A MOVE boy, about two years old, was "encouraged by one of the women to defecate in the driveway." The child did as he was told.

John Africa's revolution was, his followers boasted, "On the MOVE!"

The "MOVE lifestyle" had taken shape by 1974. Headquarters in Powelton Village had become a haven for unwanted animals—but particularly for a score of unvaccinated dogs—for roaches, termites, and every other sort of insect. The man or woman who was attracted to MOVE in those days was apt to have a problem with drugs, or else be a two-time con; homeless or alone, a seeker after wisdom or perhaps a seeker after sexual pleasure.

Progeniture was the order of the day at Headquarters. Sexual potency on the part of MOVE's men and childbearing on the part of its women were encouraged as part of "the natural order of life," the "Wisdom of Mama." Vincent Leaphart had had no children. Now, Alberta Wicker Africa, a diminunitive, slightly cherubic, light-skinned black woman, became the master's "MOVE wife." For his part, John Africa was figurative father now to the whole MOVE family, where in his former life, he could be father to no one.

MOVE's women were expected not only to bear many children, but to give birth naturally, licking their babies clean, biting off the umbilical cord with their teeth, then eating it. There would be no birth control practiced here, no obstetricians, no gynecologists, no abortions. Science, John Africa had said, "is a trick." In MOVE, there would be no such tricks. John Africa taught to "DO AS, be like the principle of life." What could be more a part of the principle of life than the constant conceiving and birthing of babies?

Every MOVE child was a veritable *tabula rasa* for the implementation of John Africa's philosophies. Unlike the adult members of the organization, MOVE children would grow up completely free of the "addictions" of the "System lifestyle." MOVE children would dress as God had meant for them to: naked beneath the summer sun's rays, no more than lightly clothed in winter. Their food would consist solely of raw fruits and vegetables. They would grow up without ever being contaminated by the taste of meat and fish. They would be pure and unaddicted as none of the parents could possibly be.

There would be no need for "Distortion Days," the infamous "D-Days" that the parents craved, when the master allowed his adult followers to indulge themselves in all the junk food and meat that they could eat. MOVE's kids would have no such needs, for they would never have known the taste of "perversion."

"The MOVE lifestyle" that the adults led forbade bathing with soap, commanded males and females alike to grow their hair to its fullest, "natural" length in thick, unwashed dreadlocks in the style of the West Indian Rastafarian sect. It encouraged one and all to eschew meat, become vegetarian, dress alike (blue jeans, blue denim jackets, heavy-soled men's boots), and chew garlic for its natural medicinal properties. There would be frequent "meetings" at which John Africa would teach his followers the "Wisdom of Mama." And there would be "activities" handed out. One MOVE person might be "assigned" to buy groceries, another to help with the street-side car wash that helped pay for the food, another to exercise the children outdoors, still another to picket at a demonstration. MOVE people would be given titles like "Minister of Defense," "Full Naturalist Minister," "Minister of Communications," "Minister of Information," and the like. John Africa alone would be known as "The Co-Ordinator," the giver of all these assignments. The meaning of his nickname, "Ball," is less clear, but it certainly suggests the symbolic sexual potency of the father of MOVE.

The ramshackle Headquarters at 309 North Thirty-third in Powelton was turned into a compound. The whole of the front lawn was made into a stage for MOVE's drama. A wooden platform extended from the front porch all the way to an eight-foot high outer fence. Electric bullhorns were mounted in tree tops, and the neighborhood was treated to frequent lectures via the powerful sound system. Extemporaneous reading from *The Teachings of John Africa* blared through the night and into the early morning hours. Neighbors who dared complain soon found themselves denounced openly, loudly, and obscenely. Under such circumstances, powerful drama unfolded almost daily on North Thirty-third Street.

In the early-to-mid-1970s, MOVE people had been transported between the Powelton Headquarters and their latest demonstration in a rickety yellow school bus. Later, there would be a van and a stationwagon and a towtruck. The battery-powered, portable bullhorns, the pickets, and the rhetoric, though, were the constants in MOVE's struggle against the evils of "the System." In those days, especially, there was always something to demonstrate against: scientists, universities, visiting circuses, Jane

Fonda, Gerry Ford, Governor Shapp, Buckminster Fuller, Jimmy Carter, even nuclear non-proliferation.

Hospitals, doctors, and veterinarians were particularly singled out for abuse. The veterinarian, for example, was described in a MOVE document from 1974 as "a sadistic, scalpel-wielding pervert, butchering animal life, a disguised intruder, illegally trespassing on private property, a madman driven by the inoculating needle . . . a pus-infected [sic] pimple on the loin of life."

By this time too, run-ins with the law had become common for MOVE people. MOVE demonstrators were frequently arrested, often harassed, and nearly always regarded with unconcealed disgust and contempt by Philadelphia policemen. With their unwashed, garlic-reeking bodies, dreadlocks, and impenetrable and obscene harangues, MOVE people were a constant affront to a police force that was (and is) largely white, ethnic—in the main, Irish, Italian, or Polish—and Catholic. As much as anything, the Philadelphia cops were baffled by what they saw and heard. A MOVE leaflet from 1974 proclaimed that the civil disobedience squad of the Philadelphia Police "will tell you that MOVE is unlike any other organization they have ever seen—and they have seen a lot."

Other MOVE papers document the problems the organization was having with the Philadelphia police in the early seventies. The notebook of Disciple Beawolf Africa, for example, lists the names of police officers said to have committed various horrors against MOVE people: the cop who "struck Del," another who is described as "vicious as usual," a third, a captain, who "tried to strangle Conrad."

The Philadelphia courts were by this time jammed with MOVE-related cases, most of them misdemeanors. In a single seven-month period spanning the winter and spring of 1973–74, some forty different MOVE people were arrested a hundred-fifty times, fined approximately $15,000, and sentenced for up to several years in jail each.

Even then, John Africa's people went to court prepared. Disciple Beawolf Africa recorded the master's advice on how to behave in court: "Speak to the panelist, judges, kings, etc., just like you speak to people you're familiar with. Don't consider their position, status, job titles. The wisdom of John Africa undercuts all of it. MOVE status in court ain't no different than cops, they are there to establish they are right, and so are we. So the cop is on trial."

Between 1972 and 1976, this was the pattern of MOVE's public "activities": demonstrations anywhere and anytime, using pickets and bullhorns, followed by arrests, usually for obscenity, loitering, unlawful demonstration or some other minor charge, followed by lengthy and often noisy court appearances. Not surprisingly, there were dozens of arrests and almost as many court cases involving MOVE people.

The pattern was substantially altered in March of 1976 when MOVE's spokespeople announced that a three-week old baby boy named Life Africa had been killed, crushed to death, during a clash with the police. The true story—Life Africa's very existence, much less death, remains shrouded in doubt—may never be known.

What is certain is that the incident began in typical MOVE fashion. At about four o'clock in the afternoon of Sunday, March 28, the familiar yellow school bus pulled up in front of MOVE headquarters in Powelton. Inside the bus were seven MOVE members who had just been released from jail. The busdriver honked his horn loudly, and MOVE people came rushing out of the compound to greet their newly freed brothers. A very noisy and lengthy celebration ensued to the dismay of the neighbors. Complaints were lodged, and Police Civil Affairs Unit officers were sent to 309 North Thirty-third Street.

Chuckie Sims Africa began the confrontation by shouting obscenities at the cops: "We're sick and tired of you people. Leave us the fuck alone." Officer Daniel Palermo told reporters that as he was walking back to his car, a brick sailed through the air and caught him on the back of his head. More bricks flew through the air. Bedlam followed. A neighbor living across the street from the compound, Barbara Gale, said that, "It was the worst thing I ever saw, it was really awful. I think they [the police] were really provoked, but I think they were overreacting. I've never seen such brutality."

By the time the melee had ended, six Philadelphia cops had been taken to the hospital and six MOVE members were under arrest, the charges against them included aggravated assault, riot, resisting arrest, and reckless endangerment. Three of the men—Gerald Ford Africa, Delbert Orr Africa, and Conrad Hampton Africa—had only been freed from jail that morning.

The next day, Beawolf Africa showed photographers a broken and bloodied police nightstick along with a policeman's regulation blue hat. Merle Africa announced to reporters that Life Africa, the three-week old son of Janine and Phil Africa, had been killed in the scuffle.

Janine Africa graphically recounted how the police had drawn their guns and billyclubs and begun to beat everyone present. The police, she said, "were going crazy," swinging their nightsticks, pushing and shoving the MOVE women away in order to get at their men. When Janine, the baby Life in her arms, tried to shield Phil, she too was pushed, then fell heavily to the ground. After that, the "cops stepped all over me and on me." Life Africa lay crushed to the earth.

Sitting on the steps of the compound alongside Janine, Merle Africa explained what then happened. "The baby was taken care of. He didn't have no fancy clothes. He didn't have no embalming. He was taken care out in the country, put in a blanket, and left."

Dust to dust.

Police Department officials denied the story and hinted strongly that no such child as Life Africa had ever existed. There were, after all, no hospital records of the child's having been born.

MOVE people laughed: *Hospital* records?

A few days later, an *Inquirer* photographer received a phone call from Robert Africa. Could he and a reporter come for dinner at MOVE Headquarters that night, Friday, April 2? The request was unusual for few non-MOVE people had ever been allowed, to say nothing of being invited, into the house itself. He was asked to bring his camera with him.

The photographer and a reporter arrived in front of the compound sometime after 5 P.M. They were asked to wait outside. The night was cold and clammy even for early April, and rain was pelting down. At 6 P.M. West Philadelphia City Councilman Lucien E. Blackwell, his wife Jane, City Councilman Joseph E. Coleman, and the Rev. Wrennie Morgan of the Philadelphia Human Rights Commission arrived. All were asked to wait as the rain continued.

At 6:30, the party was ushered inside the compound. What they saw stunned them. Pressed against various windows were the faces of thirty or more howling dogs.

The party was led down some steps into a cement basement lighted by candles that hung above two long wooden tables. The effect was "like entering another world." Seated at the two tables were twenty or more MOVE people. Dinner itself was "formal, almost ritualistic," the food consisting of chicken, rice, spinach, corn, and fruit.

As the guests prepared to eat a dessert of watermelon, they were passed a slip of paper. Their hosts explained that they were afraid to speak out loud for fear the police were bugging the house. Written on the piece of paper was an invitation to view the corpse of little Life Africa.

Stunned, the guests were escorted upstairs to a small room, about ten feet square, at the front of the house. Two desks and a chair were the only furnishings. An open cardboard box stood in the middle of the room. One guest recalled that, "It was so dark I was bumping into stuff." For light, there was only the faint glow that came from three candles.

Then, said another, "The stench hit me, and I backed up." In the cardboard box, about five feet away from her, lay a dead baby, of unidentifiable sex. Councilman Blackwell quickly looked away from the cardboard box and began to rattle on about the size of the rats running loose in the house.

None of the guests had been prepared for what they had just seen.

MOVE people explained how they had that night brought the body of the Life Africa to Headquarters from its "resting place." *That* was why the guests had had to wait so long in the rain.

The mother, Janine Africa, was not permitted to speak to the visitors. This was "out of respect for her feelings." Later, when federal authorities offered to investigate the "death of Life Africa," they asked to have an autopsy performed. The MOVE people demurred. Their organization was opposed to the perverted work of scientists and doctors. No, MOVE would not allow an autopsy. Life Africa would pass back into nature, would "cycle" with the seasons.

By September of 1976, there were reports that John Africa had decided to abandon the course of peaceful resistance. Leaphart, one newspaper article noted, had "told his followers to prepare for a showdown with police." And so it was about this time that MOVE members began doing calisthenics, practicing boxing and martial arts, and most ominous of all, stockpiling weapons and ammunition.

Louise James recalled how in the early years MOVE members had not been armed with weapons. "We were armed only with [the] truth. But when the System decided that we were disturbing the peace, didn't want to hear it, they started to beat MOVE's people, and every time we opened our mouths, we were beaten, bludgeoned, kicked, stomped, babies killed, rifle butts up besides our head. . . . Finally, MOVE decided we weren't going to get beat anymore. We were now going to fight back."

On the inside back cover of his notebook, Disciple Beawolf Africa scrawled, "From Uranium Come Plutonium." Police sources claim that it was around this time that MOVE attempted to make or acquire an atomic bomb. A National Guard atomic-weapons demolition specialist was asked to help them in this fantastic attempt. He refused.

The years 1975 and 1976 were marked by more protests, this time from MOVE's neighbors in Powelton. MOVE's bullhorns disturbed their peace. Neighbors were the object of public humiliation. Some were merely harassed, others complained of physical threats. A college professor, his own home near the MOVE Headquarters, charged that Glassey and Leaphart had obtained the property on North Thirty-third Street by intimidating the previous owner. The same source told reporters that another neighbor, a sixty-two-year-old man, had died of a heart attack after having been verbally abused by MOVE people.

There were plenty of other complaints from other neighbors. Human as well as animal waste was being dumped in the backyard of the MOVE compound. A score of unvaccinated dogs and cats posed a health hazard. City Health inspectors were sent to investigate the complaints. They were refused admittance to the house. Licenses and Inspections official Joseph Della Guardia told a reporter from the *Bulletin* that MOVE "had threatened to kill themselves and even their children if their premises were inspected." Sue Africa was quoted as saying that, "We won't let our children fall into their hands." She added cryptically that, "They'll see just how committed we are to our religion." John Africa's "MOVE wife," Alberta Wicker Africa, told reporters that, "We will not let these inspectors come in and contaminate our environment. If they violate the sanctity of our home, we will cycle our children before we let them take the children away."

The city pressed on. In September of 1975, the city solicitor's office filed suit against Glassey as legal owner of the property at 309 North Thirty-third Street—the other half of the twin structure, Number 307, although long-occupied by MOVE was not legally acquired until August of 1977 when the Delta Management Company signed papers giving it away for free—charging him with violations of city health, housing, fire, zoning, and safety codes. The city's legal case against Glassey and MOVE dragged on in the courts through the next eleven months. In July of 1976, the Supreme Court of the Commonwealth of Pennsylvania upheld a lower court order mandating an inspection of the house. MOVE members at once began construction of an eight-foot high stockade fence around the Headquarters in Powelton.

Friday, May 20, 1977, marked the beginnings of the first full-scale "confrontation," as John Africa would call it. The confrontation began when word spread that sheriff's deputies were coming to evict the MOVE people from their Headquarters. As it happened, the deputies had come to evict a MOVE member living at 3301 Powelton Avenue. In an ensuing altercation, Chuckie Sims Africa was arrested on weapons charges and held in lieu of $25,000 bail.

A half-dozen or more MOVE members, wearing khaki, army-style uniforms, almost immediately began a demonstration at the compound. Openly brandishing sawed-off shotguns, rifles, pistols, and crudely fashioned clubs, the MOVE people paraded about the platform or stationed themselves at the barricaded front of the house.

At the height of the standoff, MOVE's demands, a contemporary newspaper report noted, "were shouted into a microphone, blaring, and through loudspeakers mounted in trees in their yard. Those demands, in addition to the release of several jailed members, included the return of the man arrested earlier in the day, with his gun and ammunition; an apology from Mayor Frank Rizzo and a statement from President Carter guaranteeing that city police would leave them alone."

An unidentified MOVE person took the microphone and announced that, "the only way they [the police] will come in our headquarters is over our dead bodies. If those motherfuckers come in here, they're going to have to kill everyone in here to do it."

Some two hundred armed policemen, many of them flak-jacketed members of Philadelphia's SWAT team, the Stakeout Unit, surrounded the house for most of that afternoon. By 10:30 P.M., nine hours after it began, the "confrontation" was over. While Chuckie Sims Africa joined the incarcerated MOVE people in jail, other MOVE members took their weapons back inside the house. Commissioner of Police Joseph F. O'Neill then ordered his men to leave the area.

Afterwards, neighbors told reporters how they had been trying "for years" to get MOVE out from their midst. One neighbor recalled how he and others had written to Mayor Rizzo to complain of "rats the size of cats." The kids in his neighborhood, he said, were "petrified."

He was tough and he talked tough. He was a cop.

Frank Rizzo joined the Philadelphia Police Department in 1943 and had served as its commissioner for four years (1967–71) under Mayor James J. Tate. Colorful, macho, always good for a line in the next day's newspapers, Rizzo had been the leading figure in an otherwise lackluster administration.

During the final years of the Vietnam War, at a time when life in America's cities was increasingly marked by racial conflict and radical protest, Police Commissioner Rizzo, though nominally a Democrat, was an unabashed fan of President Richard Nixon. As late as 1976, Rizzo could still say of Nixon that, "I think he was the best president we ever had." Rizzo was for keeping the streets safe, putting the punks in jail, and sending a message to the liberal media. He was also the leading candidate to succeed Tate as mayor.

In the 1971 mayoral race, the *Inquirer* supported U.S. Representative William J. Green III. Bill Green was handsome, Irish-Catholic, the son of the city's late, longtime political boss, and close to the Kennedys. The newspaper had its doubts. "His record in Washington is hardly distinguished. His campaign, however, has been more impressive." More to the point, Bill Green was not Frank Rizzo.

In the May 1971 Democratic primary, Rizzo was the victor in an election that was fought on ideological, ethnic, and racial lines. The vote wasn't even close. When it was over, Rizzo had won with over 175,000 votes to Green's 127,000.

Four years later, Rizzo again faced the voters. Warning of the imminent demise of his political rivals, he announced that he was "gonna make Attila the Hun look like a faggot after this election's over." The *Inquirer* this time endorsed a candidate with no chance of winning, black attorney Charles Bowser. "We win some and lose some this way, but we sleep well at night," an *Inquirer* editorial noted at the time. Rizzo took nearly sixty percent of the vote, and carried with him candidates for District Attorney and City Council. Only three opposition councilmen were elected that year, and all were black: Joseph E. Coleman, Cecil Moore, and former state representative Lucien E. Blackwell.

In a city that is largely blue-collar, ethnic, and Catholic, Rizzo was clearly "the Man." No one had any doubts whatsoever about who was running Philadelphia when Frank Rizzo was the mayor.

F. Gillman Spencer, a native Philadelphian, became editor of the afternoon *Daily News* in September of 1975, having been awarded the Pulitizer Prize for editorial writing in 1974.

Spencer tells a story about Zack Stalberg, his eventual successor as editor at the *Daily News,* then a beat reporter at City Hall: "So Rizzo's on the phone, and he says, 'What I wanta know is who the fuck told you that? I know who told you, but I wanta hear *you* tell *me.'* And Rizzo pauses for a long time and then says, 'Cocksucker. I'll get that rat cocksucker.' "

You knew where Rizzo stood.

On Monday, May 23, Mayor Rizzo held a press conference. This was by no means a good time politically for the former police commissioner. The influential, liberal *Inquirer,* never a particular friend, had just run a highly critical series of editorials about police brutality in the city ("Is There a *Good* Place to Beat Up Citizens?" was the title of the most recent editorial on the subject), and this followed a four-month long *Inquirer* investigation of police brutality. The series found "a pattern of beatings, threats of violence, intimidation, coercion and knowing disregard for constitutional rights in the interrogation of homicide suspects and witnesses."

The U.S. Justice Department had recently announced that it would investigate civil rights charges against the city's police department, and State Senator Hardy D. Williams' subcommittee was scheduled to begin hearings on police brutality. The heat was very much on the mayor and his favorite city department.

Sunday morning's big news, following the MOVE confrontation, had been the recent Democratic primary. Quite unexpectedly, a young prosecutor named Edward Rendell had defeated his former boss, incumbent District Attorney F. Emmett Fitzpatrick, Jr. The *Inquirer* boasted that "the once powerful political machine of Mayor Frank L. Rizzo, a machine that won him re-election by more than 175,000 votes in 1975, came to a sputtering halt last week." Fitzpatrick lost by a vote of almost two-to-one.

At a press conference at City Hall, a dour Rizzo reported that he, along with his cabinet and West Philadelphia City Councilman Lucien E. Blackwell, had just met with "twenty-five fearful Powelton neighbors of MOVE." After talking to the neighbors, Rizzo was very much "concerned about the loss of life. We don't want to precipitate anything. We don't want anybody hurt or killed. We don't want violence." But the mayor had a warning for MOVE, "If there is any violence, they'll start it. And if they start it, I guarantee you we'll finish it." In the meantime, the mayor could offer little hope to MOVE's Powelton Village neighbors. "We're going to sit and wait it out," he said. The situation had by now become a stalemate. In MOVE terms, David had stymied Goliath.

Rizzo's parting words had a hollow ring. "MOVE," the mayor said, "has had its day. They're going to be removed from the community for a long time."

One Powelton Villager complained bitterly to the press: "It makes me sick that our society has broken down to this point. MOVE has intimidated the neighborhood, the whole city, the politicians, and the mayor. They're so gutless." Other residents said that they felt "reassured" by the mayor's worlds.

Jim Gould, an attorney who lived in Powelton, spoke the words that many probably felt. "We don't want a bloodbath," he told reporters.

Neither, however, was Gould satisfied. He, personally, had been complaining for three years to city officials, yet nothing had been done to stop MOVE people from dumping their garbage on the lawn, drawing rats and insects to the neighborhood, keeping fifty or so unvaccinated dogs in the back, directing "a stream of obscenities at residents, sometimes through their loudspeaker," and operating an illegal carwash in front of the house.

Mayor Rizzo replied that the only way he could "send in guys from L & I"—the city's Licenses and Inspections Department—would be with police protection. On this score the mayor was emphatic: "And I'm not sending in police for L & I violations."

At the same meeting, City Managing Director Hillel S. Levinson made it clear to the residents that the city had no intention of shutting off water to the MOVE compound, despite nonpayment of bills. MOVE, Levinson said, "would interpret that as an act of war," and "the way they would respond to an act of war would be to kill their own babies."

The next day's newspapers reported quiet at the MOVE compound: "The only weapons visible yesterday were an automatic pistol on the belt of one MOVE member and baseball bats and clubs lined up against the front porch."

Ishongo Africa told reporters, "We want to make it clear that our weapons are only for self-defense. We will not fire unless we are fired upon."

Seventy-five-year-old community activist Maude Roberts told reporters that she was attempting to negotiate some kind of settlement between MOVE and the city. Roberts was no particular admirer of the MOVE organization, but she wanted, she said, "to make sure these people don't die because of this. I think they are intelligent people who could help the black community, but they are just misdirected. They don't deserve to die for it though." Roberts was convinced—rightly, as it turned out—that true confrontation between MOVE and the Philadelphia police would inevitably mean bloodshed.

And still it dragged on: the demonstrations, the court cases, the bullhorns, the scuffles, the beatings, the obscenities. This was the reality of John Africa's revolution. For most of the neighbors, it amounted to a stay in purgatory, a stalemate between heaven and hell. But where was heaven, and what was hell?

2

Confrontation

T he May 20, 1977 confrontation gave MOVE the kind of credence that it had never possessed. News out of Powelton now played on front pages of local newspapers, and Philadelphia television stations often began their news broadcasts with MOVE coverage. In a single day's time, MOVE had become a Story. The possibility of violence commanded attention as no amount of bullhorns and pickets ever could.

Some of the effects of that day are calculable. Round-the-clock police surveillance of the compound began on May 20 and continued throughout the next ten months. The *Daily News* reckoned that the surveillance alone cost the city nearly a million and a quarter dollars, most of it earmarked for police overtime.

Eleven MOVE members, including Chuckie Sims Africa, were charged with Pennsylvania weapons code violations stemming from their participation in the confrontation. The gun taken from Chuckie Africa was traced, in turn, back to its date and place of purchase. Records kept by a suburban Newtown Square gunshop, Leslie Edelman, Inc., showed that two shotguns and two hundred rounds of ammunition had been purchased there on March 10, 1977 by a man using a stolen driver's license for identification. The purchaser of those shotguns was subject to federal criminal prosecution, as the Treasury Department's firearms regulations had been violated. Now, for the first time, agents of the Alcohol, Tobacco, and Firearms Agency—the ATF—would be directly involved with MOVE.

The "guns on the porch" day at MOVE Headquarters in Powelton. Wide World Photos.

Chuckie Sims Africa addresses neighbors. The *Philadelphia Daily News.*

The purchase forms were dusted for fingerprints, and the handwriting on the forms analyzed. Both fingerprints and handwriting were found to belong to Donald J. Glassey.

Glassey was arrested at his home, 8006 Mars Place, at seven o'clock on the evening of Friday, June 3, 1977. The Philadelphia District Attorney charged Glassey with possession of marijuana. The U.S. Attorney charged him with falsifying information on the firearms forms. Bail was set by a federal magistrate at twenty-five thousand dollars. Glassey was unable to post bail.

Outside the Powelton Village Headquarters, Delbert Africa was busy "putting out information," minimizing Glassey's current and former roles in MOVE. Glassey, Delbert told reporters, had once upon a time been a MOVE "sympathizer," but he had never been in "the above-ground confrontational unit" of the organization. If he *had* been a member, his name wouldn't have been Donald Glassey, it would have been Donald Africa. Delbert claimed that the last he had heard of Glassey was sometime back in 1972 or 1973, when "the professor" was still teaching social psychology at Philadelphia Community College.

Asked point blank if Glassey had ever bought weapons for MOVE, Delbert grinned slyly and said, "We accept donations from many persons and many organizations."

A major frontal assault against MOVE was not long in coming. On July 21, 1977, federal agents raided two cars parked in a narrow alley running behind some houses on the 7500 block of Woolston Avenue and Rugby Street in the West Oak Lane section of Philadelphia. In one of the automobiles, a 1970 model blue Toyota, agents found eight high-powered rifles, a handgun, two shotguns, and one hundred rounds of ammunition. Inside the second car, a gray-colored 1964 model Lincoln, they found eleven pounds of black powder, seven time-bombs, three twelve-inch-long pipe bombs, and the parts necessary to construct another forty or so bombs. Alongside the various weapons, lay copies of *The Anarchist's Cookbook,* an OSS manual, an Army fieldguide to the use of high explosives, and *The Silencers, Snipers, and Assassins Handbook.* Arrested at the wheel of the gray Lincoln was a man named William Smith, also known as "William DeWitt Africa," who gave as his address the MOVE Headquarters, 309 North Thirty-third Street. Behind the wheel of the blue Toyota was the face of the man described in the next day's newspaper accounts as "Donald J. Glassey, 30 . . . of the 8000 block of Mars Place, Southwest Philadelphia."

Unknown to the press, the circumstances of the raid, though not the weapons seized, had been contrived. Facing a possible five-year term in federal prison, Glassey, sometime during the weeks immediately preceding the raid had "turned." In exchange for a reduced sentence, a recommendation for early parole, and a place in the Federal Witness Protection Program, Glassey had become a mole within John Africa's Revolution.

Earlier that morning, Glassey had gone from one MOVE location to another, picking up much of the organization's guns, bombs, and ammunition. Federal agents had only to raid two cars parked and waiting, and the small arsenal of illegal weapons would be their's. They did, and it was. As a result of the raid, federal arrest warrants were obtained against Vincent Leaphart and prominent disciple Alphonso Robbins, better known as "Mo" Africa. MOVE's latest fugitives were, however, a very short jump ahead of the law, eluding an arresting party of federal agents in Philadelphia by hours, perhaps by minutes, then disappearing into "the underground," the counterculture's labyrinth of mutual causes and safe houses. Leaphart was on the move; his whereabouts over the next four years was the object of intense speculation by city, state, and federal law enforcement agencies.

Even if from afar, John Africa was still very much coordinating MOVE activities, and action was heating up at Headquarters from within and from without. Mayor Rizzo had come under increasing pressure, both from MOVE's Powelton Village neighbors and from the media, to do something about the problems there. The *Daily News* had further embarrassed the Rizzo administration by running a detailed analysis of the financial burdens that MOVE had forced upon the city: unpaid gas and water bills, backtaxes, and police overtime being the most prominent costs. The *Inquirer* found that over a three-year-period (1975–78) there had been more than two hundred and fifty trials involving MOVE members. The numerous and all too frequently extraordinarily lengthy MOVE cases had, in turn, delayed another two thousand cases from coming to trial on time. Thanks to MOVE, an already overloaded court system had virtually stalled, while the cost to the taxpayers of Philadelphia was on the order of two hundred-fifty thousand dollars, at a minimum.

Rizzo responded in textbook cop fashion by showing strength while avoiding the need to put that force to the test. On March 1, 1978, attorneys from the City Solicitor's office went before Judge G. Fred DiBona of the Court of Common Pleas and asked for permission to form a blockade surrounding the MOVE compound. The city's attorneys cited nonpayment of water and gas bills and noted that officials from the Philadelphia Licenses and Inspection Department were still being denied access to 309 North Thirty-third Street. DiBona granted the order for the blockade, and on March 16, the Supreme Court of the Commonwealth of Pennsylvania upheld his decision. Construction of the blockade began at once, as hundreds of Philadelphia police moved into Powelton to cordon off a four-block area, while city workers shut off gas and water lines to the MOVE Headquarters.

MOVE members, having planned for just such an eventuality, had stockpiled provisions, including water and food. And so, for the next fifty-six days, a well-publicized stalemate ensued. MOVE was still very much a good story, and its members clearly relished their long sought-after first page status. From their front-porch platform at the compound in Powelton, they continued to play to crowds of curious onlookers drawn like bees to honey.

On May 3, Managing Director Hillel S. Levinson, the city's highest-ranking appointed official, announced that a compromise had at last been reached. That morning, City Solicitor Sheldon Albert and Oscar N. Gaskins, acting as counsel for the MOVE organization, had signed a ten-point agreement, the provisions of which were made public. MOVE agreed to turn over its remaining weapons and allow police to search the Powelton compound. In return, eighteen MOVE members, charged with felonies and misdemeanors, would be freed from jail on their own recognizance. The MOVE organization would then have a ninety-day grace period—or until midnight, August 1, 1978—to vacate 307–309 North Thirty-third Street entirely. At that point, all outstanding charges would be dropped against the freed MOVE members.

It sounded like a good deal for both parties. MOVE would get its people back, and the city would, presumably, rid itself of MOVE. A search was mounted by the city and by black community groups to find a new home for MOVE, a home somewhere other than Powelton, somewhere other than West Philadelphia, somewhere other than Philadelphia.

Wouldn't MOVE be happier settled in the countryside somewhere? No, they said, they wouldn't. MOVE spokespersons said that the group feared being massacred out there in the countryside, away from the protective eye of the press. The search for a new MOVE Headquarters quickly stalled.

Tuesday, August 1, 1978 came and went. Despite relentless press coverage, most Philadelphians were more concerned with Pete Rose and his record forty-four game consecutive hitting streak than with what most of them still perceived as the antics of a group of hair-brained, if also somewhat violent, radicals. City officials knew better. No one had left Headquarters, and MOVE spokespeople were quoted as saying that, "MOVE gonna move when we ready to move." Delbert Africa announced that the organization had changed its mind. MOVE had no intention of handing over its Headquarters to Frank Rizzo and his "Gestapo."

Chuckie Sims Africa was quoted as saying that, "If you want to find us housing, and it suits us, that's fine." Otherwise, MOVE would stay where it was.

The 12:01 A.M. deadline passed, and MOVE was still in Powelton. Rizzo spoke to the press later that morning. The city, he warned, would "forcibly evict" MOVE from 307–309 North Thirty-third Street if the organization was found in contempt of court. "I believe this government has been tolerant enough," Rizzo said. "There will be no more bargaining, no more conversations, meetings, or agreements." MOVE's people, Rizzo said, "represent nobody but themselves. They're complete idiots." It was pure, vintage Rizzo.

The touch that followed was not. The people at 307–309 North Thirty-third Street, Rizzo added, "name the game. We don't." In this, the mayor was absolutely, perspicaciously correct.

Later that morning, in the course of a forty-minute hearing, Judge DiBona asked attorney Gaskins where his clients were. "I have no idea," Gaskins replied. DiBona nodded and signed arrest warrants for twenty-one MOVE people. The judge's order stipulated that the Philadelphia Police would have ten days in which to secure the arrests. How this was to be done was the city's business, not the court's. City Solicitor Sheldon Albert told reporters that, "The city will not discuss tactics, means, or methods." Forcible, perhaps violent, arrest and eviction was the widely expected course of action.

At Headquarters, the dreadlocked quartet of Chuck, Janine, Janet, and Delbert Africa appeared outside the compound to talk with reporters and passersby. While Janine stood silent her hands on her hips, Chuckie and Delbert harangued everyone within earshot. MOVE, Chuckie said, had no intention of moving. As for Judge DiBona, well, the hell with him. As MOVE's dogs scampered about them, the four paused for lunch: raw potatoes and spinach. Across the way in a vacant building, a dozen police officers surveyed the strange scene.

When two plainclothed Civil Affairs Unit officers showed up in front of the compound to read Judge DiBona's order, Chuckie Africa interrupted them, shouting: "When you started World War II, you had legal papers. Everytime you want to kill black people you make it legal." The cops just looked at one another and kept on reading.

Delbert lambasted the mayor—known during his cop-on-the-beat days as "the Cisco Kid"—"He has still got the Cisco Kid image. We're not giving up. He's going to get his fat face punched all over the fucking United States as the killer of black women and children." The message was clear. There would be no eviction, no arrests without a show of violence. MOVE was putting out information, preparing the press and the public for something horrible, a holocaust involving its women and children.

There were reports in the newspapers that "a very rich Algerian" had offered to lease five properties in North Philadelphia to MOVE, if only its people would vacate the Powelton compound. Nothing came of the stories. The op-ed page of the *Inquirer,* meanwhile, ran a piece entitled, "Now Is the Time for MOVE to Move On." It noted that MOVE was never beyond compromising when it suited their purposes. For example, they loudly declared that "they would never surrender" to police, then compromised, in return receiving "favorable arrest procedures that no ordinary citizen could get." They seldom were forced to submit to hand-cuffing and instead received "incredibly speedy, gentle treatment by the police." As to their vaunted diet of raw vegetables, MOVE members could frequently be found eating at neighborhood delis and or else at Tippy's Tacos.

MOVE's claim "is that evil justifies evil. If Rizzo is a racist, then it's okay for MOVE to break its commitments. If our legal system treats black people unfairly, then it's okay for MOVE to do whatever it wants." Such a policy, the *Inquirer* maintained, was all too likely to result in a bloodshed of innocent neighbors and of MOVE's own children. If MOVE's refusal to vacate 307–309 North Thirty-third Street were to bring about a police raid, "and if a massacre or a race riot results, it is all justified because that exposes how evil the System is." Something hot and terrible was in the air, and John Africa's people were fanning the flames of a disaster.

The prospects, if you lived in Powelton, were not good. You were trapped between the will of two armed and exhausted forces.

By Thursday, August 3, the tension had built to a point obviously intolerable to some. Sharon Gale Penn, 23, who with her twin infant sons had lived through the blockade, emerged from the compound in Powelton and asked to be taken before Judge DiBona. Later, in a courtroom in City Hall, Penn tearfully renounced her membership in MOVE, then fled down a cavernous hallway, and into a waiting freight elevator, her days in the spotlight at an end.

Back at MOVE Headquarters, Chuckie Africa told reporters that Sharon Penn was "not as strong" as the remaining members of MOVE.

The same system that "harassed her and made her weak" had finally "taken her over." Sharon Gale Penn had sold out, and in return, all charges had been dropped against her. That was how the System worked.

That same day, black City Councilman Cecil Moore amused reporters with the story of how he had recently ordered MOVE members out of his City Hall offices. So frustrated had Moore become with his recalcitrant, longwinded, and obscene guests that he had drawn a pistol on them and ordered them out. "My only regret," Moore chortled, "is that in the Marines when you pulled it out, you got to use it."

Both the *Inquirer* and *Daily News* were calling editorially for MOVE to leave 307–309, yet the group had at least a few supporters left among local politicians and activists. Walter Palmer, chairman of the Citywide Black Community Coalition for Human Rights, was one. Legal procedures, Palmer argued, were contrary to MOVE's "religion." MOVE, he said, was "a different kind of social movement." Precisely what kind of social movement he had in mind, Palmer never ventured to say.

Over the next few days, the Philadelphia public's attention continued to be focused elsewhere. The news of Pope Paul VI's death filled the Monday and Tuesday editions of all three newspapers. A pope was dead, and a city that is heavily Catholic went into mourning.

A short, one column article lay buried in the metropolitan section of the *Inquirer*. "Two MOVE Members Arrested," the headline read. MOVE's sister organization, "The Seed of Wisdom," in Richmond, Virginia, had been raided on August 6; and two of its women, Gail and Rhonda Africa, had been apprehended on bench warrants issued by Judge DiBona for the parts they had played in the "Guns on the Porch Day."

Rhonda Cheryl Harris was little more than sixteen years old when she married in 1971. Her husband, Andino R. Ward, was but a year older at the time. Their only child was born that same December. The child, a boy, was given the name Oywolffe Momer Puim Ward. Fourteen years later, Andino Ward, by then a portly, bespectacled, conservatively dressed black man, would recall that Rhonda had chosen the name. "Oywolffe," Ward believed, was an Arabic word meaning "prince." What the other words meant, he could no longer remember.

Andino and Rhonda Ward separated in 1973. Within a year's time, the two had gone their own, very different ways in the world: Andino, into the Air Force; Rhonda, into MOVE. In 1977, while assigned to an Air Force base in England, Andino Ward took a brief leave and returned home to the States. He wanted, he said, to see his son.

Ward had only to return to Philadelphia to find his former wife and child. MOVE Headquarters in Powelton Village had for the past three years been home for Rhonda and her son. They were now part of the family of John Africa. The boy's new name, Rhonda told Andino, was Birdie. Birdie Africa.

For all but one of the next eight years—a year spent in a foster home —whether in Powelton or in Richmond or again much later on Osage Avenue, Birdie Africa's life would be twined with that of his mother Rhonda and with MOVE. "The House That John Africa Built"—and others like it—would be all the real home that Birdie would have. His diet would be a MOVE diet of raw vegetables, and his body would grow slowly due to a lack of protein and vitamins. His clothing would be scant. He would never learn to read or write, although he could, Birdie later told investigators, write the single word "MOVE." The only father he would know in this period of his life would be a man named John Africa.

And as for Rhonda, she would end her life in another house surrounded by other cops. Her faith was undeniably stronger than Sharon Penn's had been. Birdie, alone among a half dozen MOVE children, would survive the holocaust which claimed his mother.

Another kind of scene was being played out in Philadelphia. As the early morning editions of August 8, 1978's dailies were hitting the streets, hundreds of policemen were massing in Powelton. At 307–309 North Thirty-third Street, the Confrontation that John Africa had so confidently predicted was in progress.

If Vincent Leaphart ever had a goal in becoming John Africa, and if that goal was a full-scale confrontation with the City of Philadelphia, then he was succeeding.

As the the August 1 deadline approached, Philadelphia police commanders began preparations for an operation against MOVE Headquarters. Preliminary planning had taken place as early as May 1978, but the "ultimate plan," as Police Commissioner Joseph F. O'Neill later called it, was put together during the last two weeks of July and the first week of August. The chief planners included the commissioner, his deputy, the commanding officer of the Stakeout Unit, the head of the Bomb Squad, and Inspector George Fencl, head of the Civil Affairs Bureau.

The final plan called for two to three dozen specially trained, heavily armed officers from the Stakeout Unit to be positioned close to the

MOVE compound. Another hundred or more officers would be assigned to patrol an outer perimeter, man barricades, control crowds, and provide other logistical services.

Fencl, using a portable bullhorn, would read the search and arrest warrants. The MOVE members would be given a reasonable amount of time to leave the house. Monsignor Charles Devlin of the Cardinal's Commission on Human Relations and Walter Palmer, the chairman of the Citywide Black Community Coalition for Human Rights, would be on hand to guarantee fair play.

If the MOVE members refused to leave 307–309, Stakeout Unit officers would first bulldoze the wooden stockade that surrounded the compound. Smoke, but not tear gas, would then be lobbed into the house. (Commissioner O'Neill, after conferring with the city Health Commissioner and the police department surgeon, had quickly vetoed the use of tear gas for fear of its effects on the lungs of the children.) Finally, if necessary, fire department personnel would be on hand to pour water into the basement of the compound in an attempt literally to flush out the MOVE members.

O'Neill's goal, simply put, was to insure a bloodless confrontation. The former police commissioner later recalled, "We did things, really, by the numbers. We knew that they had children in the house, and we knew there were some women in the house, some of whom we believed did not really want to be there. We determined that we would do something that you really should not do in an operation of this type. We telegraphed. We told them exactly what we were going to do, prior to doing it."

When asked what he meant by "telegraphing," O'Neill explained, "that means, that prior to us moving our bulldozer in, for example, we told them what we were going to do. It means that prior to us using the water, we told them what we were going to do. It means that prior to using smoke, we told them what we were going to do."

At about 4:30 A.M., on Tuesday, August 8, 1978, a force of what would eventually number some three hundred policeman and fire department personnel began placing barricades and moving in equipment six and a half blocks away from MOVE Headquarters in Powelton Village, their meetingplace a vast, dusty, vacant lot in West Philadelphia—all that remained of the former Philadelphia General Hospital, the birthplace of Vincent Leaphart.

Back at MOVE Headquarters, Janine Africa told a reporter to "stick around." Outside the compound, a half-dozen or so MOVE supporters sat on benches and milk crates. Two signs on the stockaded walls boldly proclaimed the same message, "Long Live the House that John Africa Built!"

MOVE's loudspeakers were turned on. Chuckie Africa had a message for all those who were bound for Powelton. "Testing, murderers, testing. You're trying to kill breastfeeding mothers and breastfeeding children. We're not backing down. If you want us out, you'll have to bring us out dead."

MOVE, Chuckie said, had the power of the hurricane on its side, the power of the floods. "We're hardy, and we're healthy!"

Despite the humidity of an August morning in Philadelphia, a light breeze fanned the riot-equipped policemen as they unloaded by the dozens from buses and vans.

"Who's crazy?" bellowed Chuckie, his voice rendered demonic by the loudspeakers. "Tell the world Rizzo killed black babies for a health violation."

Other voices on the loudspeakers wanted to know if the cops had their life insurance policies paid up. There would be a lot of widows, they warned, collecting their insurance money after today.

The cops continued to pour into Powelton.

Police Commissioner O'Neill came on the scene just before 6:00 A.M. Firemen ran across Thirty-Third Street, setting up deluge guns. At 6:04, Fencl grabbed a bullhorn, "You have exactly two minutes in which to come out."

MOVE voices taunted, "The gate's open. Stop playin' games."

Four minutes later, the bulldozer went to work on the stockade fence that surrounded the compound. Across the street from the headquarters, Fencl, squatting behind a pile of sandbags, tried again: "Come on out. No one will hurt you. Come on, Del. Come on, Chuckie. Give up." Fencl handed the bullhorn to Father Devlin. "Come on out!" Devlin shouted. "No one's going to get hurt. Let me come in, and I'll walk out with you."

"Fuck you priest!" came the reply.

Then, the sound of infants crying, coming from within MOVE headquarters, their tiny voices, the stuff of nightmares as they passed through the loudspeakers set up in nearby trees.

Other voices, the voices of adults, soon followed: "What are you killers waiting for? Our door is wide open. Your pictures are going to be plastered nationally."

Then a chorus of voices chanting, "Baby killers! Baby killers! Black baby killers!"

Several MOVE members suddenly appeared on the porch of the

compound, gas masks in their hands. Just as suddenly, they disappeared back into the house.

Police pressed for the release of the children. The response from MOVE, "Why don't you take gasoline and set fire to us?" From inside, the moaning of children continued to drift into the humid morning. Plaintively, they chanted, "Long Live John Africa! On the move!" And then, "Baby killers! Baby killers! Black baby killers!"

Outside the compound, MOVE's dogs and cats scampered about as city dogcatchers chased after them with their nets.

Over the bullhorn, police urged MOVE to take down the barricades from the windows. There was no response. At 6:29, a battering ram smashed through one of the boarded windows of MOVE Headquarters. When the ram struck the porch, rats gushed out of the house like water from an open hydrant.

Devlin, with Fencl and O'Neill at each side of him, made an appeal for the release of the children and the women, "in behalf of everything that is sane and honest." Nearing the compound, a policeman shouted to

Philadelphia police before the Powelton shootout. Wide World Photos.

those inside, "Uniformed officers are are now approaching the house. They will come into the house and take you into custody. Any force will be met with force." The cops behind him were armed with crowbars and sledgehammers.

At a few minutes before seven, Fencl again called for the MOVE members to surrender peacefully. "You still have a chance to surrender. Please come out with your hands above your heads. Any force will be met by force . . ." There was no reply. More dogs ran out of the house. A group of cops edged their way across the porch and entered the house. Two minutes later, their number was doubled. Almost thirty flak-jacketed cops were inside the compound.

One of the MOVE children shouting "don't shoot" as she leaves the Powelton house. Wide World Photos.

Two MOVE women and four children leaving the Powelton house after the shootout. Wide World Photos.

They met with no resistance. The residents had barricaded themselves in the basement.

Fifteen minutes later, firemen with axes began hacking away at the heavy, wooden slats that covered the basement windows.

Palmer once more offered to accompany the MOVE members to safety. "Hey, Delbert! This is Walt Palmer. Nobody's going to kill you. Come on out. . . . Can you come to the window? I'll stay here. I'll come in and come out with you." Then Devlin took the horn, "Delbert—now —anybody—can you hear me in there? This is Devlin speaking. They're not trying to kill you. If you want, I'll come out with you . . ." Devlin, with O'Neill at his side and Stakeout police huddled under the basement windows, walked to the front door of the compound.

The only sounds coming from the house were the sobs of the children.

The police announced that MOVE members had two more minutes to surrender and that water was about to be pumped into the house.

Then a gun was spotted, protruding from a basement window of the compound.

"Put that gun down!" officers shouted. "Put it down!"

Deputy Police Commissioner Solomon shouted, "Water, water!" One of the fire department's big deluge guns began to blast through a partially

Police drag wounded officer James Ramp out of the line of fire. Ramp later died. Wide World Photos.

opened basement window. The force of the water was terrific. In five minutes time, the basements of 307 and 309 were more than a foot and a half deep with water.

Then gunshots. The time was just about 8:15.

Policemen and reporters scrambled for cover. Notebooks and cameras, purses and pencils, helmets and hats soon lay scattered about the grounds.

Within seconds—a minute and a half, perhaps two minutes at the most—the shooting was over.

On Pearl Street, across from the compound, a policeman lay sprawled alongside a deep pool of his own blood. Another officer, wounded but at least still alive, writhed on the ground nearby.

In the midst of all this destruction, a tiny girl's face peered out of a basement window at MOVE Headquarters. "My mommy's dead," she could be heard saying. "Help me, please." An adult, "You killed my baby. You goddamn motherfucker, you killed my baby!" Two policemen raced across the porch and up to the window, where they coaxed the child out, then grabbed her and carried her to safety.

Beginning at 8:30 and lasting for the next half hour, the deluge guns continued to pump away into the basements of 307–309. At 9 A.M., Fencl spoke into the bullhorn again. "Come out with your hands up!"

Five minutes later, a naked child in front of her, two smaller, equally naked children following her, a woman in dreadlocks climbed out of a front basement window and began to walk slowly towards the police positions.

Within minutes, the rest of the MOVE members had emerged from the watery basement: first the children, then the adults carrying the babies. In little groups they walked towards the cops, hand in hand, the children usually well in front of the big people.

Only Delbert Orr Africa did not leave the house in this manner. Instead, he crawled out of a Powelton Village through a basement window on the Pearl Street side of the house. Newspaper photographs bore witness to his exit. Through them, you see him, shirtless, arms spread out, about to be beaten. An unidentified policeman, clothed in a bullet-proof vest and a baseball cap, stands at Delbert Africa's side, pointing a semiautomatic rifle at his chin. A second officer has an arm cocked, ready to deliver a blow with his riot helmet. The blow forwarded, Delbert hits the ground, only to be grasped by the hair and wrenched from the grass to the sidewalk, where he is kicked by another policeman. After this battering, he is taken into custody where, nearing the police wagon, fellow policemen constrain yet another officer from causing more injury to the apprehended MOVE member.

Philadelphia policeman kicks Delbert Africa after the Powelton shootout. The *Philadelphia Daily News.*

Their provocation was obvious: Officer James J. Ramp, 52, was dead, mortally wounded by a bullet fired from a .223-caliber Ruger rifle.

The wounded included Police Lieutenant William H. Krause, gunshot wounds of the abdomen and right arm; Policemen Thomas A. Hesson, gunshot wounds in the chest; Charles Stewart, gunshots wounds to the right shoulder, head, and leg; Harry Mackel, bullet shots to the buttocks; Albert Crane, puncture wound to the foot; Charles Geist, smoke inhalation; and Robert Hurst, smoke inhalation. Four firemen were wounded —John Welsh, shot in the neck and head; Robert Snead, pellet wounds to the face; Dennis O'Neill, wounds to the left arm; and Robert Lentine, pellet wounds to the face. Two other firemen suffered minor injuries. Chuckie Sims Africa, received gunshot wounds to the arm. The other MOVE casualties suffered minor injuries. The little girl's "mother," presumed dead at first, was not only very much alive, but uninjured as well.

Who started the shooting and where did it come from? MOVE members still contend that they were unarmed, and that the police, under orders from Commissioner O'Neill, later planted weapons and ammunition inside MOVE Headquarters. Observers outside the MOVE house on the morning of August 8—police officers and most of the reporters present—maintain that the first shot appeared to have been fired from a basement window of 307–309.

Three of the eleven MOVE children present on August 8—Cassandra Davis, 8 (the daughter of Sandra and Michael Davis), Janine Johnson, 5 (the daughter of DeVita Life Johnson), and Malicai Austin, 5 (the son of Merle Austin)—were questioned the next day about the shooting. Cassandra Davis told officers that the MOVE adults "all had guns." Malicai said that he saw Phil, Eddie, Delbert, Janet, and Merle fire their weapons. Janine and Malicai agreed that they had fired first. Why? "Cause cops ain't wanna shoot," Malicai said.

The arrested MOVE members numbered eleven. All now faced murder charges in the slaying of Officer Ramp. These were: Michael Davis, Sandra Davis, William "Phil" Phillips, Delbert, Eddie Goodman, Janet Holloway, Merle Austin, Janine, Debbie Sims, Consuela Dotson, DeVita Life Africa (the former DeVita Johnson), and Charles "Chuckie" Sims Africa.

At a news conference late in the afternoon of August 8, Commissioner O'Neill showed reporters and photographers the weapons which he said police had found in the house. These were identified as two .45-caliber semiautomatic pistols, a .45-caliber carbine, three .232-caliber "Ranger" carbines, two 12-gauge shotguns, two .30-caliber carbines, and a .765 caliber Argentine Mauser.

All the weapons were "operable."

When questioned by reporters about the Delbert Africa beating, O'Neill defended his men. "If you are referring to the member that crawled out with a cartridge clip in one hand and a knife in the other and was hit on the top of head with a steel helmet—if that's being overzealous, so be it."

Rizzo, at a late afternoon press conference, bellowed and cursed reporters, especially those from the *Inquirer.* "Every week in your goddamn newspaper, every weekend, they have headlines in your paper about policemen did this, did that, murder, murder, murder. . . . That's what's wrong with this city. . . . You're destroying it. The people you represent are destroying it."

The tragedy struck deep cords in the former police commissioner. His men, Rizzo said, had shown "incredible restraint for months." As for MOVE, "Here is a group who for months have said that the police were out to kill them. The only people hurt were the police. Only in a democracy would they get away with what they've done."

The *Inquirer's* lead editorial next day was entitled, "The Finale at MOVE." The newspaper praised the "remarkable" restraint shown by law-enforcement officers, yet blamed the mayor for having polarized "the city on racial lines," with the result that "when an incident such as yesterday's tragic events occurs, hatred and mistrust spread throughout the city." That, the *Inquirer* concluded, was the last thing that Philadelphia needed now.

The house had been filthy.

There were dogs everywhere. The rooms were said to be "full of dogshit." Rats ran about. There were crocks or vats of urine on the floor. There was no plumbing. A hole in the floor served as the house toilet.

In the kitchen was a wood-burning stove made out of a large steel drums. There were frying pans, and there were cooking utensils.

The furniture consisted of plastic milk crates, and there were blankets pitched on the floor. Dog droppings lay near the blankets.

In an hour of fury, all that had been was destroyed. As the police bulldozer completed its work of tearing down 307–309, the last of the MOVE banners fell beneath its treads, crushed and splintered.

The words on the fallen sign rang hollow: "Long Live the House That John Africa Built!"

3

Trials, 1979-81

Sometime in January of 1979, Airman First Class Andino R. Ward learned that his former wife Rhonda had been extradited to Philadelphia to face charges stemming from the June 1977 confrontation at Powelton. Ward again flew home to the States in search of his son. The effort proved futile. Oyewolffe Ward, now known as Birdie Africa, was nowhere to be found, and Rhonda refused to tell her ex-husband where the child was being kept.

Andino Ward went to the local media for help. His son, Ward told reporters, was "seven years old and probably can't even read or write." Airman Ward was correct. His son could not even read a watch. A lifetime in MOVE, Ward feared, might do untold damage to the child: "I don't want to see him end up like his mother, either for himself or for society."

Ward was again correct. There was abundant evidence that the boy's very life was already in danger.

For a time, Ward tried to gain custody of his son through the court system. Ward gave up when MOVE members told him that they would "cycle" Birdie before they would hand him over to the courts.

There was no way, Ward was told, that MOVE was going to give up one of its children to the System.

The fate of the eleven MOVE members arrested in 307–309 North Thirty-third on August 8 still had to be decided. Pre-trial hearings took place in early January 1979, then again in March 1979, and again from May 31 until September 5. All charges against DeVita Life Africa were dropped on September 18, 1978 as a result of insufficient evidence. Two other MOVE women, Consuela Dotson and Cassandra Davis, chose to have their cases separated from the others and be tried at a later date. That left nine MOVE defendants.

Three of the nine—Michael Davis, Janine Phillips, and Debbie Sims—had already been convicted on May 21, 1979 of terroristic threats and disorderly conduct and given sentences of from one to two years in prison by Judge Stanley L. Kubacki.

On Monday, December 10, 1979, proceedings against the nine began in room 253 of City Hall, the courtroom assigned to 68-year-old Judge Edwin S. Malmed, an archetypal white-haired, gentlemanly occupant of the bench.

Charged with murder, attempted murder, conspiracy, and aggravated and simple assault arising out of the August 8, 1978 confrontation, the nine defendants—Charles "Chuckie" Sims, Debbie Sims, Michael Davis, William Phillips, Janine Phillips, Delbert Orr, Eddie Goodman, Janet Holloway, and Merle Austin—waived their rights to a jury trial and chose instead to have Judge Malmed rule on their fates.

One by one, the defendants pled innocent to all charges. Each would act as his or her own counsel, in keeping with the tenets of MOVE doctrine. Phil Africa explained that he had been taught, "A free man has no choice but to represent himself." "An attorney," said Delbert, "does not believe as I believe." Merle put it more bluntly. "Seeing as I ain't got no choice," she said, "cause you ain't gone to let us go home, I'll take the judge."

Malmed asked each defendant his or her name, age, occupation, and educational background. Delbert gave as his age the year one. As for an occupation, "I float with life," he said.

The first three days of the trial went more or less quietly, the only significant evidence offered being the police videotapes of the August 8 confrontation. These were played in open court, after which the trial was recessed for the holidays.

When trial resumed on Wednesday, December 26, its nature shifted perceptibly. Chuckie Africa took exception to some of Malmed's rulings. "That don't make it right, cause *you* say so," he snarled. "We understand this thing is rigged." After a point, Malmed declared, "I have heard all I want to hear," and ordered Chuckie Africa removed from court.

The next day, Officer John Sigmann of the Police Department video unit took the stand. When Sigmann couldn't answer a number of Delbert

Orr Africa's questions, Africa acted puzzled. He wondered if the witness understood English. Perhaps the witness spoke Spanish instead.

As the trial entered another week, Prosecutor Wilhelm F. Knauer, Jr., the son of Nixon White House counselor Virginia Knauer, bumped into Delbert Africa at the courtroom railing. Chuckie took exception. "If one MOVE member pushed, all MOVE member pushed," he announced. "You gonna arrest this man?" Delbert shouted.

No, Malmed said. I am not. "Well," Delbert said, "the next assault charge I get, I'm going to earn it."

The next day, January 3, Eddie Africa and Chuckie Africa were ejected from the courtroom. The witness that day was police department photographer John Yagecic. Merle Africa asked Officer Yagecic if "cops lie?" The prosecution objected, and the court sustained the objection. "You're cutting me off," Merle cried. "You bet I am," the judge replied.

For the better part of a week and half (January 7–14), the Commonwealth's witness was Chief Inspector George Fencl. Asked where the first shots had come from on August 8, Fencl testified that he heard firing coming from "beneath my feet" as he was leaving the first floor of the MOVE compound.

Were MOVE people given an adequate chance to surrender to police on August 8?

"Walt Palmer asked them to surrender," Fencl said. Chuckie Sims, whose voice he recognized, then replied according to Fencl, "Fuck you, nigger! We're not going to do nothin'! Come down and get us!"

Police tapes from August 8 were played in court: "I plead with you, let the children be allowed to come out," Father Charles Devlin was heard to say. Profanities shouted from the basement of the compound were the only reply. In the background, dogs could be heard barking.

On Tuesday, January 8, first Merle Austin Africa, then Delbert Africa, were ejected from court. As deputies attempted to lead them out, Delbert began a scuffle, and soon, the other MOVE defendants were on their feet shouting, cursing, throwing punches. When order was restored, Malmed tossed out four more defendants and described the scene he had just witnessed as "a general riot." Chuckie Africa and Phil Africa, in particular, were to be banned from the courtroom until they agreed to behave properly.

The next day, all nine defendants were back in court. Chuckie and Phil agreed to behave as John Africa had taught them.

When trial resumed for the week of January 14, Room 253 was exchanged for a larger fourth-floor courtroom in order to accommodate the growing audience. The crowd at the moment was particularly restive, for early that same day, at 4 A.M., Frank James Africa had been arrested while in the act of breaking into a West Philadelphia house near Thirty-ninth Street. Already wanted by the Philadelphia police for weapons charges arising out of the "Guns on the Porch Day," Vincent Leaphart's young nephew now faced multiple jail sentences.

The atmosphere was again charged when the next day MOVE people learned that police had raided their Richmond, Virginia chapter, "The Seed of Wisdom." The court order for the raid had been signed by Judge Malmed. Phil and Chuckie Africa loudly and longly cursed the aging jurist, who then banished them from his courtroom. As his brothers were led away, Delbert Africa shouted, "Your kids spread syphilis, Malmed!" He too met with expulsion, as did Eddie Africa.

"The Seed of Wisdom" was housed in a two-story Victorian home; its more permanent occupants consisting of MOVE members Sharon Sims and Valerie Brown, along with a dozen or more ill-clothed and undernourished children.

Patrick Bell was a commonwealth's attorney in Richmond, Virginia, at the time of the raid. Since 1976, she had been handling complaints from neighbors concerning "The Seed of Wisdom." Its occupants had bullhorns, and they had guns. Their children slept on pallets and under-neath furniture coverings and ate raw vegetables and eggs, "in keeping with *The Teachings of John Africa.*" The neighbors claimed to have watched aghast as the Seed's children cracked egg shells open and sucked the yolks. All were reported to have distended stomachs, like "refugee children," some said. The house they lived in smelled of garlic.

Brown and Sims, on the other hand, slept in an upstairs bedroom, where they watched television and "ate any kind of junk food they wanted," according to Bell.

Years later, Bell recounted to the Philadelphia *Daily News* how she had many times in the past confronted the MOVE mothers: "I'd say to Sharon Sims, 'Hey, you're eating good. You're eating McDonald's and all that. Why do you make your kids eat like this?' And she'd say that they were junkfood addicts and it was the fault of the system, and they were trying to purify the children. You couldn't get them to make sense."

This was the world in which Birdie Africa had been raised.

Stakeout Officer Charles Stewart, wounded in the Powelton shootout, testified that same day (January 15) that he had seen "muzzle flashes" coming from the basement of the MOVE compound. Fellow Stakeout Officer Robert Hurst (later to be the president of the Fraternal Order of Police—the FOP—at the time of the May 13, 1985 confrontation) told of seeing Chuckie Sims with a Ruger Mini-.14 carbine in his hand. Nearby, on a table off to Chuckie Africa's left, were two handguns.

On Friday, January 18, all nine defendants were removed from court after a particularly raucous session. Malmed ordered the "back-up" counsel to become "actual counsel." While being led away, Delbert shouted, "Come on, Malmed! Come out here! Let's get it on!"

Court again recessed as the "back-up" counsel, comprised mostly of young public defenders, asked the Pennsylvania Supreme Court to rule on the propriety of the order.

The question which the back-up counsel posed was this: Could a judge order an attorney to act as actual counsel against the expressed wishes of his or her client? The Pennsylvania Supreme Court, on Tuesday the 22 of January, announced a decision. The justices found that the defendants had "forfeited their rights" when they refused to abide by acceptable courtroom behavior. Henceforth, back-up counsel would conduct the cases for the defendants.

The pace of the trial was not abetted by the addition of back-up counsel. The defendants remained abrasive, loud, and disorderly. Ejections and gaggings became the stuff of day after day, week after week in Courtroom 453. Knauer and fellow Assistant District Attorney John Straub argued the Commonwealth's case before Judge Malmed. Relying in part of the research of a young law school intern named Bradford Richman, the two prosecutors constructed a strong, if largely circumstantial, case against the Nine.

Detective Nicholas Vivino claimed that he was twenty yards from the MOVE house when he saw and heard Delbert Africa say, "Come on in. You've been wanting to come in. But call home first and make sure your insurance policy is paid up." At this point, none of the MOVE defendants was in court—they were now being held in a seventh-floor waiting cell—so Vivino was shown a blown-up photograph of Delbert Africa and asked to identify the person shown there. Defense counsel objected, and the MOVE defendants were sent for, then seated as a group in the jury box. On discovering why he had been sent for, Delbert Africa, suddenly furious, shouted, "Bring the witness upstairs!" Merle Africa began to scream insults at her court-appointed counsel, Norris Gelman, calling him a "Jew coward." "I'm not a coward, Merle," Gelman replied. "*You're* a coward."

Knauer asked Vivino to identify the man he saw on August 8. Vivino pointed at Delbert Africa, who was standing with his back turned to the officer. Vivino then left the witness stand and walked over to the jury box. Again, he pointed at Delbert Africa. "That's him," Vivino said.

Another policeman, Officer Samuel Hatch, Jr., said that he saw Michael Davis Africa armed with a Ruger Mini-14. Hatch testified that he was on the first floor of 309 at the time and was peeping through a hole in the door to the basement.

Officer Robert Archer testified that he had been on the porch of the MOVE compound at the Thirty-third Street side when he saw two women and a man in a basement window. The two women were holding babies up in front of them. The male was armed with a rifle and a hand grenade. Officer Archer identified the man with the weapons as Chuckie Africa.

Officer Andrew Kalmar said that he was with Officer Hurst when they waded into two to three foot-deep water in the basement of the MOVE compound following the confrontation. The Stakeout officers, Kalmar testified, found plenty of ammunition and weapons down there: a .223-caliber Ruger Mini-14 (at the northeast end of the basement); another Ruger Mini-14, two shotguns, a 7.65-mm rifle, 200 rounds of .50-caliber ammunition, 10 rounds of shotgun ammunition, 50 rounds of .357 Magnum ammunition, 50 rounds of .45-caliber revolver ammunition, 45 rounds of 9-mm pistol ammunition, 13 rounds of 7.65 rifle ammunition, 100 rounds of .30-caliber carbine ammunition, 36 rounds of .32-caliber pistol ammunition, and 81 rounds of .22-caliber ammunition, along with two gas masks (towards the middle of the basement area).

Officer Gale Clements was the first witness to testify to seeing a MOVE member fire a weapon on August 8. Clements was posted about fifteen feet from the Thirty-third Street side of the MOVE compound when he saw Chuckie Africa kneeling with a carbine in his hands. Shortly afterwards, Clements witnessed "flashes" coming from the rifle. The weapon appeared to be aimed at Officer Salvatore Marsalo, who was crouching, partially hidden behind a nearby tree. Clements saw bark "ripped" from the tree by rifle fire that day.

Officer Marsalo, the forty-fifth witness to be called, testified that he saw Phil Africa stooped behind a basement window with a rifle in his hands. Marsalo also testified to seeing muzzle flashes.

Officer Robert Hurst again testified that he was no more than two feet away from a basement window when he saw Chuckie Africa "in a crouched position with a carbine-type weapon in the port-arms position." Chuckie's face was in the window and he "gave me a sarcastic grin." Hurst told him to drop his weapons. "I called him by name." Sims Africa dropped out of view moments later, Hurst testified, just as "semiautomatic fire" began coming from that same window.

A Philadelphia Police Department firearms examiner testified that ballistic tests had shown that a Ruger Mini-14 taken on August 8 from the MOVE house had been the weapon used to kill Officer Ramp. The same weapon, the examiner said, was responsible for the wounding of Officers Thomas Hesson and William Krause.

U.S. Treasury Agent John L. Smith, Jr. testified that three Ruger Mini-14s and a .30-caliber carbine had been purchased in May 1977, May 1978, and June 1978 at Edelman's Gun Store shops in suburban Montgomeryville and Newton Square. The weapons were signed for by one "James W. English."

On March 10, three MOVE supporters—Michael Abdul Jones, 25; Raymond Brennan, 33; and Kenfer Abdul Mulik, 22—were arrested and charged with resisting arrest, aggravated and simple assault, and disorderly conduct. The three had engaged in a mini-confrontation of their own with sheriff's deputies and policemen in the hallway outside court.

The trial droned on. Joseph Grimes, a fingerprint expert for the Philadelphia Police Department, told the court that Phil Africa's palm print had been found on the federal weapons purchase form at Edelman's. Three such forms had been signed "Ricardo White," a fourth bore the signature, "James W. English." Clerks at Edelman's were asked to identify the purchaser or purchasers of the guns. They could only say that he was a black male.

Each Monday the MOVE defendants were taken into court and again asked to pledge to obey the judge's orders. On Monday, March 17, Delbert Africa shouted at Malmed, "We're going to hunt you down." Eddie Africa told the judge that, "Wherever we find sickness, our job is to stamp it out. And you are sick. We're going to exterminate you." The defendants were taken back to the seventh floor pen.

In mid-April, eight defense witnesses disputed police claims that the first shot had come from the MOVE basement. John McCullough, a Powelton neighbor, said that he saw a "white man with a rifle" in a third floor window on the west side of Thirty-third Street near Pearl. Howard Bycer, a student, testified that he had been standing at the northwest corner of Thirty-third and Pearl when he heard "a shattering of glass" and turned around just as glass began falling from a third floor window of 312

North Thirty-third Street. "I know of two shots that came from that window," he said.

The next day, April 14, McCullough was back on the stand. He told the judge that he had seen a man in a third floor window with a rifle in his hands. A few minutes after the shooting began, McCullough said he saw police take "a white man with a gun" out of a building at 310 North Thirty-third Street. Assistant District Attorney Straub showed McCullough an aerial photograph. The address he had given—310 North Thirty-third—was a vacant lot.

Wynne Alexander, a reporter for radio station WDAS, had been at the northwest corner of Thirty-third and Pearl when the first shot was heard. "I looked to my right. That's where the shot came from."

On April 16, Larry Rosen, a reporter-editor for KYW radio, testified that he had been at the west side of Thirty-third Street between Pearl and Baring, when he heard someone "screaming something containing an expletive. I heard two shots behind me. I turned over my right shoulder, looked up, and saw a hand, part of an arm, and a pistol. . . . After I turned, there was another shot fired from the window. Then there were scattered shots." Rosen believed that a third shot came from a second floor window in the building on the west side of Thirty-third Street that fronted onto Baring.

A tape from KYW radio was played. A reporter could be heard saying that there was "a man leaning out a window on the west side" of Thirty-third Street, "shouting obscenities . . . and fir[-ing] a pistol."

Rosen testified that he saw two or three black men taken forcibly by policemen from the building he had described.

Paul Bennett, a former KYW reporter, said that he had been on Pearl Street at the northwest corner of Thirty-third. He testified that, "the first shot came from my left." That would have put the first shot coming from a northerly direction.

John McCullough was called back to the stand to correct his earlier testimony. The first shot, he now testified, came from a building on the northwest corner, rather than the southwest corner, of Thirty-third and Pearl. There were now three witnesses—McCullough, Bycer, and Bennett—to this effect.

On April 17, Walter Palmer, one of the "negotiators" on August 8, testified that he had been standing on the curb on the east side of Thirty-third Street when the shooting began. "I heard a single shot, and I hit the ground immediately." The first shot, he believed, "came from the back of my head," out of a westerly direction. Palmer claimed not to have witnessed any gunfire at all coming from the MOVE basement.

The police had the murder weapon, but no fingerprints. Witnesses had seen Officer Ramp put his hand to his throat and crumple backwards to the ground, but that was all. No one could testify to seeing someone pull the trigger.

After sixty-four days, one hundred witnesses, two hundred exhibits, and three hundred motions for dismissal, the trial of the MOVE Nine had, by May 1, reached closing arguments. The various attorneys for the defense led off. Each did his best to counter the charges—third degree murder, attempted murder, conspiracy, and seven counts of aggravated assault. All sought to remind Judge Malmed of how circumstantial was the case before His Honor. How could the judge convict nine men and women for the murder of one man when there were no fingerprints, no eyewitness accounts, and no positive identification of the killer or killers? The defendants, counsel argued, should be set free.

Straub and Knauer presented their closing arguments on Monday, May 5. Straub emphasized that the record showed that MOVE members had purchased three high-powered .232-caliber Ruger Mini-14 carbines during the summer of 1978. These same three rifles were found in the basement of the MOVE compound on August 8, 1978, along with two thousand rounds of ammunition. One of the Rugers had been positively identified as the weapon used to murder Officer Ramp.

Judge Malmed returned with his verdict three days later on Thursday, May 8, 1980. The defendants—Merle Austin Africa, Michael Davis Africa, Charles Sims Africa, Edward Goodman Africa, Janet Holloway Africa, Delbert Orr Africa, Janine Phillips Africa, William Phillips Africa, and Deborah Sims Africa—were guilty as charged. Sentence would be set on August 4—a minimum of thirty to one hundred years in prison, as it turned out, for each of the Nine. (At the close of a separate trial, before Judge Levy Anderson of Common Pleas Court and a jury, on February 22, 1982, Consuela Dotson Africa would be convicted and sentenced to 10–20 years in prison, while Sandra Davis, who renounced her MOVE membership in court, would be acquitted of the August 8 charges filed against her.)

As Malmed pronounced sentence against him, Delbert Africa shouted, "Liar!" The other MOVE defendants cursed and screamed obscenities at the judge, the cops, the prosecutors, the press, the politicians.

As the Nine were led away in handcuffs, Michael Africa shouted, "Come on, Malmed. Get your ass out here!"

Delbert Africa hollered, "Come on, gangster. Come on with it!"

"You racist maniac!" Chuckie Africa screamed.

Eddie Africa shouted, "You'll pay for this!"

Phil Africa got in his licks. "Hey, Malmed!" he hollered. "You're nothin' but a disposable trash bag for the System."

Malmed glared, then left the bench and went back into his chambers. Straub, Knauer, and their young assistant, Richman, beamed and posed for photographers.

The trial of the MOVE Nine was over.

Yet another, more controversial, trial arose in the aftermath of the August 8, 1978 confrontation. The defendants this time were the three police officers accused in the beating of Delbert Africa. Charged with aggravated and simple assault and with official oppression were Officers Joseph Zagame, Charles Geist, and Terrence Patrick Mulvihill. A fourth officer, Lawrence D'Ulisse of the Stakeout Unit, was identified by name in newspaper accounts, but never indicted. (At a pre-trial hearing before Judge Charles L. Durham on 24 October 1979, Delbert Africa shouted, "Where's D'Ulisse? You all know who he is. I know who he is. Why is he hiding if he didn't commit no crime?")

For the prosecution, Assistant District Attorney L. George Parry relied heavily on the widely seen newspaper photographs and television footage of the beating. A three-minute video tape from the local CBS television affiliate was shown to jurors, and newspaper photographers were put on the stand. A *Daily News* photographer recalled how he had seen Delbert Africa emerge from the MOVE basement with his hands in the air. Delbert, the photographer testified, made no attempt to resist arrest.

The defendants were portrayed by their counsel, Richard A. Sprague, as good cops and good citizens. The jurors were reminded of the severe pressure under which the policemen had had to do their jobs on August 8. Officer Geist, for example, had been injured slightly in the course of the gunfight, while Officer Zagame had been a close friend (and a pall-bearer at the funeral) of the late Officer Ramp.

Chief Inspector George Fencl testified that on August 8 he heard MOVE members single out Officer Zagame by name. MOVE people on their loudspeaker talked "about who was fucking his wife while he was there."

Pat Warren, a television news reporter, testified that she saw what she believed at the time to be a gun in Delbert Africa's hand as he emerged from a basement window on the Pearl Street side of the MOVE compound.

Defense attorney Sprague then called Delbert Africa and Phil Africa to the stand. As he was led handcuffed and shackled past the jury, Delbert shouted at Judge Stanley Kubacki, "*You* in charge of this courtroom, man?" and sneered at the man he called "a criminal" and "an extortionist."

On Tuesday, February 3, 1981, as the case against the three officers was drawing to its conclusion, Kubacki made an unexpected announcement from the bench. "Philadelphia," he said, "is bleeding to death because of the MOVE tragedy." Kubacki therefore ordered a directed verdict of innocent on all charges against the three defendants. "No verdict," the judge said, "will staunch the flow of blood. It can only be stopped by setting up a lightning rod. I will be that lightning rod."

It was a line that MOVE members would remember for a long time to come: *I will be that lightning rod.*

In the early spring of 1977, two young black men arrived in Rochester, New York, in search of property. One of the men, gaunt to the point of being rail-thin, introduced himself as Jimmy Lee Phart. His friends, he said, called him "Jimmy Slant." The other, sociable and stout, was known as "Ernie." The men said they were looking for inexpensive real estate for their uncle to invest in. The uncle was the guy with the money; he would be along shortly.

A rundown property on Flint Street appealed to the newcomers. It was cheap. The neighborhood was not the best—it was nearer to derelict—but the price was right. In a city that was largely poor and more than a third black, "good buys" in real estate were abundant. A purchase price of less than five hundred dollars was agreed to, and the papers were signed in the name of the uncle, "Vincent Lee Phart."

"Jimmy Slant" was Alphonso Robbins Africa. "Ernie" was Gerald Ford Africa. The missing "uncle" was Vincent Leaphart.

There would be other purchases, using other names. Eventually, MOVE's Rochester properties would number seven, none costing more than five hundred dollars.

Philadelphia's pattern became Rochester's. The new neighbors did odd jobs to make ends meet, such as shoveling snow free of charge, and kept large numbers of unvaccinated animals in their homes. Some of the old neighbors were willing to put up with the newcomers. Some were not. The new people lectured their new audience about their diets and their "System lifestyles," talked up the merits of their own "non-System lifestyle," and kept house in their inimitable fashion. Rats and roaches were soon breeding with indigenous rapidity. Following complaints about the usual stench and noise, Dennis Sims and Vincent Leaphart were briefly hauled-off to the local stationhouse on disorderly conduct charges. Assuming aliases, the two were released on their own recognizance. Smiling broadly, the man known locally as "Master John Africa" simply walked out the door of the stationhouse. And so MOVE life went on as it had begun in Rochester for nearly three years.

Then, following another pattern, everything changed. In the early morning hours one fine spring day in 1981, three large U-Haul trucks rolled slowly onto Flint Street. Behind them came the usual rush-hour traffic, cars and a few vans. Overhead, a helicopter's blades sang.

On signal, the three trucks pulled to a halt, and three teams of twenty or more federal, state, and local cops, all heavily armed, came rushing out of the rears of the trailers.

Three neighboring houses and a vacant Citgo service station were entered and searched. Six persons were arrested either in the houses or in adjoining yards. Others were arrested where they were found. Raymond Foster was walking down the street. "Ernie" and Alberta Wicker were jogging together outside the Rochester art museum. Only Sue Levino remembered to scream, "Long Live John Africa!" No weapons were found anywhere.

"Uncle Vincent Lee Phart," dressed in blue jeans and a gray sweatshirt, was apprehended as he walked a dog and two children. Cognizant of his imminent arrest, he picked up his "children" and held them in front of him. At his booking, he would state that his name was not Vincent Leaphart, but Vincent Life. His age, he said, was one.

Leaphart told ATF Agent Walt Wasyluk—his counterpart in the sense that Wasyluk so often coordinated police actions against MOVE —that he had been looking forward to meeting him for a long time now. "Funny," Wasyluk said, "but I feel the same way about meeting you."

The others arrested that day were Alphonso Robbins, 33; Gerald Ford, 33; Dennis Sims, 28; Carlos Perez, 23; Conrad Hampton, 32; Sue Levino, 31; Alberta Wicker, 33; and Raymond Foster, 46. Conrad and Mo Africa gave as their place of work the local Sear's garage.

The date was May 13, 1981.

At their arraignment on May 27, Leaphart's bond was set at $750,000, the others at $100,000 each. Leaphart and Mo Robbins faced federal bombmaking charges. Perez and Dennis Sims were held on Pennsylvania warrants, stemming from their participation in "The Guns on the Porch

Day," May 20, 1977. Mo Africa announced that he was ready for whatever was to come: "I'm my own lawyer. I represent myself. I'm legally educated by John Africa."

Leaphart's trial was held in Philadelphia later that same summer in the court of U.S. District Judge Clifford Scott Green. Two hundred prospective jurors were questioned and dismissed before a panel could be formed. Then, on Thursday, July 2, the trial began.

The former Jeanne Africa testified that Vincent Leaphart was known as "Charlie" by fellow MOVE members. "Charlie," whom she also identified as "John Africa," had told her that her husband, Ishongo Africa, would be put on the front line against the cops in any upcoming confrontation. Ishongo, Charlie said, was almost sure to die as a MOVE martyr, for the confrontation would probably be bloody. Otherwise, Ishongo would be killed by his fellow MOVE members. John Africa had lost faith in him. Leaphart then ordered her to "marry" Eddie Goodman Africa. She refused and left the organization in December of 1977. Sometime afterwards, Jeanne got word to Ishongo, and he too left the MOVE Headquarters on April 16, 1978, well before the August 8, 1978 confrontation.

Samuel Sanders, convicted and sent to prison for three years on the same 1978 federal charges of conspiracy and weapons violations that Leaphart and Robbins now faced, testified that he had made bombs for the MOVE organization at the direction of Vincent Leaphart. Sanders said that he had planted bomb threats at the Benjamin Franklin Motor Inn in Philadelphia in 1977.

The star witness for the prosecution was, of course, none other than Donald J. Glassey. Wearing a navy blue blazer, khakis, a blue shirt and a rep tie, Glassey tried to look the part of a junior faculty member at a small college. He had, he testified, known Vincent Leaphart since 1971. Together they had founded MOVE in 1972. MOVE in its early years, Glassey said, had been essentially non-violent, but beginning in September of 1976, Leaphart had ordered its members to arm themselves. Leaphart, Glassey testified, "said he anticipated a confrontation with police and wanted to be ready."

In October of 1976, Glassey and other MOVE members planted timing devices and bomb threats in hotels across the United States. Glassey himself left threatening letters at hotels in Washington and Boston. Leaphart intended, Glassey said, to "set up an extortion scheme in various cities to have it appear that MOVE had a large underground."

Glassey testified that he was ordered by Leaphart in March 1977 to purchase two shotguns. He did. Afterwards, he brought the weapons to Leaphart's apartment where he saw what amounted to "an arsenal of weapons. There were fifty weapons, half rifles and half handguns."

In mid-May of 1977, a few days or so before the May 20 "Guns on the Porch Day," Leaphart called a "meeting." There, John Africa announced that the confrontation which he was planning was about to begin.

Agent Wasyluk testified that the July 21, 1977 raid on the two MOVE cars had produced a total of twenty-four fully intact bombs, plus seventeen more unassembled bombs. The cars, Wasyluk said, were parked near the Mount Airy home of the sister of the defendant, Mr. Alphonso Robbins.

The prosecution rested.

Leaphart remained seated and generally silent throughout most of the trial, yet frequently made hand signals to MOVE witnesses to stay calm, to speak up, to lower their voices. And always, the MOVE members did as they were instructed. In this way, Leaphart silently "coordinated" the defense.

Mo Africa, on the other hand, actively carried on a defense, putting on the stand a series of witnesses to testify to the curative power of John Africa. Anything at all—drugs, marital discord, physical deformities, sterility, epilepsy—the master could cure.

The recently convicted William Phillips was put on the stand and described himself as "Minister of Defense of the MOVE organization and Co-ordinator of the MOVE Underground." Donald J. Glassey, Phil Africa, said, was both a "coward" and a "liar." (Later in the trial, Mo Africa would ask Glassey face-to-face: "How does it feel to be a traitor?")

Delbert Africa, called as a defense witness and dressed in his prison fatigues, was asked to describe the various beatings that MOVE people had suffered at the hands of Philadelphia cops. As Delbert began to describe one particularly brutal beating outside the old MOVE headquarters, Leaphart shouted, "Stop it!" then buried his face in his hands and cried. Almost immediately, Mo Africa began to cry, and soon, MOVE people throughout the courtroom joined in the weeping.

Frank James Africa, already convicted on 1977 charges of riot and conspiracy, testified to his position as "a full Naturalist Minister of MOVE" and referred to the defendant as "Brother Vinnie."

Halfway through his own defense, Mo Africa asked to read a prepared statement to the jury. Judge Green granted the unusual motion. "Before this trial is over, you'll see how sick Don Glassey was to betray MOVE,"

Mo told the jurors. "He was real sick to just go and spill his guts all over the place about John Africa after all he did for him."

A day later, Mo Africa played excerpts from MOVE telephone conversations taped by federal agents in 1977. ATF undercover agent John Minichino could be heard discussing the sale of explosives to MOVE members Gregory Howard and Samuel Sanders, both of whom were later convicted in 1978 in a federal court trial that relied heavily on the use of the tapes. Other tapes were heard involving telephone conversations between Glassey and MOVE members, including William Whitney Smith. Smith, another former MOVE member who turned informant, had subsequently been found drowned in the Schuylkill River which runs between the downtown area and West Philadelphia. Smith's death was ruled a suicide.

The defense rested.

Leaphart delivered his own closing arguments. "I'm not a guilty man," he told the jurors. "I'm an innocent man. I didn't come here to make trouble or to bring trouble, but to bring the truth! And goddamn it, that's what I'm going to do!

"I'm fighting for air that you've got to breathe. I'm fighting for water that you've got to drink, and if it gets any worse, you're not going to be drinking that water. I'm fighting for food that you've got to eat. And, you

John Africa upon his acquittal. The *Philadelphia Daily News.*

know, you've got to eat it, and if it gets any worse, you're not going to be eating that food.

"Don't you see, if you took this thing all the way, all the way, you would have clean air, clean water, clean soil, and be quenched of industry. But you see, they don't want that. They can't have that."

"They," needless to say, were the leaders of the System. And look what the System had brought with it. Look what the System had done to the innocent creatures of nature: "Deer don't run down people, but people run down deer. Monkeys don't shoot people, but people shoot monkeys. Yet monkeys are seen as unclean and people as intelligent. You can go as far as you want in the forest and you won't find no jails. Because the animals of the forest don't believe in jail. But come to civilization, that's all you see."

Five and a half days later, on July 22, the jury returned with the verdicts. Vincent Leaphart and Alphonso Robbins Africa were found innocent on all counts. Leaphart bent forward and spoke into a microphone at the defense table. "The power of truth," he said, "is final."

John Africa beamed and hugged Alberta Wicker. Then he walked over and shook hands with Walt Wasyluk. "No hard feelings, Walt."

As free as the deer, John Africa walked out of the courtroom.

Four years later, in the fall of 1985, Louise James recalled to an investigator how, "The ATF Agency arrested a person whom they identified as John Africa. However, they could not arrest John Africa because arrest means stop, and you cannot stop the truth. Therefore, they did not arrest John Africa."

James explained how John Africa had "seemingly presented himself in the form of a human being." But the police and the prosecutors, unmindful of the truth, mistook this man, who was her brother Vincent Leaphart, for John Africa. "However, this person was only Vincent Leaphart."

After John Africa "presented himself," Vincent Leaphart ceased to be "in communication" with her and her family. James said she did not know what had happened to her brother. She only knew "that they are two human beings."

The baffled investigator asked James's attorney if *he* understood what his client was saying. "I am totally confused," was his reply.

4

6221 Osage Avenue, 1981-84

ollowing his acquittal in 1981, Vincent Leaphart went underground. A high proportion of MOVE's members, including some of the most impassioned and volatile, such as Delbert Orr and Chuckie Sims, were now confined to state prisons for lengthy, and perhaps indefinite, terms. Other MOVE members, though receptive of lesser sentences, were nonetheless off the streets and inclined to prolong their stays in prison. MOVE's jailhouse protests were frequent and all too liable to turn violent. On December 3, 1981, MOVE members and recruited hangers-on at Holmesburg State Prison attacked their guards with sharpened sticks and bricks. Seventeen guards and ten inmates were injured. As a result of this kind of activity, any number of MOVE inmates could expect to remain in prison forever.

MOVE's Headquarters had been demolished after the August 8, 1978 confrontation. Two of its "chapters," in Rochester, New York and in Richmond, Virginia—"The Seed of Wisdom"—had been raided and effectively crippled if not altogether shut down. And so, the questions, for those on the outside, were no longer ones of confrontation, but rather, of survival. The most pressing question: Where to set up housekeeping?

Number 6221 Osage Avenue, a row house in predominantly black West Philadelphia, situated between Sixty-second Street to the east and Cobbs Creek Parkway to the west, thirty blocks or so from the old Headquarters in Powelton Village, had belonged since 1958 to Louise L. and Frank R. James. Following their divorce in 1968, the property had become her's alone. James, Vincent Leaphart's sister and one of the first converts to his movement, now resided there with her only child, Frank, Jr.

Little or no strategy went into the decision to transform this trim rowhouse on Osage Avenue into the next MOVE headquarters. There was, as Louise James has said, no better place for MOVE to go. The children of several of the MOVE members convicted after the 1978 confrontation had been kept at the house since 1980–81. Now, and in very short order, 6221 Osage became not only a nursery for its children but the command center of all MOVE activity. For the next four years, the little house on Osage would be the home for at least a dozen adults and children, the actual number shifting frequently. Foremost among the new boarders was John Africa himself. Others included Birdie Africa and his mother Rhonda.

The three-story row house, set along a neat, narrow, tree-lined street, was anchored in one of the more pleasant neighborhoods in West

MOVE members addressing neighbors at 6221 Osage Avenue. Ramona Africa is on the far right. The *Philadelphia Daily News.*

Philadelphia, its residents embodying the best of the old clichés: middle-class, hard-working, family people; good, solid citizens. Many had lived in the West Philadelphia neighborhood for decades. Some had lived on the block itself for twenty and thirty years. Husbands worked, wives worked, their children would work, dreams would be fulfilled. There was little fear that this pattern would be interrupted.

In the fall of 1983, the pattern changed.

MOVE members had for some time been working on the south side of their house. A large cart, constructed from bed rails, was used to hold a nearby parking space for MOVE's supply deliveries. For some reason the cart had been moved when Butch Marshall, who resided at 6223 Osage, returned from work on September 4. Marshall made the mistake of parking his car in the empty space.

One of the brothers rushed out of 6221 and began cursing loudly. What the fuck did Marshall think he was doing, taking MOVE's space? The motherfucker knew better than that. Gonna put some MOVE heat on his motherfuck'n ass.

Blows followed. Marshall was struck and fell to the ground, hitting his head on the step of 6228 Osage, the home of the Nichols family. He then picked himself up and began to walk groggily down the street, where he was assaulted by three MOVE women. Eventually, Marshall was rescued by neighbors and taken to the hospital. When he returned, bite marks showed on his face. He had been bitten by the three women not only on the face, but in the back and in the groin.

In October of 1983, after an assault on yet another neighbor, the residents, led by Carey Foskey, of 6213 Osage, and Inez Nichols, of 6228 Osage, drew up a petition, which had begun as a letter addressed to then-Mayor William J. Green. Mrs. Foskey later enumerated some of the complaints listed in the petition, as "Garbage placed open to feed animals. Too many animals—dogs and cats running loose. Rats. Feeding animals on other peoples' property. Throwing raw meat or any other garbage outside. Feeding pigeons and building pigeon coops. Blocking a private driveway with debris at 6221 Osage Avenue. Presenting of fire hazards. . . . Vending produce in a residential area. Attacked a neighbor over a parking space . . ."

The neighbors met with a number of local black politicians, including State Representative Peter D. Truman. Truman, though professing great sympathy for the neighbors, pleaded for their endurance and silence, at least until the mayoral election was over. Once Wilson Goode was secured in office, Truman said that he himself would tear that fence down. Shortly afterwards, Wilson Goode was elected mayor of Philadelphia. As one of the neighbors later remarked, "We haven't seen Peter Truman from that day to this."

In December of 1983, several of the neighbors saw Frank James, axe in hand, chase his mother down Osage Avenue, and reported this to the police. That same December, on Christmas Day, MOVE turned on its loudspeakers, apparently for the first time on Osage Avenue. Beginning at a time near dawn and throughout the next several hours, MOVE speakers loudly and obscenely denounced the System and called for the freedom of their imprisoned brothers and sisters.

Betty Mapp had seen twenty-three Christmases pass in her home at 6241 Osage Avenue. On this Christmas morning, while playing Santa Claus with the children, the Mapps heard a loud noise. At first, they thought someone was singing Christmas carols. They went to their door to investigate and discovered that the noise was coming from the MOVE loudspeaker.

The neighbors decided to call the police. Mrs. Mapp soon saw a police car arrive. She watched out her window as it traveled slowly past her house and down to Sixty-third and Cobbs Creek Parkway. The car stopped, yet no officers alighted. The MOVE speakers went on with their obscene business. The Mapps coped. That was how they spent Christmas Day, 1983.

In February of the new year, Louise James and LaVerne Sims also turned to the police for help. The two sisters talked to Civil Affairs Unit officers about John Africa and what he had wrought within their own families. According to a Department memorandum, the sisters told officers that, "When John Africa walked away from his federal trial, he became obsessed with his own power, telling his followers that he had outsmarted the whole United States."

The same memorandum revealed what life had become for the sisters of Vincent Leaphart. As John Africa, Vincent Leaphart had demanded that Gail Sims, LaVerne's daughter, marry a MOVE member. When she heard the news, LaVerne telephoned her brother. After the phone call, Leaphart directed Frank James to beat Louise in front of other MOVE members. "Frank complied. Louise was being punished for her sister's disobedience."

Once, after a MOVE member had written from prison to reproach Louise, Leaphart insisted that his sister read the letter aloud before the whole group. The letter was filled with obscenities, and Louise was not able to continue reading for long. Leaphart then ordered Frank to beat his mother, which he did, until Louise began to vomit. Frank James covered his mother's face with a pillow, turned to Leaphart and asked if he wanted his mother "cycled." "No. Not now," Master John Africa replied. The torturer ceased his work. The son pulled the pillow off his mother's head.

Louise James moved in with LaVerne Sims in October 1983, but did not escape her brother's wrath. MOVE members and supporters were commanded, as their "activity," to place phone calls to Louise at Sims's home, calls which sometimes numbered fifty and sixty a day.

James later significantly altered her version of the departure from 6221 Osage, claiming that she moved for reasons of privacy, permitting the MOVE members to remain. She considered her departure a temporary one, believing that those remaining had no intentions of assuming permanent residence at her home. Frank, she claimed, was displeased with her retreat.

On April 13, a City Water Department employee, assigned to turn off the water to 6221 Osage for nonpayment, was asked by a policeman assigned to the area if he was aware of who owned the house. When informed that 6221 was a MOVE house, the city employee asked if the police department would back him up. He was told that they would not. And so, he noted on his form that the house belonged to MOVE and submitted it to his supervisors. This was the last attempt made by the Water Department to shut off the water at 6221 Osage Avenue.

On April 27, City Managing Director Leo A. Brooks and several black politicians met with police officers for a briefing about the situation on Osage Avenue. Nothing came of the meeting.

On May 3, a black-hooded MOVE member armed with a shotgun was spotted atop 6221 Osage, from where he soon began crossing from one roof to another. More than forty policemen were called to the neighborhood, and for more than an hour and a half, there was a stalemate. Eventually, the gunman disappeared back into the MOVE house, and the police left. No charges were filed, although the incident was prominently reported and photographed. Mayor Goode said at a press conference that, "We do not want to do anything that will cause an unnecessary confrontation. . . . I prefer to have dirt and some smell than to have bloodshed."

Clifford Bond, a schoolteacher who lived in the neighborhood, recalled, "When an individual was on the roof with the mask and shotgun, my daughter was in our picture window, and she said, 'Daddy, what is the man doing on top of the roof with the gun?' And I didn't have an answer. She asked, 'Isn't that against the law?' And I said, 'Yes.' "

MOVE members in front of their 6221 Osage Avenue Headquarters speaking through loudspeakers. Wide World Photos.

Ten days later, on May 13, and for the ensuing two weeks, MOVE began carrying out a series of weekend "activities." The loudspeakers on top of 6221 boomed twenty-four hours a day. The mayor was denounced, the cops were denounced, the judges were denounced. The Osage neighbors were denounced. There were threats of violence. The voices were loud and brutally obscene. The point of all this remained as ever: LET OUR PEOPLE GO.

On Mother's Day, a crowd of sixty or more neighbors, MOVE sympathizers, and passersby gathered in front of 6221, as yet another series of vitriolic speeches were broadcast via the loudspeaker. Outraged over MOVE's defilement of another holiday celebration, thirty-five year old Milton Williams, a nine-year resident of Osage Avenue who worked the late-night shift driving a delivery truck for the United Parcel Service and depended on daylight for sleep, along with a few other neighbors challenged MOVE's men to a fist-fight. "Come on off the porch and let's get it on. Let's fight it out, OK? We're sick of this mess," Williams shouted at the MOVE neighbors.

Up until that time, Williams said, "We tried to talk to these people like neighbors. We tried to reason with them, to find out what their problems were. . . . You know what they told us? 'John Africa told us not to respect your rights.' "

Another holiday became the occasion of another acrimonious meeting for the neighbors, this time with Mayor Goode at City Hall. On Memorial Day, 1984 (May 28), fifteen Osage area residents insisted that the City had to take some action on their behalf. We can't take it much longer, they asserted.

Betty Mapp was one of the people present that morning in the mayor's conference room. "He came out. He introduced himself, and everybody gave their names. And then, one by one, we start[ed] telling him what was going on. . . . The MOVE people had been telling us that on August 8 that they were going to have this confrontation . . . regardless [of] whether we went to the political people and got help from them or not, and that they were sorry that we were in the middle of it, but they were going to have it.

"I said to the mayor, what am I supposed to do if something was to happen on August 8, if I'm supposed to go out and go to work just like I have been going every morning and leave my family there in the street? So he said, 'I suggest to you to go on and do as you usually do.' I said, 'What about my kids?' He said, 'I'm not concerned about the kids.' I said, 'My kids?' He said, 'My only concern is the MOVE kids.' "

Goode later recalled that the neighbors had been "very upset and emotional." He told them that he was doing the best that he could under the circumstances: "I said to them that I will, over the next few days, research as to whether or not there is a legal basis for the city to do something about the problem that you have brought to us . . . and we had a discussion about my concerns, and I expressed that my overall concern was not to, in an unprepared manner, end up with a confrontation on that street that would cause the loss of lives, that would have innocent people, perhaps, injured or lose their lives and property damaged unnecessarily.

"Therefore, any plan which I used would be well thought out."

As mayor, Frank Rizzo had had his detractors, and they were not all, by any means, black. A growing number of Downtown executives thought the Mayor out of step with the times, resented his old-fashioned, "unprofessional," hands-on style of governing the city, and were determined to halt the city's economic decline.

Michael Pakenham, now the editorial page editor of the New York *Daily News*, was for thirteen years (1971–84) an associate editor at the *Inquirer*. As Pakenham views it in retrospect, some of the newer powers in the Downtown Establishment—Sam McKeel, the Southern-born president of Philadelphia Newspapers Incorporated, the Knight-Ridder-owned publisher of the *Inquirer* and *Daily News*, Harold Sorgenti of Atlantic Richfield, and "their crowd," many of them corporate members of the Greater First Philadelphia Corporation, an influential non-profit organization—were determined to give a new face to Philadelphia politics.

"They'd all read Digby," Pakenham says of E. Digby Baltzell, the influential sociologist and author of *Puritan Boston and Quaker Philadelphia*. What McKeel, Sorgenti, and the others found in Philadelphia society and politics "was all the worst things that Baltzell said and more." A spirit of deeply ingrained complacency, entrepreneurial inertia, intellectual sluggishness, and the worst possible degree of inbreeding had combined to rob Philadelphia's existing leadership circle of vigor. The result was a longstanding legacy of mediocrity.

"McKeel and the others were hired managers, not second and third generation proprietors," Pakenham recalls. "They were the CEO generation. None was a Philadelphian by birth. They weren't any of them geniuses, but they were good managers. And they didn't like what they saw. Manufacturing had fled."

The census figures bore out Downtown Philadelphia's worst fears. Philadelphia County's population had shrunk precipitously between 1970 and 1980. A 13.4 percent decline in population, the loss of Congressional districts and state house seats, and the prospect for even worse corporate and political losses were all proof that something had to be done to shake up the city's economic and political scene.

Frank Rizzo had given Philadelphia an image as a city that was tough, abrasive, ethnic, and decidedly blue-collar. In an age in which corporate America was beginning to shift its investments from heavy industry to high technology, Philadelphia had largely failed in its appeal to the future. The necessary talent for such a conversion to a highly technological society lay, seemingly, elsewhere, in Boston or in the Sillicon Valley. Not in Philadelphia.

The city itself was fragmented, with its neighborhood pockets of Irish, Italian, and Polish Catholics, its well-to-do Jewish professionals, and more and more, its black and Hispanic inner-city dwellers. Despite the marvellous old railroad terminal that is Thirtieth Street Station, despite the

University of Pennsylvania and its great hospital, despite Drexel, despite a wealth of lovely—if mostly decrepit—nineteenth-century homes, West Philadelphia was practically a ghetto. Downtown was a mess. A comparison of Chestnut and Market Streets with New York's Fifth Avenue was ludicrous. The public-owned bus and rail lines were antiquated almost beyond hope of renovation. A great deal, probably most, of the city's wealth lay outside it, along the Main Line, still white, Protestant, and comfortably Republican. Philadelphia was a city without a true center, a city with a weak tax-base, and a city with a damaged pride.

The face, if not the substance, of Philadelphia government changed dramatically with the election of William J. Green III as mayor in November of 1979.

Rizzo had been prohibited by law from running for a third successive term, and Bill Green was, from the beginning, a near shoe-in. A *Daily News* editorial noted after the May Democratic primary that Green had "won with a smooth, safe, money-to-burn campaign . . . won with the support of idealistic liberals who saw him as an extension of themselves and their philosophy . . . won with the support of a motley collection of anti-liberals who saw him as a winner and thus someone a whole lot better to be with than against."

Green's opponents in the 1983 general election were Republican David W. Marston and Consumer Party candidate Lucien E. Blackwell, the West Philadelphia city councilman. As U.S. Attorney, Marston had played a key role in the ABSCAM probe into political corruption and kickbacks. As a candidate for mayor, he now played an unlikelier role as the advocate for a major black political voice in Philadelphia politics.

"Marston was intelligent, he was decent, he was honest," says Pakenham. "He was better than anyone they'd ever had in that job. It was a fluke that he was good. [President Jimmy] Carter called his Attorney General [Griffin Bell] in and told him that [former U.S. Rep. and later ABSCAM victim] Josh Eilberg said that Marston was making his life miserable and Carter told Bell to get rid of him. He did, and Marston decided to run for mayor on the Republican ticket.

"Marston came out early in the campaign and said that he would name a black as his Managing Director and this put pressure on Green to do the same. Green got really scared. Now whether he should have gotten scared or not about Marston is another thing. And he started calling around town, asking people for advice, trying to find someone to be his Managing Director. . . .

"I don't think he'd ever met [Wilson] Goode."

Yet, Wilson Goode, it was.

The *Inquirer's* endorsement of Green followed shortly. The *Inquirer* made it abundantly clear that any of the candidates—Marston, Green, or Bowser—would be infinitely preferable to Rizzo. All three, the newspaper noted, offered "great promise for helping to bring this city out of its long, dark, often violent night of maladministration, corruption, and bitter divisiveness."

The November 7 headline said it all: "GREEN WINS IN LAND-SLIDE."

Suffice it to say that Bill Green did not look like Frank Rizzo, nor did he talk like Frank Rizzo. Green was a still youthful forty-two years of age at the time of his inauguration, handsome in a distinctly Irish sort of way (lantern jaw, wide smile, dark, thick, wavy hair), and dressed in horn-rimmed glasses and pin-stripes. His wife was beautiful. His children were beautiful.

Green took office on the strength of his massive electoral victory, at the head of a widespread coalition, and with plenty of political good will. But his enemies, and some of his friends, whispered that he did not work very hard at being mayor.

As the associate editor of the *Inquirer's* editorial page, Pakenham was close to the new mayor and admired him. "I thought Bill Green had great promise," he says, echoing what many observers believed at the time. In retrospect though, Pakenham has some second thoughts. Bill Green, he now concedes, "was a great disappointment as mayor. Bill had a remarkably quick mind and great charm, but he seldom tried to charm.

"Green had an unreasonable conflict over the role that his father had played as the consummate politician. The two great influences in his life were his father's death too soon and his meeting and drawing close to Bob Kennedy. These were absolutely antithetical influences.

"Bill Green's father was an old-fashioned Irish ward boss. Just the opposite of Bobby Kennedy, who was the politician as Puritan. Bill Green never felt comfortable with the backroom types that his father charmed —didn't trust them, by and large didn't like them. He despised [City] Council, and he made no effort to hide his disgust with individual members."

But Bill Green looked right, and he helped give Philadelphia what it wanted. "Image" and "self-image" became entrenched in Philadelphia's vocabulary. Green received help from other sources as well. The Flyers had become big winners in the Rizzo years. The Eagles (for a brief time), the Sixers, and the Phillies, all turned themselves around. Philadelphia started calling itself the "City of Champions."

No one profited more by all these success than Green's managing director, W. Wilson Goode. Born to a family of rural sharecroppers in North Carolina, Goode had moved with his parents, Albert and Rozelar Goode, to Philadelphia at the age of fifteen. His 1957 Bartram High yearbook described him as "Willie Wilson Goode, 6026 Locust Street."

Educated at Morgan State University and the Wharton School of Finance and Commerce at the University of Pennsylvania, Goode had made a comfortable middle-class life for himself, his wife—Velma Goode was by now an administrator at Penn's Veterinary School—and their three children.

Wilson Goode projected what Philadelphians needed their first black mayor to project: an almost excessive competence, mirrored in extreme attention to his personal appearance. His speech swollen with the jargon of management decision, he seemed the Wharton Man to the nth degree, whether as president of his own firm, as chairman of the state Public Utilities Commission (PUC), or as managing director of Philadelphia. As President and Chief Executive of the Philadelphia Council for Community Advancement, Inc., Goode, for almost a decade (1969–78) developed an intricate relationship with Philadelphia's black community and its Democratic machine. He had worked behind the scenes for State Senator Hardy D. Williams, for State Representative David P. Richardson, and for City Councilman John F. White, Jr. Moreover, as he liked to remind people, Wilson Goode was a Christian gentleman, a deacon at the First Baptist Church of Paschall. Deacon, father, businessman, politician, seemingly the consummate manager, Wilson Goode worked hard developing an image of working hard. "Goode has said he needs only five hours sleep a night," a *Daily News* profile noted of him in 1983.

The *Daily News'* Gil Spenser has a version of Goode's ascendance: "Bill Green took the lumps for Goode. And Goode used the damn thing for all it's worth. . . . He made more speeches than any mayor ever made, showed-up at every ribbon-cutting there ever was, did all the ceremonial stuff that Bill Green hated—and you know at least half of being mayor is the ceremonial stuff.

"Then Green bugs out! *Why?* Who knows? . . . Jesus, that's what everybody wanted to know at the time. He coulda got re-elected. Who knows? I don't think he liked it. He was tired of the shit. He created Wilson Goode. That's his gift to Philadelphia."

Bill Green, still in his mid-forties, surprised almost everyone when he announced on November 2, 1982 that he would not run for re-election. One day later, Wilson Goode surprised no one by announcing that he was running. Goode counted on and received not only the support of black political figures—attorney Charles Bowser, Henry Nicholas of the power-

ful Hospital Workers Union, Councilman John F. White, Jr., and the rest
—but of much of white Downtown Philadelphia.

Despite his glaring lack of humility and overbearing self-confidence, Goode was nevertheless an attractive figure to the more reform-minded CEO's of Downtown Philadelphia. According to Pakenham, "They didn't know Goode, not personally. But they saw a guy who visibly tried harder to control himself than any man they'd ever met. They saw that he had a speech impediment, and by sheer dint of will, managed to control it.

"He was so concentrated, so hyperfocused that he was working all the time. He had been a perceivably effective administrator under Green, and they perceived that he was basically of the same breed as them.

"Meanwhile, Green faded out of the major roles of the mayor, while Goode showed up at every ribbon-cutting you could imagine.

"They'd come to the conclusion that in four years, or if not in four, in eight, Philadelphia would have a black mayor. That was the inevitable. And they were not about to have what was happening in Chicago"— where the racially divisive election of Mayor Harold Washington over two white candidates from rival factions of the Chicago Democratic machine had just taken place—happen to them. They might have put up another white liberal this time or next time, but with Wilson Goode, they had what they wanted now.

"It was feel-good politics in that it made our liberal consciousness hum, if not sing."

The idea of Wilson Goode running for mayor carried strong prospects for success. If you were black, the Goode campaign bore an overly simplistic message: he was a brother, he understood as the white politicians could not hope to understand. He had been there. In a city that is more than forty percent black and overwhelmingly Democratic, yet is bankrolled by white Main Line businessmen, the result of this kind of allure was all too clear.

Rizzo, no longer barred from election, was also off and running. The election promised to be nasty. It wasn't. Rizzo, unbearably tame and careful in the face of a black opponent, was stripped of the greatest strength of his old image, further enhancing Goode's chances. Only on occasion was the Old Rizzo heard from, such as the time he said of Goode, "I wouldn't let him manage my doghouse." It wasn't enough.

The *Inquirer* gave its most heartfelt endorsement to the former managing director: "One stands above the others in promise of leadership, professional effectiveness and experience in the complex administration of public policy. He is W. Wilson Goode. . . . Mr. Goode has emerged as a thoughtful man who is pre-eminently knowledgeable about urban problems, sensitive to diversity and dedicated to professionalism. . . . He has energy. He has a vision for the city which promises to draw it forward and upward—and together—in a very trying time."

Despite the usual voting irregularities, a more or less honest vote was held. The election was not that close. As of January 1984, Philadelphia had its first black mayor.

The figure of a black demon—"Nigger Willie" as MOVE members would call him—had found a place in MOVE iconography.

5

"Only an Act of God"

On May 30, 1984, the mayor, managing director, police commissioner, and city solicitor met at City Hall with District Attorney Rendell, U.S. Attorney Edward S. G. Dennis, Jr., and officials of the FBI and the Secret Service. The mayor wanted to know if the MOVE problem wasn't something that the federal government ought to handle. No, he was told, it was not. The U.S. Attorney could think of no possible grounds for any action on the part of the United States government. Moreover, he warned that the Philadelphia police should strenuously avoid violating the civil rights of the residents of 6221 Osage. The mayor left the meeting, as he had entered it, still very much in a bind.

Goode next tried to dump the problem into the Philadelphia District Attorney's lap. The mayor said that he needed legal advice as to what to do. On June 22, Rendell informed Goode by letter that legal grounds already existed for the arrest Frank James Africa. A warrant had been issued on June 6, 1984, for parole violations. Rendell wrote to say that, "I would reiterate, however, what I expressed to you at our first meeting, that I believe it is important to do something as quickly as possible before the situation grows worse. . . ."

Yvonne B. Haskins was district supervisor of the Pennsylvania Board of Probation and Parole at this time. Amongst her more troublesome—and delinquent—"clients" was Frank James Africa. On March 24, 1984, Frank Africa had failed to appear for his required appointment at the local parole board office. Three days later, on March 27, Haskins sent a State Parole Board agent to 6221 Osage. His report states that, "At the residence, agent was met by a man who identified himself as the client [Frank James Africa]. Entry into the residence [6221] was not permitted. Therefore, an interview was conducted on the front steps. During the interview, agent was subjected not only to verbal abuse and insults but also to the stench and filth of two garbage cans nearby. After about fifteen minutes, the man who stated he was the client, identified himself as Conrad Africa. At that point, agent's patience was exhausted. Agent gave his business card with reporting instructions written on it (Report 3/28/84, at 11 A.M.) to Conrad Africa and requested that he give it to the client. Agent then proceeded to walk towards his auto. At that moment, the client came out of the house. Evidently, the client was listening to the conversation from behind the front door. Agent took his business card (with reporting instructions written on it) from Conrad Africa and gave it to the client. Client was also verbally instructed to report to agent's office on 3/28/84, at 11 A.M. The client replied that he was not going to report, that he does not recognize the Board's authority and that he was in confrontation with the system. Agent did not reply to those comments. As this agent was entering his auto, the client stated, 'If you come back, you better be armed because I'm in confrontation with the System.' "

On April 4, a certified letter was sent to Frank James Africa at 6221 Osage Avenue instructing him to report to his Prison Board agent on April 12. The agent later reported to his superiors that, "Said letter has not been returned. . . . It is obvious that the client still resides at [6221]. It is equally obvious that he has no intention of reporting as instructed. It appears to this agent . . . that the client and his organization (MOVE) desires [sic] a confrontation with the 'System.' Agent believes that this matter cannot be resolved in the usual fashion."

Haskins ordered the Board to declare James "delinquent" on May 3. On June 5, 1984, she met with Chief Inspector Robert A. Wolfinger and Captain James Shanahan of the Philadelphia Police Department. Wolfinger argued that the situation on Osage Avenue was explosive. The residents of 6221 Osage Avenue were ripe for confrontation, Wolfinger said. Haskins was warned not to make any further attempts to serve the warrant.

Haskins complied, instructing her agents to stay away from the MOVE house. "We had to assume that we would not have [police] assistance, as far as a planned arrest." Frank James Africa was only to be arrested if seen "on the street." The warrant was never executed.

Marie Fields, 39, lived with her postal worker husband Ronald and their two children, ages 19 and 17, at 6230 Pine Street across the alley from the MOVE house. "They kept to themselves, and I kept to myself.

I minded my own business and didn't worry about their's." The Fields decided to celebrate July Fourth, 1984, with a barbecue. Midway through the festivities, the MOVE loudspeaker thundered. "MOVE heat" was being put on against "all those motherfuckers out there celebrating a white man's holiday." "I ignored it," Mrs. Fields said, but she added that the summer of 1984 had been "rough, really rough."

The mayor met again with the neighbors on July 4. This time, he told them, the city would do something. Psychological counseling, as well as recreation facilities, would be made available to neighborhood children. The neighbors couldn't believe their ears. *This* was what the mayor was going to do about MOVE?

On July 13, Louise James called the police department. She told Officer Dolores Thompson that Vincent Leaphart was insane, a madman. Her son Frank James now served as the "naturalist minister" to Leaphart. The title gave him the power to mete out punishment to MOVE members at will—a preprogative which beforehand had belonged exclusively to John Africa. James feared for her own safety, feared her own son.

Louise James was, by now, desperate. She told Mayor Goode that she would prefer to see her son in prison—where he would at least be alive —than allow him to continue to dwell under John Africa's roof. Could her son be picked up on the street? Could her son be "deprogrammed"?

Milton Garnett, a man in his mid-sixties, had lived at 6242 Osage since 1960. At first he had gotten along fine with the MOVE people. "I used to talk to them, and they acted like real people. They were talking just like people in the street, different things, places they've been, but they didn't talk about violence." By the summer of 1984, all that had changed. "They just do what they want to do," he was quoted as saying at the time. "All they know is John Africa, John Africa, the same thing over and over. Here's a real nice neighborhood, and when they get on their bullhorns, it runs the devil crazy."

Lloyd and Lucretia Wilson had lived at 6219 Osage for ten years. They had never experienced anything quite like this though. According to Mrs. Wilson, "As time went on and conditions just grew worse, then we had to contend with things inside our house. Bugs that you couldn't do anything about. . . . I mean they just totally . . . took over our house. We had just decided that we were going to stay there. We were not going to be run out of our house, and that was it. So we had to adjust to the situation. And some of the adjustments I had to make was—exterminate all the time, until it got like the air was like heavy with smells and extermination in our house. And it did no good. . . .

"And my kids—it got so bad, my children woke up in the middle of the night from bug bites, crying from things biting them in their beds. . . .

"My oven—to cook dinner, which I was just determined I was going to do because that was my way of life, I had—before I could cook on it, I had to turn the stove on and let the bugs evacuate. This was daily. . . .

"I spoke to Conrad [Hampton Africa] . . . about it. He went completely berserk. You know, the bugs are our brothers and sister. If you exterminate the bugs, you exterminate us."

Lloyd Wilson talked to Frank James Africa about the problem. He also spoke to "the other heavy gentleman, the Minister of Defense," Gerald Ford Africa. Wilson told the MOVE members that he intended to set off sulfur bombs. "They told . . . me, if I set those bombs off, that when the revolution started, our doors would be the first ones to be kicked. . . . Our family would be the first to go."

Cassandra Carter was having her own problems with MOVE. "That year [1984], we were going to exercise [class], and we would leave—it just happened that our exercise started at 7:30. So we would leave at seven. And they [MOVE] pretty much knew everybody's schedule. You know, working, whether you were home or whatever. Because they would just watch everything. And this evening, when I came back home everybody was saying, 'They got you tonight,' I said, 'Pardon me?' And they said, 'They got you tonight. They talked about the blonde and the alley.' No one would tell me exactly, other than the description was me. I don't know what they said because—I guess the people that were telling me probably they figured, well, maybe if you tell her she might go up there."

Carter brought her problems to John White, Sr., who had directed the Philadelphia Community Development Program since February 1981. Working out of the office of City Managing Director Leo A. Brooks, White was also charged with supervising the work of the Community Intervention Program. Both Carter and White attended the same church, and White became quite familiar with her stories of woe.

White tried to help Mrs. Carter with her problem "in many ways." For example: "The time that she came to me I merely suggested to her if she had some relative with whom she could move with, during that time, to move with them. . . . That was my help. That was the best that I could do for her."

White assumed someone else was working on the problem. He told no one of the conversation he had with Mrs. Carter.

The neighbors were not the only ones having problems with MOVE. In the late summer of 1984, a Philadelphia Gas Works crew was servicing the 1600 block of South Fifty-sixth Street, near another MOVE house. The crew suddenly found itself being yelled at by the residents. The police were called. Their advice to the PGW workers was, "Look, stay away from these four addresses unless there's an emergency and you've got to go in." "All four of those addresses were known MOVE addresses and one of them was 6221," a PGW spokesman said.

Jules Pergolini, a district supervisor of Licenses and Inspections, noted on an L&I form concerning the house at 6221 Osage Avenue, "Do not make any inspection unless cleared with Jules, Rudy, [Rudolph Paglia, Chief of District Operations of the same agency], or the Commissioner [of L&I]." "MOVE PROPERTY," in big, black letters, headed the form. The instructions, initially written in pencil, had been traced over in red ink.

There were more meetings later that summer between city officials and the neighbors. At one such meeting on July 28, Mayor Goode emphasized that he would act only when forced to by MOVE. Three days later, on July 31, Goode met with Louise James and LaVerne Sims at City Hall.

James articulated her belief that a confrontation was imminent, as well as her fear for her son's life. Goode asked if the two sisters could give him any advice as to how to quell the possible confrontation. Neither could help him. James couldn't even tell him how many people were in the house.

Her son's death might be prevented, James said, if she herself picked him up for the parole violation sometime when he was outside of the house. Goode asked her if she thought this might be provocative of a confrontation with the rest of the people in the house. After thinking about it, James agreed, but added that she could not live through another August 8. Couldn't Goode try to obtain a pardon from the governor for the imprisoned MOVE members? Goode said he could not, and that the governor would not. Could he at least try? Goode said he would get back to her.

Another meeting was called between the mayor and the neighbors. There, Goode assured the neighbors that, as one of them recalled, "He was on top of the problem, but he didn't specify what he would do. He said he was working on it."

If MOVE was preparing for a confrontation, it was generally agreed that the likely date for it would be August 8, the sixth anniversary of the Powelton shoot-out. MOVE members had taunted the police on their loudspeakers at 6221, promising that, "Come August 8, we will take care of you people." The police department was ordered to prepare for such just an event.

Sergeant Herbert Kirk was assigned by Commissioner Gregore J. Sambor to develop a tactical plan for August 8, 1984. The planning began in late May of that year.

As Kirk later described his plan, "At that time [the MOVE people] had a trap door of about three foot by three foot cut into the roof of the Osage house, and around the trap door were placed wooden skids or pallets in a barricade fashion . . . between three and four feet high.

"I had the Fire Department bring their high-pressure lines on this truck—the squrt gun—to the Fire Academy . . . [to] see if the power of the squrt gun would move these pallets and drive them off the roof, and the squrt gun did accomplish this, it would move the pallets. Our plan being that we were going to try a rooftop assault to deliver tear gas into the property. . . .

"[Next] I contacted the Bomb Squad . . . Lieutenant Frank Powell, commanding officer of the Bomb Squad, and asked him if his people could design an entry device. . . . An entry device being something that we would breach the rooftop with, to deliver tear gas. . . .

"The plan was for one assault team to scale to the rooftop after the squrt guns had done the job of knocking the barricades away from the trap door.

"When the rooftop team secured the roof, the water would then be turned off, the entrance device placed on the roof, detonated, and the tear-gas generator would start to deliver tear gas into the property. The tear-gas generator delivers a high volume of gas in a very short time. It would have filled the house in a matter of minutes, thus driving anyone inside outside unless they had breathing equipment. And the longer the gas generator ran, the more the oxygen would be displaced. So, even if they had gas masks, sooner or later they would have failed."

The managing director, Leo A. Brooks, was in overall command of the city's forces on August 8, 1984. After a distinguished career in the U.S. Army, Major General Brooks had retired, at age fifty-one, as the commanding officer of the sprawling Defense Personnel Support Center in South Philadelphia. Shortly thereafter, in January 1984, he was named managing director of the City of Philadelphia by newly elected Mayor W. Wilson Goode.

General Brooks was described by associates as, "an honorable man, a Christian man, a church-going man." He had been married for over thirty years to his wife, Naomi, and it was said that she loved Philadelphia. And so, the couple had chosen to make this city their home.

As the highest-ranking non-elected official of the City of Philadelphia, General Brooks was charged with oversight of all departments, fire as well as police. Sometime, according to Brooks, "during the months of June and July there was a growing feeling, and it was reported to me several times by the Police Commissioner, that he had received it through his intelligence sources, that [the MOVE members] were going to make a public excitement on that day. . . . There were implications that there might be hostage-taking, that there might be all sorts of things, fire, whatnot, explosives, and whatnot."

Brooks later contended that he did not know at the time that Kirk's plan called for the use of an "explosive device," and that he only learned of this in August or September of 1985.

Commissioner Sambor, however, claimed that he himself had informed Brooks that it might become necessary to blow a hole in the roof, using explosives. "His [Brooks's] concern was for the safety of the occupants. And I assured him, as I had been assured by my personnel, that there was no danger, that it was only that minimal charge which would be necessary to do what had to be done."

Police Commissioner Gregore J. Sambor was a thirty-four-year veteran of the Philadelphia Police force. The son of a Ukrainian immigrant father, Sambor was born in Philadelphia in 1928. His father died in the midst of the Great Depression, in 1938, and his mother was forced to send her two sons to the Hershey Industrial School for orphaned boys. The mother eventually remarried, and Sambor, by this time a junior in high school, was transferred to Northeast Catholic High School.

Following his graduation from high school in 1945, Sambor entered in the Oblates of St. Francis de Sales as a novice studying for the priesthood. After four months in the cloisters, Sambor resigned and enlisted in the U.S. Army. He would remain in the Army Reserves until 1981 when he retired with the rank of major.

Sambor's police department career began in 1950 and was marked by a swift rise following his promotion to lieutenant in 1964: captain in 1966, inspector in 1971, and chief inspector in 1974. As commanding officer of the Police Academy, Sambor was mentioned as a possible commissioner under incoming Mayor William J. Green in 1979, but passed over for Deputy Commissioner Morton B. Solomon.

Meanwhile, Chief Inspector Sambor continued his education, earning both a bachelor's degree in social welfare in 1971 and a master's degree in public administration in 1974. While serving as head of the Police Academy, Sambor continued to work for a Ph.D. in political science at Temple.

Gregore Sambor's time came at last in January of 1984 when newly elected Mayor W. Wilson Goode named him to head the department. As commissioner, Sambor was frequently in the news, not least for his handling of the corruption scandals which had dogged the department for years. Sambor's own deputy commissioner, James J. Martin, was soon named in federal indictments as the alleged leader of one such police corruption ring and was forced to resign within months of taking office. Martin was eventually convicted on federal racketeering and bribery charges.

Commissioner Sambor was never accused of anything other than a certain gruffness. A profile in the *Daily News* noted that, "Sambor's military bearing was emphasized by his preference for the Commissioner's uniform, marked by four stars on the collar of the white shirt, and a full braided cap." The commissioner was well known for his spit-and-polish military style.

And so, at 6 A.M. on August 8, nearly three hundred police and firemen began assembling at the parking lot behind the Walnut Park Plaza Geriatrics Center and Sixty-third and Walnut Streets. Fifteen police wagons, two armored cars, the bomb disposal unit, a K-9 team, a mounted patrol, fire trucks, and rescue units were moved in. Neighbors were asked to leave their homes for the day, and many did. At the MOVE house, the loudspeaker blasted. "We're here. We're not going anywhere. You can't push us away," a woman shouted over the loudspeaker.

The day ended as it began. Pronouncements could still be heard blaring from the MOVE loudspeakers as nightfall set. Neighbors gradually moved back into their homes. Police and firemen packed up and began to leave the area.

In retrospect, one can only wonder at the size of the force that was employed on August 8, 1984. What exactly had been expected of MOVE? And what was the intent of the police planners? Was the display of an immense force of police and firemen intended as merely a defensive response? Or was the expectation, all along, for a fight to the finish? As it was, August 8, 1984 had merely been the dress rehearsal for a disaster.

Late that evening, Lloyd Wilson and his wife were on their way home from yet another neighborhood meeting. The TV cameras and lights were still very much present on Osage Avenue. So were MOVE's members. "And as we walked, we would always speak whether they spoke. We gave them the courtesy, them being other human beings, that we would speak to them. And I spoke and Frank [James Africa] said to me, 'I want to talk to you.' My wife continued on up the steps. They had a platform at that point. So he was on the platform, and I was standing, looking up, talking to him.

"He said, 'You went to the cops about this wood.'

"And just to back up a little bit, they had brought a lot of wood in. It overflowed into our property. And we had a lot of people that come to our house for meetings, and so we asked, 'Will you please clear that walkway so people can come in?' He said he would.

"What happened, I think, a couple of days later the wood was still there. So I went back to him again and asked him, would he remove the wood? It still stayed there. So that night, on August 8, coming in, he said, 'You went to the cops, and you told them that I wouldn't move the wood.' I said, 'Frank, the police were standing right there. The Civil Affairs Unit was standing right there when I said that to you. You don't have to go to the cops to tell them that I asked you to move the wood again.'

"He got very indignant and very violent and told me I was a traitor and I would not help support their cause. He really got violent. . . . He grabbed me, and Mrs. Foskey kept screaming down the street, 'Help him! Help him!' "

There were policemen at the corner, near the television cameras. They offered Wilson no assistance.

"So I was very upset. The next morning—we left the house that night and we got a hotel room. I might have done something stupid that night."

The next morning, August 9, Wilson went to see Mayor Goode at City Hall: "The Mayor was coming out of a conference with Police Commissioner Sambor and Managing Director Brooks. And I said, 'Look, this is it. Last night, I was actually attacked by Frank James. . . . I'm at his mercy. What are you people going to do?' They whisked me off to a little office to the side, and the mayor continued with what he had to do and he left me with Mr. Sambor and the Managing Director.

"And we [Wilson, Sambor, and Brooks] sat down, and we had a lengthy conversation. . . . And I asked them, what kind of plans did they have to deal with the situation, what kind of protection do we have living right next door to them? A lot of times, I would have to travel, and I would be gone. So I was concerned about my family." The conversation went on in this vein for a lengthy period of time.

As Wilson recalls it, General Brooks at last turned to him and said, "Only an act of God could change this."

6

A Sense of Foreboding

On October 2, 1984, the police department officially confirmed a report by the neighbors that a "wooden shack" was being constructed on the roof of 6221. By mid-December it was all too obvious that some sort of fortified emplacement was being built there. Officers in the Civil Affairs Unit and in the Major Investigations Division (MID) were aware that lead pipes, half-inch thick sheets of steel, and tree trunks were being carried into the house at 6221 Osage on a daily basis.

Howard Nichols, Jr., 30, lived at 6228 Osage, and said that MOVE had been "hauling that stuff in daily for the last year. They took it in in broad daylight. Quite frankly, it got to the point where you'd see it and not see it, it was such a daily occurrence. It was not secret. You'd have to be stupid not to know that. We could see them building the bunker. They'd get on the bullhorn to tell us, in case we didn't know, that they were going to be ready for the cops when they came." Cassandra Carter, of 6232 Osage, said that the neighbors reported the construction work to police, but, "I don't think they believed us. I don't think they took us seriously."

On December 17, Superior Court upheld the convictions of the MOVE members involved in the August 8, 1978 shootout. At 6221 Osage, construction work continued.

Throughout the fall and winter of 1984–85, West Philadelphia City Councilman Lucien E. Blackwell received numerous complaints from the Osage neighbors. These, he forwarded to the office of the district attorney, believing that if he were to go to the scene, he would be giving MOVE what it wanted. So he stayed away.

Managing Director Brooks did not believe the city had adequate reason to move on 6221 Osage during this time: "You see . . . it was otherwise a relatively dormant neighborhood, relatively. And in that state, if they had constructed the thing in steel, except for it having a gun through a parapet or something of that nature would probably not have precipitated a crisis. . . . I do not believe, nor was there ever any legal advice, nor was there ever anything by the D.A. or by anyone else that said, 'Because they are building on that roof, it is a criminal act for which you can attack.' "

The police commissioner disagreed. "I was always of the opinion . . . that the longer we wait the worse it could get." By February of 1985, he was certain that something was being built on the roof of 6221 Osage. He knew, from discussions with Louise James and LaVerne Sims, that Frank James Africa had grown increasingly violent and that he resided in the house. He knew that Conrad Hampton Africa, whom he considered to be one of the leaders of the organization, was also in the house. And he had arrest warrants for both of them.

In February and March of 1985, the neighbors organized themselves as "The United Residents of the 6200 Block of Osage Avenue." On April 25, thirty or so residents met at the Cobbs Creek Community Center to protest the MOVE presence in their neighborhood.

Four days later, on April 29, MOVE put on another show at 6221. Spectators and Civil Affairs cops listened as MOVE members denounced the police and the neighbors and threatened to kill the mayor. Officers were told by one neighbor that armed men had been seen inside the shack atop the roof.

The story was prominently displayed in the next day's *Daily News,* which accurately reported, as it turned out, that there were about twelve adults and children, along with fifteen to thirty dogs and cats, inside the MOVE house at 6221 Osage. Four plainclothes Civil Affairs officers were said to have taped the voices heard on the MOVE loudspeaker on Monday, and two members of the Community Intervention Team of the Managing Director's Office were also observed on the block.

The neighbors claimed that three area residents had been assaulted by MOVE members, and that MOVE members had committed burglaries in the neighborhood, burned wood on the roof of 6221, blocked the driveway in the back of the house with a nine-foot high fence constructed out of tin and wood, and pitched rat meat to their animals.

Clifford Bond told reporters that, "Everybody sees it from the city's side and MOVE's side. I'm seeing it from the homeowner's side. I'm not going to go through this again this summer." Howard Nichols added, "We will support any action that will remove MOVE from this block."

Press Secretary Karen Warrington, responding for the mayor, said that the city could not do anything "unless the MOVE persons break a law."

The next day, April 30, Commissioner Sambor began planning for the confrontation. Those present in the commissioner's conference room that day included a number of ranking officers, yet, curiously, the tactical planning for the operation was turned over to Lieutenant Frank W. Powell, the head of the Bomb Disposal Unit (BDU), and Sergeant Albert Revel, a firing range instructor at the Police Academy. As Powell later recalled, "At that time, the police commissioner requested Sgt. Revel to look into the feasibility of using the [August 8] 1984 plan for the MOVE compound at 6221 Osage Avenue. During this meeting, the commissioner also requested that [Powell] assist Officer Revel in setting up this plan and to check the feasibility of the 1984 plan and get back to him by Friday, the first of May."

Forty-one-years old and a seventeen-year veteran of the Philadelphia Police Department, Frank Powell had commanded the Bomb Disposal Unit since 1984. Prior to that time, Powell had served for two and a half years as a police officer, three years as a detective, two and a half years as a street sergeant, and the remainder of the time as a lieutenant assigned to the Juvenile Aid Division and the Moral Sex Squad. In January of 1979, he was assigned to the Stakeout Bomb Unit, the combined Stakeout Unit and Bomb Squad. Powell's intimacy with explosives was limited to a five-day FBI seminar which he had enrolled in, called "Bomb Commanders." He was not a certified explosives technician.

Despite Powell's lack of expertise in the area of explosives, Sambor's designation of a member of the Stakeout Bomb Unit as head planner for the operation rendered the use of explosives almost inevitable.

On that first day of May, Powell discussed the August 8, 1984 "Kirk Plan" with Sergeant Revel and Officer Michael Tursi at the police firing range. Despite Powell's familiarity with the plan, it became necessary for him to call Kirk, as the group had no written plans to work with. According to Powell, Kirk neither returned his call nor forwarded the plans.

Powell came to the conclusion that the 1984 plan was no longer workable. It would be impossible for policemen to get to the roof of 6221 Osage, blow a hole and insert tear gas without being discovered and perhaps attacked now that the bunkers with their gun ports were in place.

Powell composed a memorandum to Commissioner Sambor relaying his feelings, adding that he, along with Revel and Tursi, would compose an operable plan.

Tursi had come to the initial meeting with his own plan, according to Powell, which consisted of the establishment of four posts, two on Osage Avenue and two to the rear of Pine Street. Thereafter, two entry teams would slip into the houses on either side of the MOVE house and simultaneously insert gas into the house into the basement and second floors through holes created in the walls. According to Tursi's plan, said Powell, no matter where the MOVE members were, they would be forced onto the first floor and then have to proceed outside where they would be apprehended.

Powell, along with Lieutenant Dominick Marandola of the Stakeout team, chose the Stakeout and Bomb Squad team members for the operation. According to Powell, the overriding criteria used in the selection of these officers was skill.

That same day, May first, the United Residents called a press conference in which they requested the aid of Republican Governor Dick Thornburgh in resolving the problem on Osage. They announced that they could no longer co-exist with MOVE. Block Captain Clifford Bond handed out a statement in which the neighbors demanded that outstanding warrants for MOVE members be served by the State Attorney General's Office.

Lloyd Wilson said that he had met with Mayor Goode, Commissioner Sambor, and Managing Director Brooks after his alleged beating on August 8. "I asked them what they could do," Wilson said. "They said, 'It's up to God'. . . . I think what's gonna have to happen is something drastic. And then, maybe an act of God will happen."

"Mayor Goode says he does not know what to do about MOVE. We find that totally unacceptable," said Howard Nichols. "Our other elected representatives have either given us empty promises or have ignored us completely. And we find that reprehensible."

During the night, Betty Mapp would wake as the row house roofs were trod upon by MOVE members and their animals. The summer before, one of the MOVE cats fell through a skylight and landed in the Mapp's bathroom. Life with MOVE had become, she said, too much for her to bear.

Back at City Hall, Goode announced that he could find no "violations on which we can make arrests. . . . I don't have anything to hope for at this point. . . . I've said that I cannot, in order to protect the rights of

Gasoline being pulled up to the roof of the 6221 Osage Avenue MOVE Headquarters. Wide World Photos.

a group of people, violate the rights of a single person to do that. And my big concern is that I don't have a legal basis at this point to remove the problem from the neighborhood."

When a reporter asked if the mayor would take action against MOVE if he could, he replied, "The answer is yes. Do I wish I had a way? The answer is yes. Do I at this point? The answer is no." Interviewed that morning on a radio talk-show, Goode put it more bluntly, "There is no legal basis for arresting MOVE members."

On May 2, neighbors reported that they had witnessed a five-gallon gasoline can being hoisted to the roof of 6221. The Associated Press carried a photograph of the event on its wires. In the photograph, the can is clearly labelled "GASOLINE."

Captain James Shanahan, the head of the Civil Affairs Unit, claimed that he "generated a paper" that very day regarding the gasoline can. According to Shanahan, though, the paper did not go up the chain of command.

Captain Edward McLaughlin, head of the Major Investigations Division, contended that Shanahan's paper did reach the command levels of the Department. McLaughlin himself prepared a paper which he knew to have reached at least as far as the desk of Deputy Commissioner Robert Armstrong. McLaughlin was uncertain whether Commissioner Sambor ever received his report, but he knew that the gasoline can was discussed at a subsequent meeting in Sambor's conference room on May 9.

Powell, accompanied by Tursi and Revel, made a trip to 6221 Osage on either May 2 or May 3. Powell says that trip was taken in order to determine the positions of the entry teams and the fire post. No surveillance photographs were made.

By May 2, Mayor Goode had come to the conclusion that an armed conflict between MOVE and the neighbors was probable. District Attorney Rendell was subsequently asked to ascertain the legal grounds necessary for the City to move on 6221.

The developments, or lack of them, on Osage Avenue were by now beginning to attract the attention of a public that had grown tired of hearing about MOVE. The lead editorial in May 3 *Daily News* succinctly described the situation: "Everybody who had brothers and sisters knows the technique. Every family has a kid who avoids doing things everybody else has to do by kicking up such a fuss that the parents stop asking. It works if nobody's got the will to enforce the rules. The clowns with the guns at MOVE have taken that technique and perfected it.

"The Mayor says he wants to do something about MOVE, but that he cannot, in order to protect the rights of a group of people, violate the rights of a single person. An assistant city solicitor says that MOVE would use court appearances to serve their ends. The solicitor says the courts are slow. The Commissioner of Licenses and Inspections says he's not planning any inspections of MOVE's house.

"What the hell are these people talking about?" The editorial called on the mayor to act.

After three years, the neighbors were at last being heard.

Back at the Police Academy, work on the plan was continuing. On May 3, Sergeant Revel began handing out equipment to Stakeout and Range personnel. According to Lieutenant Powell, the weaponry at this time included high-powered rifles equipped for sharpshooting, M-16 assault rifles, and the Israeli-made Uzi submachine guns.

Later that day, Rendell, Sambor, Brooks, City Solicitor Barbara W. Mather, and Councilman Lucien E. Blackwell met with Mayor Goode and his Chief of Staff, Shirley B. Hamilton, to discuss the options available to them. According to Rendell, there was talk at this meeting about the possibility that MOVE might have wired the neighboring homes with explosives. Rendell left the meeting convinced that the City was ready to act.

Goode testified before the MOVE Commission that, "At that meeting we talked about what we knew about what was going on out there and the potential for confrontation. . . . I asked Mr. Rendell that in view of what we have now . . . can you go back and re-examine whether or not there are additional legal bases for taking steps against people in the house than there were a year ago. . . . At that meeting there was a great deal of discussion about the fact that . . . explosives [had been stolen] from Chester County, and that it was the feeling of the people present that tunnels had in fact been dug underneath the houses. And there was in fact some concern expressed at that meeting that there may very well be explosives planted under the houses."

On May 5, the district attorney's office conducted interviews with nineteen of the neighbors to support applications for search and arrest warrants. Deputy District Attorney Bernard L. Siegel was given sworn testimony from the neighbors, which included assertions of the stockpiling of weapons at 6221. Siegel later claimed that the neighbors presented no evidence of explosives, except that, "The people inside [6221 Osage Avenue] said they had it and would use it."

Birdie Africa was asked by homicide detectives if he had ever seen guns or explosives in the MOVE house. No, the boy replied, he had seen neither. He had, however, seen Frank James Africa crossing the neighboring roofs with a "long gun" in his hands. Asked why he thought Frank had done this, Birdie replied, "He wanted to let the cops know we had guns in the house."

Were there places in the house at 6221 Osage where the children were not permitted to go?

"Yeah," Birdie said. "We couldn't go in a closet in the back room on the second floor. It was locked and had a sofa in front of it. The adults told us not to go in it because the cats would get locked in." The kids, Birdie said, thought that maybe that was where they big people kept their guns.

Two days later, on Tuesday, May 7, Goode met at City Hall with Chief of Staff Shirley B. Hamilton, Managing Director Brooks, Police Commissioner Sambor, Councilman Blackwell, representatives of the city solicitor's office, and District Attorney Rendell. It was at this meeting that Goode first officially authorized Sambor to prepare and execute a tactical plan, under the supervision of the managing director. According to Deputy District Attorney Siegel, the mayor at one point turned to Sambor and said, "You are the professional. You need not keep me informed of the details." Siegel says that he "was somewhat surprised" by the mayor's attitude.

Goode claimed before the MOVE Commission to have given the following instructions at the meeting: "Number one, we wanted to make sure that the protection of police officers and firefighters and the occupants of the house were paramount, that we did not want any loss of life. Secondly, we wanted [Police Commissioner Sambor] to handpick the officers who in fact would be in charge that day, would be out there, all the police officers. We did not want persons involved who may have a hot temper, who may have emotionally been attached to 1978 for some reason, and we did not want—we wanted the people there to be handpicked who would go in and do an expert and professional job."

But Sambor, who was at the time aware of the beating of Delbert Africa during the 1978 confrontation, as well as the subsequent acquittal of the police officers involved, has maintained that no special guidelines were dictated. There was, he says, no instruction that certain police officers should be excluded from the operation. The selection of officers was, according to Sambor, left completely up to his discretion.

Brooks has also denied that Goode expressed the necessity for eliminating particular officers from participation in the planned operation against MOVE. He does recall, "That there would be the utmost of care in the selection of individuals, so there would be people there with the greatest of maturity, and that we not have an embarrassment or a confrontation over the issue of how we handle the people when they come out."

Rendell also has denied Goode's assertion: "I don't recall a specific instruction. I think there was just a general sort of agreement that it ought to be personnel with a degree of sensitivity. . . . The Stakeout police and the police who handled both 1978 and this incident are extraordinarily capable at what they do, in my judgment." With Rendell that morning were Deputy District Attorneys Bernard L. Siegel and Eric B. Henson. Both have agreed that there was "no specific directive by the mayor to the police commissioner to handpick the personnel."

Mayor Goode also claimed that at this meeting he gave instructions to Police Commissioner Sambor to pick up the MOVE children as soon as possible. The removal of the children from the MOVE house had been discussed before this meeting, but it was not until May 7 that Goode put forth the formal request. Sambor, however, has said that he was not provided with the orders to pick up the children until the tenth of May, and that he had no legal authority to do so before then.

The result of the meeting, according to Rendell, was "a general agreement by everybody that we should proceed to draw up search warrants and arrest warrants.

"I was asked how long it would take. I said one day. Mr. Henson, who had to do the work, corrected me and said two days. For some reason, the managing director said, 'Oh, it's going to take more than that.' I said, no, it wouldn't. . . . I knew that given the material we had, we could have literally, if we wanted to keep secretarial personnel and everything involved late that night, late Tuesday night, I think we could have done it on Wednesday."

The same day, one of the inhabitants of 6221 Osage, Alphonso Robbins, better known as Mo Africa, stood in the City Hall courtroom of Judge Samuel M. Lehrer, charged with making terroristic threats against a police officer. The case against Robbins Africa involved an incident inside the Sixty-fifth and Woodland Avenue police station on June 19, 1984. At the time, Mo Africa was arrested for the assault of police

Sergeant James McDonnell with a tire iron after McDonnell stopped him for a traffic violation in West Philadelphia.

According to the transcript of his June 19 preliminary hearing, Mo Africa, who acted as his own attorney, "stopped questioning McDonnell and said, 'Beat me, be prepared to die. If I don't get [you] . . . M-1, MOVE Underground, will kill you.' "

Mo Africa was additionally accused of cursing and threatening an officer and was arrested again after the hearing. Africa told the jury that he made those threats because McDonnell had lied about the June 10, 1984 incident.

MOVE, Mo Africa told the jurors, had been harassed by the police for seventeen years—since 1968, or four years before the group's actual founding in 1972. The cops, he said, "are licensed killers and MOVE don't know nothing about killing." From now on, though, "if they come for us, they better come ready to die too," he announced. "I will fight to my death. I'm willing to take six bullets."

That afternoon, at 2:00, at the Police Academy Range, there was a discussion of the use of explosives for what was already being called "Operation MOVE." Inspector John Tiers was present along with Lieutenant Powell, Sergeant Revel, Officer Tursi, Captain Kirchner, Lieutenant Rambo, Detectives Benner and Boyd, Bomb Squad Officers Angelucci and Klein, and other men from the Stakeout Unit.

According to Tiers, Powell mentioned the use of "shaped charges" and talked about placing a "small charge" onto the walls adjoining 6221 Osage in order to create a three-inch hole. Revel and Tursi added that there was also talk of using powdered gas, CS or CN, on the rooftop of 6221 Osage. The purpose of this, said Revel, "was only to neutralize any possibility of anyone being on the roof." At one point, Revel continued, there was discussion of delivering the powdered gas by helicopter. Eventually this possibility was discarded as too costly and as too likely to "contaminate the neighborhood."

On Wednesday, May 8, Republican City Councilwoman Joan Specter, the wife of U.S. Senator Arlen Specter, charged that MOVE's "terrorists" owed more than $1500 in unpaid gas and water bills to the city. (The city-owned Philadelphia Gas Works, known as PGW, later announced that MOVE owed more than $1600 for gas alone). At a City Hall press conference, Specter said that, "It is outrageous that this city is being held hostage by MOVE, but it is even more outrageous that city residents are unwittingly subsidizing those terrorists."

PGW officials would not comment on Specter's charges.

City Water Commissioner William Marrazzo divulged that one of his crew had gone to 6221 in April of 1984 to turn off the water but was turned back on the advice of police officers after being "harassed by occupants of the property."

City Revenue Commissioner Eugene L. Cliett announced on the same day that his department twice had sent investigators to 6221 to serve notice on delinquent water bills. A female investigator was "threatened and intimidated" in February 1985. Cliett said that the Water Department's own shut-off unit informed him during the previous month that they "won't touch" MOVE properties.

The mayor, forced by now to address the Osage Avenue question at a news conference, characterized it as "very, very explosive." He acknowledged that MOVE was in violation of the city housing code and probably other codes. Cited as the most obvious example of this was the "bunker" which crowned the MOVE residence, in clear violation of Licenses and Inspections codes.

Nevertheless, Goode contended that he was still searching for a legal basis to move against 6221 Osage. "The issue," he said, "is whether or not the people who live in that house can continue to remain there. . . . Yes, we can turn the water off. Yes, we can probably turn off electricity, but that's not going to solve the problem the neighbors are faced with out there."

The mayor was confronted at his news conference by Howard Nichols, who again cited the neighbors' complaints and demanded action. "Three residents of that block have been beaten by MOVE members, and the police department has had that information. . . . Are you waiting for someone to be killed in order to act on that, Mr. Mayor?"

Nichols praised Joan Specter and Democratic State Rep. David P. Richardson, for supporting the neighbors in their struggle. "It's ironic," Nichols said, referring to Councilwoman Specter, "that the second elected official to come to our aid would be a woman who is a Republican."

Another neighbor, Oris Thomas, said, "Since the news media got involved, something is going to be done now. . . . We can't go through another summer like the last one."

Meanwhile, back in Judge Lehrer's court, the jury, having deliberated one hour Tuesday and six hours Wednesday, brought in a guilty verdict against Alphonso Robbins Africa.

During his closing arguments, Mo Africa told the jurors that he knew their names and would sue each of them if convicted. Enemies of MOVE had "suffered heart attacks or a bullet in the head," he warned.

MOVE was "going to put a lot of heat on the city of Philadelphia."

"You're prejudiced like all the rest of the judges," Mo Africa told Judge Lehrer, "and you're going to suffer and pay for it. You did everything you can [sic] to make sure I was found guilty. You are going to suffer dire consequences because of the action against us. I'm not talking about somebody just tripping or falling, I'm talking about a heart attack. . . . You ain't fair. Your system ain't fair. You should have thrown yourself off this case before it was over. This case should never have went as far as it went. You know I'm innocent."

"You finished?" Judge Lehrer asked. "If you ever sat still for a half hour . . ." Mo Africa broke in again, and Lehrer told him to, "Just keep your mouth shut. Be quiet for a little bit. If you learned to control your mouth and keep quiet you might learn something." Robbins Africa replied, "You're the one that should learn about MOVE."

"Send me a letter," Lehrer said.

Lehrer revoked Alphonso Robbins Africa's $20,000 bail and ordered him taken to the Philadelphia Detention Center pending a June 20 sentencing, the maximum term being two years in prison.

Meanwhile, at the Police Academy, Powell was making some telephone calls. Several were placed to Paul Geppert of the Geppert Construction Company. Powell did not reveal his conversation with Geppert to Sergeant Revel until October of 1985. According to Revel, Geppert told Powell that it would be possible to use a crane to remove the bunker, and that it would cost $6,500. Powell told Revel that that he had informed Sambor of the conversation on Friday, May 10. "Lieutenant Powell said to me that he had told the Police Commissioner that Mr. Geppert thought that he could do the job, it would cost $6,500. The commissioner's response to Lieutenant Powell was: I will have to check with the mayor to see if we can get the money and Lieutenant Powell said he was called back by the commissioner and said that the mayor would not okay the $6,500."

Both the mayor and the former police commissioner have vigorously denied that any such conversation took place.

The morning began with yet another planning session in Commissioner Sambor's conference room in the Police Administration Building at Seventh and Race Streets. Present were Powell, Revel, Tursi, Sergeant Edward Connor, Fire Commissioner William C. Richmond, Deputy Fire Commissioner Frank J. Scipione, and numerous police officers of command rank. Powell says that Sambor instructed that one officer each be placed in command of each of the entry teams. Powell was designated to lead Team A, and Connor, a street sergeant in the First Police District, who had previously served on the Bomb Squad was chosen to lead Team B.

Revel remembered that, "My hopes were dashed," when Fire Commissioner Richmond told him at the May 9 meeting that he did not believe the bunkers could be pushed off the roof using the squrts. "The fire commissioner felt that because of the distance where they [the squrts] would have to be placed and the construction as I had described it to him and shown him in pictures that he would not be able to knock it off the roof." Therefore, the use of water amounted to little more than a "diversion," intended to obscure the vision of MOVE members. Revel relayed this information to his superiors.

Powell similarly remembered that Fire Commissioner Richmond announced at the meeting that his department would have to use two squrt guns, instead of the originally designated equipment, as it was not working. Richmond stressed to others at the meeting that the bunkers could not be removed by the two squrt guns.

The plan nonetheless remained basically intact, according to Powell. As it now stood, the two entry teams, under cover of smoke and gas, would go into 6223 and 6219 Osage Avenue, and deploy shaped charges on the walls creating holes in the second floor and basement levels of 6221 Osage. A "pepper fogger"—a machine that disperses tear gas—would then be placed through those holes and the residents of 6221 Osage would be forced outside, through the main floor of the house. The use of the squrt guns by the fire department would ensure that MOVE would be unable retreat to the bunkers. Powell still believed it feasible, despite Richmond's conclusions, that the water might force the bunkers off the roof.

Sambor has subsequently claimed that he had no knowledge of the specific weaponry involved in Operation MOVE, no idea that it would include M-60s, an anti-tank gun, or .50-caliber weapons, and was unaware that in order to obtain the M-60s and the BARs, the department was forced to turn to sources outside of its own arsenal.

Revel has another story. For twenty-six years a policeman, with face and voice reminiscent of Wally Cox, Revel, 47, had joined the force on Aug 17, 1959. Thereafter, he had worked in the Second and Fifteenth Districts in his native Northeast Philadelphia; as an undercover cop on anti-crime teams; as a sergeant in the K-9 unit; and since February 1985, as a weapons expert, assigned to the Firing Range.

At the end of the May 9 meeting, Revel says, he, Powell and Sambor did indeed discuss weapons. "What I heard was that the commissioner wanted to know what we had in our armory as [to] the availability of automatic weapons. And [Sambor] was told we have . . . all the [M-]16s, Uzis, and the .50s." Lieutenant Powell then said that, "he had the availability of getting some other heavy automatic weapons and he wanted the advice of [Sambor] whether he thought it necessary for them to get them." The commissioner, according to Revel, replied, "If you can get them and they can be transferred legally . . . get them." It was clear, Revel says, that Powell was talking about, "an M-60 and three BARS [Browning Automatic Rifles]."

The conversation between Powell and Sambor was "intense," Revel recalls. "I think when you're dealing with something like that, it's an intense conversation."

Powell also has acknowledged the discussion of weaponry with the commissioner, his recollection of the commissioner's reply, the same as Revel's.

A Philadelphia Police Department memorandum addressed to Captain John Donnelly at the Police Academy from Powell reads:

Subject: BORROWED WEAPONS & AMMUNITION
RE: MOVE TACTICAL OPERATION
1. On 5-9-85, Lt. Frank Powell # 176, Bomb Disposal Unit, requested permission from the Police Commissioner to borrow certain special weapons from Mr. Andrew Tabas, 1414 Willow Avenue, Melrose Park, Pa., for the MOVE Operation. Mr. Tabas is the owner of Sportsman's Emporium and had offered the weapons for our use.
2. The Police Commissioner granted permission and Lt. Powell contacted Special Agent Ron Hubbard, A.T.F. [Alcohol, Tobacco, and Firearms Agency, U.S. Treasury Department], about obtaining permission to transfer the weapons.
3. Upon receipt of the information on the weapons, S/A Hubbard made the necessary arrangements and transferred the weapons.
4. The weapons and ammunition borrowed are described below:
   A. Weapons Borrowed
      (1) Three (3) Browning Automatic Rifles, caliber 30-06
      (2) One (1) M-60, .30 caliber
      (3) One (1) 20 mm LAHTI Anti-Tank Gun
   B. Ammunition Borrowed and spent

CALIBER	AMOUNT BORROWED	AMOUNT SPENT
30-06	2,100 [rounds]	120 [rounds]
.30 caliber	7,413 [rounds]	1,000 [rounds]
20 mm	111 [rounds]	-0- [rounds]"

That same day, General Brooks left town for Virginia. The ostensible purpose of the trip was to attend his daughter's graduation from college. Brooks had not been at work at all on May 8. Before leaving, he had no discussions with Sambor concerning the progress of the plan. Similarly, he had no discussions with Mayor Goode, because, he said, "We left the [May 7] meeting with the understanding that it would take from one to two weeks to prepare—to obtain the warrants, and after that we would begin, we would work up the operation. We would begin the planning now, but not begin [the operation] until after the obtaining of the warrants." He left for Virginia, he says, under the impression that the MOVE operation would not take place until the next week, the week of the thirteenth. "I had no idea that anything would happen on May 13."

There was no one in Brooks's office, according to Goode, who was filled in on the planning for the operation or left in charge. Goode has said that he was by now "dealing direct with the Police Commissioner." Brooks, Goode's designated man in charge of Operation MOVE, returned on Sunday, the twelfth of May, sometime around 6:00 P.M. The Osage neighborhood had by then been evacuated.

Mayor Goode met with Police Commissioner Sambor on Thursday, May 9, for a private briefing concerning the tactical plans to be used against 6221 Osage Avenue. According to Goode, Sambor gave him no written plans. "I asked him where he stood with the plan. He said he was going to take the steps to do it on May 12, and then with May 13 being the day. I asked whether or not he thought, since May 12 was Mother's Day, he wanted to wait a few days beyond that. He said no, that he felt May 12 was a good day. . . . The Police Commissioner made the decision and informed me that . . . he thought [May 13] would be the best date. And that is consistent, by the way, with my instructions.

"What I said to him, what I instructed him was, 'Go and develop a tactical plan. You pick the date, and you pick the overall plan that you want to use. I'm not a police professional, I'm the mayor, and I must rely upon you to go and do a proper kind of plan.'

"He [Sambor] told me essentially the plan had these components, that he had a number of police officers who were well trained, who were handpicked by him. . . . He would start on Saturday, May 11, even prior to May 10, it may have been that he would start, to put people into the adjoining houses and that they would have listening devices where they would listen in on what was happening inside of the house to determine what movement, what preparation, where the people were in the house . . . where the children were. . . . So that they could have some basic kind of intelligence in terms of what was going on.

"He explained to me that it was his plan as the Police Commissioner at 0600 that morning, which is 6 A.M., to proceed to the site, to announce and read off the names of those persons who in fact were under arrest in the house, that he would await their response for a given period of time. . . . And at the end of that given period of time, that he would repeat it again, and if there was no response after a given period of time that he would then proceed to use water, to begin to force the residents out with water, that he also would use tear gas that he would use to put in the house.

"And thirdly, that he would use what he called a stun gun. He described a stun gun to me as something which would temporarily immobilize persons who would be inside the house in the event they got close enough to the house that it would enable them to go in and take those inside the house.

"He also indicated that they would put holes in the adjoining walls of the two houses at some point during the day. And they would put tear gas in from the two adjoining houses.

"And that was the basic plan which he outlined to me. He told me on May 9 that the plan was not firm at that time. There was going to be a meeting all morning on Saturday [May 11], lasting perhaps five or six hours, where every detail of the plan would in fact be gone over, and that he would get back to me on Saturday afternoon."

Goode says that he and the commissioner did not, at any time, or in any context, discuss the use of explosives.

Revel said later that contingency plans to put explosives on the roof of 6221 Osage had been a clear part of a two-page tactical plan, "MOVE Operation," which he himself had written. Revel had seen the written plan "on the table" in Commissioner Sambor's conference room on May 9. Under the heading of "Operation," the plan read: "If for some reason entrance is NOT gained through the walls for the gas teams, bomb men will go onto roof and drop gas into 6221. Shaped charges, 4 locations on or at hatch entrance." Revel and Officer Michael Tursi both say that they were never told that the plan was secret. "This piece of paper was out and available." Both officers agreed that Lieutenant Powell had ordered the plan typed and copied. Powell gave them copies early on the morning of May 9.

Sambor does not remember whether or not he discussed the use of explosives with Goode at the May 9 meeting. As for the existence of written plans for May 13, he has said, "There were tactical plans, as far as the deployment of personnel, but there were not tactical plans as to the insertion teams for the employment of gas or the use of explosives, and the reason why these types of plans are not prepared and put on paper or disseminated, except on an absolute need-to-know basis, verbally, [is] because the ability to restrict this dissemination of information to unauthorized personnel is virtually impossible. . . . I feel very strongly about that, that too much information gets out."

Goode remembered asking about the possible harm to the children inside the MOVE house due to the use of tear gas: "I was told that they felt that the tear gas being used would not in fact be fatal to the children. . . . Harmful, fatal. I use the words as the same."

That same afternoon, Thursday, May 9, in the mayor's conference room, Goode and Sambor met with District Attorney Ed Rendell, who informed them that warrants had been prepared but not yet signed. According to Rendell, this was also the first time that he heard that May 13 had been chosen as the date for the operation.

The district attorney proposed the idea, first suggested by his deputy Bernard L. Siegel, of placing hidden microphones ("spike mikes") into the walls of 6221 Osage. Goode and Sambor were both immediately receptive to the idea. Rendell promised to assign Deputy District Attorney Hanson the task of arguing for the use of such microphones before a Superior Court judge.

The somber meeting at an end, Rendell left the mayor's office "with an enormous sense of foreboding." His worst fears would, in the end, come all too true. That nightmarish reality was almost at hand.

7

Mother's Day

By Friday, May 10, the situation in the Osage neighborhood had made the front page of the *Inquirer* under the headline, "Living with MOVE: Endless Trauma."

Lucille George, a 62-year-old neighbor with a serious heart condition, had attended a meeting of the United Residents on Wednesday night at the Cobbs Creek Recreation Center: "Thirty minutes into the meeting, another neighbor ran into the room with a breathless report that a MOVE car had blockaded the street, and the group exploded.

"People began to shriek. Several women trembled and cried. Others bolted from the room, sprinting the three blocks back to Osage.... And in the midst of all this, Lucille Green began gasping for breath."

The next morning, Green was reported "resting comfortably" in Lankenau Hospital, suffering from "a serious aggravation of her heart condition."

As it happened, the MOVE members were not blockading the street, but only stopping to unload food at 6221.

That same day, Maude Roberts, one of the would-be negotiators during MOVE's Powelton Village days, eighty-three-years old, visited the steps of 6221 Osage and told reporters that she intended to return the next day in order to help bring about a peaceful solution to the problems. The women in the house, she said, seemed willing to listen to reason, but a man "sounded very desperate in his talk. He said he doesn't care if he dies."

Three or four MOVE members could be seen working on the bunker

Two MOVE members working on the rooftop bunker at 6221 Osage Avenue.
The *Philadelphia Daily News.*

most of the day Friday, nailing on additional layers of wood and cutting peepholes.

Civil Affairs officers could be found stationed at the corner of Osage Avenue and Sixty-second Street. Police Department sources told the *Daily News* that 24-hour coverage of the MOVE house would begin on Saturday, and at noon, Monday, the complement would "be doubled to fourteen detectives."

A very different picture was being painted that same Friday afternoon, as Sambor met with Mayor Goode and District Attorney Rendell in the mayor's office. According to Sambor, "The discussion was that we . . . would try and get the warrants prior to the weekend. . . . I started going into details about the plan after giving the general overview, and to the best of my recollection, at the time that I was going into the details, the mayor indicated that he at that stage was not interested in the details, that that rested with the managing director and myself. . . .

"The general description of the plan was the water, the gas, and the smoke, that we would establish a perimeter, that we would if possible, evacuate."

The rooftop bunker. Wide World Photos.

The back yards of 6219–6221 Osage Avenue. The *Philadelphia Daily News.*

Later that afternoon, block captain Clifford Bond met with Mayor Goode at City Hall for about fifteen minutes. Afterwards, Bond said that the mayor had agreed to attend a community meeting already scheduled for next Saturday night at St. Carthage Church, Sixty-third Street and Cedar Avenue. Bond said that Goode had disclosed to him "a favorable plan" for dealing with MOVE. The mayor, Bond said, planned to make the details public at the community meeting next week. Goode, however, refused to comment about his meeting with Bond.

At 8 A.M. on Saturday, May 11, Police Commissioner Sambor met in his conference room at the Police Administration Building with Fire Commissioner William C. Richmond, agents of the Federal Bureau of Investigation, and some two dozen police commanders. The meeting lasted for approximately three hours. At that meeting, according to Sambor, the Fire Department was "confident" that its squrt guns would "probably" be successful in the removal of the bunkers from the MOVE house. The use of those squrts, Sambor contended, "was one of the essential elements of the plan."

Fire Commissioner Richmond's version of the Saturday morning meeting differs. "I think we made it quite clear that we could give no guarantees . . . and when we got out there on Monday morning [the use of the squrts to remove the bunkers] turned out to be just not tenable. . . . I made it clear that I couldn't guarantee it would do what they wanted to do and that is to dislodge the bunker." Richmond was unclear as to the absent managing director's role in the operation, but assumed that General Brooks would act as "commander-in-chief."

There was no written plan distributed at the meeting, according to Lieutenant Powell, who also claimed that a written report was not composed until several weeks after May 13.

There was no discussion of the use of explosives on the roof of the MOVE house at the May 11 meeting, according to Sambor, nor was there any discussion of weaponry. "I did not know of any weapons that would be on the scene, other than the fact there would be automatic and semiautomatic weapons and handguns available."

Despite Sambor's recollection, Powell has said that it was made clear at the meeting that holes would be blown in the walls of the MOVE compound and the adjoining row houses via explosives charges, so that the pepper fogger machine could be inserted. Those present, Powell says, were informed that if it became necessary for the entry teams to get into 6221 Osage, or to evacuate their positions, detonating cord would be used to blow holes through the the appropriate walls. Neither Tovex nor C-4, both high explosives eventually utilized in May, were discussed.

On that Saturday, the Osage neighbors were to have met with State Representative Peter D. Truman at 10:30 A.M., an appointment which, the neighbors say, Truman himself arranged. When Truman failed to show, Howard Nichols and Cliff Bond declared that they were "outraged." Truman later claimed that the meeting had been rescheduled for twelve o'clock noon, at a time he could not attend. He had other commitments. However, he added, "In short order . . . it will come out that Pete Truman was in the forefront to solve this thing all along."

Anthony Dennis Jackson, an attorney, announced after meeting with fifteen of the neighbors that morning for over an hour that they had agreed to file a civil suit to force the city to apply the laws to MOVE. Howard Nichols said that the United Residents had offered to provide another house for MOVE members, "where they can live as they wish." The neighbors asked only that MOVE find its new house somewhere outside the city of Philadelphia. Cliff Bond was asked if the suit would jeopardize his Friday agreement with Mayor Goode. He replied, "I don't really know, and I'm not concerned. . . . I've been victimized."

At about 2:30 P.M., Goode and Sambor again discussed the plan. According to Goode, Sambor "indicated to me that they had had a good, long, thorough meeting, that the items that he had indeed explained to me in my office were all items that they would proceed with."

Sambor has said that at that meeting, he "went into the operational details of the plan. I told him [Goode] about the evacuation. I told him the time would commence somewhere around ten A.M. on Sunday; that we hoped to have the majority of, if not everybody, out by ten o'clock that night. . . . I also went into the plan itself. . . . I told the mayor about securing the outer perimeter; that I would be exercising strict discipline and control of the interior forces; that unlike '78, the exterior ring of the perimeter would be kept from moving into the interior portion of the perimeter, and that we would have the various teams located in strategic locations for cover, and that I planned to notify them that we had warrants for their arrest and to give them time, and also that the plan called for, generally, water, smoke, and gas. . . .

"I told the mayor that the insertion teams were going to use explosive charges to breach the walls so that they can insert tear gas through the holes into the 6221 Osage Avenue."

Sambor has testified that that the mayor understood the plan for Operation MOVE. Of that, "I had no doubt."

Goode has denied that any information about the use of explosives was imparted to him by Sambor.

It was his understanding, the mayor has testified, that "the essential

part of the plan in the beginning would be not to fire at the house.
. . . It was my feeling that if in fact there was some confrontation directed
between a MOVE organization member and a police officer, of course,
they would return the fire. But my understanding was that they would not
simply fire into the house."

There was plenty of activity within and without 6221 Osage that
Saturday. For at least three hours that morning, MOVE members could
be seen reinforcing the building with planks and heavy wooden boards.

Detectives and uniformed police were again observed keeping tabs on
MOVE activity. As with Powelton Village six and a half years earlier, it
was obvious that something was about to happen, probably something
bad.

Meanwhile, three "community activists," Charles L. "Charlie Boo"
Burrus of the Inner-City Organizing Network, Inc. (ICON), Fareed
Ahmed, and Robert Hamilton, husband of Mayor Goode's private secretary and Chief of Staff Shirley B. Hamilton, were authorized by the mayor
to try to negotiate with MOVE. They were not allowed into the house
at 6221 and instead carried on most of their negotiations with Burrus's
childhood friend, Gerald Ford Africa.

It was during this same day, Saturday, that policemen were given a
letter addressed to Mayor W. Wilson Goode at City Hall. The writer was
Ramona Johnson Africa. The letter said in very brief part that, "The raid
will not be swift, and it will not be clean. It's gone to be a mess. If MOVE
go down, not only with everybody in this block go down, the knee joints
of America will break and the body of American will soon fall. We going
to burn them with smoke, gas, fire, and bullets. . . . We will burn this
house down and burn you up with us."

Meanwhile, that evening, officers from the Stakeout and Bomb Disposal Units under the direct command of Lt. Dominick Marandola were
in the process of trying to place the so-called "spike mike" listening device
into the wall between 6219 and 6221 Osage.

Officer Charles T. "Reds" Mellor, an eleven-year veteran of the Stakeout Unit regularly assigned to the decoy unit, the so-called "Granny
Squad," was summoned to Major Investigations Division headquarters at
7:30 P.M. for a meeting headed by Powell, Marandola, Connor, and Revel.
It was there that he received his assignment for Operation MOVE.

The meeting lasted for less than an hour, according to Mellor. It
included a discussion of the Court Order which had been signed by Judge

Hoffman, granting the police department permission to place a bug in the wall of the MOVE house. After the meeting, Mellor, along with Officer James Berghaier, Mellor's partner in the Granny Squad and a twelve-year veteran of the Stakeout Unit, and Officer Marshall ("Jesse") Freer, drove in an unmarked car, to Sixty-second and Osage, arriving at about 8:00 P.M. Lt. Dominick Marandola was in charge of the operation. All were armed with Uzi submachine guns.

Berghaier, Freer, and Mellor, were met by Officers Dennis Pharro, William Blackman, and Paul Tolbert. Blackman and Tolbert went into 6219 Osage in order to drill the hole in the wall. During this time, recalled Mellor, a MOVE member emerged from 6221 Osage and handed the Civil Affairs officers assigned to watch the MOVE house a note which stated that MOVE would kill the policemen if they attempted to blow the walls of the MOVE house. Soon thereafter, Blackman and Tolbert departed from 6219 through the rear alley, saying, "Let's get out of here, they know we're here." Marandola believed that the sound of Blackman's and Tolbert's drilling was responsible for MOVE's detection of their presence.

Nevertheless, "Operation MOVE" was definitely on. Earlier that morning, Judge Lynne M. Abraham of Common Pleas Court had signed the search and arrest warrants prepared by the district attorney's office.

The MOVE children inside 6221 Osage Avenue could now be taken into protective custody.

They never were.

On Mother's Day morning, Sunday May 12, police began the scheduled evacuation of the Osage neighborhood. By nightfall, most of the neighbors had departed. They were told by Civil Affairs officers to be prepared to spend the next twenty-four hours with relatives or friends. Most left their homes with a single change of clothing.

At 6221 Osage, work continued around the rooftop bunkers, uniformed policemen manned nearby barricades, "negotiators" for the city —Charles "Charlie Boo" Burrus, Novella Williams, Robert Owens, Bennie J. Swans—came and went, while the MOVE children carried out their own "activity" for the day.

Birdie Africa, later described in an interview with fire marshals, how the children spent the day. "We was all out back and a cop came back there with a machine gun, straight up like that, and then we ran in the house and we told, and then they told us to go out and look out for them, and we was looking out, and then it got nighttime, no, they was keep coming back there and pointing at us and laughing and stuff. And then it go night, some nighttime and the cops got all they bags and stuff, and they started coming up there, and I think that was a cop and he was (inaudible) 'no come back,' he told them to all come back, then they started coming back, then they told them to go on Pine Street, and they went on Pine Street, then we was out there for a while, and they keep. . . . they had raincoats on, then they was sneaking up, 'cause they didn't see us, and they were sneaking up, then they saw me, then they started running back around the wall, and then we went, I went in and then everybody came in."

On that Sunday evening, at about ten o'clock, Robert Owens began his negotiation attempts. "Myself and Mr. [Bennie] Swans went to 6221 Osage Avenue in an effort to work out some type of negotiation. Prior to going to the MOVE house (8:30 P.M.), I talked to Gerald Ford Africa on the phone. He is their minister of information. We talked about the possibility of ending the whole thing with a peaceful solution. He said that he didn't believe there was a chance that anything could be prevented. He said that I could go and talk to Conrad and give it another shot.

"Later that evening, me and Swans went to the MOVE house. I talked to Ramona Africa about talking to Conrad. At first she was reluctant to let me talk to him and went back in the house. She came back twice and the second time that she came to the door I observed an adult male and a small child about six years of age inside the house.

"Conrad then came out and we talked. We talked about resolving the whole thing peacefully and he informed me that already there had been a fight in the basement and that the 'motherfucking' cops had tried to come through the walls last night and they [MOVE] had sent 'their ass back.' He then said that he didn't see any way this could be resolved and that he was wasting time talking and that he had to go back in the house and prepare himself for their defense. I then told him that this would probably be the last time I would see him and he said if that was God's will, so be it. . . . I was warned by a Police Officer not to smoke near the house because there might have been flammable material in or near the house."

Swans's account is much the same. "We (Bob Owens and I) checked with Commissioner Sambor, and he said he would try anything to try to avoid a confrontation. We had Lieutenant Pritchett meet us on Sixty-second Street at Pine at 9:50 P.M. and [Pritchett] escorted us to Sixty-second and Osage. . . . Lieutenant Pritchett advised us not to smoke in front of the house because the house contained flammable liquids."

Earlier in the evening, at about 6:30, General Brooks had returned from Virginia. With Sambor present, Brooks briefed the mayor at about 9:00, via the telephone. Both Sambor and Brooks have said that Goode was made aware, in the course of the conversation, of the use of explosives in the plan. Goode has insisted that he was not told.

Whether the mayor was aware of it or not, the use of explosives was a very real part of the plan as envisioned by the "experts," Lt. Frank W. Powell and Officer William Klein of the Bomb Disposal Unit.

Powell had reported to the Bomb Disposal Unit at 8:00 that morning, leaving at four in the afternoon. At 9:00 P.M., he returned to the Academy, where, for the next two hours, other police officers also arrived. Connor, Tursi, and Powell briefed Teams A and B at the Bomb Disposal Unit headquarters at 11:30 P.M. The assembled teams were informed of the main components of the operation, which were, according to Powell, to enter 6219 and 6223 Osage Avenue, blow holes in the basement and second floors of the MOVE compound, and insert tear gas through pepper fogger machines.

Powell was outfitted in a two piece black SWAT suit, vest, tear gas mask, and baseball cap with the Bomb Squad's emblem. He was issued a Smith and Wesson model 39 with a four-inch barrel, a semiautomatic pistol, and carried a clip in the pistol for 25 rounds of 9-mm ammunition. He also carried a mini-Uzi machine gun for which he had four clips with 32 rounds in to the clip.

Officer William C. Klein, a 38-year-old former Marine, had been a member of the Police Department since 1971, and of the Bomb Disposal Unit since 1977. While stationed at the Engineer Training Center in Camp LeJeune, North Carolina, he had enrolled in several courses in explosives demolition. From 1966 to 1967, while stationed in Vietnam, Klein used the high explosive C-4 on what he says was a daily basis in "opening up tunnels, destroying fortifications, removing booby traps, blowing up caches of weapons and various other tasks as directed."

In his own judgment, Klein was more familiar with C-4 than any other member of the Bomb Disposal Unit. He has characterized C-4 as "a plastic explosive, easily transported, not round sensitive [not reactive to exploding gunfire] and although it will burn, it will not detonate without an explosive charge. Because it is pliable like putty, it is very desirable to use in making up charges in the field. It is usually detonated with a blasting cap or with detonating cord. It either comes in two-and-a-half-pound or one-and-a-quarter-pound blocks. These blocks are wrapped in plastic and the explosive itself is light in color." Klein attained the rank of Gunnery Sergeant while enlisted and obtained a Military Occupational Specialty in Explosive Ordnance Dispoal.

According to Powell, both Tursi and Revel were aware that the tactical plan for Operation MOVE called for the use of stun grenades, as well as shape charges and detonating cord to blow holes in the walls of 6223 and 6219. Sergeant Connor, the officer assigned to lead B Team, had demonstrated the use of the stun grenades at the meeting held on May 12 at 11:30 at the Bomb Disposal Unit headquarters, at which both Revel and Tursi were present. FBI Special Agent Richard Harrison and Alcohol, Tobacco, and Firearms Agent Macy, the commanding officers of the federal Swat Team based in Philadelphia, had a separate meeting with Powell, Revel, and Tursi, in which, according to Powell, the entire plan was gone over and given the agents' sanction. Neither C-4 nor plastic explosives were mentioned at the meeting.

The members of the Bomb Squad to whom Powell had given the task of constructing the shaped charges and stun grenades were, most likely, Officers Blackman, Boyce, Klein, and Muldowney. Powell, despite his supervisory status, claims to remain uncertain as to which officers were assigned this important task. Nor is he able to recall how many such explosives "devices" were composed.

Preceding the MOVE operation, according to Klein, the Police Academy magazine contained one block of C-4, which weighed about one pound. The block, contained in a piece of Tupperware along with samples of other explosives, was, Klein has said, "old and ratty-looking."

Commercially made "shaped charges" and detonating cord, along with homemade "stun grenades" and "water charges," were the "assigned" explosives, carried by the members of Teams A and B. Each of the teams carried five shaped charges. As for the water charges, Powell claims that he cannot remember who was assigned to make these up. The water charges, Powell explains, were composed by putting a small charge inside a plastic container along with detonating cord and DuPont data sheet, which he describes as a plastic explosive similar to C-4, but less powerful. Similarly, Powell claims not to remember who constructed the stun grenades. He does know that one of them had a time fuse, blasting cap and a plastic explosive called dexoprime booster. The other, more powerful than the first, contained a one-third pound explosive booster. There were, he has said, about twelve grenades, six for each team.

"We all decided what we needed based on our own experience," said Klein. Powell, he continued, gave the teams no instructions as to the use of specific explosives. The explosives technicians assigned to Teams A and

B were each responsible for their own explosives. Klein, attired in a jump suit, combat boots, Bomb Squad cap and gas mask, carried a .357 Magnum, a 9-mm city-issued Model 39 automatic pistol with two extra magazines, a mini-Uzi submachine gun with four magazines, a Marine Corps K-Bar knife, demolition tools, a half-mile light and a flashlight, two canteens of water, a gas mask, a military backpack and a pepper-fogger.

He also carried some, though he does not remember how many, small shaped charges, commercially manufactured, each about four inches high and one and a half to two inches wide at the bottom, as well as two or three ounces of blasting powder. Klein had never before used this kind of shaped charge, which he believed to be a DuPont product called "Jet Taps." Klein planned to construct his own shaped charges using explosives available to him, including the pound of C-4.

Other explosives carried to the scene, according to Klein, were Tovex, PETN boosters, detonating cord and data-sheets, and two kinds of stun grenades, which he called "oversized firecrackers," that sounded a loud bang intended to deafen, certainly frighten, and absolutely impair its target.

There were also some "little red things," used as concussion devices, with a six- or seven-second time fuse and a blasting cap wrapped in red plastic booster material. These had been tested at the Police Academy Range, but Klein himself did not carry or throw any during the MOVE operation. Team A also brought two linear charges, which, according to Klein, were composed of detonating cord imposed on three inch by two inch cardboard sheets. One of the charges had five strands of detonation cord taped to it; the other, three strands, to be used as breeching charges, if holes had to be blown in the wall of the rowhouse so that the team could escape.

Powell has maintained that he was ignorant of whatever explosives the other members of his team carried, other than the authorized wall and shaped charges, and the stun grenades. The members of his team, he has said, were experienced bomb technicians and were each capable of deciding what explosives to bring with them. None had been authorized to carry plastic explosives, including C-4 and Tovex.

Officer James Laarkamp, a thirteen-year veteran of the Philadelphia Police Department, had been assigned to the Bomb Disposal Unit for the past eight years. He reported to the Academy on the evening of May 12, at eleven o'clock. Assigned to Team A, Laarkamp was outfitted in plain dark blue overalls, a flak jacket, and the Bomb Squad baseball cap, and issued a Smith & Wesson Model 39.9-mm semiautomatic pistol and a fully automatic 9-mm Uzi submachine gun. For ammunition, Laarkamp was given two clips of 32 rounds and one clip of 20 rounds.

During the previous week, at Powell's instruction, Laarkamp, along with other members of the Bomb Disposal Unit had constructed shaped charges for use in the MOVE operation. These charges were intended to be used in case the team needed to gain access to 6221 Osage Avenue, and were made, according to Laarkamp, with Tovex-TR2. Having been put into a plastic funnel—which would concentrate the energy of the explosion—the Tovex would then be placed against the wall and exploded, thereby creating the entrance hole.

Like the other men of Teams A and B, Officer Laarkamp was ready for whatever came. Operation MOVE was on.

8

In the Dawn's Early Light

Weather Forecast for Monday, May 13, 1985
Weather: Sunny, hot, and humid. Near 90°
Sun: Rises at 5:48 a.m., sets at 8:07 p.m.

Frank Powell, along with the rest of Team A, left the Police Academy for the Walnut Plaza at Sixty-third and Walnut Streets, some few blocks away from 6221 Osage. This was to be the assembly site for Operation MOVE. There, Powell and Sergeant Connor would attend a last minute briefing before the operation began in earnest.

Commissioner Sambor, Fire Commissioner Richmond, and various police commanders were present at the briefing. Though Powell later claimed that he was unable to remember the details of the meeting, he did recall that the plan of operation was gone over by Sambor. There was, said Powell, no discussion of using explosives on the roof of the MOVE house. Neither was there any attempt made to improve upon the plan. Everyone present agreed that the plan for Operation MOVE was a good one.

The log of Detective William Stephenson—assigned to keep the official police chronology of Operation MOVE—is revelatory of something else: "0340 [3:40 A.M.]—Command Post—Walnut Park Plaza, Cobbscreek Pkwy & Walnut St. Briefing by Pol. Comm. He was asked about State [Police] Helo [helicopter]. He responded that it was not requested at this time.

"Sgt. Edward Connor, Lt. Frank Powell explained attack plan to staff who were present: To place explosive shape charges (C-4) on both sides of 6221 Osage in an attempt to activate tear gas."

Sambor, asked later if he knew Detective Stephenson, said that he did not. When told that Stephenson, during the meeting, had recorded, "(C-4) on both sides of 6221 Osage in an attempt to activate tear gas," Sambor denied that the powerful military explosive had ever been mentioned.

Detective Stephenson has continued to stand by the accuracy of his notes.

The final briefing adjourned, Powell and Connor joined their respective teams at the adjacent parking lot. From there, they headed to Sixty-second and Osage, parked the bomb disposal truck, removed their equipment, and waited for Sambor to deliver his ultimatum to MOVE.

Interviewed later, Birdie Africa said that with him in the house were, "Raymond, Conrad, Frank who we call Nick, Theressa, Ramona, and Ronda [sic]. They were the adults. I call the children my sisters and brothers, but they are not from my mother. Their names are Tree. Her real name is Katresse [sic]. Her mother is Consuella [Dotson Africa]. She is older than I am. Tomosa is a white male boy. His mother is Sue [Levino Africa]. Melissa is a black female about the same age as me. Her mother is Janet [Holloway Africa]. Phil is younger than me. He is black and his mother is Jenine [Janine Phillips Africa]. Consuella, Sue, Janet, and Jenine are in Muncy Prison."

Birdie stated that although he knew John Africa, he had not seen him since he was a baby.

Much later, Birdie was again asked to identify the people in 6221 Osage. This time, the boy named Conrad Hampton Africa ("Rad"), 36; Frank James Africa ("Nick"), 26; Rhonda Harris Ward Africa, 30; Raymond T. Foster Africa ("CP"), 50; Theresa Brooks Africa, 26; Ramona Johnson Africa ("Mona"), 30; Katricia Dotson Africa ("Tree"), 15; Zanetta Dotson Africa ("Netta"), 13; Phil Phillips Africa ("Phil"), 12; Delitia Orr Africa, 12; and Tomasa Levino Africa ("Boo-Boo"), 9. To this list, he added another name, that of the man they called "Ball"—Vincent Leaphart, now aged 54.

Ball had a gray beard, said Birdie, and had a bald spot on top of his head. "Sometimes he would come visit," the Osage Avenue house, and when he did, "they had meetings." Yes, Birdie continued, he had heard of Vincent Leaphart; he was "Ball." "I heard it in the newspapers, and his name was Vinny."

Asked on May 14 to describe the adults as they had appeared on the day before, Birdie replied that Frank "had on a pair of shorts, old sneakers, no shirt, moustache, and beard and goatee. Raymond had on long pants (jeans), hair cut short, no shoes, no shirt and teeth missing in the back. Conrad had on short green pants, high top white sneaks, blue and white short sleeve shirt, dreadlock hair, goatee and small moustache. . . . Rhonda had on a blue shirt with flowers, shorts, blue sneakers and real long dreadlock hair."

Police Academy firearms instructor Edward Furlong was assigned to Post No. 2 at 6232 Osage Avenue. His equipment consisted of a Browning Automatic Rifle (often referred to as a "BAR" gun) and a .357 Magnum. During the early morning hours of May 13, with the aid of binoculars, Furlong saw what he believed to be a MOVE member "on the front west edge of the roof at 6221 Osage. It was a black male and he was wearing a red shirt with a gray sweatshirt over the red shirt, dark trousers and dreadlocks." The man, Furlong reported, "was dark complexioned" and stood between 5'7" and 5'10"."

Later, sometime towards dawn, Furlong "saw two black males going into the bunker at the front of the roof at different times. One went in and then the other followed about a minute or so later. Both were moving quickly so I couldn't make out what they were wearing but they both had dreadlocks. They were carrying something and were walking bent over as if they were carrying something with both hands. All of this was going on while whoever was on the bull horn responded to Commissioner Sambor's ultimatum."

Officer Dominic Folino of the Stakeout Unit was also assigned to Post No. 2. He was equipped with a 12-gauge shotgun, his service revolver, and a .37-mm tear-gas gun. During the course of the confrontation, Officer Folino would fire both his tear-gas gun and his shotgun. In the early morning hours of May 13, before the shooting had begun, Folino observed two men on the roof of the MOVE house. "I watched them for about 10 minutes with binoculars. All I could see was their head and shoulders. . . . Both had dreadlocks and both had dark shirts on. One had a sleeveless shirt and the other had a short sleeve shirt on."

Stakeout Officer Carmen Iacuzio was in Post No. 2, along with Officers Furlong and Folino. Iacuzio was armed with his service revolver and an M-16 assault rifle. He fired the M-16 during the course of the day. Sometime before the confrontation, he too saw activity at 6221 Osage. A MOVE member "was on the roof around the time the commissioner gave his statement to MOVE. He was a black male, approximately 25–35 years, medium cut hair (no dreadlocks) he was around 5'8", 160 lbs., [and was wearing a] gray heavy sweater. I did not see any weapons on him. He was standing outside the front bunker."

Officer James Farley was assigned to Post No. 6, a rooftop rifle position, and was armed with a .357 Magnum along with a 30/06 rifle with scope. During the course of the gunbattle, Stakeout Officer Farley would fire his rifle, but not his revolver. In the early morning hours, before the shooting began, Farley also reported seeing atop the MOVE roof, "two black males. Number One had dreadlock hair, dark complexion, either a dark shirt or no shirt—I'm not sure if it was a dark shirt or his skin. He looked to be in his thirties. Number Two appeared to have gray short hair, about fifty years old. He was wearing a gray sweatshirt. He had something around his neck that was red which was either a scarf or another shirt underneath the sweatshirt."

Stakeout Officer Joseph Thompson was assigned to the rooftop detail at 430 South Sixty-second, Post No. 5. He carried his service revolver, a .357 Magnum, a 30/06 rifle, and an M-16 assault rifle with nighttime "star-scope." He fired some or all of his weapons at the MOVE house on May 13. Early in the morning though, he saw, "two of the MOVE members on the roof of the residence walking between the two bunkers. This was before light and was with the use of a startrom [night scope]. All I could say is that one of the MOVE members had on a white shirt and the other appeared to be wearing a light green shirt, or what it appeared to be in the scope. . . . They were males. . . . Neither of these males had weapons."

On the roof at that time, said Birdie, were "Rad and CP and Nick." Just what they were doing, Birdie never knew for sure.

That morning, said Birdie, "We were all asleep on the second floor when Commissioner Sambor came and told us to come out. Frank told the cops we were not coming out. Frank is the leader. He tells everybody in MOVE what to do. Ramona told the cops that they had put gas on both sides of the MOVE house. Then Frank told all the women and children to go downstairs. We went downstairs and the men stayed upstairs."

In its late afternoon edition, the *Daily News* on May 13, reported that Commissioner Sambor had issued his ultimatum at 5:35 A.M. via a bull-horn. According to the newspaper account, Sambor began with the words:

"Attention, MOVE! This is America! You have to abide by the laws of the United States."

The commissioner was dressed in blue pants, a blue windbreaker, a blue baseball cap, and a flak jacket. Throughout the day, he carried an M-16 slung over his shoulder. According to Detective Stephenson's log, Sambor's ultimatum elicited the following response from MOVE: "0535 [5:35 A.M.] . . . 'We ain't got a motherfucking thing to lose, come and get us. Remember we killed Ramp. Is your insurance paid up, your wives will cash them in after today, Motherfuckers.' "

Conrad Hampton Africa and Ramona Johnson Africa were on the bullhorn shortly after Sambor delivered his message, according to Birdie. "They were saying that Wilson Goode had sent the white cops out to get killed because they had gotten on his nerves. Any cop that wanted the job come on and get killed. When the cop die his wife would get another man. The white cop's wife would get a nigger, and the nigger would fuck his wife and daughter and get the white cop's money and be riding around in the big boat that the cop bought. When the cops come and try to kill MOVE, MOVE would shoot back and get sticks and beat the cops to death and the cops would fuck around and get their heads blown off. MOVE would take ten bullets just to be able to put one bullet in Wilson Goode's head to prove their point."

In a later interview, Birdie said that he and the other children were awakened by the commissioner's voice on the police bullhorn. They had all been asleep in the second floor hallway. Some of the adults were upstairs, some were downstairs. Birdie shortly afterwards heard Ramona on the bullhorn. "I heard her say they put—at first we heard a glass breaking and then she said, 'Did you all hear that? We are putting gas in all these houses.' And she said, 'If one house get it, all of these houses are going to get it.' " She was referring to fire, the child added.

"Then," said Birdie, "they got on the mike and started giving the cops information, and then . . . we went to sleep. And then, it was half way nighttime and I heard Commissioner Sambor on the mike, and he was saying, telling them to come out, and they heard him, then they got on the mike and started talking to him, and then, then . . . they told us to go in the cellar, in the garage, and we went in the garage, and we had to put wet blankets over our head, 'cause they were shooting tear gas in and then we was laying all, all over top of each other, and then they started shooting water and tear gas in, and we heard shooting and stuff, that's all."

The James's home on Osage was, as a MOVE Commission document later put it, "one of 17 houses on the north side of the block between Sixty-second Street, to the east, and Cobbs Creek Parkway to the west. . . .

"6221 was the fifth house in—86 feet—from the east end of the block and the 13th from the west end—approximately 230 feet."

Louise James described the house that Birdie Africa had been sleeping in on the morning of May 13, the house into which Teams A and B were about to try to put tear gas.

If you entered the house from the front steps, you would come into an enclosed front porch with an arched passage leading into the living room. In the living room was another arched passage which led into a large dining room. A door on the left side of the dining room led into the kitchen. Behind the kitchen was a "shed kitchen" into which could fit only two trash cans. A door at the rear of the kitchen led to this "shed kitchen." It was impossible to get outdoors from the kitchen or the shed kitchen, as there were no doors from those locations to the outside.

To get into the cellar, you would go through a door in the kitchen and descend some long wooden steps. In the cellar was one room, with panelled walls in the front. This room was under the first floor dining room. Through a door at the back of this room, you would be led into a laundry room, which lay beneath the kitchen. The rear driveway was accessible through a door in the laundry room. There were, according to James, no yards around the house.

A stairway on the left of the living room led to the second floor. There were three bedrooms on the second floor, one over the front porch with a bath, one middle bedroom, then a rear bedroom.

There were two bunkers on the top of the roof, according to Birdie, made of, "tree wood and regular wood and then we put steel on it and then we put plyboard on it." Mo and Rad had built the bunkers, with the help of the children. "Like the bunker was halfway over the roof . . . and you could look down, you could see up the street and all over." There were little "windows" in the bunker, he said, "they had real thick glass." There were also holes in the steel parts of the bunker. Asked what they were for, the child replied, "They were shooting holes."

The other bunker, "didn't have no steel on that. They only had steel around where the holes were." It did, he said, have trees inside.

It was still early on the morning of May 13. Birdie was fully awake now. The commissioner had finished reading his ultimatum, and MOVE had made all the reply it was going to make. It was at this time that Birdie first heard gunfire, "a lot of shots. Then Conrad came downstairs and told Rhonda that the cops had some mean bullets, and he went back upstairs." Birdie and the other children, along with the women, "stayed down there" for the rest of the day. And all day long, huddled with the others in the cellar, Birdie would hear explosion after explosion rock the house above them as tear gas filled the room in which they lay.

"And it was like I was going to die," he said.

9

"They Got Some Mean Bombs"

On the morning of May 13, 1985 the men of Team A, along with the weapons they carried were:

Lt. Frank W. Powell, Commanding Officer of the Bomb Disposal Unit (BDU): 9-mm sidearm; Uzi submachine gun.
Officer William Klein, BDU: 357 Magnum; 9-mm sidearm; Uzi; explosives.
Officer James Laarkamp, BDU: 9-mm sidearm; Uzi.
Officer Raymond Graham, BDU: 357 Magnum; 12-gauge shotgun.
Officer James Berghaier, Stakeout Unit (S/O): 357 Magnum; 12-gauge shotgun.
Officer Charles T. Mellor, S/O: 357 Magnum, Uzi.
Officer Terrence Patrick Mulvihill, S/O: 357 Magnum; Uzi.
Officer Lawrence D'Ulisse, S/O: 357 Magnum; Uzi.
Officer John J. Reiber, S/O: his sidearm and a shotgun.

Typical of the group was Officer Jim Berghaier, who carried with him a military type flak jacket, his police-issued protective vest, a speed loader for his revolver and a military gas mask. Like all the men in Team A, he had rubbed vaseline around his neck and wrists to protect himself from tear gas. Again, like the others, Berghaier, wore surgical gloves.

Mulvihill and D'Ulisse, partners on Team A, were two of the four Philadelphia policemen alleged to have beaten Delbert Africa on August 8, 1978. Once again, they found themselves part of an operation against MOVE—this time, though, on the front line.

Asked pointedly by homicide detectives when his men had begun their assault on 6221, Lieutenant Powell replied, "There never was any assault on the MOVE residence." This was to be both the standard question asked by and the standard reply given to homicide detectives—after the fact of May 13.

By 5:50 A.M., fifteen minutes after Commissioner Sambor ordered the MOVE people in 6221 Osage to surrender, the men of Team A were poised at their "jump-off" location (along the west side of 6245 Osage) in the back alley between Osage and Pine Streets. The squrt guns on Sixty-second Street were now turned on, filling the air with cascades of water intended, it was said, to dislodge the bunkers on top of the MOVE house and to provide cover for the insertion teams. Three minutes later,

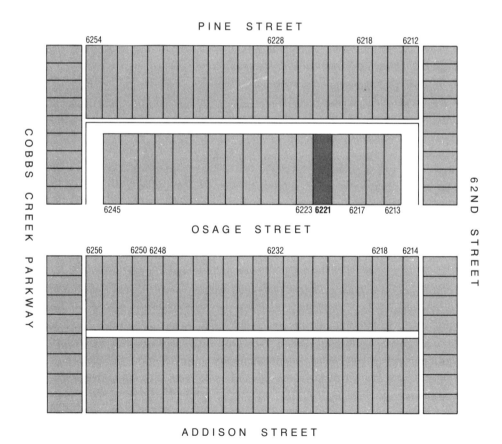

Stakeout officers began firing and throwing tear gas cannisters into the front and rear of 6221. At the same time, Powell said, "yelling" could still be heard coming from the MOVE loudspeakers.

Lieutenant Marandola, at Command Post One, at this time gave Powell the signal for his team to head towards 6223 Osage Avenue. When Team A reached the alley, they put on their tear-gas masks and steeled themselves for what was to come. Berghaier remembered Powell saying, "Let's go." With that, the men of Team A began their approach towards 6223 in single file.

Before passing behind the MOVE house, now entirely hidden by smoke, Berghaier recalled that Powell asked, "Well, who wants to go first?" No one, Berghaier said, volunteered. While still in the alley, Berghaier heard the first shots, single fire. They were coming, he said, from the MOVE house.

The time was approximately 6 A.M.

Members of Team A, after forcing the door to 6223 Osage open, searched the basement, then the first floor living room, and then the second floor. Having secured the house, the various team members rendezvoused in the basement. Powell could still hear pistol shots coming from the MOVE house. The shooting, which was initially single fire, soon escalated to rapid fire, and sounded as though it was coming from a .38-caliber weapon. The gunfire, Powell said, continued for at least five or six minutes.

From inside the MOVE house, Birdie Africa could hear that, "The cops were drilling holes in the walls next door, and Frank and Conrad were banging on the walls with their hands and then with sticks." Birdie subsequently clarified this: "When the cops started drilling in the walls, Frank knocked holes in the wall with his hand and with a stick."

According to Powell, it was at about this time that Klein put a shaped charge on the wall of 6221 from beneath the cellar steps of 6223. The firing had already stopped. The team then vacated the basement and proceeded to the second floor of the house, while Klein detonated the explosive. The charge destroyed the steps of the basement, yet curiously the hole it created did not fully penetrate the wall.

Klein then stacked some of the disassembled basement steps and used them to climb to the first floor of the house. Laarkamp, on the second floor, meanwhile put another shaped charge against the wall at the top of the stairs. The other members of the team, according to Powell, retreated to the front bedroom closet while the explosive was detonated. Once again, the results were a failure, the explosive having blown a hole which did not penetrate the wall. The team was preparing to set off yet another explosive in the same place, when work was interrupted. Bullets began tearing *through the wall* of the MOVE house. Team A was again under fire.

The time was now approximately 6:18 A.M.

According to Laarkamp, who was at the time in the rear bedroom along with other members of the team, the gunfire they received from the MOVE house was rifle fire. The shooting was coming, he said, through the wall of 6221 into the bedroom of 6223; it was neither outside fire nor cross fire from police positions across the way. When asked how small caliber fire could penetrate the same wall that an explosive had failed to open, Laarkamp told investigators that he could think of no explanation. That was just the way it was.

Powell believed that the shots, which were rapid fire and of such force that they soon created a three foot by three foot circle on the wall near him, emanated from automatic weapons. And so, in retaliation, Powell fired his Uzi through the wall in the direction of the incoming bullets. Other members of the team, he said, followed suit.

Mayor Goode was at his home in the Overbrook section of West Philadelphia, along with City Council President Joseph E. Coleman, Councilman Lucien E. Blackwell, State Senator Hardy D. Williams, and State Representative Peter D. Truman. The five powerful black politicians sat in the family kitchen, drinking orange juice, discussing the progress of the morning. Coleman would later recall how the group had watched Operation MOVE live on Channel 10 television. Coleman, however, claimed to have had no knowledge of the explosions that morning—this despite the fact that Channel 10 reporters several times noted the sound of what seemed to them like heavy explosions. (At one point in the videotapes from that morning, an explosion is heard, the ground shakes, and the television picture wobbles badly.) The mayor, on the other hand, has said that he was able to hear gunfire from his back porch. "We could in fact hear gunfire, yes," Goode has said. "And it sounded like a war zone out there."

Birdie Africa was still in the cellar, in "the cement room," so called because the floor there was made of cement. Water had begun to flood the basement as soon as the shooting started. By now, "It was kind of deep, and it was running out of the drain in the garage floor." The women and children lay hidden in the pitch black of the basement under blankets soaked with water. Birdie shared one with Tree. He was afraid during the shooting, "but the older people said that when we get scared to say, 'Long Live John Africa!'" And so the children frequently shouted, "Long Live John Africa!"

It was probably between 6:30 and 7:00 A.M. Posts 3 and 4 (located on Pine Street diagonally across the rear alleyway from 6221) were engaged in heavy firing aimed at the roof and second floor of 6221. The back of 6223 Osage Avenue, where members of Team A were, remained directly in the line of fire.

Berghaier thought the firing coming from the MOVE house was probably .22 caliber. The rounds were hitting a wall near him, creating a large circle. When he was asked whether the source of the incoming fire could have possibly have been police weapons, not MOVE weapons, Berghaier replied that, "Anything was possible!" Berghaier did not return fire. "I didn't have anything to fire at."

Commissioner Gregore Sambor, when informed that the Police Department had in the course of Operation MOVE used no less than "20 rounds of .22-caliber rifle fire out of 10,000 rounds that were taken [to the scene]; 30 rounds of .45-caliber Thompson machine gun rounds out of 2,000 taken; 2,240 rounds of M-60 machine gun fire, which required additional rounds being received, or obtained, from the Police Academy; 1,500 rounds out of 4,000 rounds of M-16 .223 caliber out of 15,000 rounds that were present at the scene" replied that, "I have no understanding as to the amount of ammunition that was used."

The firing into 6223 continued unabaited. So heavy was the shooting that, according to his own account, Officer Charles "Reds" Mellor crawled across the second floor and into a closet for shelter against the incoming bullets. Before very long, Mellor had company: his closet was soon packed with what must have seemed like all of Team A. There was hardly room to budge. And it was hot in there. It was very hot.

According to Powell, while Klein was trying to set off the second explosive against the wall, he was hit by "flying debris" from the party wall of 6221. Klein hit the floor, having been struck in the arm, the leg, and possibly, said Powell, the shoulder. Several members of the team, including Powell, dragged Klein into the closet with them.

Berghaier, while in the closet, noticed that Laarkamp was getting dizzy, his eyes rolling back into his head. Because of the tear gas and the mask Laarkamp was wearing, Berghaier concluded that he was hyperventilating, and so escorted Laarkamp out of the house through the back. Team A was now two men short and worse off than ever, still very much under fire, its initial mission—to place tear gas into 6221—yet to be accomplished. Something had to be done. Not surprisingly, high explosives were again deployed.

Klein set off another explosive in the same place where the second charge had failed. Once again, according to Powell, the charge failed to go off. The lieutenant then ordered the rest of his team to retreat from the second floor to the first floor, while Klein attempted to detonate the device manually. For the first time, said Powell, an explosive fully penetrated the wall of the MOVE house.

The resulting explosion opened a hole that was at least eighteen inches in diameter. (Commissioner Sambor would later claim that he had authorized the use of explosives capable only of creating holes less than three inches in diameter.)

Klein has said that he and Powell were able now to see into the MOVE house. There, they noticed a wall composed of wooden beams and railroad ties covered with creosote. Gunport openings were prominent in the wall.

The MOVE Commission document, " 'A' Team," notes that: "Klein is the ony person to describe such an interior fortification on 6221's second floor. His description matches all other accounts of the bunker inside the first floor of the MOVE house. It must be noted that Fire Marshal's Office investigators, on May 14, examined the west wall of 6223, which was still standing after the fire. These observers have told the [MOVE Commission] that *they saw no evidence of any breach of the second floor wall—they saw no hole.* This is supported by partial analysis of photographs, but is flatly contradicted by the predominance of statements from A Team members."

Soon thereafter, according to Klein, the team was again assaulted by gunfire. Klein and Powell now retreated to a second floor back room in order to take cover. Powell, Klein said, retaliated by firing his Uzi, and the gunfire from the MOVE house quickly came to a halt.

Mellor told investigators that after the successful third explosion, the so-called "pepper fogger," a device to fan tear gas, was inserted into the wall and turned on. The machine then pumped tear gas into the second floor of the MOVE house for fifteen or twenty minutes. This, Mellor said, was verified by a radio report to the effect that tear gas could be seen coming out of the front windows of the second floor of 6221 Osage.

Powell, to the contrary, has contended that the pepper fogger, having been damaged during the gunbattle, was no longer in working order. This, Powell claims, was why he and Klein were forced to hurl tear gas grenades for about half an hour through the hole.

While Powell and Klein either hurled gas grenades or else looked after the pepper fogger machine, Mellor went down a stairwell to the first floor, in search of Mulvihill and D'Ulisse. He found them, huddled behind a chair against the west wall of the living room, protecting themselves from gunfire. D'Ulisse believed that much of this was cross-fire which "came from our own people." It sounded, he said, like heavy caliber machine-gun fire, "like the M-60. A lot of it."

Mellor ran back upstairs with the news that Mulvihill and D'Ulisee were under fire. Powell and Klein then started downstairs in order to help the two officers. What about the pepper fogger? asked Mellor. The ostensible purpose of the morning's explosions, after all, had been to open a hole sufficient in size for the pepper fogger to be inserted and tear gas pumped into 6221. Should they now simply abandon the pepper fogger? "Don't worry about it," Powell told Mellor. "Leave the damn thing there."

When Powell and Klein got downstairs and met the other members of the team, said the lieutenant, they discovered .22 rifle fire coming from the MOVE house. They could also hear a helicopter flying above their location. Using a walky-talky, Powell informed Lieutenant Marandola at Command Post One of his predicament. Marandola asked about the possibility of finding another means of getting tear gas into the MOVE house. Powell replied that he thought that they might use water charges combined with detonating cord or DuPont Data sheets—explosives, which by Powell's own admission, had not been authorized for use in the operation against 6221. Officers Boyce and Blackman were soon dispatched to 6223 with the required explosives from the Bomb Squad truck.

(Commissioner Sambor has since testified that he neither approved, nor had any knowledge of, the use of any explosives other than those authorized in the original plan for Operation MOVE.)

The commanding officer of the Stakeout Unit, Captain Richard Kirchner was with Lieutenant Marandola in Post One when a radio message came from Powell in 6223. According to Marandola, Powell's suggestion "was that he prepare some type of charge to propel through the side wall on a downward angle, protruding through the floor of [6221], and that would make sort of a chute effect where he could get gas from the first floor of [6223] into the basement of 21. . . . He made the suggestion to me over the radio, and I told him he would have to wait a minute, and I would have to check further." Marandola said that he then checked this with "the Captain [Kirchner] and the Police Commissioner [Sambor]. . . . The Captain and the Commissioner were in the parlor. . . ."

Kirchner continued, "The Lieutenant turned around, and was going to relay the message to me. And the police commissioner was standing right alongside of me. And before I made any comment at all, the Police commissioner instructed Lieutenant Marandola to ask Lieutenant Powell —I believe his words [were]—was it a high or low [level of explosive charge]."

Sambor, according to both Marandola and Kirchner, gave Powell permission to use the "low order" explosives.

Mellor recalled that Officer Ray Graham of the Bomb Disposal Unit arrived about this time and began to discuss something with Powell and Klein. Graham left and soon came back with Blackman and another Stakeout officer whose name Mellor could not remember, as well as a bag of explosives, which they put on the dining room table. There, Powell, Klein, and Graham made another explosive device, the composition of which has yet to be ascertained. Powell then went up to the second floor along with Mulvihill.

There, through the hole in the wall which the third explosive had opened, Powell and Mulvihill began throwing stun grenades and tear-gas grenades. After a time, the two returned to the ground floor, where they met with Graham and Klein, who had by this time composed some kind of explosive for use against the living room wall facing 6221. Mellor, who contended that he was unfamiliar with explosives, was later asked by investigators to describe the device. To the best of his recollection, he said, there had been a three-foot by two-foot piece of cardboard on which detonating cord was placed in a circular fashion. In the middle of the cardboard was added another explosive, this one about four- to six-inches wide, with wooden "legs." Klein told Mellor that the explosive would be used against the opposite wall of the living room if the team had to get out of the house. It was, said Mellor, put on the east wall, several feet from the front door. Klein and Graham put it there.

Berghaier had by this time returned from Cobbs Creek Parkway, having carried Officer Laarkamp to safety. He now brought with him a fire company ladder, which he used to climb from the basement to the first floor. There, he too found Graham and Klein busily engaged in making some sort of explosive device.

Berghaier, who also claimed to be unfamiliar with explosives, described the device constructed by Graham and Klein as a two-by-three-foot piece of cardboard with what he thought was detonating cord taped on. Attached to the device, Berghaier said, was a strangley shaped thing with "little wooden legs" on it. Berghaier, like Mellor, watched as Graham and Klein taped the cardboard to the party wall between 6223 Osage and the MOVE house, some three or four feet from the front door of the house.

Having evacuated the house through the basement, Klein set a five-minute delayed fuse. He then heard an explosion and what he believed was a "counter-explosion."

(It has been suggested that the "counter-explosion" may well have come from the second satchel charge thrown by Team B's Officer Muldowney, from 6217, into the first floor MOVE bunker.)

Powell also said that he heard two explosions. He, as well as Klein, believed at the time that the second explosion came from inside 6221 Osage. The air conditioner, which had been running in the first floor dining room of 6223 Osage, was blown through the window and landed in the driveway as a result of the second explosion. Powell later claimed that it was impossible for the team to get back into 6223 Osage, as the wall against which the explosive had been set had collapsed and the floor seemed to be caving in.

James R. Phelan, a former bomb and counterterrorism specialist with the Federal Bureau of Investigation, was an expert witness before the MOVE Commission. Phelan has testified that the damage done to the front porches of 6219, 6221, and 6223 Osage on the morning of May 13 was "not consistent" with what should have been caused by detonating cord. The twisted metal and shredded wood shown in police photographs from that morning indicated to Phelan that "high explosives were used." It is not unlikely that the mining explosive Tovex—or perhaps the vastly more powerful military-grade C-4—had already been utilized before noontime of the morning of May 13.

After climbing the ladder which he had brought with him, Berghaier observed that the front part of the MOVE house seemed to have moved, and a hole was visible in the living room wall at the front. He overheard Marandola complimenting Powell via the radio. What he heard Marandola say to Powell, was, "You should have seen what that last charge did to the front of the house. You really did a job on it."

In its chronology of May 13, the Philadelphia *Inquirer* reported that at 10:35 A.M., "Explosions . . . are felt a block away from the house." Videotape from a local television station confirmed the time of the explosion.

Birdie Africa remembered Conrad Hampton Africa saying of the police that, "They got some mean bombs out there."

After members of the team got back into the dining room of 6223 by using a ladder, Klein reported that he could see into 6221 through the hole blown in the first floor wall. There, about three feet inside the MOVE house, stood a wooden bunker with gunports. Yet curiously, the team did not at the time receive gunfire from this interior bunker.

Because the pepper fogger machine was no longer working—if again, we are to believe Powell and Klein and not Mellor on this score—Klein said that tear gas could only be introduced into 6221 by hand. He had used all of his shaped charges by this time, but only one of the linear charges. Klein was still in possession of an undetermined quantity of C-4 and some blasting caps.

Outside the house, Officers Powell, Graham, Reiber and Mulvihill worked to tear down a barricade made of plywood, old fencing and sheet metal, and fencing that blocked the alley behind 6221. The work took no more than five minutes, after which the men could see "a large timber laid in a barricade fashion" where the garage door to 6221 would be.

After taking down the fence in back of the MOVE house, Powell and the others stationed themselves by the back door near the MOVE garage. According to Powell, they could hear movement and talking coming from the people inside.

A four-inch vent protruded up from the rear basement of 6221 Osage. For a time, Powell seems to have pondered the idea of dropping tear gas or stun grenades down the vent.

Klein said that he and Graham could hear the voices of women or children coming from the vent, and so they rejected the use of gas.

Berghaier noticed two five-gallon kerosene cans, either blue or green in color, standing by the fence. Both, he believes, were empty.

Powell now contemplated blowing the door to the basement of the MOVE house. The notion, he says, was again rejected because of the possibility of harming the children. And so the members of Team A returned to the alley and headed towards Cobbs Creek Parkway, their mission a nearly total failure.

The time was approximately 12:30 P.M.

In one of the many, remarkably routine interviews that Philadelphia homicide detectives carried out days after the fact, Powell was asked what injuries he sustained in the course of Operation MOVE. He replied that, "I twisted my ankle while pulling down the rear fence of the MOVE residence on 5-13-85 at about 1 P.M. I twisted it while walking on the debris in the rear of that residence. The elbow I just don't recall how that occurred." His ankle though was "still a bit tender."

After conducting a very different sort of investigation, explosives expert James R. Phelan told the MOVE Commission that he considered the members of the Philadelphia Bomb Disposal Unit "quite professional" in performing bomb-disposal duties, but "completely unqualified" in the use explosives as tactical weapons.

MOVE Commission member Neil Welch, a former assistant director of the Federal Bureau of Investigation in its post-Watergate, post-Hoover period, interjected, "If they *are* qualified, it's not evident by the results." Phelan had to reply, "No, it is not."

The Philadelphia *Daily News* reported on May 14 that, "One team of officers made it into an adjoining building and detonated a charge of [C-4] plastic explosive . . . but it failed to blast open a significant hole because MOVE had fortified the walls of the house."

Members of the Bomb Disposal Unit, the *Daily News* continued, "were assigned to enter the adjoining houses, detonate the C-2 plastic explosive, and pour tear gas into the house. Stakeout Unit officers were assigned to accompany them.

"Shortly after 7 A.M., a C-2 charge was set off in a house adjoining the MOVE structure."

The *Daily News* article, with its curious and telling reference to "C-2" remains remarkably suggestive. Perhaps *that*—or rather, C-4—was what was attached by the "little wooden legs" to the cardboard strung with detonation cord. In its account the *Daily News* cited neither politicians nor Osage neighbors nor angry MOVE members, but **unidentified police sources**.

Managing Director Leo A. Brooks, the retired two-star army general and "commander in chief" of Operation MOVE, has testified that he was unaware during the late morning and early afternoon of May 13 of the extent of the damage which had been caused by the insertion teams' use of explosives. He had no idea, Brooks has said, that, for example, the front of the MOVE house had for the most part been destroyed or that a brick wall in front of the house had been penetrated by explosives.

Yet, at approximately 1:30 P.M., General Brooks, Police Commissioner Sambor, and Fire Commissioner Richmond were taken to a second floor window of Post One, a position which faced 6221 diagonally across narrow Osage Avenue. The morning's explosions had all occurred long before. In official police photographs taken from precisely the same vantage point at very nearly the same time, you can see clearly what General Brooks says he never saw: the whole of the porch areas of 6219, 6221, and 6223 Osage Avenue had by this time been blown away.

Considerably after the fact, Birdie Africa was asked by investigators to describe what an explosion was like. He replied: "Like if somebody threw a bomb, and it busts like, and it would be all like—break stuff up like." A child's definition of a horror, it said all that really needed to be said.

The boy Birdie Africa was still in the "cement room" of the cellar with his mother Rhonda, along with the other women and children, when Conrad Hampton Africa came downstairs with news of the damage done by the explosions. "Rad," Birdie has said, "was talking to Rhonda . . . [and he] said they blew half of the porch away."

And what did Rhonda say?

"She was laughing," Birdie said. "She was just laughing."

And so the great confrontation of May 13 had come to this: the most fatal possible combination of mayhem and madness.

10

"You Won't Believe This!"

These were the men of Team B, along with their weapons on the morning of May 13:

Sgt. Edward Connor, Bomb Disposal Unit (BDU): 9-mm sidearm; Uzi submachine gun.

James Muldowney, BDU: 357 Magnum, explosives.

Daniel C. Angelucci, BDU: 9-mm sidearm; Uzi; no. 37 tear gas rifle; gas.

Salvatore Thomas Marsalo, Stakeout Unit (S/O): .357 Magnum; Uzi.

Marshall Freeman Freer, S/O: .357 Magnum; shotgun; Uzi.

Alexander Draft, S/O: .357 Magnum; Uzi.

Michael Ryan, S/O: .357 Magnum; Uzi.

Known to his fellow officers as "Jesse," Marshall Freeman Freer had been on the Philadelphia Police force for more than eight years, the last three years and ten months in the Stakeout Unit's decoy operation, the Granny Squad.

On May 12, 1985, Freer reported to the Police Academy Range at noon and remained there until about four or five o'clock in the afternoon. He spent the day, he said, "getting to know" the Uzi submachine gun, shotgun, and handgun he had been assigned for Operation MOVE. Other Stakeout Officers were similarly engaged at the Range, familiarizing themselves with shotguns, nightscoped rifles, M-16s, Uzis, and the heavy .50-caliber machine guns, the expelled shells of which Freer helped clean up.

At ten o'clock that evening, Freer, along with Officers Berghaier and Mellor of Team A, reported to the Bomb Squad headquarters, where he outfitted himself in navy blue coveralls, vest, gas mask, and ballistics helmet. He also picked up a .357-caliber Magnum handgun and an Israeli-made Uzi.

Eight years a cop, the last three in the Stakeout Unit, Officer Michael Ryan discovered his name on a notice posted on the bulletin board at Stakeout Headquarters on May 10. "It was an assignment sheet for the MOVE Operation," he recalled later. Officer Ryan found that he had been detailed to Team B.

And so, on May 12, 1985, Ryan too, reported to the Bomb Disposal Unit. There, he was issued blue overalls, a baseball cap, tear-gas mask, and a ballistic vest. His sidearm was a Smith & Wesson .357 Magnum, for which he carried eighteen rounds of ammunition, .38-caliber "police special + p." He was also assigned at that time a Winchester model 1200, 12-gauge police shotgun and a single bandolier holding twenty-four rounds of buckshot and ten rifle slugs.

Officer Salvatore Thomas "Sal" Marsalo had been on the Philadelphia Police force for nearly twenty years, the last sixteen and a half in the Granny Squad. Marsalo had previous experience with MOVE on August 8, 1978, when he was assigned to the "assault team," whose responsibility it had been to enter the old MOVE Headquarters in Powelton Village "in a forceful manner if it was required of them to act in this manner." On Friday morning, May 10, Marsalo had begun to sharpen his skills at the Range in preparation for another confrontation with MOVE.

While practicing at the range, Marsalo fired an Uzi machine gun, a .357 Magnum revolver, an M-16 assault rifle, and a .12-gauge shotgun. On Sunday, May 12, Sgt. David Liebert suggested that Marsalo again join him at the Range "in order to practice firing the Uzi." Because it was Mother's Day, Marsalo told investigators, he declined the sergeant's invitation.

That same day, Officer Marsalo was told to report to work at 10 P.M. He had been assigned to Operation MOVE.

At about eleven o'clock that night, Marsalo reported to a classroom at the Police Academy, where Lieutenant Powell, Sergeant Connor, and Officer Michael Tursi went over the assignments for Teams A and B.

Marsalo understood his team's plan to consist of entering 6219 Osage Avenue, after first blowing a hole in the wall of 6217 Osage to gain access.

In 6219, the team would drill small holes in the party wall adjoining 6221, through which gas from the pepper fogger, which they would hang on large nails on the wall, would filter into the MOVE residence. When asked by MOVE Commission investigators to describe the pepper fogger, Marsalo replied that it looked like a large gasoline-powered chain saw with a big nozzle through which tear gas was emitted.

For fourteen years a policeman, Officer Daniel Angelucci had received four Merit Commendation Awards and the Distinguished Hand Gun Medal of the Philadelphia Police Department. His current posting was in the Bomb Disposal Unit, and his assignment for May 13 was as an explosives technician with Team B.

For Operation MOVE, Angelucci was armed with a 9 mm hand gun and a 9-mm Uzi submachine gun. In a utility bag, he carried a no. 37 tear-gas rifle along with six tear-gas cannisters. Angelucci told MOVE Commission investigators that he carried some other things in his utility bag as well, but he could not remember exactly what.

Officer James Muldowney, not yet forty years old, had been a policeman since March of 1970. Like, Daniel Angelucci, his partner in the Bomb Disposal Unit, Muldowney was assigned to Team B for the May 13 operation.

Muldowney arrived at Bomb Squad headquarters at about ten o'clock that Sunday evening, where he too was outfitted in coveralls and a protective vest. He was issued a .357 revolver, two high explosive shaped charges, pepper foggers and tear gas canisters, as well as other equipment for "breeching and gassing."

Sgt. Edward Connor was a former head of the Bomb Disposal Unit. There have been many cryptic allusions made to Connor's past. "He does have prior Bomb Squad experience and for many years was attached to that unit before some type of disagreement, and he was then transferred to the 1st District" as a street sergeant, Powell told investigators. What that disagreement was about and why Connor was transferred from the Bomb Squad in the first place have never been properly answered. Nor has it ever been explained just why Connor was chosen for such a sensitive assignment as Team B leader. According to Powell, it was decided as late as the May 9 planning conference that, on "the recommendation of the Commissioner, Sergeant Connor was going to be placed in charge of entry team B." The one thing that should be clear from all this is that at every important turn, the man who called the shots in Operation MOVE was the commissioner, Gregor Sambor. He, far more than the "commander in chief" General Leo Brooks, was the man in charge on May 13. These were, after all, *his* men.

Angelucci could not remember what Commissioner Sambor said to the MOVE members over the loudspeaker, but he does remember MOVE's response, which he said contained a lot of profanity. "Hope you Stakeout motherfuckers have paid up your insurance because you're not going to make it out of here." He remembered this most of all.

Under cover provided by smoke and the Fire Department's water squrts, it took Team B about two minutes to get into 6217 Osage Avenue, according to Freer.

Connor had selected his old friend Officer Sal Marsalo to lead Team B up the street. Together, Marsalo and Connor reached the house about fifteen seconds before the other members of the team. Marsalo's task was to cover Connor's entrance into the house.

Marsalo, as assigned, knelt down and covered Connor with his Uzi, while the sergeant opened the door to 6217 Osage with a key which Detective Ben Walker, MOVE's improbable near next-door neighbor, had given to him. After entering 6217, Connor, in turn, provided cover for the members of the team who followed.

The time was approximately 5:55 A.M.

"We never wanted to assault the MOVE residence," was Officer Daniel Angelucci's rote response to the question posed by homicide detectives. There was no assault on the MOVE house. No one had ordered an assault. So no assault was ever made.

Officer Alexander Draft, a Granny Squad member of the Stakeout Unit since 1979, was Marshall Freer's partner on May 13. "We did not assault the MOVE residence," he replied when asked the same question.

Freer's own account differs somewhat. Asked when he left his post to begin the assaulton the MOVE headquarters, Freer answered, "My assault was made sometime around 5:45 A.M.—6:00 A.M. and right after the smoke had been set off in front of the MOVE residence." Sergeant Connor, he said, had given the orders for the assault to begin.

Officer Michael Ryan, asked the same pro forma question, replied,

"We never made an assault on the MOVE compound itself." One sentence later, however, Ryan added that he did help "blow the common wall that separates 6217 and 6219."

The time was approximately 6:18 A.M.

Connor has testified that the original plan called for the manual removal, using a sledge hammer, of the walls which separated 6217 and 6219 Osage Avenue. The plan changed, according to Connor, after the application of a so-called "hatch charge," which created a hole in the porch wall. Why the "hatch charge" was used and the sledge hammer discarded has never been adequately explained.

Marsalo later recalled watching as Connor, along with Officers Muldowney and Angelucci, placed explosives on a "large cardboard structure" which they then attached to the wall of 6217 Osage. A small explosion followed not long afterwards, and Marsalo watched as a four-foot by five-foot hole was blown in the wall.

Freer, looking through the newly opened hole, could now see into the interior of 6221. There, Freer observed a "bunker type construction," about two or three feet high, composed of wooden planks, on the front porch of the MOVE house.

The interior of 6219 was dim, smoky and unlit, and Freer and the other men of Team B had to peer through the goggle-eyed faces of their military-style gas masks. Thus it was difficult for Freer and the others, he says now, to determine much about what they saw that morning. But he was able, Freer has said, to discern gunports in the "log cabin," as well as muzzle flashes and the vague outline of human beings behind the fortifications.

Muldowney believed that the MOVE members fired weapons of at least three different calibers. The shooting came, he said, from both high and low positions inside 6221. From the patterns of bullet holes in the walls of 6217, he identified two of the calibers as double-ought buckshot and .22 caliber. He believed as well that there was MOVE gunfire coming from inside 6219 Osage.

Angelucci recalled how heavy gunfire erupted from inside the MOVE house, passed over the heads of the team by less than two feet, and pinned the officers down. Connor, said Angelucci, then hurled some kind of "noise-making device" at the bunker in 6221, in hopes of interrupting the MOVE gunfire. Connor later explained that what he had thrown was a "concussion device," and hastened to add that such a device ought not to cause injuries to its intended target.

(Marsalo remembered how Connor had given him two "flashbangs," either very late in the evening of May 12 or early in the morning of May 13. These homemade "flashbangs," Marsalo explained, were similar to hand grenades, except that they exploded without shrapnel. They were cylindrical, four or five inches in length, with a five inch fuse at one end, and an activating pin at the other. Marsalo, who had initially suspended the flashbangs from his vest, was told by Connor not to place them there or in his pocket, lest they be hit by a bullet and explode. Connor told him, he said, to set the flashbangs down inside the house once he had entered it, and to keep them away from his body. Marsalo didn't want to blow himself to bits, did he?)

After the hole had been blown in the wall of 6219, Connor hurled a flashbang through it. As soon as it exploded, Freer said, gunfire began coming from the MOVE house into 6217 Osage. Connor returned fire, this time with his Uzi, through the same hole. Freer, from his front porch position in 6217, attempted to provide cover fire for Connor, who was now exposed on the south side of the same porch and hemmed in by MOVE gunfire. Connor hurled another flashbang—or "stun grenade," as he also called them—through the hole, seemingly effecting a pause of a few seconds in the MOVE gunfire, and then lept past the hole in the wall.

Suddenly Connor cried, "I'm hit, I'm hit!" Spun round, the sergeant had been knocked forward and to his knees. There was a bullet in his back.

Freer "reached out and grabbed" the sergeant, sprawled now on the floor, and pulled him into the living room area of 6217 Osage. Connor was, Freer continued, "in pain, and I examined his back and saw that he had been hit with one single shot dead center in the back of his vest. I was also able to see that the bullet had cut through his jump suit and into his vest." Fortunately for the Connor, the bullet had lodged in his protective vest. Where a pool of blood might have been, there was only a nasty purple welt.

Freer, in order to prevent MOVE members from entering 6219, stayed at the porch door of 6217. While Connor was being looked after by other members of the team, Freer pitched two more stun grenades through the hole and into 6221. There was only a momentary lull in the firing.

Freer, according to Connor, who was watching him, "threw another concussion device towards the wall of 6221 Osage Ave. This device also detonated." The incoming fire continued. Connor, back on his feet, now "returned fire at the upper gun port where I could see muzzle flashes. I could hear screaming from 6221 Osage Avenue, however, the gunfire continued from that location."

The voice, Connor has said, was that of a female screaming inside the first floor bunker of 6221. According to his own, earlier accounts given to investigators, Connor fired his Uzi in the direction of the scream, and the screaming stopped.

According to Officer Michael Ryan, Connor, Freer, and draft were by now all firing their Uzis in the direction of 6219 and 6221. Ryan too was firing his shotgun in that direction.

Freer recalled that they took turns firing their Uzis in order to conserve ammunition. He himself estimated that he fired three thirty-round clips of ammunition from his Uzi and six or twelve rounds from his service revolver, a .357 Magnum.

Before the team entered 6217, according to Angelucci, several explosives had already been constructed, one of which was eventually thrown by Connor. At Connor's direction, Angelucci and Muldowney now made up a "high" explosive with a six-second delay, containing an igniter, time fuse, detonator, and an amount and type of explosive material which Angelucci was unable to recall.

Angelucci gave this explosive to Muldowney while the team was under fire. Positioned against the wall of 6219, kneeling over Muldowney, Angelucci gave cover fire, while the prone Muldowney threw the bomb towards a wall opening between 6219 and the MOVE house.

Connor concurred with this account, and said that, "Muldowney laid on his back in the living room of 6217 and was pushed out onto the porch." From his prone position, Muldowney "threw the device against the wall of 6219–21."

According to Ryan, the three Bomb Squad officers ran in and told the other members of the team to leave the kitchen and hit the floor, because there was going to be an explosion. A loud explosion followed by only seconds, and afterwards, having gone back to the front porch, they saw with their own eyes that the party wall between the living rooms of 6219 and 6221 had been destroyed. The fortification—which some called a "pill box," and others called "the log cabin"—could now be seen plainly inside of the MOVE house.

This movable, interior bunker, Connor has said, consisted of "tree trunks, railroad ties, and what appeared to be mortar." Connor could plainly see gunports in the bunker, both top and bottom. Team B was still being fired upon.

Midday, May 13, 1985, after devices exploded at 6221 Osage Avenue. The *Philadelphia Daily News.*

6221 Osage Avenue as seen from the police vantage point across the street. The *Philadelphia Daily News.*

Repulsed again, the mean of Team met in the living room of 6217 in order to determine what kind of explosive might now be employed to penetrate the fortification. Connor again directed Muldowney and Angelucci "to prepare a device in an effort to effect the removal of the bunker on the porch of 6221 Osage Avenue." This device, Connor has said, was to be "delivered in the same manner as the device that had just removed the porch wall of 6219–6221." That is, Muldowney, prone on his back, would again be shoved forward and would then pitch the device at the bunker. This is precisely what happened next.

The homemade bomb, thrown through one of the gunports of the bunker, "successfully removed . . . the East wall of the bunker, pushing the front of the bunker out towards the street" and exposed the wall between the porch and living room of 6221.

This last explosion, Officer Michael Ryan has said, was so intense that the entire house shook with its force. When he looked into the MOVE compound, Ryan could discern no activity within.

According to Freer, only "minimal" fire was returned by MOVE after the explosion. It was impossible at the time, Freer said, to tell whether MOVE members were crying out in pain. The members of the team were, after all, wearing earplugs and earmuffs. They could hear nothing, Freer has said, save for the noise of their own explosions.

While peering at the partially destroyed bunker, Connor observed "what appeared" to him "to be a body covered with a green material with an arm hanging down and a white glove on the hand."

The body "appeared to be face down on what had appeared to be what had originally been the bottom portion of a crawl space constructed below the porch roof." At very nearly the same time, Connor saw something else: "what appeared to be the side of a head at a position approximately between the buttocks and knees of the body and behind the body."

Later, Connor would change his testimony. He now only *thinks* that this was what he saw. He now believes that his first impressions may have been incorrect: No white glove, no green material, no decapitated head, no dead body.

The MOVE Commission's special consultant on forensic pathology was Dr. Ali Z. Hameli, Chief Medical Examiner for the State of Delaware and a past president of the National Association of Medical Examiners. Hameli would later find evidence of buckshot pellets in the chest and buttocks of a body identified as that of Vincent Leaphart. The corpse of the man whose human form John Africa had assumed in this all too mortal life had been discovered, headless, in a corner of what had been the front porch of 6221 Osage Avenue.

Marsalo, while stationed in the kitchen, overheard radio transmissions between Connor, Powell, and Marandola. At one point, Powell ordered Team B to retreat to the rear of 6217. Team A was about to set off a "large" explosion. Some five minutes later, a loud explosion from 6223 Osage was heard. Marsalo then overheard Lieutenant Marandola at Command Post One tell Powell to, "Come around here. You won't believe this!" Marsalo assumed that Marandola was referring to the wooden fortification near the front of the MOVE house which Team A's bomb had revealed.

Then again, perhaps what Marandola really meant was simpler and more obvious. Perhaps he was saying to Powell: You won't believe what that bomb just did.

The time was now 10:40 A.M.

The members of Team B spent the rest of the morning in 6217 wondering among themselves why they had received no new orders to attempt to enter 6219.

Marsalo said that Connor was asked sometime later in the day, via the radio, to determine whether or not the delivery of a "satchel-type device" on the bunker on the roof of the MOVE house would be possible. According to Marsalo, Connor took a step ladder to the second floor of 6217 and attempted to get on to the roof of the house. In order to see the roof of the MOVE house, Connor used a simple kind of periscope which he shoved through the skylight of the bathroom in 6217. Connor then informed either Marandola or Powell that it would be possible for him to deliver the explosive to the MOVE bunker, but warned that he might well be exposed to gunfire from 6221. The operation, Connor told his superiors, would be very dangerous. Connor was told, Marsalo recalled later, to forget it. The men of Team B were relieved by the news.

Sometime between two and four o'clock in the afternoon, Team B left 6217 Osage through the back door, retreated down the rear alleyway, and eventually found themselves near Cobbs Creek and Osage Avenue, breathing easily for the first time in a long while. The gas masks came off, the Uzis and the gas guns and the shotguns were laid aside, hot coffee and sandwiches awaited. Everyone was dead tired.

Operation MOVE was stalled.

11

No Alternative to Failure

The long afternoon of stalemate was drawing to a head when, at about 3:00 P.M., Lt. Frank Powell was ordered to report to Sixty-second and Osage. Upon his arrival, Powell was met by Inspector John Tiers, Cpt. Richard Kirchner, Cpt. Edward McLaughlin, and Commissioner Gregore J. Sambor. Together with Lt. Dominick Marandola, these six were the ranking tactical commanders involved in Operation MOVE. All now faced the possibility of an extended stalemate—or else the prospect of some new and potentially deadly assault against 6221. Given the history of August 8, 1978 and the realities of this day—the bunkers and the interior fortifications and the possible presence of gas and explosives within the MOVE house—all should have been both sufficiently wary and prudent. The evidence, however, is quite to the contrary.

Commissioner Sambor ran the makeshift planning session. His question was whether or not Powell could place an explosive on the roof of the MOVE house in order to remove the front bunker. A secondary goal, according to interviews with both Powell and Sambor, was to create a rooftop hole through which tear gas could be inserted, the need for which in retrospect seems rather strange given the fact that the first floor front facades of 6221 and 6219 Osage were by now almost completely blown away.

Powell says that he told Sambor that such a plan would probably not work. Connor was contacted via walky-talky radio. He agreed with Powell. The plan was at best risky. The officers charged with planting the device,

Connor said, would be subject to great danger. They would have to leapfrog from the rooftops of neighboring houses onto that of 6221. In the process, they would be in a direct line of fire from the bunkers.

The message was relayed by Powell to Sambor. The commissioner, however, remained adamant. A plan would have to be devised, Sambor insisted, to explode a hole in the roof of 6221.

The whole mission, as defined by Sambor and Powell, seems strangely improbable. What purpose could possibly have been served by putting tear gas through the rooftop of 6221? Had tear gas not been pitched, shot, and fanned into the house throughout the day? Had Powell himself not reported that MOVE's people were burrowed in the cellar of 6221? Was no one aware of the possible presence of gasoline, kerosene, and explosives in that house? And what of the children's safety? The questions are as alive today as they should have been on May 13, 1985.

"Negotiations," meanwhile, went on.

At about 4:10 P.M., a gray van pulled up across from the MOVE compound. For the next thirty minutes or so, a number of friends and "negotiators," including Mary Clare Leak, the mother of Theresa Brooks Africa, were given permission to try to talk to the people in 6221 Osage.

Crouched behind bushes at the corner of sixty-second and Osage, Mrs. Leak called out over a bullhorn provided by the police, "Theresa, respond to me. This is the only chance I have to talk to you. Please come out with the children. You can't do this to the children, Theresa. Come out. Please, before it's too late. Theresa, bring the children out. Please, they're innocent victims. Give them a chance to let them come out. They don't have a chance. They're innocent babies. Send the children out. What's the matter, they won't let you talk to your mother? For no other reason, send the children out, darling." There was no response.

Stanley Vaughan of the Urban Coalition took a turn with the bull-horn: "Ramona, I'm your friend. Can't we negotiate? It's me, Stan, Stanley Vaughan, from the Urban Coalition. Would you want to talk to LaVerne and Louise? I'm here to help you. Can't we negotiate? Yell out yes or no. We have met with Wilson [Goode] and he's willing to negotiate with you." Yet another of the negotiators called out, "Anyone in there answer me if you can. Conrad, please let the children out."

None of the residents of 6221 Osage were seen or heard from. The children were still in the cellar.

Back at City Hall, Mayor Goode spoke at a late afternoon press conference. He was ready now, he said, "to seize control of the house . . . by any means necessary."

At about the same time, Officers Klein and Powell were meeting with Commissioner Sambor, Fire Commissioner Richmond, and Managing Director Brooks. The hour was approximately four o'clock; the place, Sixty-third and Walnut Plaza. According to Powell, the topic of this meeting was the proposed delivery of an explosive device onto the roof of the MOVE house. The use of a construction crane and ball to smash a hole in the roof of 6221 had been briefly considered and quickly discounted. Osage Avenue was probably too narrow to accommodate the massive equipment necessary for such a plan. More to the point, the crane's operator would be subject to considerable danger. That still left the very real possibility of employing some sort of explosive "device."

According to Sambor's later testimony, it was at this meeting that, "We mentioned the [explosives] testing that had gone on [during the planning stages]. . . . Whether it was Lieutenant Powell or myself, I don't know. It was part of the general discussion . . . that they had tested explosive materials on simulated roofs, tar paper and wood and wall board, to the best of my recollection."

General Brooks's recollection of the meeting differs from Sambor's in several instances. There was, for example, no discussion of any such prior explosives testing, according to Brooks. There was, instead, "Confidence. I had confidence that Lieutenant Powell, who was described to me as being an expert with great training, significant amount of experience knew how to handle that." It was Sambor, said Brooks, who described Powell to him as an expert.

Sambor, according to Powell, first suggested using a police helicopter to deliver the explosive. Powell told the commissioner that he thought such a plan would work, and added that he had already obtained the explosives for the task. He would do the job himself.

(Powell, having decided that the commercial mining explosive Tovex TR2 would be the best agent to employ against the bunkers, had, according to his own testimony, already instructed Officer William Blackman of the Bomb Squad to return to the Police Academy and pick up the necessary ingredients. This, Blackman did, though how much Tovex, as well as what other explosives he might have obtained, Powell later claimed not to know.)

Commissioner Richmond was properly skeptical: "I turned to Lieutenant Powell, and I said, 'I have one question about this. Is this thing incendiary in nature or will it cause a fire?' And his response to me was, 'No.'" Skeptical or not, Richmond acquiesed to the plan.

As to the composition of the "device," Sambor has testified that it was at this meeting that the use of Tovex was first discussed. "And I remember asking what was Tovex. We were informed that it was an explosive, a relatively new explosive that had been developed for use in mining, that was safe to handle."

Brooks, however, has claimed that he did not hear the word "Tovex" mentioned until, "The next day [May 14] on television."

Neither Sambor nor Brooks ever asked what kind of explosive he was planning to use, Powell has contended. They only inquired as to his ability to do the job.

At a City Hall press conference on the night of May 14, Commissioner Sambor first revealed to the media and the public that the "device" dropped from the helicopter had contained Tovex. "The explosive was tested extensively at the Police Academy and the Fire Academy," said Sambor, "and never during any of these tests was there any fire."

When asked if its use against the bunker made the satchel charge "a military device," Sambor replied tartly, "It was not!"

Mayor Goode later recalled that, "It was at five o'clock roughly . . . when I received a call from Leo Brooks to indicate to me that the crane was found not to be workable, that there was two problems with the crane, one was the problem of the security of the operator and he could not find any operator who would send an operator there to operate the crane and therefore that was one reason.

"The second was there was some issue or problem of getting close enough to the house itself with the crane in order to remove the bunker.

"He, therefore, said that we have decided, and I use the terms that I recollect he used with me, we have decided to blow the bunker off and to blow a hole in the roof and to put tear gas and water in through that process.

"I, after he said to me he was going to blow the bunker off, I paused, I guess, for thirty seconds to absorb what he was saying to me and the next word I said to him was: Does Mr. Sambor know about this?

"He says: Yes, it was his idea.

"And I said, number two, do you feel it will work?

"He says, we feel that it will work. And that we will be able to put the tear gas and water in from the roof area and proceed with our plan.

"I said: Okay. Keep me posted."

This is Brooks's account of the same conversation:

"Without saying very much more, I turned—I was sitting in a chair —I turned and picked up the phone, dialed the mayor, described to the mayor that we had reached the conclusion. That the commissioner can find no other way to get the device onto the roof and that's what he intended to do, and there was a short pause and the mayor said, 'Okay.' "

Goode has testified that General Brooks never mentioned what was going to be used to make the hole in the roof. Instead, the mayor recalls that it was his "impression" that, "They were going to use some type of explosive when he said blow a hole."

General Brooks told the mayor that the explosive would be dropped from a helicopter, according to Sambor. The mayor, however, has said that he remained unaware that the bomb had been delivered by helicopter until about 6:00 P.M. That would have been half an hour after the event —this despite the fact that the bombing was shown on live television. Brooks, for his part, has steadfastly maintained that the mayor was explicitly told that a helicopter was to be used. "I'm positive," Brooks has said that he told Mayor Goode that, "There was going to be a helicopter. A helicopter would be there."

At a press conference later in the week, Goode was questioned about the use of a bomb dropped from a helicopter onto a row house. He replied, "If . . . someone called on the telephone and said to me, 'We're going to drop a bomb on a house;' would I approve that? The answer is no. What was said to me was that they were going to use an explosive device to blow the bunker off the top of the house."

The *Daily News'* Pete Dexter, the most eloquent and ascerbic of Wilson Goode's critics, warned his readers on May 14 and 15, that, "In the next few days, of course, Wilson Goode is going to tell you that he was unaware of the seriousness of the problem. He has, as a matter of fact, already starting minimizing the number of complaints his office got. He will probably deny that the police have been operating under a different set of orders when dealing with MOVE than they were for everybody else. He will deny he knew the extent to which MOVE was armed. And if he says those things, he will be lying. He will probably say that as soon as he became aware of them, he acted. And if he says that, he will be lying again."

Dexter went on, in the same scathing vein: "I want to talk to you a little bit about MOVE again today, and Wilson Goode, and what Wilson Goode thinks is irresponsible, and about dropping bombs into residential neighborhoods. But I have just watched a television interview with Police Commissioner Gregore Sambor—the man whom the mayor credits with planning overall strategy on Osage Avenue—and there is something that needs to be said first. Gregore Sambor is dumber than wallpaper."

In Sambor's own words before the MOVE Commission, "The use of the device itself gives me the least pause. It was selected as a conservative and safe approach to what I perceived as a tactical necessity. I was assured that the device would not harm the occupants.

"What has imprinted that device on the mind of this city is, in fact, the method of delivery. If it had been carried or thrown into position, or if it had been dropped from a crane, the perception of that action would be quite different. But its intent and essential nature would be the same."

Goode said later that he, "believed that there was a possibility that there were gasoline cans on the roof and that in fact there had been gas poured on the roof as well."

Sambor was not concerned. "From my knowledge of explosions, most of the explosive efforts go up and out as opposed to down and in. The bunker was very sturdily constructed and, as I said, they had direct access to the second floor through the bunker, through entries that they themselves had constructed. So that I felt that as a result of having been driven off the roof by the water, and the continuing water until almost immediately before the device was dropped, and because of all of this, and understanding that this was the operation, I did not feel that someone was in danger of losing their lives because of that device."

Following his meeting with the managing director, Powell says that he told Klein to return to one of the police vehicles and there construct an explosive using a pair of two-inch by sixteen-inch sticks of Tovex TR2, placed in a satchel.

Yet, the *Daily News* reported—more or less accurately, as it turned out—on May 14, "*Police sources* said the bomb that dropped from the state police helicopter was a two pound C-4 plastic explosive, packed in a satchel resembling a child's canvas book bag. . . . The satchel contained a C-4 plastic explosive charge constructed by the Philadelphia Police Department's Bomb Squad." (Authors' italics). It was this news account that Mayor Goode deemed "irresponsible."

Officer Klein, after receiving his orders from Lieutenant Powell, proceeded to the Bomb Disposal Unit truck, where he composed the two "explosive devices." Aside from the work of Officer Ray Graham, who constructed the fuses, Klein has said that he received no help in assembling the two bombs.

For the first explosive, Klein told investigators that he put two tubes of Tovex TR2 inside a tear gas cannister bag, on top of which he taped a one and a quarter pound block of C-4. A blasting cap was inserted into the C-4, and the flap of the cannister bag was closed with tape. Klein then taped a fuse to the strap of the bag. The explosive weighed about 3.25 pounds. Neither the Tovex nor the C-4, Klein subsequently claimed, presented much risk of inciting a fire.

Powell, Klein said, had requested that he use two pounds of Tovex. Such a limited amount, Klein believed, would not be sufficient both to blow a hole in the roof and dislodge the bunker. Klein thought, moreover, that he was better qualified to make such a judgment than Powell was. This is why, he said, he added the C-4. "I am still convinced," Klein told MOVE Commission investigators, "that if the charge had been properly placed on the roof, it would have accomplished its purpose."

The explosives consultant to the MOVE Commission, James R. Phelan, later determined that as much as three and three-quarters pounds of C-4 were contained in the "device"—more than double the one and a quarter pound that Klein himself admitted to using.

When Powell returned to the Bomb Squad truck to pick up the explosive, he met Officer Graham, who he said told him that the fuses he had been working on had a duration of forty-five seconds, and that he believed that this should give Powell adequate time. Klein and Powell then drove to the Sixty-third and Walnut parking lot, where a State Police helicopter was waiting. Commissioner Sambor introduced them to Corporal Morris Demsko and Trooper Richard Reed, members of the Pennsylvania State Police Aviation Patrol. According to Powell, Klein handed him two bags, one green and the other white, and told him to use the green one first. Should the green satchel fail, or if Powell found himself in need of more explosives, he should use the white one, Klein said.

Klein told investigators that the second explosive, which he placed in the white canvas bag, contained one tube of two-by-sixteen-inch Tovex TR-2. It was similarly taped closed with a time fuse coming out of the Tovex. Klein explained that he "made up the second bag just in case the first one did not do the job."

The contents of the white bag would eventually be disassembled at the Bomb Disposal Unit at about 9:30 that evening, according to Powell.

With him at the time were Sergeant Connor, Officer Blackman, Officer Klein, Officer Laarkamp, Office Muldowney, Officer Boyce, and Officer Angelucci. Powell claimed that after dismantling the explosive on top of his desk, he determined that it had been composed of four 1 ¼-by-8-inch tubes of Tovex. There was no C-4 present in the white satchel—*if* we are to believe Powell—yet, this was certainly not the "device" as described by Klein.

It was sometime around 5:00 P.M. when Powell met with Lieutenant Dominick Marandola on Cobbs Creek Parkway and told him that an explosive device was to be dropped onto the roof of the MOVE house. Marandola was told that he had about twenty-five minutes "to pull back his Stakeout Unit personnel or find sufficient cover." The bomb would then be dropped and detonated.

By 5:15, Marandola had radioed orders to exacuate all posts. No reasons were given, although the rumor was widespread by this time that a helicopter was going to drop a bomb. The Stakeout officers were told to "standby."

Powell said that the State Police pilots were "pretty upset" when they were told that they were going to drop a bomb on the roof of 6221. They were also, Powell added, "a little reluctant." Reluctant or not, the pilots went along with the plan. Powell, himself a licensed pilot, hopped into the helicopter, which at once headed towards the MOVE house.

Using the helicopter's so-called "150" radio, Powell remained in contact with Lieutenant Marandola on the ground. Shortly after five o'clock, Marandola reported that two MOVE members had been spotted on the roof of 6221 Osage Avenue. Detective William Stephenson's official log confirms this. Stephenson noted that at 5:10 P.M., "2 Black/Ms observed on MOVE roof by Stake Out."

Sometime after 5:15 P.M. and before the dropping of the bomb at 5:27 P.M., Officer John E. McCauley of the Stakeout Unit peered inside a Channel 10 News truck at the corner of Sixty-second and Pine. A woman inside the truck told him that if he looked on her monitor, he would see a MOVE member on the roof. On the monitor, McCauley said, he saw a black male, walking west across the row house roofs. After crossing about three roofs, the man stopped, turned around, and walked back toward the bunker on top of the MOVE compound, into which he disappeared.

After receiving the information about the MOVE members, the helicopter pilots changed their course and waited for further instruction.

Lieutenant Frank W. Powell of the Philadelphia Bomb Squad about to drop explosives onto the roof of 6221 Osage Avenue. *Philadelphia Daily News.*

After five or ten minutes had passed, Marandola radioed that the roof was clear, and so the helicopter turned back towards the MOVE house. Having passed over the roof a few times, the helicopter stopped directly over the top of the house. It was then, Powell said, that he pulled the fuse igniter and, leaning out of the helicopter, hurled the satchel down on top of the bunker.

The time was 5:27. The temperature was eighty-two degrees, the humidity sixty percent, the wind out of the southwest at twenty miles an hour.

The green satchel had landed.

12

A Large, Bright Ball of Fire

Frank Powell watched as the bag laden with Tovex (and C-4) landed on target atop the roof of the MOVE house. His job was nearly finished now. The device had only to do its work.

Yet, Powell was helpless as he watched the down draft from the helicopter blades blow the bag off target and towards the right rooftop party wall of 6221. So strong was the down draft that Powell feared for a time that the satchel would fly off the roof.

Powell's fears went unfounded. As the State Police helicopter reached a point a few blocks from the house, Powell heard, and was able to see, the explosion that the "device" in the green satchel had created.

Detective William Stephenson witnessed the same explosion from the ground. His log reads, "1728 [5:28 P.M.]—My position is at tree line, Osage & Cobbs Creek, with clear view to the drop. A loud explosion occurs on the roof of 6221 Osage Ave, followed immediately by a large bright orange ball and [debris] that exits the roof going above the front bunker in a southerly direction. The bunker shakes briefly. There is a small amount of both black and white smoke and a small flame on the roof."

The State Police helicopter flew back several times over the roof of 6221 Osage Avenue, while Powell conducted a reconnaissance of sorts. From where he sat, Powell could now observe a two-by-two-foot hole in the roof. The bunker, however, remained fully intact. Powell later told investigators that he considered dropping the second bag of explosives on the roof. In the end, though, he decided that he should leave that decision up to Commissioner Sambor. The helicopter therefore returned to the ground, its ostensible mission—to dislodge the bunker—a failure.

Lieutenant Powell found the commissioner near Sixty-second and Osage. By this time, though, the MOVE house was obviously ablaze, and Powell thought it unnecessary to recommend using the white satchel. Perhaps his mission hadn't been a failure after all.

Sambor ordered Powell to get back into the helicopter. An accurate assessment of the damage to 6221 was in order, and so Powell was handed a 35-mm camera and told to take photographs. Lieutenant Powell, joined now by Officer Klein, met the State Police pilots at Sixty-third and

A view from across the street as flames engulf 6221 Osage Avenue. Wide World Photos.

Walnut, where they all climbed back into the helicopter. As the chopper passed over the MOVE roof, Powell could see heavy smoke and fire emerging from the vicinity of the bunker.

No hoses had yet been aimed at the blaze. The Fire Department's two "Squrts" had briefly been turned on between 5:20 and 5:25 P.M. in order to provide cover for the helicopter. The powerful "squrts," high-pressure water cannon mounted atop movable booms, were stationed on Pine Street. Each was capable of pumping a thousand gallons of water per minute. Both were now silent.

Detective Stephenson's log reported that at 5:51 P.M., "Massive amounts of black smoke and a small flame" could be seen coming from 6221. By 5:59, the flames had spread "to [the] front of MOVE house with 10' high dark orange flame." "A slight breeze," Stephenson noted, appeared to be fanning the flames westward.

Fire Commissioner Richmond later testified before the MOVE Commission to the obvious effect that his men "were mentally prepared to fight the fire. And as I say again and again, we had no reason not to fight the fire."

Mayor Goode said that the fire on the roof was apparent to him, "at about ten minutes of six." He was, at the time, watching a television set at City Hall: "I saw initially a small fire on the roof. I saw what appeared to be as some water coming in. I determined later that was not water at all but that was basically the kind of snow on my television screen and after about five minutes of watching that, I indicated to my office [to] get Leo Brooks on the phone, and at sometime close to six P.M. that day, I gave what was my first orders of the day, which was to Leo Brooks, which was: Put the fire out. He indicated to me at that time that he had already given that order two minutes earlier."

According to General Brooks, "It must have been about five minutes to six by the time I got [Commissioner Sambor on the telephone]. . . . My question to him was, 'We have accomplished a mission of penetrating the roof, . . . The face of that bunker is now on fire. Why don't we put the fire out?' And I then said, 'Let's put the fire out.' And he left the phone, left the radio to go to put the fire out." That, at least, was what Brooks thought Sambor was going to do. What the commissioner did, on the other hand, was something altogether different.

Fire Commissioner Richmond, who met with Sambor sometime shortly after his conversation with Brooks, remembers asking him,

The fire spreads from 6221 Osage Avenue. The *Philadelphia Daily News.*

" 'What do you want to do about the fire?' or 'What are we going to do about the fire?' " Both men had in mind, as Richmond later recalled, "the criticality of that bunker . . . as it relates to the tactical operation. I knew that as long as that bunker was up there, there were police and firefighters who were, without a doubt, in jeopardy."

And so it was, Richmond remembered that, "Commissioner Sambor said to me something to the effect, 'Can we control that fire?' And my response—and I'm a cautious person by nature, I said, 'I think we can.' "

A critical decision had been made. A memorandum written after the fact by the mayor's press secretary in conjunction with the police and fire commissioners would record the essence of their discussion. Quoting Sambor, the memorandum reads, "Let the bunker burn."

Richmond claimed later that he had been unaware of the presence of gasoline cans on the roof of the MOVE house. Had he been aware of their existence, his response to Sambor, Richmond said, would have been quite different.

At the time though, standing beside Richmond at the corner of Sixty-second and Osage, Sambor asked, "If we let the fire burn to get the bunker, [can] we control the fire?" Richmond, Sambor says, "stated we could."

"Almost simultaneously," Sambor has testified, "we agreed, one or both of us, that it would be a good idea to put the water on either side of 6221 to prevent the spread of the flames. And that was in the time frame of approximately ten of, five of [six], when we first knew that there was fire on the roof. Because I was still desirous of removing the bunker."

Richmond, on the other hand, has contended that the decision to let the fire burn was Sambor's to make. There was, Richmond has testified, "a recommendation, a strong recommendation from the police commissioner, and I concurred."

At six P.M., Richmond was still unaware of any order from the mayor or from Managing Director Brooks to extinguish the fire. Richmond has, moreover, testified that he received "no order directly or indirectly from General Brooks to extinguish that fire," during the entire course of the evening.

Of Sambor's contention that he relayed the order to put the fire out, Richmond said, "I categorically deny that. I had no knowledge of an order from General Brooks to extinguish that fire."

The squrts went off and on, but mostly stayed off. The fire gained momentum and spread.

When asked by the MOVE Commission whether he considered the actions of his department heads "insubordinate," General Brooks replied,

Police Commisioner Sambor (in flak jacket) on the scene, May 13, 1985. The *Philadelphia Daily News.*

"I don't think, you know, I did not know why, but I don't think Commissioner Sambor or Commissioner Richmond—and I think I know both of those individuals well enough. . . . I don't think either one of them is enough of an animal to do that."

By 6:04 P.M., according to Detective Stephenson's log, the front bunker was on fire. The growth of the fire is chronicled in the log, which continues:

[6:19 P.M.]—20' high flames and black smoke are coming out of the 2nd floor window of 6221 Osage.

[6:20 P.M.]—Rear bunker now engulfed in flames.

[6:22 P.M.]—50' high flames and a large amount of black smoke is coming from 6221 Osage Ave.

[6:24 P.M.]—6219 is now in flames. 100' high flames, now coming from MOVE house.

[6:26 P.M.]—Entire MOVE house now appears to be engulphed [sic] in flames.

[6:39 P.M.]—Rear bunker fell into the MOVE house.

[6:58 P.M.]—The front of 6221 Osage fell inward.

Mayor Goode told the MOVE Commission that he perceived that a catastrophe had developed by about 6:30 that evening: "I wanted to go to Sixty-third and Walnut all day long. . . . My gut always says to me, be where the action is, be at the scene. That's something which is very natural to me." Continuing in this vein, the mayor said that he believed, "It is far better for a mayor to be perceived as being out there on a scene with hands-on than not to be and, therefore . . . I think I lose points from that vantage point." Wilson Goode, points or no, remained far from the scene.

On Tuesday night, May 14, the mayor, fire commissioner, and police commissioner were on hand to answer reporters' questions at a press conference held at City Hall. The mayor said that, "The decision . . . to explode the bunker at the top of the house was indeed a conscious decision. It was felt by all [the] experts, all the professionals, that it would not cause a fire, and it would only cause damage to the part that it was hit on." The mayor was confident that, "In fact, if you watch the films, as I've done, what in fact took place there was an explosion, the bunker was in fact destroyed, and then a fire ensued from that point on. The unexpected part of that was the fire itself."

Goode told the MOVE Commission that he had gone "through very deep emotions at that time. I cried because I knew at that point that lives would be lost, and I knew that homes would be destroyed, and I knew that despite all our good intentions that we had . . . an absolute disaster. And I can't explain to you or to anyone the kind of emotions that I went through, because everything about me is about preserving life and to know that any plan that I've had anything to do with would, in fact, bring about the cessation of life, was very tough."

The fire, which had begun with a bomb dropped from a helicopter onto one row house, spread to other row houses. The immediate result of the decision to "let the bunker burn," was the destruction of sixty-one homes and the homelessness of two hundred fifty-three human beings.

13

The Violet Hour

The geography of 6221 Osage Avenue is vital if you are to make any sense of what happened in the early evening hours of May 13, 1985. The horror is inexplicable without these banal details. Reader, carry these facts with you in your mind's eye.*

In the spare wording of a MOVE Commission document:

"Running behind 6221 was an alley, 16 feet wide, accessed on either end of the block by 10-foot-wide driveways out to Osage on the south, and 3-foot-wide walkways out to Pine on the north.

"The alley was approximately 340 feet long, with a slight, downward slope from east to west, from the Sixty-second Street end down to Cobbs Creek. Bordering the alley along the rear of homes fronting on Pine was an elevated 3-foot-wide walkway with a wrought iron fence mounted along the edge of a concrete wall. The top of the fence was almost 5 feet above the pavement."

What you must not forget is that the backyard of 6221 was hardly a yard at all it was so small, and the alley was narrow, and the walkway narrower still and its fence high. It was very high to climb, if you were a child—even a teenaged child—and if you were malnourished to begin with and undersized, and if your lungs were filled with gas and smoke, and if you were scared. And you were probably scared out of your wits. You were scared that you were going to "cycle." Scared that you were going to die.

* See diagram on page 116.

There were Stakeout Unit firing posts on Pine Street at diagonals across the alleyway from 6221 Osage. Post 3, commanded by Sergeant David Liebert, was situated just west of 6221, at 6228 Pine Street. Post 4, under the command of Sgt. Donald Griffiths, lay to the east, at 6218 Pine. Post 4 was but four houses down from the 400 block of Sixty-second Street.

Stakeout officers were posted at each end of the alley, and at least one policeman (Officer Harry Young)—and perhaps others, as well—was on the nearby rooftop of Pine Street. All told, more than four dozen police officers, most of them from Stakeout, were either in the alley or else in adjoining buildings during the time between seven and eight o'clock P.M.

The front bunker had begun burning at 6:04 P.M. Within a very few minutes, the fire had spread across the neighboring rooftops to the east and west. As the bunkers began to burn and the fire reached downward into the house at 6221, heavy smoke began to pour out the windows. The front steps of the house had been blown away that morning. If the MOVE members were to try to exit 6221, then the route of escape would almost inevitably be through the rear and into the narrow alleyway that ran between Pine and Osage.

Officer Salvatore Marsalo remembered that while he and Officers Draft and Ryan were on Sixty-second Street, Sergeant Connor along with Officers Freer, Muldowney, and Angelucci ran towards them, with Freer shouting, "Come on, let's go!" Marsalo, Draft, and Ryan hurried after them, halting finally behind the house at 418 Sixty-second street. Like the other men of Team B, Marsalo anticipated that the MOVE members would soon be forced out of their home by the fire. After a few minutes, Marsalo saw that hoses had been turned on and aimed from Sixty-second Street to the north side of Osage, where the fire had become quite concentrated. The hoses, according to Marsalo, were turned on and off several times. He and the rest of Team B left the area for Sixty-second and Osage when the heat of the fire became intolerable.

While positioned at Sixty-second and Osage, Marsalo heard over the radio of a "command-type" officer that MOVE members were exiting the compound. He soon noticed a lot of policemen heading toward Pine Street, leaving very few officers at Sixty-second and Osage. Marsalo then hid behind a large tree, from which point all that was visible were the inflamed houses on Osage. He did not, he said, hear or see any gunfire.

Officer Daniel Angelucci, while in 6217 Osage, also heard radio reports of movement and sightings of MOVE members on the first floor of the MOVE house, as well as a report that there was a possibility that one of the MOVE members wanted to leave the house. Stakeout officers, Angelucci recalled, were instructed over the radio to allow anyone who wished to leave the house to do so—and to apprehend them as soon as they were out. Angelucci saw no MOVE members. After some twenty minutes, Sergeant Connor received a report concerning the spreading fire within the MOVE house. Team B was soon thereafter ordered to leave the premises. According to Angelucci, Team B had spent about forty minutes in 6217 Osage before evacuating.

The men of Team B then proceeded to 6214 Osage, where they took a "blocking position" and waited, hoping to apprehend anyone leaving the MOVE house. Angelucci could see flames on both the roof and second floor of the MOVE compound; flames which were spreading quickly. None of the Fire Department's deluge guns had been turned on. Angelucci and the rest of the Team remained at 6214 Osage until the heat of the fire became such that their weapons became hot, at which point they left in the direction of Sixty-second Street. Soon, Angelucci said, he overheard a report of gunfire near Post 4, as well as a radio report that the MOVE members were exiting the premises.

Officer Jesse Freer's recollection is similar to Angelucci's. Freer heard a loud explosion when the bomb dropped and saw debris being blown from the MOVE compound. Before the debris had even hit the ground, Sergeant Connor, Freer recalled, ordered the members of the Team to go back into 6217 Osage with him. They did so, entering the house from the back, and remained there, along with some relief officers, in the hopes that MOVE would leave 6221 Osage, and approach 6217, where they would be apprehended. When it became apparent that no one was leaving the MOVE house, Connor ordered the officers to leave 6217, which was just beginning to catch on fire. They left through a door at the rear of the house, eventually ending up in an alleyway behind 418 Sixty-second Street. According to Freer, none of the members of the Team attempted to get into 6221 or 6219 in order to seek out the MOVE members.

Freer remembered how his Team remained in the alleyway for about half an hour, until they heard shouts from other officers to the effect that gunfire was coming from the 6221, which was completely in flames at that point. Freer subsequently heard other reports of MOVE members leaving 6221 Osage as well as accounts of their entering homes on Pine Street. Freer, and several other officers, departed for Pine Street and searched the homes, to no avail.

The members of Team A, largely if not altogether unsupervised now, took up "blocking" positions in the rear alleyway. While Team B's men took the east end of the alley (towards South Sixty-second Street), the men of Team A were deployed in pairs near Cobbs Creek Parkway on the west.

Minutes after the bomb drop, Team A was ordered to report to the west end of the alley. The Team was thus stationed for possible entrance into 6223 Osage as well as for the prevention of the escape of MOVE members via this route. Officer James Berghaier remembered that Officers Mulvihill, D'Ulisse, Mellor, Graham, Reiber were with him then, at the rear of 6245 Osage.

Berghaier said that Officer Michael Tursi joined them sometime around six o'clock. Flames and smoke could be seen coming from the MOVE compound, and it was decided that they should position themselves further down the alley in order to see the MOVE compound more clearly. The others took position on the north side of the alley: Mulvihill and D'Ulisse were stationed near the back of either 6246 or 6248 Pine Street, Graham and Reiber near 6326 and 6238 Pine, according to Berghaier's recollection. Berghaier was stationed on the south side of the alley, along with Tursi and Mellor.

Berghaier recalled that immediately before the men took their new positions, Fire Battalion Chief Dyer crawled toward them shouting something like, "We have lines to run back here, how about it?" Dyer was told by the Stakeout officers that it would be less risky to run the hoses from inside the houses; and with that, he crawled back to safety.

Birdie Africa was in the garage when the fire started, under a blanket with his mother Rhonda and the boy Phil. All of the rest of the MOVE women and children were similarly hidden under blankets. Theresa, Birdie recalled, was with Tomasa. Smells of smoke and tear gas filled the cellar. It was all Birdie could do to breathe, and he was uncomfortable and scared besides. The blankets were wet, having been soaked in a bucket of water earlier in the day in preparation for the confrontation.

All of the men, said Birdie, were downstairs when the bomb was dropped. He could hear them talking. Rad was near the garage door.

The adults told the children that if they got out of the house, they should stick together. They failed, however, to tell the children exactly where to go. The adults were, by this time, perhaps just as confused as their children.

The children did not attempt to leave the house, said Birdie, until the fire started: "Conrad, no it was Frank, came downstairs and told us that we can't get out the front because the bomb had taken half the step off and that we would have to go out the back."

Investigative documents, along with eyewitness accounts, suggest that movement was apparent inside 6221 at approximately 5:35 P.M. From a police log: "Movement at front door, three (3) people at 6221, one of which is a female." From a Fraternal Order of Police log: "There is a report that came over the Radio of shadow movement on the first floor." From the MOVE Commission's official chronology of May 13: "Two men and one woman observed inside the front porch 6221 Osage."

Birdie could not see in the pitch black of the "cement room." But he could hear Conrad panting, "Give me the monkey wrench, give me a monkey wrench." And he could hear Raymond, Frank, and Conrad talking to each other now: "Get the monkey wrench," he heard them saying, over and over.

After opening the rear garage door with the monkey wrench, Conrad opened the front basement window, which faced Osage Avenue.

Although Birdie still could see nothing, he again heard the big people: "They, they all started sticking their heads out the window, I think, and started yelling, 'Bringing the kids out!' " They were yelling, Birdie said, out of the Osage Avenue side of the house. They were also yelling, he added, out the back.

According to Birdie, the adults told the children "to go out, and we said we didn't want to go, we wanted to be with them. And then they said, we will see them, and then we was going out and Rad was taking Tomasa out. Then the cops started shooting again. Then they locked the things up and waited for awhile. Then the fire got all—all that smoke started coming in and you could hear the stuff dropping upstairs. And then, that is when they started just hollering things: 'The kids coming out!' and stuff."

In another account of the same story, Birdie recalled that, "[Conrad] was on his knees, and he had Tomasa around his stomach like that." Conrad was crawling on the garage floor. When Conrad opened the door, the police started shooting. Conrad did not have a gun. The sound Birdie heard went, "Do-do-do-do-do-do, like that . . . Like going off—like bullets were going after each other." The shooting, Birdie said, went on for "a little while."

Fireman Joe Murray, a Vietnam veteran, was inside 412 South Sixty-second helping to spray water onto the houses on Osage Avenue. He heard what sounded like automatic fire coming from the rear of 6221 Osage when he arrived at the scene, at about 7:15 P.M.

Captain Joseph Jackson was at 6244 Pine Street during the time. At about 7:10 P.M., he heard "a lot of single shots." Stakeout officers moved him from his post immediately afterward, Jackson said. The reason they gave for the move was obvious—gunfire.

At least seven firefighters in the immediate vicinity of 6221 Osage reported hearing gunfire at some time during the fifteen minutes between 7:00 and 7:15 P.M. Their accounts vary in exact particulars, but all agree on one important score. There was shooting going on in the alleyway. From six of the accounts, we learn that there was: "a lot of gunfire," "single shot," "several bursts of single gun shots," "popping sounds," "a lot of single shots," "automatic, quick bursts." The majority of the reports placed the gunfire within a five minute period between 7:10 and 7:15 P.M.

Having been met by police gunfire upon opening the garage door, Conrad retreated back inside 6221 and handed Tomasa to Rhonda. Insofar as Birdie could tell in the darkness of the cement room, Tomasa did not appear hurt. He could see no bleeding, he told investigators. Yet how much of anything Birdie could see in such conditions remains questionable.

Tomasa was awake, and, "he was crying." Conrad shut and bolted the the garage door and sat down with Rhonda and Tomasa.

"Then we were sitting down," Birdie recalled. The adults "was just talking, and then all that smoke and stuff was coming in. That is when the fire was getting heavy and all that stuff was coming in." The "stuff," Birdie said, was coming "from everywhere."

Rhonda had Tomasa on her lap. The child lay on his stomach. "He was crying and then I didn't hear anybody," Birdie said. Soon, Tomasa stopped crying, and then he stopped moving. "Rhonda smacked him . . . on his back." Tomasa cried one time, and then, "He stopped."

Stakeout "Granny Squad" Officers Markus Bariana and William Trudel were stationed at the second floor rear window of Post 4 at 6218 Pine Street, directly overlooking the alleyway. Both were equipped with M-16 assault rifles. With them was Sergeant Donald Griffiths of the "Granny Squad," their post commander, who was equipped with a walky-talky (a so-called "150-type" police radio), his service revolver (a .357 Magnum) and an M-16. Officers James Gillespie and John Roussel—equipped with service revolvers, tear-gas gun, and shotgun—were also on the second floor of the house, and Officers Tim Lynch and Kenneth Brown were downstairs with Firearms Instructor William "Pumpkin" Stewart, who was armed with a silenced .22-caliber rifle. At some point, Officer John McCauley was also "on post" at 6218.

The MOVE house at 6221 Osage Avenue was fully ablaze when Officer Lynch reported hearing "screaming coming from the MOVE house," and Officer Trudel heard "chopping and banging sounds" from the behind the barricades at the compound. The time was approximately 7:25 P.M.

Birdie Africa told Police Department investigators that, "the fire did not get in the cellar." There was, though, "a lot of smoke and water" in the cellar, and "it was hot, but it didn't catch on fire." The point when the "cement room" would catch on fire must have seemed near, for Birdie recalled in another interview that, "When the fire got real heavy and we smelled all that smoke and we couldn't breathe, that is when we started yelling, 'The kids coming out.' "

"Rad, Nick, Rhonda, Theresa, and Mona," Birdie recalled, were the ones doing the yelling. They were yelling "loud," the child said, and they were again shouting at both the front window of the house and the cellar window. From the garage, Birdie could hear gunfire. The adults instructed the children to join them in yelling, "The kids coming out!" Birdie said that children cried, "We want to come out!" from beneath their water-soaked blankets. All of the children were crying.

Birdie felt as though he "was getting ready to cycle." He and the other children continued to yell "loud." The words they yelled left no doubt about their desire: "We want to come out, we want to come out!" they shouted.

That was when the "big people" again opened the garage door and the cellar window.

Stakeout Officer Markus Bariana recalled that, "By this time, all the residences from the MOVE house on down were on fire, as was the house I was in [6218 Pine, Post 4]. I heard a woman screaming that she was coming out with her kids. I yelled, 'Come on out, no one was going to shoot.' The woman screamed back that she was coming out."

From his station inside 412 South Sixty-second Street, Fireman Joe Murray heard Stakeout Officers shouting, "Come out with no weapons, we're not going to shoot you!" Murray believed that the policemen were calling to a female MOVE member. Murray reported what he had just heard to Fire Lieutenant John Vaccarelli, who quickly left in search of more policemen. Within moments, according to Fireman Murray, two Stakeout officers arrived on the scene and joined the attempt to coax the woman out of 6221.

Back inside the MOVE house, there was bedlam. Birdie recalled how, "Rad opened the door back up, and then Rhonda got Theresa, no, I mean Tomasa. And then we all started shouting, trying to come out, and trying to all come out, and then Rhonda had Tomasa and then we was all coming out, running and stuff and then we started going out. And then Mona went out and she said, it is all right now, we could come out, and then we all started running, trying to come out."

Fire Lt. John Vaccarelli was back inside 418 South Sixty-second Street, directing water onto the rear of homes on Osage, when he saw a woman and a child emerge through the cellar door of 6221 Osage Avenue and run west down the alley, quickly disappearing from his sight.

A couple of minutes later, three people, whom Vaccarelli, in his account to fire marshal's investigators, said he believed to be men left the MOVE house from the rear. The "men" surveyed the area, then ran back into the house. According to Vaccarelli, the "men" carried no weapons.

Over his radio, Sergeant Connor heard someone say, "They are coming out of the back!" and then, "They're firing in the rear!"

Officer James Berghaier of the A Team recalled hearing someone shouting, "They're coming out, they're coming out, they're shooting!"

Officer William Trudel, stationed at the second floor window of Post 4, observed "approximately five people come from the rear basement of the MOVE house, from like a garage door that a hole was punched in for them to get out." It looked to him, Trudel said, "like an adult male and female and three children."

Trudel continued his account, "I believe the first one out was a male child wearing a tee shirt and, I believe, blue jeans. He was about nine to ten years old. . . . At this point, what appeared to be a female adult came out, crawled out on her hands and knees. She stood up approximately eight to ten feet from the back of the MOVE house. She was looking around. She looked up at us. We were hollering for her to just put her hands up, nobody would shoot. She turned and faced the MOVE house and waved withher hands, like for somebody else to come out."

The woman, Birdie has said, was Ramona; the first child out, the girl Tree. Then came Phil, then Birdie.

According to Trudel, "At this time, another child came out, smaller than the first one, [and] started running around in the yard. The stuff was still falling down. The female knelt down and grabbed the child and was holding the child."

Ramona, Birdie recalled, "was putting Phil and Tree up in the alley." She was "near the house . . . on the walkway." Ramona was able to get Phil and Tree onto the walkway. Then, "they [Phil and Tree] was running. She told them to run." Birdie saw them run down the alley, towards Cobbs Creek. "And then she tried to get me, and I didn't make it. Then I fell and I kept on running again. And I tried to climb up the wall part, and that is when I fell and fainted. . . . I didn't see nothing."

Officer Charles Mellor, his position now midway up the alley from Cobbs Creek Parkway, saw Birdie fall and strike his head on the cement walkway while Ramona was attempting to pull him over the fence.

Birdie, recalled Officer James Berghaier, "actually came out of the fire. . . . There was a board on fire that he had to step over or hop over. This board was not flat on the ground, it was on an angle. Then he started walking west towards us out of the driveway. He then met up with Ramona and she attempted to lift him up from the driveway up on to the walk where she was at which was about three feet and then there was a fence on top of that. This was all taking place [at] approximately 6229 Osage Avenue in the rear driveway on the north side. Ramona put her hand down and attempted to lift the child. . . .

"While Ramona was trying to help the kid Birdie up, he either fell or slipped, falling back, landing straight on his head, striking the concrete."

When asked if he ever saw Phil and Tree again, Birdie replied, "Un —uh." No.

Fireman Murray had observed a woman leaving the MOVE house, followed immediately by a child. The woman, he said, ran up the alley towards Cobbs Creek; the child—almost certainly not Birdie, who, like Ramona went westward towards Cobbs Creek—ran down the alley towards Sixty-second Street.

Officer Trudel's recollection is of, "Child number one, a nine- to ten-year-old male. He stood there for a second, [while] burning debris was falling, and it appeared like he got hit with something on the arm. He ran towards the back wall."

He got hit with something on the arm. This may account for the fate of the boy Phil, the second child out by Birdie's reckoning. Or perhaps, again, it was Tree, with her dreadlocks, mistaken for a boy. The particulars do matter—if ever they can be properly sorted out by a judge and a jury —for both children were to die on the night of May 13.

From inside his post at 408 South Sixty-second Street, Fireman John Hamilton saw a lone and disoriented MOVE child at about 7:30 P.M. moving back and forth in the alleyway, obviously not knowing where to go. Hamilton informed his supervisor, Captain Anthony Roman, and a Stakeout Officer of what he had seen. As a result, said Hamilton, the Stakeout cop yelled to the other officers stationed in the rear alley of the 400 block of South Sixty-second Street.

Then, Hamilton saw that a stream of water had been aimed at the child. Because of the density of the smoke, fire, and water, the firemen quickly became blind to the whereabouts of the child.

The child—perhaps Phil, perhaps Tree—had gone in the direction of Sixty-second Street, a route that led beneath the upstairs windows of Post 4 at 6218 Pine.

Conrad had been the first out, Birdie recalled. "He had to open the garage door. He had to take some long screws out of the garage door. Frank hollered to the cops that the kids were coming out. We ran out through the garage door. Ramona, Tree, and Phil was behind Conrad, and I was behind Phil. Phil's skin was melting."

Phil, Tree, and Ramona all "ran up to the upper alley." When Birdie last saw Phil and Tree, "They were running towards Pine Street. I don't think the cops saw them." It was about this time that Birdie "fell in some stuff that was burning, and I passed out. Ramona was calling for me to come up there with them, but I fell and passed out."

In fainting, Birdie may have unwittingly saved his own life. Passed out amid the burning debris, seemingly dead, but in fact relatively uninjured, Birdie was in a sense protected from what followed. And, almost certainly too, his path—towards Cobbs Creek and Officers Mellor and Berghaier —was the right one.

Birdie has said that he does not know what happened to Conrad. Nor does he know what happened to the other children.

According to Officer William Trudel of Post 4, "It appeared like another child came out with what appeared to be a male right behind. The male stood up beside the female who was holding the child. The child that had come out in front of him was directly in front of him. The male was stooped behind the child and firing the rifle in my direction. He fired four to five quick shots."

Officer Charles Mellor's accounts of what actually happened throughout the day frequently conflict with those of other police witnesses (particularly Lt. Frank Powell and Officer Michael Tursi). Mellor, who was cited in MOVE Commission interviews for his general veracity, recalled how, "at the same instant" that he witnessed Ramona leaving the burning house, he too had seen what appeared to be "a large black male dart towards the same pile of debris. It looked like he was trying to get up to the fence also. He ducked back down again and after he ducked back down, I didn't see him anymore, but I also didn't see him go into the house." The man Officer Mellor saw "was a MOVE member and he appeared to me to be big." He was also, Officer Mellor has testified, unarmed.

Officer Bariana described the same black male as being "in his late twenties, 160 pounds, dark-skinned, [and wearing a] dark top." The man he saw, Bariana has said, "carried a rifle in both hands across the front of his body . . . [and] fired approximately four times toward Post 4." The shots, Bariana told investigators, sounded as though had been fired from a .22-caliber rifle.

Officer Michael Tursi, in describing what was obviously the same young black man and child, recalled observing, "a tall, black, lightskinned, shirtless male carrying a rifle and pulling a black child from the same area that the female had appeared in." The adult male, Tursi continued, "was moving in the same direction, a northerly direction across the driveway. He continued to move and began firing his weapon. I could tell from the report that it was a .22-caliber rifle. He fired in a northerly direction, toward the rear of the homes in the 6200 block of Pine Street. He fired three shots in that direction."

When the shooting started, Officer Trudel recalled, "It seemed like everyone got down on the ground." *Everyone* meant Conrad, Ramona, and the three children. No policeman stationed directly in or overlooking that alleyway has so far admitted to firing his weapon or witnessing other officers fire their's. Yet, Trudel remembered how the MOVE people were now "crawling in different directions." Some of them perhaps already had been hit, the rest obviously were doing their best to avoid being shot.

"When they went on the ground," Trudel has said of the escaping MOVE people, "it looked like one of the children crawled back into the house. The female tried to grab the child. The male that fired the shots crawled over to the concrete wall that would be the rear of the house on Pine Street. I don't know the address, but I lost sight of the male at this point. The smoke was very heavy."

Officer Michael Tursi, who was standing immediately to the left of Officer Mellor on an elevated walkway contended that from his position, "As he reached the top of the debris in the driveway, [the black male adult] turned in my direction and fired another three to four rounds. The child was behind him at that time."

Both the child and the man, Tursi said, "fell back into the debris."

Officer James Gillespie, stationed on the second floor of Post 4, recalled how the adult male MOVE member, who must surely have been Conrad Africa, "appeared to go down in the right hand side of the yard. The female and [two] children went to the rear fence of the yard. She ran back into the fire, followed by one of the kids. I saw her return from the garage again and go towards the fence. I then left my post and went up a few houses and kicked in a few doors to try and get to the rear alley to get the kids." Like Officer Mellor, Officer Gillespie saw no MOVE members carry weapons into the alleyway: "I didn't see any of them armed."

General Leo Brooks was "moving back and forth up and down Pine Street and up and down Sixty-third Street. . . . I was going around supporting the police officers, you know, pepping them up and whatnot who had been there all night long, particularly the Stakeout and the Bomb Squad people who were still in the area—and a police officer said to me, 'We saw individuals and the individuals turned and went back. The first, the boy, and the woman dropped to the ground; someone fired over their heads. They went back into the smoke.'"

The General believed that, "Someone from out of the back [of] the MOVE house, in the alley," had fired the shots.

Brooks' driver and bodyguard, Police Officer Louis Mount, recalled that at 7:30 P.M., while standing on Pine Street, he heard three shots, which he thought came from a revolver. Someone then shouted, "They got one, they got one!"

A haunting account in the Philadelphia *Daily News* told of "One firefighter, Doug Jonathan . . . [who] spoke of human forms fading in and out of the smoky alley behind the flames that consumed the row houses on Osage Avenue. Jonathan, who was inside a Pine Street row home across the street from MOVE, said he was almost certain the shadowy figures were MOVE members."

Fire Lt. John Vaccarelli remembered how eight heavily armed Stakeout officers reported to 412 South Sixty-second Street, where he and other firemen were stationed. Two or three of the officers went downstairs, the rest went upstairs. Soon, Vaccarelli heard one of them shout, "Come on out. Surrender. Give it up, we're not going to hurt you." The announcement was followed by gunfire, but Vaccarelli could not determine where it came from.

Lieutenant Vaccarelli was not the only firefighter to hear gunfire between 7:25 and 7:45 p.m. At least ten other firemen, all of them stationed in the immediate vicinity, reported hearing shooting coming from the alley. The following recollections were drawn from fire marshal's interviews with ten separate witnesses. The firefighters recalled hearing: "mostly single shots," "single shots," "sporadic single shots," "gunfire, ordered out of alley," "five minutes, single shots," "four or five shots," "gunshots," "gunfire," "gun shots," "five or more gunshots."

As with earlier reports of gunfire at about 7:15, the general picture is confirmed by account after account of witnesses who, on the one hand, were not Stakeout officers and so presumably had nothing to hide and no friends to protect, and on the other hand, should have been able to differentiate between gunfire and the sounds made by crackling embers and flames.

The fact of gunfire is further substantiated by the transcription of Channel 10's tapes, which note, "7:21:30 seconds: Video indicates explosion or gunfire in background."

Lieutenant Bernard Boyd was supervising fire fighting operations in the Sixty-second and Osage area. While inside 408 South Sixty-second Street, Lieutenant Boyd heard "about six shots, single fire." Then he heard Stakeout officers "in 408 South Sixty-second and other voices I presumed to be police shout, 'Throw down your guns—come out with your hands up—we won't shoot.' Then came the six shots." Lt. Boyd quickly ordered his firemen out of the house "until police allowed re-entry."

According to Fireman John Hamilton, who was stationed in 408 South Sixty-second Street, voices were heard coming from the area of 6213 Osage Avenue by both the policemen inside the house with him as well as those in the back alley.

Fire Captain Anthony Roman could also hear moaning and wailing coming from the area of 6213 Osage. The adjacent row house at 6215 Osage Avenue was already completely inflamed. Captain Roman remembered hearing policemen shout for anyone inside to evacuate the building at 6213, but it too quickly became engulfed in flames.

Where were those moans and that wailing coming from? From inside 6213? Or from the yard of nearby 6221? Or from the alleyway itself?

And whose moans had Captain Roman heard? Might he not, from where he stood, have heard the wailing of children? Or of a dying man? Or of women and more children trapped in the burning house at 6221?

While trying to scan the alley at the rear of 6221 Osage, Officer James Berghaier suddenly saw a black woman, who, having scaled the fence of the MOVE house, was walking west, approaching his position on the walkway. The woman suddenly stopped and began heading back towards 6221 Osage. Simultaneously, Berghaier noticed a young black child at the back of the house, crawling over some burning boards. Despite the woman's attempts to pull the child onto the alleyway, the child fell down. The MOVE house was now engulfed in fire, which Berghaier said seemed to be "rolling" out.

According to Officer Mellor, who was with Berghaier, the child Birdie, "got up staggering back and forth and started walking again toward him, again very slowly."

"At this point," Officer Michael Tursi continued, "the child and black female were almost parallel to each other in the back. She in the alley above the drive, and he in the driveway. Both the child and female fell to the ground. The child fell hard, the female just sort of slithered to the ground. I became concerned that this was a trap to lure us into the open. I still did not see the male. . . . They both regained consciousness in a matter of seconds, and I ordered them to crawl in my direction. As the female neared me, she pointed back towards the child and said, 'That was my brother.' "

Ramona in custody on her way to the hospital. The *Philadelphia Daily News*.

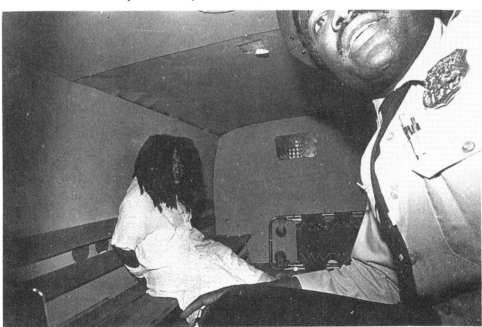

Berghaier remembered that as the woman got closer, she said, "Don't shoot, I've had enough, don't shoot, we've had enough." Officer Mellor told her to, "Keep your hands up, nobody is going to shoot you." The woman, Berghaier recalled, just said, "That's my son."

Birdie, meanwhile, had again fallen into the debris. Berghaier recalled how the boy "got up, staggering back and forth into the waste that had accumulated in the back alley. As he got further down the alley towards them, the water was getting deeper and eventually he fell headfirst into a puddle."

Berghaier could stand it no longer. "Mike," he told Tursi, "I'm getting the kid. Cover me." With that, Berghaier ran to get the boy, who was now "laying in the driveway." Berghaier "grabbed him underneath his left arm with myright hand [and] said, 'Come on, let's go.' He started to say something to me, but at first I couldn't understand what it was. As we were running and I was pulling him in the water, he did say, 'My pants is falling down.' I said, 'Fuck your pants. Let's get out of here.'"

The woman was walking slowly towards Mellor and Tursi who both kept their weapons aimed at her, according to Mellor. Mellor said that she stopped suddenly and fell to the ground, in his own words "fak[ing] a faint job." Believing this to be some kind of trick, Mellor and Tursi shouted at her to get back up and walk towards them, that no one was going to harm her. The woman got up slowly and again walked towards them. They then led her out of the alley and towards Osage Avenue, where, Ramona, safe at last, was handed over to a black member of the Stakeout Unit, Officer Walter Washington.

As for Birdie, Officer Berghaier recalled that, "I finally got him out, and then I went south through the driveway, west to Osage Avenue to Cobbs Creek Parkway. . . . The first officer I came in contact with was Inspector Bernard Small. Birdie was telling me, 'I want to eat something, I'm hungry, I'm hungry.'" Inspector Small instructed Berghaier to take the boy to a Juvenile Aid Division (JAD) Officer. Berghaier remembered Small shouting, "JAD, JAD!"

Berghaier then "started running with the child north on Cobbs Creek where I was met by a black Detective who I assumed was from JAD. Myself, along with this detective, then ran east on Pine Street to a JAD Van."

According to his own account, Officer Berghaier's last words to Birdie were: "It's all over, son. Take care."

Officer John McCauley said that he first got word of the attempted escape from the MOVE house after he had been forced, because of the

Birdie on his way to the hospital after the fire. The *Philadelphia Daily News.*

fire, to evacuate his first floor position at 6218 Pine Street (Post 4). While he was either in the driveway or alleyway between Osage and Pine, he met two firemen who told him, "They're coming out." When he asked who was coming out, the firemen replied "People coming out of the MOVE house—now." The firemen told McCauley that they "were there to fight fires, not people," and hurried off.

The scene, McCauley remembered, was by now one of utter chaos. Consequently, McCauley told investigators, he had no personal knowledge concerning the exit of the MOVE members. The Police Department, thought Officer McCauley, had done a "good job" on May 13. The "best thing about it," McCauley added gratuitously, "was that nobody got hurt."

Back in the alley, Lt. Dominick Marandola had left his position at Sixty-second Street and gone to the east end of the alley, there to take up a "blocking position." It was impossible at this point in time, Marandola has testified, for him to venture far into the alley because of the intensity of the fire. Marandola told investigators from the MOVE Commission that he knew nothing concerning the events at the other end of the alley. He remained ignorant, he later claimed, of the capture of Ramona and Birdie until sometime after 10:30 P.M., when he left the area.

Marandola did admit that he had heard an account of the attempted escape over his police radio. He also heard "popping" or "explosions," but he could not be certain whether these were caused by gunfire or by the fire itself. Marandola questioned whether anyone could differentiate between the two under the circumstances.

However, according to Officer Paul Tolbert who was with Marandola at the end of the alley behind 406 Sixty-second Street, the lieutenant flatly stated to him that four MOVE members "were lying in the back drive" of 6221.

Marandola seems to have joined the men of Post 4 sometime after 7:40 P.M., or some ten or more minutes after the gunfire ended. According to the lieutenant's own account, "I instructed Sergeant Griffiths to open up the kitchen door [of 6218 Pine]. I also instructed him to leave one man with us in the kitchen with a shotgun. We opened the kitchen door, and I instructed the sergeant to holler numerous times out the back door to instruct the MOVE members to surrender, they would not be hurt, they could escape the fire by coming in the rear kitchen door."

Sergeant Griffiths told the MOVE Commission how he had "cautiously peeked out" the kitchen door of Post 4. "I didn't see anybody out there. I yelled as loud as I could, 'Come this way, we're not going to hurt you! Come toward my voice!' At one point, Lieutenant Marandola said, 'Louder.' I heard no response. I yelled one more time and went back to the front porch."

This was what Marandola remembered when he testified before the MOVE Commission: He and Sergeant Griffiths had "stayed in the kitchen area until the kitchen caught fire. . . . Then we backed up to the front porch area, leaving the kitchen door open."

Marandola told the Commissioners that, "I have every reason to believe the MOVE members heard us."

The *Daily News,* drawing on police department resources, reported on Tuesday, May 14, that, "Three members of MOVE were shot to death in a gun battle with police Stakeout units at the rear of the cult's head-quarters." The same sources told of the bodies of three MOVE members found "lying in the rubble at the rear of the home." The gun battle was reported to have taken place at about 7:20 P.M., "at the rear of the MOVE house."

The article continued: "Three firefighters, in separate interviews with a *Daily News* reporter at 4 A.M., said they had seen several bodies in the wreckage of the MOVE house. There was another report from different police sources that the bodies of some MOVE children were in the rubble."

For the May 17 editions of the *Daily News*, a summary was pieced together, again drawing primarily upon police department sources: "Late Monday night," the article began, "three men came out of the MOVE house at 7:20 P.M. and began firing at Stakeout officers, who returned the shots, killing the MOVErs. Officers left the bodies of the man in the alley behind the MOVE house, according to the police sources."

Police sources again confirmed "that Stakeout officers had a gun battle with MOVE members."

Ramona Africa, the sources said, had "turned toward the MOVE house and started to wave her arms, walking slowly" away from 6221. Stakeout officers "in the Pine Street houses"—presumably the men of Post 4—"saw a gunman come out of the MOVE house and open fire." An anonymous police source was quoted directly: "Everyone," he said, "started shooting." Almost at once, "It became a 100 percent bona fide shootout."

According to the same account, "Three other men were behind the first gunman in the doorway of the MOVE house." Stakeout officers reported seeing "the first gunman 'blown back' into the house by a barrage of bullets and assumed that they also hit the other three MOVE men."

The fate of the "first gunman" would again account for Conrad Hampton Africa. The fate of the "three MOVE men"—or rather the two reported slain in the earlier Tuesday *Daily News* story—might well account for both Phil and Tree.

The *Daily News* report continued: "Witnesses on the scene heard a short burst of gunfire, possibly from exploding shells, at 7:10 P.M. Monday.Twenty-eight minutes later, police yelled that shooting had broken out and began clearing spectators from the 6100 block of Pine Street."

The article went on to cite videotape evidence provided by WCAU-TV, Channel 10. Anchor Larry Kane "noted at 7:23 P.M. that he just heard an explosion." At 7:31 P.M., television news reporter Harvey Clark "said that Stakeout men were scattering between Sixty-second and Osage

Avenue and Cobbs Creek Parkway. At 7:37, a Civil Affairs Unit officer "pushed Clark who was on Pine Street near Sixty-first shouting, 'Get over, they're shooting.' "

The mayor termed the *Daily News* accounts "irresponsible."

Mayor Goode held another press conference on Tuesday, May 14, at 9:30 P.M.

Fire Commissioner Richmond told reporters that all the bodies were found along the area of collapsed rear walls at 6221. But because of the destruction, Richmond said, it was difficult to ascertain whether this was the original position of the remains. "Some that I know," Richmond said of the corpses, were found "in the rear of the dwelling of 6221. Yes, that's the rear alley."

The bodybags, Richmond said, had only just been opened at the morgue. The fire commissioner detailed the known contents of the bags: "There are two males, one female adult, and parts of a fourth adult. There is one female child, and there are parts of at least one other child."

"The initial information," Police Commissioner Sambor said, "is that the MOVE members, at least one of them, fired at police in several different directions. They ran east. When they saw the police, they started firing at the east, then they turned around and started running west. When they saw the police there, they started firing at them there. We got one woman and one youngster out from those people there, and the others, under the smoke and everything that was there, disappeared from view. So where they went, how they got away, if in fact they did get away, I can't answer that at this stage."

At press conferences held on Monday and Tuesday, the mayor told reporters that MOVE members "engaged" police in gunfire in the alleyway. At a Wednesday night press conference, the mayor said that this was incorrect. Police had not, in fact, returned fire for fear of hitting their own men at each end of the alley.

At a Thursday, May 17 press conference—conspicuous for the absence of General Brooks—the mayor was asked about discrepancies in the various official accounts of what had happened in the alleyway. The mayor replied, "I said this: The three MOVE members came out of the house in the evening and shot at police. The police officers did not return the fire. Those have been my consistent statements and remain my statement at this time."

Commissioner Sambor, standing alongside the mayor, at first said that police *did* return fire. "As to whether or not we killed anybody, that information is not at present available to me."

Later in the same press conference, Sambor corrected himself. His conclusions, he said, had been based on "unconfirmed reports."

As they left the conference room, Sambor interrupted the mayor before he could answer a reporter's question:

"Dammit! Excuse me, Mr. Mayor, I've said once and for all that in the beginning I said there was gunfire returned. I did not say categorically or unequivocably that gunfire was returned, OK?"

When a reporter tried to butt in with yet another question, Sambor snapped, "Will you let me finish, dammit! Now, I said it twice. That it was unconfirmed. And now, I've confirmed it that no gunfire was returned. I hope that that is clear now. Do you want me to say it in another language?"

14

"Lack of Daylight"

Birdie Africa was first interviewed at 9:35 P.M. on the evening of May 13. His questioners were officers of the Juvenile Aid Division (JAD); the place, a room in Children's Hospital of Philadelphia. According to the official report, "Birdie was lying on his back in a bed, fully covered with sheets, with an oxygen mask over his mouth and nose." The boy, the report noted, "appeared very nervous but coherent." Treatment had already begun for second degree burns on both arms and legs. Six months later—in December 1985—there would be more doctors to see and yet more pain for the child to endure: "partial revisional [plastic] surgery," as the physician's statement put it, for Birdie's burn scar injuries.

Late in the evening of May 13, while Birdie Africa lay in a hospital bed and while Osage still burned, Mayor Wilson Goode spoke at a press conference. "This is not child's play," the mayor explained. "What we have out there is war. And I knew from the very beginning that once we made that decision to go in there, it would in fact be war. . . . I stand fully accountable for the actions that took place last night. I will not try to place any blame on any of my subordinates. I was aware of what's going on, and, therefore, I support them in terms of their decisions. And therefore, *the people of the city will have to judge the Mayor in fact for what happened.*" [Authors' italics]

But other men, following the usual dictates of history, abdicated their status for what the mayor claimed responsibility. On May 22, 1985, General Brooks submitted his resignation as managing director. He denied that his resignation had anything to do with the MOVE confrontation. The mayor attempted to bolster the claim, telling reporters that General Brooks "had told him late last month that he intended to resign."

Months later, Leo Brooks would be heard testifying before the MOVE Commission. "The fact that we didn't use the .50-caliber machine gun," he told commissioners, was a clear indication of how the planners of Operation MOVE had weighed the safety of the children inside the MOVE house.

At the same hearings, General Brooks professed ignorance of the police department's use of an M-60 and BAR machine guns in Operation MOVE. As for the Uzis and the M-16s which were used, Brooks contended that these weapons were evidence of police department prudence. In Brooks's own words, "The Uzi and the M-16 are small arms. Now, they make a rapid fire, but they're small arms." Of course, he added, "I would say that . . . if somebody has a child up at a door, that would not be safe for the child" to be fired at by an Uzi. General Brooks admitted that, yes, both the Uzi and the M-16 were "absolutely" capable of killing.

The instructions to police officers on May 13, Brooks said, "were to fire if fired upon, and they were returning fire that was fired upon them. . . . I think almost any responsible person might say—well, maybe I won't say that," Brooks stopped himself. Nevertheless, he argued, it was not "reasonable to expect a police officer . . . to be fired upon without returning fire."

He did not know, Brooks said, precisely how many rounds of ammunition were used on May 13, "but I know it was a lot." Nor did he know, he contended, that the majority of those more than ten thousand rounds were fired into the MOVE house.

On November 13, 1985, Gregore J. Sambor resigned as police commissioner of the City of Philadelphia. Characterized in a local editorial as, "the Police Commissioner who dressed as gaudily as a Third World admiral and thought about as well as your average asparagus fern . . . the guy in the flak jacket with the silly little codpiece leading troops in an assault on an entire neighborhood," Gregore Sambor found that his dismissal came swiftly and all too easily. The same editorial concluded that, "Putting him in charge of a critical city department was the decision of a leader with all the balance of Mad King Ludwig of Bavaria."

There have been times when men have recouped from great evil with great thought and certain action; the MOVE tragedy seems not to be one.

On May 14, W. Wilson Goode told reporters at another press conference, "You don't go back and cry over spilled milk. We are all very big people, and we have to understand that sometimes we win and sometimes we lose. And when we lose, we stand up and say we lost and move on."

Sambor, having moved on, later told reporters that he had been given the choice of resigning as commissioner or being fired by Mayor Goode.

The mayor responded to Sambor's charges: "The Commissioner," he said, had "retired from the department, and he indicated at that time that he retired without any coercion from anyone . . . I have indicated to you that the Commissioner retired. He indicated that he retired of his own free well, overall. . . . He was not coerced by me to retire. . . . He retired."

On the same day that Brooks tendered his resignation, Goode announced the formation of a blue-ribbon commission to investigate the events of May 13, 1985. Named by the mayor to chair the Philadelphia Special Investigation Commission—or the "MOVE Commission," as it was commonly referred to—was William H. Brown III, a prominent Philadelphia attorney and former chairman of the U.S. Equal Employment Opportunity Commission. The announcement of the creation of such a Commission was initially regarded as a ploy. The mayor's own version of the tragedy, skeptics feared, would be enshrined as the officially accepted version. But it soon became clear during the Commission's public hearings that no such intelligent and honest group of men and women could guarantee that result.

Eight days before the announcement of the Commission, Mayor Goode turned the following phrases: "I said on two occasions today that it was very sad, that it was very depressing, and that I wanted to extend my prayers to all those persons who lost those homes. . . . Now, I'm not sure I spelled the word S-O-R-R-Y, but I don't know how I could express that differently. Of course, we're sorry. Of course, we wish we could take everything back."

In the hours before Goode made his remarks, the police sifted slowly through the debris of disaster. A monotonous but harrowing account of the findings of May 14 is found in Detective William Stephenson's log:

[Four] 5 gal cans are recovered . . . in the rear of MOVE house . . . 1—Paint thinner marked Napa, 1—Green can-red label marked flammable liquid, 2 [cans] —marked weed killer. . . . One generator and a 5 gal brn. can removed from the middle of the property. . . . One (1) gal can and a 5 gal can removed. . . . [Four] 5 gal can[s] and a one (1) gal can and a water pump removed.

Two 55 gal drums, one of which is . . . ¼ full of kerosene. . . . One 55 gal drum. . . . One propane tank. . . . [yet another] propane tank. . . . One 5 gal can. . . .

MOVE proganda [sic] material recovered from rear of property and turned over to Police Intelligence Unit. . . .

The body of a female was recovered 10′ from rear door, 8′ from west wall. On her [left] foot was a black Chinese slipper and was laying on her [right] side facing the rear wall. . . . The body of a child was recovered under the female. . . . Another child was recovered same area, along with numerous other parts of the human body.

Found newspaper forged [sic] against rear bunker and held in place by wooden boards. Sandbags also found.

Human child found . . . [Left] Forearm with clinched fist recovered at door. [Medical Examiner] Patherman on scene. Attempting to recover a Human Adult.

Child found by basement rear door. . . . Human body and parts possibly located in center of basement. . . . Adult male from waist down recovered. Several small human body parts recovered rear area.

Philadelphia row houses devastated by the fire. The *Philadelphia Daily News*.

Police and firemen sort through the rubble on Osage Avenue. Wide World Photos.

Escavation [sic] discontinued until Wed[nesday] 5-15-85 because [of a] lack of day light.

Meanwhile, Birdie Africa sketched in on a police department drawing the places where gasoline cans were kept in the basement of 6221. He said that there were a lot of "big fat cans" in the cement room, as well as "them big drums"; fifty-five gallon drums of gasoline.

There were other cans on the roof. "There was three cans about this high and this round," the child said indicating the approximate size of a five gallon can, "that was red and had yellow flames painted on them. They had screw caps and a long hose inside that you could put outside." He was not sure what was inside the cans, but, "It was the color of apple juice. It was pee-colored." The cans originally, "were in the cellar and then Mo [Robbins Africa, arrested and jailed before the confrontation, so unwittingly saved from the holocaust] . . . pulled them up on the roof with a rope. That was when they were fixing the bunkers before MOVE went to jail."

There were a lot of "barrels" on the roof, Birdie said, adding, "That's what they had, kerosene, too."

At the evening press conference on May 14, Mayor Goode said, "The plan was to try and prevent the loss of life. . . . The one thing that we did not anticipate that went wrong was when the device was dropped, it caused a fire. . . . *Now, that was an accident. No one could have known that.* And I am as saddened by that as anyone else, to look at people talk with me with tears in their eyes, who lost everything. It's not easy. It's not easy for the mayor to think that children and adults may have lost their lives in the fire. It's not easy." [Authors' italics]

It is less than easy to suspend belief to the extent that fire was not anticipated, yet it remains a popular point of view. (Even if one suspends belief to the extent of trusting that there was knowledge of only one can of gasoline on that roof, a can whose path to that destination was photographed by the Associated Press, it is impossible to believe that anyone could have overlooked the reality of fire.) It is harder still to acknowledge that a plan which called for the use of an anti-tank gun, Browning Automatic Rifles, Uzis, and M-50 and M-60 machine guns—as well as "shaped charges," "little red things," "concussion grenades," "flash-bangs," and Tovex TR2—was one "to try and prevent the loss of life."

The sifting on May 15 uncovered, as Detective Stephenson noted:

Numerous bolts for logs, steel plates with apparent bullet holes removed. . . . Shotgun barrel recovered from left front of MOVE house.

. . . Metal plates, washers, 6" wood spikes. . . . Two man lumberjack saws. . . . Two addition[-al] lumberjack saws recovered, masonary [sic] tools, hammer and hand saws. . . . Shotgun magazine tube recovered. . . . .22 bolt action assembly tube found under panel left front. . . . One 10" long motor recovered from rear of 6219 Osage Ave.

Large bundle of clothing recovered east of front wall along with a large white T shirt with black letters on both sides. 'Long Live John Africa.'

One hand drill & loudspeaker was located . . . against front wall.

The body of one N[Negro]/male was lifted from the front area with his heart outside the chest area. *By CRANE.*

The use of that crane, in addition to being extraordinarily unprofessional, made certain the obscuring of any accurate translation of the surviving evidence. Bodies were dismembered, skeletal parts mixed, animal and human bones confused. The excavation of the crime scene at 6221 Osage Avenue was nothing short of scandalous.

The original sin was compounded by the Medical Examiner's Office's delay in taking tissue samples for analysis as well as its omission of the pro forma process of taking lateral X rays. It took months and the heated and public debates of forensic experts to undo the damage. It was not, for example, until outside experts had been hired by the Commission that ammunition fragments were found to be present in six of the bodies.

But Detective Stephenson's log, aided by no expert analysis, speaks clearly enough of the anticipation and arrival of the Grim Reaper at 6221 Osage Avenue. The May 15 discoveries included, "One hand . . . at rear door. . . . One Shotgun was located at rear wall lodged against bunker, weapon identified as a 500 ATT Musburger [sic] pump action.

—Strong odor of death is present at this bunker.

Sandbags removed from rear wall. . . . One child found at wall along rear bunker. . . . Five-foot-high stack of folded newspapers observed stacked against basement east wall.

One partially melted yellow container with an unidentified flammable liquid. . . . Three large sections of wood found . . . to have strong indication of being saturated with a flammable liquid. Check with sniffer.

One unidentified head recovered in rear of property 6221 Osage Avenue. . . .

The bodies of one adult female and one child recovered against rear bunker.

NOTE—The body's [sic] at this location were covered with wet blankets and sleeping bags.

Front roof bunker recovered, checked by ATF with sniffer and found to be saturated with a flammable liquid. . . . Body of one adult male recovered from front center of MOVE compound after a large beam was removed.

One large green rug saturated with a flammable liquid was recovered from middle bunker.

Had Ramona Africa poured gasoline on the roofs adjoining the MOVE house in the early morning hours of May 13? Birdie believed that, "She said she did it . . . on the microphone to the cops. . . . Uh, she told the cops that she poured, that they poured gasoline on the, in the other houses, the empty houses. So if the cops go in there, there be explosions on both sides. . . . And [Ramona] said, 'Y'all heard that skylight break?' And then said, 'That's me putting gas in this, in this house next door.' "

On Thursday, May 16, Detective Stephenson noted that, "Sifting is continuing throughout the day, two .38 caliber revolvers were recovered near east wall at middle bunker. . . . Other material saturated with flammable liquid was still being removed from 6221 Osage.

"Found also were *Teaching Aid.* 3 × 5 cards, used as outlines, directing ATTACKS against Police and Firemen who respond to fires, riots, and other disturbances. Identification and weakness."

And then, Stephenson wrote, "Sgt.[Donald] Griffith[s]: A Sgt. from Stake Out is in the rear of Osage AVE 6221, and is pointing to an area that he states, *I dropped an Adult Male from the MOVE property who fired at me when the female and child escaped.*" [Authors' italics]

Of this entry in his log, Stephenson said simply, "That's what I thought I heard." Sergeant Griffiths was standing, Stephenson claimed, "approximately fifty yards" away when he made the remark. Stephenson continued, "I was at the front of the MOVE house and the Sergeant was in the alley above the rear driveway." There was some noise, as, "the crane was operating." It was possible, said Stephenson when asked, that he could have misunderstood Griffiths.

Sergeant Griffiths vehemently denied making the remark, and claimed, "I don't know who Detective Stephenson is."

Griffiths, the commander at Post 4 on the night of May 13, *was* in the area of the MOVE house on May 16, he admitted to investigators,

". . . to check on my men who were detailed there. I went to the area of the MOVE house and was asked by Detective and Fire Department Personnel to show them where the people exited the rear of the MOVE house. I never saw them exit, but I gave them information that I received from my fire team. I told them where the MOVE members exited and also where I thought the male with the gun *had dropped* out of sight." Sergeant Griffiths added that neither he nor any other member of his team at Post 4 had fired at the MOVE members as they exited the house.

But Sergeant Griffiths and Detective Stephenson were not the only men in the area on the day in question. Battalion Chief John Skarbek of the Philadelphia Fire Department was assigned on the fifteenth and sixteenth of May to serve as a liaison to the fire marshal's detail on Osage Avenue. "I was on the step, top step of what was the MOVE house. There was a sergeant in . . . a uniform about fifteen to twenty feet away on about same level as I was, he was yelling to the crane operator, 'Dig back in that area back there,' indicating towards back driveway of MOVE house, towards Sixty-second Street side, said something to the effect, 'I shot a guy back there,' then something like he tried to jump on a porch [when] everything came down on top of him."

Skarbek described the man he overheard talking as wearing a "tailored shirt, sergeant stripes, sharp creases, very neatly dressed for that time and location. . . . White, more white with gray, middle to late forties. Trim build. Height, I could not say." The time, Skarbek said, was about 5:30 P.M., the date, either May fifteenth or sixteenth. The description fit Sgt. Donald Griffiths very neatly indeed.

Detective Stephenson recalled how he had made two copies of his transcribed notes: "I gave one copy to Sergeant James Henwood [of West Detective Division] in a sealed envelope. I kept one copy and turned the original transcribed copy over to homicide on May 28, 1985. Sergeant Henwood's copy was put in his box between May 20, 1985 and May 23, 1985. I never personally gave it to him."

As it turned out, Detective Stephenson's were notes worth guarding —and studying—with the utmost care.

The first mention of the explosive C-4 in Stephenson's log occurs in a notation made at 3:40 on the morning of May 13. This information, Stephenson got "from the briefing" held by Lt. Frank Powell, at which Commissioner Sambor was present. As to whoever actually spoke of using C-4, Stephenson remained uncertain.

The entry in Stephenson's log for 5:28 P.M. of May 13 originally read, "Had C-4, 2 ½ lbs., as being inside the satchel that was dropped." He later omitted this information, "Because I received conflicting information during the week of May 13, 1985 to May 17, 1985, and I did not have direct knowledge of what was in the device."

When he first obtained the information concerning the presence of C-4 in the "device," Stephenson "was standing at Osage and Cobbs Creek Parkway, when a uniformed Police Officer approached me and told me to cover my ears. I don't know who this Police Officer was. I asked him why, and he said, they are going to drop an explosive on the house, and it contained two and one-half pounds of C-4."

Lieutenant Powell originally said that there was no C-4 explosive assigned to him at the Bomb Disposal Unit. He later changed his mind and admitted to MOVE Commission investigators that there was a very small amount of plastic C-4 which had been at the magazine for years and was used for the sole purpose of training police dogs in bomb detection. No C-4 was issued to him while he was commanding officer of the Bomb Squad, Powell insisted. He hd no knowledge of how the C-4 came to be there.

Despite Powell's contentions, it was later discovered that in January of 1985, almost thirty-eight pounds of C-4 was delivered to the Bomb Squad by an FBI agent. Neither the Bomb Squad nor the FBI documented the delivery.

Lieutenant Powell, as commanding officer of the Bomb Disposal Unit, was responsible for maintaining all of the records pertaining to the purchase of explosives, explosives stored, and the use and reason for the use of any explosives. Powell said that according to his records, before May 13, Tovex TR-2 was stored in the magazine in two forms; in two-inch by sixteen-inch sticks and one-and-one-quarter-inch by eight-inch sticks. However, he did not know, he claimed, how much of the explosive had been stored at the magazine at that time.

A document from the Commonwealth of Pennsylvania's Department of Environmental Resources tells another story. On a License for the Storage of Explosives for the Philadelphia Police Academy at 8501 State Road, in answer to the question, "What kind of explosives do you intend to keep or store," the response reads: "Military C-4, Flex-X, Det. Cord, Black Powder, Military TNT, Dynamite, Data Sheet." The "maximum amount of explosives to be stored," was "200 Lbs." The license, dated October 15, 1984, is signed, "Lt. Frank W. Powell [Badge] #176."

Powell told investigators that he composed some standard operating procedures for the Bomb Disposal Unit when he originally became commander and that these gained the approval of then Commissioner Morton Solomon. And yet, he did not know, Powell said, what explosives were available on May 13 because he was having trouble finding the records.

But before July of 1985, Powell continued, there was no "control sheet" requiring the signatures of officers entering and leaving the magazine; therefore no records existed as to who brought in or took out what explosives before that date. One has to wonder what Powell meant by standard operating procedure.

(Powell did eventually admit to MOVE Commission investigators that there was a second, smaller magazine on the grounds of the Police Academy Firing Range. This second magazine, he said, was used by the FBI for explosives as well as evidence. Its use, Powell claimed, was prohibited to the Philadelphia Police Department.)

During initial investigative interviews with homicide detectives, Bomb Squad Officer William Klein refused to acknowledge the presence of anything "extra" in the explosive used against the roof of the MOVE house. But Captain Eugene Dooley, after watching television tapes of the explosion as well as Police Department film of tests performed on July 31, 1985, insisted to Klein again and again that there was something stronger contained in the explosive other than what Klein had so far admitted to. In early August of 1985, and very much against his will, Klein at last disclosed those "extra" ingredients to Captain Dooley.

The deaths of the five MOVE children were determined by the MOVE Commission to "have been caused by carbon monoxide poisoning, burns, effects of explosions and wounds from firearms ammunition." Deletia Orr Africa's body, a Commission's report pointed out, "contained metal fragments which the FBI laboratory and the Commission's pathology expert said were consistent with OO buckshot pellets."

In addition, "Two of the adult bodies contained metal fragments which the FBI laboratory and the Commission's pathology expert said were consistent with buckshot pellets or the cores of jacketed or semi-jacketed bullets.

"Three of the adult bodies contained other types of metal fragments thrust into them by explosions set off during the encounter."

Evidence of either buckshot or bullet fragments was found in Rhonda Ward Africa's ankle, Deletia Orr Africa's elbow, and Vincent Leaphart's chest and buttocks. Leaphart's head was severed from his body. A part of a steam valve was recovered from Frank James Africa's chest.

PART II

15

Room 253

No law school in this land could possibly prepare a judge to try a case involving MOVE, much less one involving the loss of at least eleven lives, the catastrophic destruction by fire of an entire neighborhood, and the careers of untold numbers of policemen, city officials, even the mayor of a city of the size, importance, and historical gravity of Philadelphia. Good sense, maybe, and a great deal of patience, might, just might, get an exceptional jurist through the ordeal.

No one had to remind Common Pleas Court Judge Michael R. Stiles what this case meant either to the city, the court system, or to his own career. Nor would anyone have to remind Stiles, a former first assistant district attorney, of the essential nature of the hundreds of other MOVE-related cases tried in Philadelphia courts over the past decade. Almost all of these cases, ranging from the simplest civil suits to murder trials, had eventually degenerated into shouting matches involving not only the plaintiffs, but attorneys and judges as well. Contempt citations by the score had been handed out to MOVE members. Judges had visibly aged while trying such cases, their courts had been made into lecture halls by MOVE defendants, prosecutors had shouted themselves hoarse while protesting the antics inspired by *The Teachings of John Africa*, and the judicial system itself, confronted by MOVE, seemed always on the verge of breaking down.

One glance at the organization's "Guide to Court Cases," and an intelligent jurist might know to prepare himself or herself for the worst. Designed to educate MOVE members in "proper" ways to respond to judges and prosecutors, the "Guide" states in part that:

1) When first in court, state that the constitution states you have freedom of speech and you intend to speak freely.
2) We're in the court to show you that your laws don't work not to take advantage of your law but to show that you can't use them.
3) They must back off their law or prove that it works, either way we got them because we can show inconsistency in their laws.
4) If a contempt charge is made the judge is guilty of slavery, kidnap, violation of our religion. Slavery means to take away a person's rights, freedom, against his will and slavery is against their laws.
5) If anything is out of order, then everything is out of order because if I can't speak freely neither can you and the whole thing is out of order.
6) If I got to have a lawyer, then why ain't you got a judge to advise you, because if you tell me that I can't talk to you without counsel, you're slandering me, defermation of character.
7) The instant the judge warns us for contempts, call cops and say we want arrest for a threat, and when this is not done, point out if we did it, we would be jailed.
8) When he states this is his court, tell him he don't own a goddamn thing (the indian argument).
9) If he ain't got the solution, he ain't clear, if he ain't clear, he is confused, if he is confused, who is he to judge.
10) If he say we are playing word games (symantics) tell him he is the one playing the games if he can't justify his position.
11) Around 5th or 6th trial, tell judge, ask him what he witnessed, was he there, trying people on gossip.
12) When the court asks us questions, make them admit they don't know. If so, tell them we don't want no flak from our answer.
13) To overrule is to overrule his own laws.

Patience here would probably be the key, patience and a steady stream of aspirin and the knowledge that someday it would be all over. It would be some appellate judge's problem. Then, assuming he had been very skilled and patient and clever, Michael Stiles might be able to look back and think: at least I kept it from becoming a circus.

Now Ramona Johnson Africa, sole adult MOVE survivor of the May 13 tragedy, was standing before Michael Stiles. The contrast could not have been greater, for Michael Stiles is, by all of the standards of our society, a success, while Ramona Johnson Africa is a survivor. Stiles stands about six feet tall and looks much like the NBC news correspondent Chris Wallace. He is a handsome young man, impeccably dressed, quietly well spoken, and very much the product of good schools. One feels he is an effective advertisement for the system he must represent, the "rotten ass" system which stands as MOVE's dominant enemy.

"Miss Africa" as Stiles unfailingly addresses her—virtually everyone else, from MOVE to the press corps to the usual idle and curious spectators, calls her "Ramona" or "Mona," as though all were intimates of a sort, implicated one way or another in this drama—stands something under five feet tall and is thickset, her face an oval punctuated by thick glasses and wide, broad lips often pursed in a half-open question mark. Her dreadlocks are long and bulky and extend well past her shoulders, reinforcing the impression of squareness. Her dress is habitual: blue jeans rolled up at the cuffs, T-shirt, windbreaker or sweatshirt. The shoes she wears are those of a man: heavy work boots, thick soled, tightly laced. The impression she gives is one of virility.

Ramona Johnson Africa is thirty years old, the product of a lower-middle-class black Philadelphia family of mother and daughter. Most days, her mother, Eleanor Johnson, a trim, forty-seven-year-old golden-skinned black woman who dresses neatly in well-fitting garb, will be found sitting in court next to, but silently apart from, the members of Ramona's other family. While the various MOVE elements wear dreadlocks, Mrs. Johnson, a West Philadelphia hairdresser, keeps her hair straightened and gold tipped. The MOVErs grumble loudly among themselves, mumbling obscenities. Mrs. Johnson reads constantly, carefully from a small Bible. She often closes her eyes for minutes at a time. The juxtaposition is telling: this is what Ramona came from; this is where she brought herself.

That older world ended, fittingly enough, in court. In 1979 Ramona was preparing herself for a career in the law at Temple, an urban, state-supported university that is not considered to be an institution of cultural privilege or elitism. Its student body is multiracial, and its values are those of the working middle class: industry and intelligence, up-by-your-boot-straps. Ramona Johnson was an idealistic young woman in 1979, working as a paralegal, making a little money while gaining some firsthand knowledge of the way it works outside of class.

Another story, another time, another person, another city, another City Hall, and this might be a black woman's Horatio Alger tale. But it was 1979, it was Ramona Johnson, it was Philadelphia, it was Frank Rizzo's City Hall. What she saw of the court system repelled her: the delays, the courtroom performances, the menacing presence of mostly white cops, the foreordained presence of mostly black defendants. What she saw of MOVE attracted her. It was an oppressed organization, complete with a "message." It needed strength . . . bodies. It welcomed those who were dismayed by the system, and were energetic enough to oppose it. And Ramona Johnson, easily convinced of the sordidness of the way the system works, turned to MOVE for something to believe in. The student of the law thus became the acolyte of John Africa.

Not quite a generation earlier, Michael Stiles had been across town from Temple, taking his undergraduate studies at the University of Pennsylvania. Where Temple is blue collar, Penn is blue blazer, oxford white. Penn is by definition privileged: well-heeled fraternities and sororities, crew and squash, the Wharton School, tasselled loafers and Scarsdale girls, the upper-middle class and the really rich, Main Line and Long Island, with parents who can somehow or another manage to pick up an Ivy League tab. Michael Stiles graduated from all that, then entered the Villanova Law School, from which he graduated with honors. Stiles had the very same, impeccable credentials as his former boss in the Philadelphia District Attorney's Office, Ed Rendell. Penn, Villanova Law, the Philadelphia District Attorney's office, and the Democratic Party, these were the strong links in a chain which brought Michael Stiles to this court in the very same City Hall where Ramona first became attracted to the teachings of John Africa.

Ramona knows this place well for all of the MOVE trials it has housed and for all of the offices of the privately appointed and publicly elected officials who are quartered here. Down one hall is the mayor's office, while down another is the sheriff's. Here is the press room where all the paid for or otherwise indifferent tools of a corrupt system spend their time spinning tales about MOVE.

It was here on the second floor of City Hall that for some two months the obsessed and the bored formed early morning lines, passed through metal detectors, and sat until evening.

City Hall is at once ornate and barren, sensuous and stern, elegant and decrepit. Work on the building began towards the end of the last century when Philadelphia really was Republican. A full city block square, it sits at the intersection of the two most prominent streets, Broad and Market. Broad Street accommodates the city's architectural and social monuments, the Bellevue Stratford Hotel, the Academy of Music, and the Union League, all within a couple of blocks of City Hall, all true to some old notion of what Philadelphia is. Broad Street is respectability.

Market Street thrives in its defiance of all this. It is City-backed minority retail, porn houses, gun shops. It is more than a little shabby. Ghetto boxes blast, making the distinction between the music's and the owner's hustle impossible. This is the kind of street that Mayor W. Wilson Goode was elected to govern. And it reeks of failure.

Thus in the collision of Broad and Market occurs the arrogant old building. It is Second Empire, brought to earth by routine and short-sighted changes wrought by generations of politicians and bureaucrats and their friends' firms. William Penn's statue stands atop a slender dome, warning that "we are met on the broad pathway of good faith and good will, so that no advantage is to be taken on either side, but all is to be openness, brotherhood, and love." It is difficult to determine in whose ears his message rings, though he watches over all.

Inside, the halls are cavernous and cold. The once high ceilings have been lowered to accommodate either the economy of fluorescent lighting or the compactness of bureaucrats. The days of gas lighting and tiled floors are gone, although here and there the inlaid tile of another day is revealed, unearthed by the constant footfall of boots, oxfords, and loafers on linoleum.

The offices which line the halls of this building are to be found in every City Hall and courthouse in America, but so too are the denizens of the place. Register of Wills, Licenses and Inspections, Civil Dockets, Criminal Dockets, Orphans Court: small, ill-lit or handwritten signs above mostly closed doors mark dim hallways crowded with cops, lawyers, secretaries, people with things to do. More signs, more closed doors, more signs: Judge Marutani, Judge McCabe, Judge Kubacki, and the rest, many of whom have had other, messy MOVE-inspired dramas played in their forums. Still more doors, more courtrooms, the smell of urine and perfume, polyester and linen; yesterday's and today's filth and elegance, poverty and wealth somehow one now, melded into the place itself: this is City Hall.

But above all, what distinguishes these halls is the presence of men with guns, the footsteps of the free and the chained. It is not difficult to imagine the role that this building and those at home in it have in MOVE's iconography, for here is where power defeats the powerless. This is where the system thrives.

The second floor is a maze of hallways, offices, courtrooms, bathrooms, and private passages. It is on this floor that for some two months, Ramona Johnson Africa's handcuffs are removed until evening. Some hundreds of feet directly behind her, W. Wilson Goode sits in his office. Every day, both come into and leave this building. Every day, photographers wait to take their pictures and reporters attempt to elicit responses. And every day, their faces are looked deeply into, in the hope that some understanding, some small clue might be had about the events of May 13.

There are many ways to enter City Hall, but only one for Ramona

Africa. The ubiquitous "they," the men and women with the guns, lead her handcuffed out of the prison bus through a sort of wire mesh pen and into the building proper. There she is met by a group, mostly men, mostly smoking, with pump-action shotguns at rest on a brown-clothed knee or cradled in a soft belly, pointed skyward. They take her upstairs in an elevator to a holding room or else to court.

Ramona Johnson Africa is the central figure here. It is she who withstood the bullets, the bombs, and the flames. And she, alone, is on trial. There is a lot of ennobling talk about how the city is on trial, or the cops, or the fire commissioner, or the mayor. It rings hollow, the willingness to reform being slight.

To get into room 253 as an observer, you must go through 251, past the metal detectors and the searches and the cops. But first, you must spend some time in line, queued up for the 9:30 opening of the courtroom. The line begins forming at about 7:30 when the MOVE supporters and their children arrive. Why they arrive so early is mystifying, as everyone defers to them. A handsome elderly black woman, with a quick wit and a ready picture or two of beautiful grandchildren and the story of a hard life, arrives at eight. She stands apart from the MOVE supporters. There is a thirty-five-year-old black man who sports a light mustache and the beginnings of a goatee. He has two coats, one of suede and one of some indeterminant animal origin, but equal in rattiness. His hair remains an enigma, as underneath his black velvet hat the thigh part of a pair of women's pantyhose has been sewn tightly around his head. He greets everyone everyday, everyone, that is, except the MOVE supporters, and when he is not imparting the legal advice he would give Ramona or sorting out his absolutely incoherent opinions on the matter, he informs reporters that he works for RCA in Camden at a salary of $25,000 a year and has the day off. He will have every day off for the next five weeks.

MOVE supporters are here showing their solidarity. Never much more than a dozen adults, young and older mothers, few men, different children, they wait in line patiently, talking among themselves and to those who wish to talk to them, arguing mildly with sheriff's deputies about one thing and another, and doing (the men and children, anyway) exercises, stretching, touching toes, sometimes even pushups.

For the first couple of weeks, the press also waits in the same line, first come, first served. The front row of the courtroom is similarly allotted to the press. In any case, the distinction between the working press and advocacy journalists is blurred. Besides the *Daily News* and *Inquirer* reporters, there are the infrequent television and radio types, a young woman from a Trotskyite journal in New York, a young woman and a young man who work with the *Tribune,* Philadelphia's black newspaper, a slight, light-complected black female lawyer, and an aging hack who occasionally gets a word into a couple of the neighborhood weeklies.

There is a retired high school teacher, who considers himself a "writer." He is the kind of white man who believes himself to be in sympatico with the black race. He speaks frequently of the investigative reporter Seymour Hersh. He fancies himself Hersch-like in his incessant interruptions of other people's conversations as well as of their silences. He speaks to one and all about the possibility of co-authoring with him, his selling point being something he refers to as the "MOVE dictionary," in which terms like "pepper-fogger" would find definition. No one takes his offer. He is also one of a group of people who believe that if they could only get to Ramona, the advice they have to offer her would be invaluable.

Kenneth is a black man, possessed of great physical beauty and a silent magnetic pride. He is highly intelligent, gracefully reserved, and keenly observant. He is mysterious. He has been a labor organizer in the South, a VISTA volunteer and is now a radio talk-show host who intersperses reggae music with his and his guests' interpretations of Ramona's trial. He remarks that the relationships between blacks and whites are "cooler" in the South, in Memphis and in Arkansas. They have been around each other for a long time down there and have some kind of silent pact. What he has seen in Philadelphia in the past year convinces him of the corruptness of the system. He speaks like this, in conclusions. Kenneth wears his dreadlocks up, under a hat, and fears that the cops are wondering who he is. He is afraid of going to jail. "What for?" "They don't have to have a reason. They'll find something if they want to." He speaks so softly, his voice and his words are an odd couple. And he says again softly, "But I sure wouldn't want to go to jail." He is, however, committed to "putting out" the truth as he sees it, hence his certainty in his fear.

The Widow is in her fifties, full figured, with beautiful clear dark golden skin. She traces her lineage to the Moors, and dresses in kind. She considers herself faithful to the world of Islam, outspoken in all matters, and skeptical of Ramona Johnson Africa's chance at a fair trial.

When she is not in Room 253, the Widow is at a radio station where she is the manager. Kenneth works with her. She broadcasts three times weekly, talking about, as she puts it, anything that needs talking about. Her ads say "Uplifting Fallen Humanity thru Edification, Health, and Astrology." The same ad mentions something called "The Social Strip" and has two circles at the bottom, one containing a black number "7," another with the triangle and eye of the one dollar bill. Beneath are the words, "We Will Save Our Nation." Which nation is unclear.

The Widow neither drinks nor smokes, despite urgings from a reporter that these and one other habit could make her forget about saving any nation. She breaks into a big rolling laugh—she is a creature of great joy —and throws back the noble head. She wonders if anyone would like some garlic to chew. She says it would not hurt and could certainly do some good. She laughs again, and winks, and bustles off.

And so Ramona's trial emerges as a forum for all sorts, the ones who spend lives writing long letters to the editor, the social activists, the press, the deranged, the unemployed—a family whose house now was City Hall.

Day One: Tuesday, January 14, 1986

At last, after five days spent culling twelve jurors and six alternates from a body of 165 potential candidates, the day is here. Over the objection of Assistant District Attorney Joseph J. McGill, Stiles has ruled that the courtroom will be open to all spectators, regardless of age. McGill has argued that the presence of MOVE children "is an attempt by the defense to bring extraneous matter into the courtroom to gain sympathy for her [Ramona's] position. This is characteristic of every MOVE trial." What McGill means is that the presence of all those apparently happy and healthy MOVE children is bound both to remind the jurors of the dead children of 6221 Osage Avenue and to suggest at the same time that MOVE people are family-loving peaceable folk.

So here now are the living children, the remaining free men and women of MOVE, a gaggle of rag-tag spectators, the usual and unusual members of the press, a bevy of uniformed and civilian-clad cops, the regular courtroom staff: bailiffs, stenographer, criers and the like, judge, jury, prosecution, defense. It is time to get on with things.

The charges against Ramona Africa are enumerated: single counts of criminal conspiracy and riot, ten separate counts of aggravated or simple assault—all of them arising out of the May 13 confrontation.

It is McGill's time now to present his opening arguments, proof being, after all, the prosecution's burden. The jurors have already been given some sense of what this man will be like during their own questioning and selection process, the so-called *voir dire*. Now they will get the real thing, open throttle.

For his part, McGill must somehow diffuse any sympathy the jurors may well have for Ramona, and so at once he strikes the note they will hear again and again.

Jurors, McGill declaims, you must not consider the aftermath of the morning of May 13, the bomb dropped from the helicopter that afternoon, the resulting fire that evening, the deaths. These are matters for another time, another body to consider. Miss Africa is not on trial for those actions. Miss Africa is on trial for what she did in the early morning hours of May 13 and up until mid-afternoon that day. That and that alone is what Miss Africa is being tried for today.

The organization to which Miss Africa belongs is "rigid in its resolve to a philosophy which they, in their own words, call revolution," he continues. The Miss Africa that the jurors are about to hear from—"an individual who is intelligent, articulate, and I even bet, courteous"—is the same "individual" who, as a member of MOVE, exposed the Osage neighbors to "the most hideous examples of riot, comments, shouts, [and] threats."

In his twenty-three minute argument, McGill hammers away at the violent nature of the organization, the obvious threat to the police from the bunkers on the roof of 6221, and at Ramona's participation in the whole affair. He characterizes the front bunker as "a fortress which by itself shouts resistance." Armed and ensconsed within their fortress-home, MOVE members challenged anyone who would serve warrants upon them. "What it really comes down to is a police officer with a warrant attempted to serve that warrant at a person's house. All he's doing is trying to serve an arrest warrant and somebody in there is trying to kill him." Just like that. Simplistic but effective. Slowly and emphatically, McGill draws out the impersonation he has prepared. "Don't dare to arrest me— or you are dead."

Ramona's opening remarks are surprisingly brief, lasting little more than twelve minutes. As she will at the end of this case, Ramona stands directly in front of the jurors. "My defense," she tells them, "is very simple. I am innocent."

During the few minutes which follow, she seeks to allay their discomfort, faced with a dreadlocked black woman dressed in man's clothing, reeking of garlic, a woman who is a member of what Philadelphians consider a "notorious" radical group, and as a defendant charged with conspiracy to riot and aggravated assault. "I do not wear my hair like you," she tells them. "I do not believe in the system. For this, I face more prejudice than I do being a black person or a woman." She asks the jurors to put their prejudices aside, to "make a conscious effort to sift through the evidence and see the truth."

The thrust of her argument is that "MOVE has never ever acted in a conspiracy to kill police," whereas the "police mentality" endorses "killing innocent children." The latter theme will be a constant in this trial, as will Ramona's contention that May 13 was really about MOVE's demand for justice, about, in other words, liberation for imprisoned MOVE members, "put in prison for nothing and MOVE's bitterness about that situation."

A disciple quoting the master, a child reciting his prayers, Ramona concludes invoking the words of John Africa: "The presence of truth is the power of God."

McGill calls MOVE's Osage neighbor, Milton Williams, to the stand. What as it like to live near MOVE? "Hell."

Williams testifies concerning MOVE activities in the spring and summer of 1984, a time when MOVE members went on the loudspeaker for ten and twelve hours a day, ran across neighboring rooftops, and made threats against the police, city officials, even the neighbors themselves.

MOVE threatened over the loudspeaker to "kill anyone who would get in their way." "If necessary, they would kill all of us. They had bullets with some of the neighbors' names on them. They were prepared to die." He claims that he was personally threatened. Conrad Hampton Africa vowed to "kick my door in, rape my wife, blow my motherfuck'n head off and kill my children." Like the other neighbors, Williams was the subject of "MOVE heat." Although he says he never heard Ramona make such threats over the bullhorn, he well remembers hearing her read a statement to the effect that, "if necessary, when a confrontation came, they would take the entire block with them."

When her time comes in cross-examination, Ramona returns to this. "You heard me say MOVE had the block wired and we would take the block with us?" she asks incredulously.

"You said you would take the block with you if necessary," Williams replies. The tension is hard, cold, nasty, and ominous. What is between these two is still very much alive.

The tension becomes all the greater when the next neighbor, Cassandra Carter, takes the stand. After McGill has led her through an examination to establish the horrors wrought by MOVE upon the neighborhood, Carter is faced with the old antagonist.

Would Carter repeat for the jury what Ramona had told reporters in the days prior to the May 13 confrontation? "You said your name was Ramona Africa. You were the Minister [of Information for the MOVE organization]. You knew what was getting ready to happen if the police came. John Africa had prepared you. You would not leave 6221." It is not a good question to ask; the answer is more damning than anything which McGill might have coached out of Carter, for it implies a rigid and unyielding, uncompromising faith and strongly hints at a willing martyrdom.

The neighborhood is gone, but the hatred remains.

16

"And the Knee Joints of America Will Break"

Day Two: Wednesday, January 15, 1986

McGill calls Lieutenant Donald Pritchett of the Civil Affairs Unit. On Saturday, May 11, 1985, Pritchett was stationed at Sixty-second and Osage Avenue with a surveillance team, whose purpose it was to keep an eye on 6221 Osage Avenue. At ten o'clock in the evening, Pritchett was handed a "folded message" by a MOVE sympathizer and asked to read that message. Pritchett, after reading it, turned it over to one of his superiors. McGill asks him to read the message to the jury.

" 'Take this to your people. If y'all think you're gonna come in here and suprise us, you're wrong. Thanks to the strategy of John Africa, we are prepared for anything. We know that y'all would like us to think that as long as the block ain't evacuated, we ain't got to worry about no raid so that y'all can catch us off guard. "M" ain't never off guard. We know you people will try to raid this house by coming through the walls on either side of the house and catch us off guard, by allowing the people on the block to go about their business like nothing ain't happened.

" 'We know about the plastic explosive y'all can use to knock down walls to attempt to raid us swiftly and cleanly before any of the neighbors can get hurt. This is a fucking pipedream. The raid will not be swift and it will not be clean. The strategy of John Africa prepared us for anything y'all come with. We will not be caught by surprise. To quote John Africa, the Coordinator, "Surprises only work when you succeed in surprising somebody." Long live the Coordinator.

" 'You cannot surprise MOVE when y'all come in here trying to surprise us. We gonna leave you where you stand, and the surprise is gone be on y'all. It don't matter how y'all come, through the walls, through the floor, in the basement, through the windows or anyplace else. We ain't gone be surprised. You are. Y'all can plan all y'all want to, but finally, y'all gotto come in here. To quote John Africa, "Officials making plans is like a scientist making experiments. They don't know how it's gone come. They don't know how it's gone come out. Super cops who come into an explosive situation and gain the community's trust are like the scientists in the community who have gained the community's trust until the laboratory blow up and the community catch fire." Long Live the Coordinator.

" 'In 1978, a lot of plans were made to raid MOVE swiftly and cleanly, but a lot of cops got fucked up, and the plans were a mess. We are sending this note to you because we could not send this message over the P-A system until it is repaired. However, we want to make it clear that any surprise attack on this house, like y'all intended to pull on August eighth, last year, will end in not only you planners getting fucked up, but a whole lot of these neighbors getting fucked up.

" 'We don't give a damn whether you come through the walls or come through the ceiling, long as you get the elderly and the infants out of the neighborhood. When that is done, you can come—you can come in any way you want to come, but if you try to pull some surprise while these people are still in the community, we are going to leave y'all where you stand, cause y'all to get a lot of people hurt and use that example to show how dangerous you politicians are and all you super cops with all your super plans are. Anybody who think they gone come, they gone jump on MOVE, wipe us out and leave an example of a well-organized plan is out of their goddamn mind. When you come here, it's ain't gone be swift and clean. It's gone be a mess. MOVE gone see to that. And the example that is left will be in MOVE's favor. If MOVE go down, the knee joints of America will break and the body of America will soon fall, and we mean it. MOVE ain't going down without leaving the example of power with people, and leaving you people with the example of a goddamn failure. We ain't gone fuck around. If them motherfuckers try anything next door, we gonna burn them the fuck out. If they succeed in coming through the walls, they are going to find *smoke, gas, fire,* and *bullets.* Before we let you motherfuckers make an example of us, we will burn this motherfucking house down and burn you up with us.

" 'We know about all these odorless chemicals and y'all can put through the walls for to paralyze people or put people to sleep or even kill people, but we got detectors. . . . If that detector shows signs of foreign odor in the basement or any other part of this house, if any of our canaries drop dead or if any of our seorians begins to vomit or wheeze, we are going to burn that goddamn house next door and burn them motherfuckers up in it.' " The letter is signed "Ramona Africa, Minister of Communications for the MOVE Organization."

In cross-examination, Ramona asks Pritchett how he interpreted the letter. "I would say I interpreted it as being threatening and frightening to me . . . not as an individual; as a member of a [police] department."

McGill's turn again: Yes, Pritchett interpreted the letter as indicating that MOVE would resist arrest.

McGill next calls Bennie J. Swans, Jr., the executive director of the Philadelphia Crisis Intervention Network, a "non-profit organization" which is contracted for by the City to mediate in predominantly black, community crises. Swans testifies that he had talks with Conrad Hampton Africa and Ramona Johnson Africa on the evening of the twelfth of May, and that Conrad made it clear to him that MOVE would not come out of 6221 Osage unless its imprisoned members were released. Period.

He tells Ramona what he had hoped would be the result of his being there, "Basically, a compromise that, one, that persons either in the house where arrest warrants were outstanding would come out; or two, there would be a general concession where all parties would come out and would lend itself to avoid a confrontation."

Officer George Draper is called to the stand. George Draper is a tall black man who, as an officer in the Civil Affairs Unit was assigned 6221 Osage Avenue as his beat. He was thus, to those within, a token of the system at its lowest and most obvious manifestation. He was not himself of great consequence, but he was there. The MOVE sympathizers in the audience watch him with contempt as he reads slowly, apprehensively from the transcripts of the tapes which, with two other officers he recorded from midnight until the dawn of May 13.

The tapes of MOVE's speeches on their loudspeaker late on May 12 and early on May 13 are played for the jury, then read to them. Draper, along with an Officer Jennings, made the tapes. The jury members are given headsets—and a small, bitter taste of what living next to MOVE was like.

The jury will hear only parts of the whole business. McGill has Draper read the portion of Ramona's words which the jury had heard. " 'Y'all must be out of your motherfuckin minds. This gonna be a long fight. Y'all better prepare yourself for a long motherfuckin stay. We want y'all to understand that it doesn't matter how y'all come. Come through the motherfuckin walls. Come through the door. Come through the floor. It don't matter how the fuck you come. We gonna leave you where the fuck you stand. We ain't playin no motherfuckin games. Y'all come through the motherfuckin walls. We gonna tell y'all what y'all gonna face. Y'all gonna face gas, fire, bullets, smoke. We got something for your mother-fuckin asses. We are prepared. The strategy of John Africa prepares us for any motherfuckin thing that y'all come with, however y'all come. And like I said, through the walls, through the doors, come through either, you know, on either side of us, 6219 or 6223. We got something waiting for y'all motherfuckin asses. So we want y'all to know is that y'all can plan and plan and plan, but finally, y'all got to come the fuck in. That's what we want y'all to know. You got to come the fuck in here.' "

Another tape. The voice belongs to Theresa Brooks Africa. Draper reads the words of the portion of the tape the jury has heard. "Hey, Hurst [Officer Robert Hurst, president of the Fraternal Order of Police and a Stakeout officer at the August 8, 1978 confrontation], remember the goddamn plans you made back in '78? Your motherfuckin ass take pride in being a goddamn assassin. But see, you didn't testify about how you came with them goddamn bullets into MOVE people's house . . . [inaudible] . . . motherfucker, but your goddamn buddy, that motherfuckin Ramp is dead, ain't he? And you know why he's dead? Cause, see, he came out here to do some killing. See, killing is Ramp's belief just like killing is all you motherfuckin cops' belief. Cause, see, when the motherfuckin bullets start coming at y'all, when y'all start choking on your goddamn blood and you feel your motherfuckin heart stop beating, then you gonna start crying for help. 'Oh, my God.' See, this is what it is. This is what MOVE believes. All you motherfuckin cops talking about how nasty MOVE is, how they this and how MOVE is that, and house is all fucked up. But see, when it comes down to it, when your motherfuckin life starts to leave your goddamn body, all you motherfuckers believe in MOVE law, cause all you brothers and sisters believe in life. And everybody has got to believe in life. If you motherfuckers don't believe in MOVE as MOVE did, cut your goddamn breath off . . . [inaudible] . . . But you motherfuck-ers want to breathe, don't you? But see, the ground, the air, the wind and the sun, that is our belief. That's MOVE's belief. If you don't believe in air, cut your goddamn breath off, you motherfuckers outside. All you got to do is come down here to the house, and we'll fill it the fuck up. We'll cut it off for you. Let me tell you something else. That nigger Willie Goode . . . [inaudible] . . .

"Rizzo sent all you motherfuckers out to our house in '78. He said he had protection for you motherfuckers. He had sandbags with him. He had motherfuckin . . . [inaudible] . . . on the scene. He had a goddamn tank, them cherry pickers and all of that other bullshit he brought down there to our house. But it didn't do you motherfuckers no good, because y'all walked away with casualties. MOVE walked the fuck out strong and healthy. And the same goddamn thing going to happen this time. You motherfuckers still ain't got no goddamn protection on y'all. Nigger Willie thinks that man is crazy. He's so goddamn organized, he prides hisself on being a goddamn manager, a motherfuckin organizer. But he ain't organized. This motherfucker is fighting. He ain't bought no god-damn protection up here for you crazy motherfuckers. He sent y'all up here naked. He sent y'all up here with a goddamn gun in your goddamn hands . . . [inaudible] . . .

"Where's the sandbags? Where's the goddamn shields? And what the fuck y'all gonna hide behind? Y'all gonna hide behind motherfuckin people's houses? We gonna chase you the fuck out of the motherfuckin houses. We're gonna chase you motherfuckers right in the goddamn street. We're gonna leave y'all right in the goddamn street. See, mother-fuckers, come out here to kill us. We know it. We ain't no goddamn fool. John Africa told us about you motherfuckers. John Africa told us that you motherfuckers come out here to kill MOVE people, to kill MOVE babies, to kill MOVE women, MOVE men, animals in this house, and you motherfuckers don't even give a fuck about it. Y'all don't have no feeling about it. Y'all all excited about it. You gonna tell motherfuckin Sambor, that goddamn nigger Willie, and that motherfuckin chameleon Brooks to give y'all a motherfuckin order. You're all itching to come the fuck out here, but y'all got to understand, y'all ain't got no goddamn protection. Not only do y'all ain't got no protection, but you coming out here trying to hurt innocent people, trying to hurt Godly people, righteous people who are doing the work of God, of life, and these motherfuckers try to come up against something like that.

"Y'all asking for a motherfuckin bullet, because you motherfuckers violated life, violating the principles of life. You motherfuckers going to pay, just like that goddamn George Fencl. See, Fencl always coming around MOVE headquarters smiling, doing that same bullshit he done trained little goddamn little Fencls to do. See, we know how you mother-fuckin Civil Affairs cops roll. Fencl done told y'all how to handle people, and y'all think that bullshit work. But see, Fencl smiled and he bullshitted the people, and he made small talk with people. But he ain't making small talk now. That motherfucker is suffering. He's screaming and hollering right now. He's trying to get out of that goddamn coffin. And you motherfuckers that want to be like George Fencl and you motherfuckers that don't want to be like George Fencl, y'all gone to be doing the same goddamn screaming and hollering to get out of that goddamn coffin . . . [inaudible] . . .

"Wilson Goode ain't got nothing to give you motherfuckers. But see, John Africa done put the protection on this family just like protection was on us back in 1978. That's why MOVE people are alive today, cause we got protection on us. Ain't a goddamn thing to do with your motherfuckin cops. You motherfuckers try to clear that bullshit after y'all couldn't kill MOVE. Y'all started talking about, well, y'all remember . . . [inaudible] . . . .

"Y'all . . . a lot of disgrace. Y'all Wilson Goode's . . . finest [inaudible] . . . Fuckin part time. That's a motherfuckin lie. Y'all do anything. Y'all motherfuckers. They try to kill MOVE. But you couldn't kill MOVE because Long Live John Africa. John Africa got protection on this family, cause we are right. We are doing what's right. But you motherfuckers is wrong. Y'all poison. Y'all goddamn jealous, all of you motherfuckers, and I'm not just talking about the white cops. I'm talking about the niggers, too. I'm talking about all those black motherfuckers that want to sit around here with MOVE, and make small talk with those niggers around the community and make you try to think everything's gonna all right. We gonna take care of you people. . . .

"But you motherfuckers is told some goddamn lies. See, Willie Goode and all those cops, y'all done told those niggers some more goddamn lies. But, you see, it ain't gonna be as easy as y'all thought it was. Y'all ain't gonna seize this motherfuckin house. Because y'all evacuate the goddamn neighborhood don't mean y'all gonna rush right the fuck in here and take us out of here. You motherfuckers come in this house with them goddamn guns shooting that shit in this motherfuckin house, y'all gonna get something, and we ain't talking about no goddamn talking on no microphone, neither, motherfucker. When y'all get ready to attack this motherfuckin house, y'all might as well kiss Philadelphia goodbye, cause this motherfucker is going to go the fuck up in smoke. This goddamn city is going to go the fuck up. Nigger Willie, with all your goddamn ambition, all your goddamn plans for this goddamn city, y'all order, you'll might as well forget about that shit, that goddamn Convention Center and all the rest of that bullshit you got planned. All that motherfuckin energy you burned up for the Eagles, ain't nobody gonna come to this motherfuckin city. Y'all ain't gonna get no goddamn business in this city. John Africa gonna kill this motherfucker. John Africa gonna put this goddamn city in the ground and its goddamn administrator, including you, Nigger Willie, cause you deserve to be there. See, Nigger Willie, why don't you tell the people what you told MOVE people a few years ago when we talked to y'all when we talked to you about the innocent people in jail, when you were Managing Director? You sat there with your lying black ugly broad nose motherfuckin self talking that bullshit. 'I know what happened to y'all during '78 was not right. It was not handled properly. I know that you are innocent but it's nothing I can do. I'm only the managin director. My hands are tied. I'm not the mayor.'

"So, motherfucker, you done been the mayor for a goddamn year now, and what the fuck are you doing about getting innocent people out of jail? You know the answer, motherfucker. You have the goddamn time it takes y'all to sit around talking that bullshit to the news media about we don't understand why MOVE is taking a stand. You know motherfuckin well we was right all the goddamn time. We done come to the court. We been to the goddamn politicians. We done been through every motherfuckin legal channel. It is to show that our people are innocent, just like that bullshit [inaudible] . . .

". . . you had. We didn't take them challenge cause we expected you motherfuckers to do what was right. You took them motherfuckin channels to explose you motherfuckers, to show people just what we're saying how ridiculous that bullshit legal system is to get our people out of jail. We knew it wasn't gonna work, but we did it to expose you, motherfuckers. So now, we can show people, see, we took them steps y'all talking about for MOVE to take. We took the goddamn shit right before this confrontation kicked on off, but you motherfuckers ain't have no intentions of bringing people home. Y'all got to be forced to do that shit. You got to do it because you know it's right.

"Y'all not gonna do it. Y'all not gonna do it cause you know it's right, You motherfuckers got to be forced. Y'all got to get MOVE heat under your motherfuckin ass, and that's just what y'all gonna get, nigger Willie. We understand your ass grow tired. You look like you got a lot of motherfuckin pressure on you. Well, motherfucker, when you come in this house, your motherfuckin pressure gonna activate. You ain't gonna be able to take it. Next thing you know, your motherfuckin ass is gonna be in the goddamn byberry somewhere and see."

Another voice, that of Frank James Africa, is heard now: "We got something in this house for all you motherfuckin freaks. That's right. We got something in this house for all you motherfuckin freaks. So bring your motherfuckin macho asses the fuck on down here right now and get the fuck y'all got coming. All you sick motherfucker, slimey-ass motherfuckin freaks, motherfuckin around with them goddamn guns on your hip trying to intimidate some motherfuckin body. Flying over our house all hours of the goddamn night and day with the motherfuckin helicopter, like that's supposed to do something. Y'all motherfuckers is sick. I'm just gonna ignore you motherfuckers. All you got is a bunch of motherfuckin bully tactics, intimidation tactics, and a bunch of motherfuckin plans. But see, we got something for your motherfuckin plans. We got something for your goddamn tactics, too. And that so-called strategy y'all think y'all prepared. We gonna give you motherfuckers what the fuck you asking for. See, we gonna end you motherfuckers. That's right. We gonna end you motherfuckers. We gonna finalize you motherfuckers. See this is MOVE you're dealing with. This ain't no motherfuckin . . . [inaudible] . . . We gonna make this real clear to you to y'all. This is MOVE that you're dealing with. So when you motherfuckers come, you can expect to be dealt with in a way y'all ain't never been dealt with before, cause we ain't coming in this goddamn system.

"See, we coming from MOVE law, and you freaks don't know nothing about MOVE law. But goddamn it, by the time the confrontation is over, everybody, every one of you motherfuckers is gonna be impressed with the power of MOVE law. That's right. Every one of you motherfuckers is gonna be impressed and we gonna make our impression in your motherfuckin chest. We gonna stamp our impression in your goddamn head. We gonna put our impression in your motherfuckin stomach until the goddamn blood that you got in your motherfuckin guts run like a goddamn faucet. And all you hero motherfuckers, we got something for you motherfuckers, too. That's right. Get up on the front line where we want you. We want you motherfuckers on the front line. You motherfuckers come out on the front line with your motherfuckin slapjacks. Bring your motherfuckin Uzi automatic guns, machine guns. Come on you motherfuckers, SWAT magicians. And we gonna swat you motherfuckers down. That's what the fuck we gonna do. We gonna treat you motherfuckers like SWAT. We gonna swat you motherfuckers down where you stand. We gonna drop you motherfuckers and let you swim in your own motherfuckin blood. We got something for all you motherfuckers. Bring—and we glad you motherfuckers evacuated the neighborhood, because we got something we want to bring out to all you motherfuckers. We been wanting to get you motherfuckers. We been chafing at the bit to get you motherfuckers, and we couldn't wait. Now, goddamn it, you all walking around trying to get started and hemming and hawing trying to wait.

"Bring your motherfuckin asses out of here. Bring it all, motherfuckers. Don't wait. And them motherfuckers [inaudible] . . . down the alley. Don't stand down the opposite end of the alley. Don't stand up the alley. Don't stand around on Pine Street. Come on the motherfuckin bricks. Face your motherfuckin defeat, motherfucker. All you motherfuckin freaks over them houses, across the way, over the alley, peeking through the venetian blind and sheets up at the window, well we got something for you motherfuckers, too. You ain't got to hide behind no goddamn venetian blinds.

"You ain't a peep behind no motherfuckin shit. Break your fat ass out so we can see you motherfuckers. Bring your bad-ass out, and back that motherfuckin chump shit y'all trying to portray. Back up that motherfuckin y'all attitude that y'all been fronting with. Bring your motherfuckin asses from behind those blinds. See, we ain't hiding from you motherfuckers. We ain't got to hide from you motherfuckers. Y'all know where the fuck we at, but you freak motherfuckers, you motherfuckin coward pussies. All you motherfuckers do is hide, hide behind motherfuckin badge, hide behind some motherfuckin authority. But see, we ain't gonna respect no goddamn authority. That badge don't mean shit to us. All that badge is telling us us a motherfuckin target. All that authority is to us is a motherfuckin bull's-eye.

"All that motherfuckin shit that you y'all do, that fuckin intimidation that y'all trying to use on other people. All that shit to us is more aggression. It just makes us more aggressive. All you motherfuckers is doing is feeding our motherfuckin fire. So bring your motherfuckin asses on. You ain't got to be pussyfooting around. You ain't got to walk around like ain't nothing happening. You ain't got to peep through binoculars. You ain't got to turn on your motherfuckin radio. You ain't got to talk to your motherfuckin partner and chew your motherfuckin bubblegum. You ain't got to jive back from the motherfuckin shit that you faced with. Bring your bad ass the fuck out here, cause we got something for all you motherfuckers.

"We got something for every one of you motherfuckers, all you chump motherfuckers. All you motherfuckers gonna be the first to get it. We're gonna make y'all motherfuckers' blood run like a goddamn river. That's what the fuck we gonna do for you motherfuckers. We gonna drop you motherfuckers as soon as we see you motherfuckers. We gonna drop your motherfuckin asses. That's right. You think your motherfuckin slapjacks is something, don't you. Well, we got something for that, too. You think them motherfuckin tanks is something, don't you? Well, we got plenty for that too. You think your motherfuckin helicopter is something, don't you? Well we got something for that too. You motherfuckers ain't got nothing for MOVE. That's right. You ain't got a motherfuckin thing for MOVE. You can bring all the motherfuckin shit you want. You can call the National Guard in. You can call the goddamn Marines in. You can call the motherfuckin Air Force in. I don't give a fuck who you call. MOVE has something for you motherfuckers you ain't never been hit with before. And goddamn it, when we hit you, you gonna get—you ain't gonna get the fuck up again. When we hit you motherfuckers, you gonna drop. You ain't gonna move, motherfucker. You ain't gonna never get up again. This is your last motherfuckin time that you gonna see night. You ain't never—you ain't gonna make it in the morning. We got something for you motherfuckers, all you motherfuckin tough guys, all you badge-wearing motherfuckin blacks, you motherfuckin faggots, all you motherfuckin cowards. You ain't got shit for MOVE. Y'all ain't got a motherfuckin thing for MOVE, but your goddamn system and you know your system is weak. Since your system is weak, you can expect it to die because your protection is weak. See, all y'all got for protection is your system, and this motherfuckin system is full of holes, and we gonna plug every motherfuckin hole in this goddamn system and put a plug in your motherfuckin ass for relying on this weak-ass system . . . [inaudible] . . .

"See, we got something for you motherfuckers. Y'all motherfuckers think you're gonna hide behind this goddamn system. Y'all motherfuckers want to hide behind that goddamn badge, hide behind that goddamn tin y'all call authority. But see, that shit is weak. All that motherfuckin shit is full of holes, and we're gonna give you motherfuckers something that you ain't never seen in your history before. That's right. We're gonna give you motherfuckers something that you ain't never seen in your motherfuckin history. See, since you want to come out here and fight these politicians' war, and we're gonna spill your motherfuckin blood since you motherfuckers want to come out here and try to back up what these goddamn politicians trying to do to MOVE. Then we gonna hold you motherfuckers to blame. We gonna cut through you motherfuckers to get to those goddamn politicians. We ain't gonna let nothing stand in our motherfuckin way. Since y'all motherfuckers is dumb enough, since you stupid enough, since you motherfuckers want to be flunkies behind these goddamn politicians, well, we gonna deal with you motherfuckers. We gonna give you motherfuckers what the fuck you are asking for. We're gonna give our every bit of our energy to you motherfuckers. We're gonna copter down on you motherfuckers . . . [inaudible] . . .

"These goddamn politicians. That's right. We got plenty of them for this goddamn system. We got seventeen years', going on eighteen years' worth of them for this motherfuckin system, and we're gonna concentrate on you motherfuckers. Every one of you motherfuckers gonna pay. So bring your bad motherfuckin asses out here. This ain't gonna be no motherfuckin Grenada. Ain't no more goddamn Grenada. See, that shit was in the past. This ain't gonna be . . . [inaudible] . . . so-called war plans.

"Ain't gonna be no more shit like that. This ain't gonna be no goddamn repeat of your history. We're gonna give you motherfuckers a taste of something different. You gonna get the best. This ain't gonna be no goddamn Grenada."

Ramona Johnson Africa is the next to be on the tapes: "We ain't gonna be no Grenada. The first thing we want y'all to understand that right now, if y'all come, if y'all come at MOVE, y'all gonna have to come fighting, shooting, and we gonna whip y'all motherfuckin ass. So we want you all to understand, because this ain't gonna be another Grenada. This ain't gonna be no motherfuckin Grenada. See, we know how to fight. We got the strategy of John Africa. See, in 1978, y'all thought y'all saw something. In 1985, we're gonna make Wilson Goode look ten times worse than Frank Rizzo. That black motherfucker, you know, gonna talk about the holocaust for months. Now we heard all over the TV about the Holocaust, and what we think is that black motherfuckin mayor down there is getting ready to initiate another holocaust with black folks. He gonna get a whole bunch of black folks killed. What we're saying is last night cops tried to sneak the fuck in here, tried to come through 6219 Osage and we ran them the fuck out of here.

"What we're saying is when y'all try to come in here again, y'all ain't gonna survive cause y'all can't survive MOVE. MOVE ain't never off guard. We ain't never gone—You ain't—y'all ain't never gonna catch us off guard. We're prepared for anything that you come with. Y'all better understand that. We are prepared for anything. The strategy of John Africa prepares us for anything you can come with. We know about the plastic explosives that you put in the walls. We know all about that fuckin shit. We know why y'all kept the new media away, cause y'all don't want people to see your treacherous fuckin plan, cause we gonna explose y'all. We gonna expose Wilson Goode. We gonna expose that nasty filthy ass fuckin Wilson Goode. We gonna—like I said—y'all hear that skylight, skylight breaking? Y'all hear that glass break? We are—we are letting y'all know that we put gas in each one of the houses on both sides of us, and if you come in here, we gonna—if you come in on either side of us, 6219 or 6223, we gonna burn you the fuck up. We know all about y'all plans. We know all about those plastic explosives y'all put in the walls. We know all about y'all treacherous sneaky ass fucking plans. We know all about them gasses you try to pump in on people, try to put them to sleep, paralyze them, kill them. But we're saying we are prepared. We are prepared for anything that y'all come with. The strategy of John Africa has prepared us for anything that y'all come with.

"The strategy of John Africa has prepared us for anything that y'all come with. Like I said, y'all cops better prepare yourselves for a long fuckin fight, a long goddamn fight, cause it's gonna be a long goddamn fight. Right now our brother Gerry Africa is the only communication you got with MOVE. If anything happen to Gerry Africa, we ain't talking to no motherfuckin body. If you got something to say, you want to say to MOVE, and y'all got something to say, say it to Gerry Africa. We want our brother Gerry Africa to be accompanied by Irv Homer, Barbara Grant of WDAS [radio] and Harvey Clark of Channel 10. When you got something to say, MOVE ain't asking for no communication, but you know goddamn well the strategy of John Africa put y'all in a predicament where y'all gonna have to communicate with us. What we saying is John Africa got so much MOVE people that y'all gonna want to communicate with us. And when you do what to communicate with us, you gonna have to do it through our brother, Gerry Africa."

Shortly after this, Sambor will read the arrest warrants he has for four of the residents of 6221 (Frank, Theresa, Conrad, and Ramona). But Sambor's tape-recorded voice will not be heard in the courtroom, nor will the noises which began some thirty minutes later, of tear-gas cannisters exploding, bullets fired, and water cannons blasting onto the roof of 6221 Osage.

McGill asked Draper if he can identify the last voice heard on the tape. Yes, Draper says, he knows all the MOVE people well, and that voice belongs to the defendant, Ramona Johnson Africa. McGill will later tell reporters that he played the tapes in order to establish the fact that Ramona Johnson Africa had participated in a conspiracy to riot, and had endangered the lives of all those outside the house in the morning hours of May 13. He is satisfied that he has done this.

David S. Shrager enters the courtroom and retreats with Ramona, Stevenson, McGill, and Stiles into the judge's chambers. Shrager is the attorney for Adino and Michael Moses Ward, still known as "Birdie Africa," and we remember that which we are most at a loss to deal with, the children. All of us shudder as we realize that this room too will probably have to be part of Michael's landscape. We wonder, some of us, if we will be some part of his hell.

Day Three: Thursday, January 16, 1986

Draper is back on the stand today, facing cross-examination from Ramona. Her manner towards him is antagonistic and more than slightly incredulous. She reads to him from his testimony of yesterday. Did he not quote her as saying on the bullhorn on May 13 that the city had gotten itself into a "predicament where y'all are gone to want to stop this confrontation?" Yes. Did he believe that negotiations between MOVE and the city were still possible at that point?

"It was a possibility."

"What did you do with that, if anything?"

"I didn't do anything about it."

Did Draper turn the information over to one of his superiors? Yes.

Was any effort made to negotiate with Gerald Ford Africa? Was any effort made to contact Irv Homer, Barbara Grant, or Harvey Clark?

"To my knowledge, I know of no personal contact."

And how did Draper know that that was Ramona's voice on the tape? How many times had he spoken with her? How many times had he heard her on the bullhorn before? How many times on May 13?

Draper replies drowsily. He had talked to Ramona only once before, and all she had said was, "Long Live John Africa." He heard her maybe three times on the bullhorn, twice on May 13. He was sure though, he tells McGill, that the female voice he heard that day was hers, "She has a voice you remember."

Draper is followed on the stand by Lieutenant Dominick Marandola, the second in command of the Stakeout Unit, Philadelphia's SWAT team. It is he who directed the gunfire at 6221 Osage on May 13 from across the street at Post One in 6218 Osage.

Marandola, a swarthy man with a neat black mustache, testifies that the police faced a life-threatening situation, but that they did not fire back indiscriminately. Gunfire was "controlled" on direct orders from a supervisor, who, in turn, had direct orders from Marandola at Post One. Fire was only to be returned if fired upon or in order to protect fellow policemen or firemen from being fired upon. Only in the first case might a policeman fire on his own, without direct orders.

Under cross-examination, Marandola is asked if he knows of a single case where an officer had fired on his own in the belief that his life was in imminent danger. No, Marandola answers, he knows of no such case.

Ramona seizes on the answer: "Since you've testified that the procedure was that if a police officer was in a life or death situation, that he could fire his weapon without consulting you, and since you've also testified that, to your knowledge, no police officer fired his weapon without consulting Post One, however you want to phrase it, that no officers found the need to fire their weapons in a life and death situation?"

McGill objects, and Stiles sustains the objection. But Ramona has more than made her point.

Day Four: Friday, 17 January, 1986

Officer Harry Young is a twelve-year veteran of the Stakeout Unit. On the morning of May 13, he was with Lieutenant Marandola in Post One. He testifies that he was stationed at the front porch screen door to 6218 Osage, where he both heard and observed two shots coming from the lower right hand corner of the front bunker at 6221. Soon afterwards, he saw more shooting, coming now from the top of the bunker. This, he says, would have been fifteen to eighteen minutes or so after Commissioner Sambor had finished reading the warrants at 5:35 A.M. As Marandola has already testified, it was Young who first noted the gunfire from 6221 Osage Avenue. Now, as Young testifies, it was Marandola who ordered Post One to open fire. All the while, fresh reports were coming in over the radio: Post Two (6232 Osage Avenue) was under fire, Post Five (418 South Sixty-second Street) was under fire. We were being shot at. We opened Fire.

Over the next hour and a half, there were six or seven more exchanges of sustained gunfire between the police and the people in 6221. The bags in front of Officer Young were ripped by bullets and leaked sand. Young looked over to his side and counted twenty or more bullet holes in the storm door. He is not asked to testify about the weaponry that MOVE used that day, but is asked about his own: a .37-mm gas gun (fired), a 12-gauge shotgun (fired), his service revolver, and an M-16 assault rifle with scope (three clips fired). No one asks him whether the M-16 was equipped with a silencer, as some were.

Young also testifies that he was assigned to Powelton Village on August 8, 1978. "I observed Officer Thomas Hesson and Officer James Ramp shot." McGill starts going over the weapons recovered from the MOVE headquarters in 1978. Ramona erupts. "I want to know what this has to do with the trial. For the last five minutes, this man has been questioning this witness about 1978. Am I on trial for May thirteenth, 1985 or August eighth, 1978?" The years, the confrontations are jumbled and now linked by Ramona herself. The answer to her question is: everything.

Under cross-examination, Young delivers his remarks with certainty: "I felt anyone who was in that house, any adult who was in the house was capable of firing a weapon, assaulted me."

Ramona asks, "Do you feel like every cop out that was in Powelton Village [on August 8, 1978] was responsible for beating my brother [Delbert Africa] since any cop out there could have done it? . . . . Do you feel like any cop on the police force is responsible for kicking a baby out of Alberta Africa's stomach because they are able to do it?"

Following a brief mid-morning recess, three more police officers are called to the stand. Officer Herman Mitchell is a youthful, middle-aged black man, sturdily built. Even in plain clothes, he gives an impression of strength, as though he may well have been a football player. Mitchell has spent the last fifteen years on Stakeout, and he, like Harry Young, was at Powelton Village in August 1978.

Mitchell was assigned to Post One, at 6218 Osage, on May 13, at the extreme right (east) window of the second floor. There, he testifies, he saw muzzle flashes from the second portal of the east-side front of the bunker at 6221. One bullet hit a sandbag about a foot away from him, and he returned fire on orders from Lieutenant Marandola. He subsequently testifies to witnessing five different exchanges of gunfire from approximately 5:35 A.M. until nearly 11 A.M.

Officer Joseph Szczech, of the Police Department's Audio Visual Squad, is the last witness this morning. He was assigned as official police photographer on May 13. Most of his day was spent in a first floor vantage point in 6218 Osage Avenue (Post One), often flat on his stomach dodging bullets. Four of Officer Szczech's photographs are offered into evidence. All were taken on May 13 at about the same time, 1:30 P.M. The photographs show the front porch of 6221 Osage Avenue, the first floor of 6232 Osage Avenue (Post Two), a blow-up of the previous shot which reveals a tear in a curtain, and finally, the lower front half of the door to 6232, scarred by a bullet hole. Ramona, quiet until now, is on her feet. "My position," she announces, "is that I object to this whole procedure." She is allowed to complete her objection, and is then overruled. Soon thereafter, Szczech is off the stand. It is noon.

As the courtroom clears of people, it assumes its former elegance. Its considerable gilt and cavernous Second Empire style is penetrated by brown marble pillars, which touch both an elaborate carved white ceiling and indoor-outdoor carpeting of indeterminate hue. The walls are covered on all sides with oil paintings of mostly unsmiling, aggrandized, white male judges.

Ramona is still sitting at the defense table. The microphones are off, and she is turned round, chin on wrist, facing the half-dozen or so men and women in dreadlocks who have gathered at the Rail of Justice to speak with her. There is an odd quality here of a family picnic as these people, joined by appearance and some notion of the world giggle and exchange the usual anecdotes of life. A MOVE supporter is explaining the M-16 rifle to a young MOVE boy, "Well, it's like what Rambo carries."

17

Return Fire

Friday Afternoon, January 17, 1985

Sergeant Edward Connor is this afternoon's only witness. A member of the Philadelphia Police Department since 1964, Connor is a solid, balding man whose speech is branded with the clip of Upper Darby, a white, ethnic, working-class enclave of Northwest Philadelphia. Connor, as former head of the Bomb Squad, was selected by Commissioner Sambor to lead Insertion Team B on the morning of May 13. The plan, Connor relates, was straightforward. While Team A, under Lt. Frank Powell's supervision, approached from the west end of Osage Avenue and entered 6223, Team B was to enter 6219 through 6217. Both teams would then use explosive charges to blow small holes through the walls of 6221, holes just large enough to accommodate "pepper foggers," devices which fan tear gas. There would be no entry into 6221, and so there would be relatively little danger of being shot at.

(Six hundred officers from the Philadelphia Police department, Uzis, BARs, and an anti-tank gun converge in the early hours of May 13, 1985 on Osage Avenue because there is "little danger of being shot at.")

Connor testifies as to what it was like to be a cop on an insertion team in one of those neighboring houses that day:

It was approximately 5:30 in the morning. Connor and the other members of Team B—Officers James Muldowney and Daniel Angelucci of the Bomb Squad, and Officers Salvatore Marsalo, Marshall Freer, Michael Ryan, and Alexander Draft of Stakeout—were positioned in the driveway next to 6213 Osage Avenue. From where they were, they could

hear Sambor on the bullhorn. Fifteen minutes passed, and the only response from the MOVE house was more "rhetoric." Dominick Marandola at Post One ordered the operation to commence. Connor was listening to his walky-talky as a barrage of tear-gas cannisters began to explode.
Soon the streets were filled with smoke, and water, too, now that the fire
department's "squrt" guns had opened up.

Running through smoke and water, Connor and his men quickly
reached their destination. As Connor opened the door to 6217, gunfire
was heard coming from the MOVE house. The time was approximately
5:53. Inside 6217, Connor and his men stopped to take family pictures
and knick-knacks from the west wall, next to 6219. This was the home
of a fellow officer, Detective Ben Walker. Connor had promised that
Team B would look after the Walkers' things.

Connor had intended to use sledgehammers and crowbars, first to
remove the plywood, then to "slam through the sheetrock." Instead—and
despite his promises to the Walkers—he placed a small explosive, a 50-
grain "hatch-charge" on the west porch wall. The resulting blast generated a hole 3½ by 4½ feet wide. Through the hole, Connor could see
another large hole, opened between 6219 and 6221, and through this he
saw tree trunks piled inside the MOVE house. In a flash, Connor also saw
muzzleflashes high and low, coming from gun ports cut in the wall.

"Get back! Get back!" Connor screamed as he threw a "flashbang,"
a small explosive much like a hand grenade, through the opening and
towards the tree trunks. Backing away, he was shot, spun around, and
thrown to the floor, face forward. He had been struck squarely in the
middle of the back, at the juncture of his shoulder blades. "I'm hit! I'm
hit!" he cried as he lay on the floor and watched a string of bullets slapping
the carpet at his right.

Suddenly, slowly, Connor could feel himself being dragged backward.
It was Officer Jesse Freer, pulling him to safety. The time was about 6:05
A.M.

Connor did not feel the expected wetness of his own blood, and since
he had no trouble moving, he conjectured that his armored vest had saved
his life. He was right. A spent .38-caliber bullet would later be recovered,
embedded deep in his flak jacket.

Someone from Post One was on the walky-talky. What was all the
firing about? There was supposed to be a cease-fire. Connor explained the
situation and asked for cover fire. Posts One and Two opened fire. After
a time, another cease-fire was called so that it might be seen if the people
in 6221 had decided to stop firing. They had not.

Connor now instructed Muldowney and Angelucci to make a "device" powerful enough to rip off the neighboring wall. On the walky-talky with Post One, Connor asked for a cease-fire while Muldowney, his back to the floor, inched towards the existing hole in the wall. From this position, he slung the "device."

The wall crumbled with the explosive's impact, revealing the existence of a "log cabin" made of tree trunks and railroad ties and mortar a foot to a foot and a half behind what had for some time been walls. There were gun ports top and bottom, aligned with holes which had been cut into the walls. There was more firing coming from both the log cabin and from the front bunker or else the second floor.

Another "device" was made up, another cease-fire ordered, as Officer Muldowney, again on his back, inched forward again and pitched this third bomb straight at the log cabin. The resulting explosion cleared an opening across the porch and into 6221 Osage.

Connor could now see in the upper crawl space of the partly destroyed log cabin a loosely suspended beam and beneath that a body, arms hanging limp, a white glove, and a severed head.

Gunfire again erupted, presumably from the basement at 6221. Faced with crossfire from above and below, Connor ordered Team B to pull back into 6217.

One thing was certain. The morning's work had led to an impasse.

McGill asks Connor to identify the clothes he wore on May 13: a black baseball cap, dark blue overalls with "POLICE" stencilled in white on the back, and an armored vest or flak jacket. McGill shows the jury the vest and overalls, a small neat bullet hole quite evident in both. There is also a photograph taken that afternoon showing Connor's back with its black, spreading bruise, the solid center of which is the size of a fist. Juxtaposed alongside this photograph is one of the log cabin, taken early that afternoon. The gun portals are clearly visible.

A wound, gun portals, the assailant. There is not much doubt about the first or even the second, but is Ramona the third? Does a voice on a loudspeaker shouting obscenities and inviting the police to a holocaust equal guilt in a conspiracy to riot, or, in turn imply guilt in an aggravated assault, when the actual assailant remains unknown?

For a man who was shot and, save for a piece of clothing, almost killed, Sergeant Connor elicits little reaction from either the jury or the spectators. Why this is, is not easy to say. There is a certain monotony about his testimony. Bombs keep getting made and thrown at walls that crumble more than they should. What were supposed to be little holes are somehow big holes that a man can walk through easily enough. Maybe Connor has been around bombs too long—there is, after all, the ease with which a good strong bomb solves difficult matters—or maybe we are too comfortable, too removed from the reality of being there on May 13 ever to be able to judge. Then again, maybe we just cannot think as Edward Connor does, think, that is, in terms of killing someone before he kills you. Under the right circumstances, one might very well not be feeling much pity towards the living—or the dead.

The survivor is questioning Sergeant Connor. Could he please explain how, if the initial charge was of such low yield, it blew holes not only through 6219 but also right through to 6221? The answer, he says, is simple. MOVE must have already opened a passageway into 6219. This, he says, is self-evident, for the distance across the porch from 6219 to 6221 Osage is 17½ feet. To have made two holes across that distance at one time would have required a really powerful charge. Ramona nods her head.

What was Connor armed with on May 13? An Uzi submachine gun and his side arm. What weapons were fired by members of Team B on May 13? Five 9-mm Uzis, one 12-gauge shotgun, and a Smith and Wesson revolver. A .38-caliber Smith and Wesson revolver, the same caliber as that of the bullet retrieved from Connor's flak jacket, was carried by Officer Marshall (Jesse) Freer.

Could Connor describe again how he was wounded? Well, the police were firing from the front living room, behind the porch. One officer was behind a radiator, one behind the west wall, a third beneath yet another radiator. There was an archway between the front room and the porch, and this radiator was to the right of the archway. Connor was backing out, face forward towards the east wall (6221) when he found himself spun around 180 degrees, then struck by a bullet. He does not know what spun him around, but he is sure that there was no return fire coming from his men at the time.

"And at the point that you encountered this fire," Ramona is saying, "You found yourself to be in an open position on the porch, is that correct? And you didn't return any fire?" That's right, Connor replies, there was no return fire.

Day Five: Monday, January 20, 1986

Connor is back on the stand, his story much the same.
Someone else constructed the explosives which were used to blow a

hole in the wall which separated 6217 and 6219 Osage; he does not remember who. The explosives were not concocted at 6217 Osage, as "they were a part of the plan, and they were already made up."

He left 6217 Osage at about 3:00 P.M. "I don't remember whether I was told. I believe I was told to leave—and, yeah, I believe I was told to leave." He does not remember who gave him the instructions, but the reason for leaving was to give Team B a rest.

He encountered, he repeats, heavy fire while halfway between 6217 and 6219. He was struck in the back after he had taken a few steps backward. He was still in view of the hole. He had been spun around before being struck, and was facing east. He still can not figure out what spun him around. He does know that later he found a welt under his armpit. He thinks that might have something to do with it, but is unsure.

After he was hit, he was facing east on his hands and knees. Bullets were still "bouncing all around inside the living room of 6217 Osage." He could not function. He screamed that he had been hit. Jesse Freer, of the Stakeout Unit, pulled him from the porch into the living room. When he realized he was not seriously hurt and was able to function again, he returned fire at the muzzle blasts coming from 6221 Osage Avenue and instructed his team members to do the same. He believes that all of his team members returned fire, with the exception of Officer Muldowney. They were using a twelve-gauge shotgun and Uzis submachine guns. Jesse Freer was firing .38-caliber ammunition.

Yes, it was his understanding that he was not to assault the MOVE residence; his purpose was to pump tear gas into the house. After encountering fire from the MOVE house, he "pursued several other options" for placing tear gas into the house, but none of them was feasible.

The detonation of the second explosive, which removed the wall between 6219 Osage and 6221 Osage, was part of the strategy for gaining access to 6221 Osage or pumping the tear gas inside. The inside of 6221 was still not visible, and the team was still encountering fire from the house. "Just inside the porch wall was what appeared to be fortifications, composed of tree trunks and railroad ties. They extended from the ceiling to the floor, from the wall of 6221 that separated the porch from the living room out to the front of that property." It was from behind this fortification that the firing from MOVE was coming.

The purpose of the third explosive, which Connor says was more powerful than the second (which was more powerful than the first), was to remove the fortifications from the porch of the MOVE house. Officer Muldowney threw this one, while lying on his back on the porch of 6217 Osage. The explosive was constructed on site by Officers Mudlowney and

Angelucci, at Connor's request. The explosive missed the wall, and "disappeared in the general direction of the gunport, in the upper left-hand corner of the fortification."

Yes, the third bomb would have caused injury to MOVE members "if they were immediately behind the fortification . . . I would say serious injury." Yes, it is still Connor's testimony that his assignment was not to assault the MOVE house. He never received any change in that assignment from anyone else. It was not his intention to assault the MOVE house, "I intended to neutralize the fire that was coming from inside the fortification of 6221 Osage . . . and prevent the individual or those individuals who were firing at my team from having a place of concealment from which to fire at my team."

McGill asks Connor why the members of his team were armed as they were. "There are several reasons, sir. Going back to 1977 and 1978, we had knowledge that during the '78 MOVE confrontation, the MOVE members were armed with weapons such as the Ruger Mini-14 assault rifle, two .23 caliber and .45 caliber semiautomatic Thompson submachine guns. I also knew, from past experience, that there were nine weapons outstanding that were traced to the MOVE members, and had not yet been taken into custody by the police.

"In 1977 and '78, there were a total of forty-one explosives and explosive components seized by the Philadelphia Police Bomb Disposal Unit and agents of the Bureau of Alcohol, Tobacco, and Firearms. These were seized from MOVE members.

"Statements attributed to several MOVE members, including Ms. Africa, stated that this situation was going to be worse than 1978; that they would blow up the entire neighborhood; that we had better come ready because they were better prepared in 1985 than they were in 1978."

When Ramona gets back to him, Connor adds that after the detonation of the third explosive, the gunfire "seemed to be coming from two positions. We know for certain it was coming from what appeared to be the basement level of 6221 Osage, and also from the trajectory where we could watch the bullets striking the curtains and the windows and around the doorknob. The trajectory could only be coming from inside 6219, so we felt that we were taking fire also from 6219 Osage."

He requested cover fire, which was delivered from Posts One and Two, after he had instructed Team B to return fire at the first floor of the MOVE house. This occurred before Team A set off the second and third explosions. The cover fire lasted only for a few seconds, and then Post One called for a cease fire. This was called because the cover fire did not seem to be having any effect on the firing that Team B was receiving.

Officer Alexander Draft, a member of the Stakeout Unit, was assigned to Team B with Connor on May 13. After Sambor's fifteen minutes, and the retaliatory speeches from the MOVE loudspeaker, Draft entered 6217 Osage through the first floor and from the kitchen descended to the cellar. The house had to be inspected from the cellar to the second floor in order to be certain that no one else was in the house. Draft then returned to the first floor, where Connor and other Stakeout members were. There, other members of the team were preparing the explosive charge which would enable them to enter 6219 Osage.

He describes his encounter with gunfire. "We were setting up in the living room of 6217, and we were setting as two-men intervals, seconds. We had a second to count, and take off into the doorway. And as we set up, lined up, we all—by the time we got to the porch, we entered to go into the hole, the gunfire started from the location of 6221 Osage." Connor was in front, but they were not able to enter 6219 because of the gunfire. He and the other members of the team hit the ground, and crawled back into the living room. Connor was left in front; he threw a flashbang toward the gunfire.

"As he turned, what may have turned him, I observed him slump his back against the—he made a statement like, 'I'm hit.' " Freer then pulled Connor to safety.

Draft says the gunfire was coming from the bunkers of the MOVE house. "I observed the flash as I looked through the hole [between 6217 and 6219]. You can observe the flash coming from the bunker area, and you can also look through the hole and you can see portholes in the walls of 6219." The gunfire was heavy: "What you see when you know there's shots, as you look down, you would see flashed, which is—which was muzzle flashes. I was coming in the direction myself, and as I looked—and you can hear the sounds. And you look on the wall, you can see the rounds bouncing around. That's how I observed that the shots we were receiving were coming at us from 6221, because as I looked down the hallway, I could see muzzle flashes coming towards my direction."

He also observed gunfire from 6219 Osage and thinks he saw someone's shadow within that dwelling, but is not certain.

He repeats much of Connor's testimony, but contends that Officer Muldowney also returned fire to the MOVE residence.

Officer John W. LaCon of the Stakeout Unit follows Draft to the witness stand. LaCon, Connor, and Harry Young are the three officers whom Ramona is charged with having assaulted on May 13. LaCon was stationed at one of the windows at Post Two, 6232 Osage, across the street and three houses to the west of the MOVE compound.

At about 5:00 A.M., after Sambor delivered his message, LaCon observed "two males on the roof of 6221 Osage Avenue. One of the two males was standing very close to the edge of the roof. The male just behind him moved in and out of my field of vision. But the male that I described as first, the initial male, stood at the edge of the roof and, very slowly, surveyed Osage Avenue in that block, methodically looking east, then west, checking each house and each roof for the duration of their time on the roof." The men then moved toward the rear of the bunker, and disappeared from LaCon's sight.

At about 6:00 A.M., Post One delivered smoke, and immediately afterward, LaCon's team did the same. "In our case, Officer Folino delivered the smoke, and I was immediately to his right. After the smoke was delivered, there was a brief lull of several seconds, and then I heard what sounded to me like a shotgun blast. It was a short, flat blast, indicative of a shotgun blast, emanating from the area of the bunker. There was, again, a slight delay of a second or two. At that point, I was observing the west side of the bunker . . ." After hearing the shotgun blast, he saw "a series of muzzle flashes. The muzzle flashes were such, they were indicative of someone hold—pulling a trigger repetitively, very quickly. There were several such flashes, almost in continuity." The fire was coming from a gunpoint in the bunker. Soon, LaCon and other members of Post Two saw a muzzle flash from "the southernmost firing port."

He reported this to his immediate supervisor, Sergeant Hall, and then to Lieutenant Marandola at Post One. LaCon says that he would like to add, that "at this time that in conjunction with the muzzle flashes, there was almost an instantaneous impact at our location. . . . That impact was on the transom above the screen door directly in front of us. That is to say, approximately seven feet above my head. The bullets impacted on the transom, causing the curtain on the transom to move. Shards of glass struck the wall, and the bullets passed on through, striking the upper wall." Then Marandola, through Hall, instructed Post Two to "open fire on the positions where we observed muzzle flashes."

LaCon says that "to the best of his recollection" there were about five exchanges of gunfire "varying in duration and intensity" between the residents of 6221 Osage and Post One. They would fire until ordered to stop or until the firing from the MOVE house ceased.

Yes, he was injured at about 7:30 A.M., during one of these exchanges. He was struck in the back of the neck by a bullet. The bullet hit his helmet first, "cutting the fiberglass liner and border," then "richochetting off the helmet and striking me in the back of the neck, cutting a chain on which I had a miraculous medal." The bullet fell behind him.

There is much snickering among the MOVE supporters when LaCon testifies to being saved by his "miraculous medal": "Boo-shee-it, motha-fucker."

Later, LaCon and the other officers with him counted thirty-three entry holes "on the border of our position around our door, in the transom, in the dropped ceiling, in our sandbags and in the glass at our left and above." These bullets holes were made during a five-and-a-half hour period in which LaCon reckons there were five episodes of gunfire exchanged.

LaCon was stationed at Post Two until 5:30 P.M. McGill asks him to tell the jury what occurred at 4:00 P.M. "This is approximately quarter to four. Out of our field of vision, east, at Sixty-second and Osage Avenue, we heard someone endeavoring to address the occupants of the MOVE compound. They were doing so by some form of sound amplification or bullhorn. It was a woman's voice. And she was directing her statement towards someone in the house. She referred to a girl's name. I don't remember what the name was. She addressed her by name and pleaded with her. She implored that they come out of the house, and that they had proved whatever they wished to prove. There was no response from the house.

"Immediately thereafter—and what remains very fresh in my mind about that was the same woman now used a different focus. She asked whomever she was addressing in the house to let the children out of the house. Irrespective of their particular posture or whatever they wanted to do for the remainder of the day, she said, 'Let the children leave the house.'

"Now I know that whoever was in the house heard her, because it was very quiet at that point. There was no shooting. The shooting had been done for some time, and the sounds emanated from Sixty-second and Osage directly about our position.

"Also, corresponding with that, in conjunction with the statement, a window, one of the slatted windows on the second floor [of 6221 Osage], opened out . . . and I was conscious of a female, through those slats, stick her head out the window and look east on Osage Avenue. . . . She stayed in that position with that slatted window open for several minutes, looking east on Osage Avenue, and then pulled her head back in and shut the window. There was no response from the house during the course of this communique."

Ramona inches over everything that LaCon has already testified to, but does get LaCon to state that he fired about three hundreds rounds of ammunition. His weapon was an M-16.

Officer William Trudel, also of the Stakeout Unit, is the last to take the stand today. He was stationed at Post Four (6218 Pine) in the evening hours of May 13. From his position at a second-floor window, Trudel could look directly across the alley that separated the backyards of Pine and Osage Streets. Because the window was at the west side of the house, Trudel was angled towards the MOVE yard, a mere two houses west of his position. He saw Ramona Africa leave the house at 6221 sometime around 7:30 P.M. Officer Trudel is the first witness to have placed Ramona Johnson Africa in the house at 6221 Osage on May 13, 1985.

Day Six: Tuesday, January 21, 1986

Officer Anthony McBride is on the stand. Like a stage-struck comedian, he tries to get over his jitters by ingratiating himself with the jury. Waiting to be sworn, he constantly shifts in his chair, first grinning at the jury, then the audience. It is hard to tell who he is trying to please. The effect is disconcerting to some on the jury; most turn from Officer McBride's looks, others stare at the ceiling.

McBride is asked to identify a plan of the basement area of 6221, a receipt for the bullet casings found there, and over twenty photographs taken of "the crime scene." The photographs are of large timbers, badly charred wood, metal plates with holes large enough to accommodate gun barrels, the interior of the basement's east wall as it was on the morning of May 14, stacks of still intact newspapers found in the basement of 6221, and various "metal objects," "metal plates," "charred wood" sifted out of the rubble. One hints at the care taken by police at the crime scene: it shows a large crane at work. Another group records something else. These are photographs of weapons: a "weapon recovered in the rear garage area"; a Charter Arms revolver; the same revolver, its barrel now open; the barrel of a rifle, "in bent condition"; three barrels of weapons recovered inside the MOVE house, a Smith and Wesson revolver.

In all there are five weapons which police claim to have found in 6221. Officer McBride is asked to identify where each was found, placing red ink marks on the sketch of the basement. A shotgun, is placed at the rear opening of the basement, standing upright against what is left of a cinderblock wall; the Smith and Wesson revolver, near the east wall; the barrel of a .22-caliber rifle, towards the middle and back of the house; a second shotgun, underneath the front porch area; the Charter Arms revolver, in the front area of the basement's south wall. McBride concedes that two of the weapons were removed from the house via the crane and that another was actually found in the street, but he believes that he has placed them as accurately as possible on the sketch.

As for recovered ammunition, Officer McBride testifies that twelve fired cartridge cases were found near the front of the house along with six live rounds. Some 140 rounds, comprised of cartridge casings as well as live rounds, were found near the north wall, south wall, and east wall. These were rounds of .38s, .22s, and shotgun ammunition.

Another 40 to 45 casings were found in 6217 Osage. Why, when there was so much firing at 6217, so few casings? McBride speculates that this could be due to the intensity of the fire, and that with the amount of water from the squrts, numerous other casings could well have gone down drains and culverts in the rear garage area.

As McBride looks at photographs of the bunker, a Sergeant McCall of the Mobile Crime Detection Unit wheels in a large laundry basket full of burnt offerings, plastic bags, and metal plates. A large piece of plywood, badly charred at the edges, sits up in the basket, dominating the whole. The plywood is nicked and dented with numerous pockmarks surrounding a square portal. It is a nasty looking thing, ominous and menacing.

The evidence boxed by the laundry basket is shown piece by abstruse piece: rectangular metal plates, five holes to the plate—one big hole in the center (big enough for a shotgun), surrounded by two little holes (big enough for pistols), and two medium-sized holes (big enough for rifles); timber from the top bunker; the plywood with its portal; more strips of metal; three thick metal plates, this time with a large hole in the center and four small holes near the corners; a metal strap from the east side of the bunker; large bolts recovered in the rear of 6221, from along the cinderblock wall.

Taken together, the contents of the laundry basket deliver a silent discourse on the banality of evil. Their inherent horror is provocative of no sensation. The holocaust is survivable; and this is the proof: scraps of metal, charred wood, stacks of newspapers, and Ramona.

After lunch, McBride again faces Ramona. The comedian of the morning is gone, replaced by a man whose hands and shoulders are shaking. When were the photographs taken? May 14–16. Did he take all of the photographs? Some of them, less than half. Did he see the others taking the photographs which have been entered into evidence? Is he testifying from information he was given? Where exactly were the weapons found in relation to the debris?

The Smith and Wesson was at the very bottom. One shotgun was found near the bottom. The .22 was found maybe three quarters of the way down towards the bottom, at or about the same level as the shotgun in the front and the Charter Arms revolver. When was this sketch prepared? May 15. And when was the cinderblock wall at the rear demolished? May 14. Oh, and the casings, couldn't they have been dumped there by the police?

Objection, objection sustained. Ramona's cross-examination is rambling; not incoherent, but rambling all the same. She pursues almost none of her points. Her aim is clear, but the jurors are getting confused.

What McGill is up to, on the other hand, is patently clear. On redirection, McGill turns again to the sketch of 6221 Osage Avenue. Officer McBride is asked to locate the bodies of the adults in the rubble of the house. One by one, the bodies are located on the sketch, the individual bodies very near the marks in red ink that are weapons. A dead body here, red ink there.

The last questions of the day belong to Ramona. Could Officer McBride describe how the bodies were unearthed? Was he present when they were found? Yes, he was there, and he goes on to describe how the crane was first used, then the shovels, and how, "some debris did fall out" as the crane did its work. What condition were the bodies in when they were found? Some were fully intact, some were not. In the front middle of the basement, Officer McBride thinks it was, he saw, he thinks, a fully intact body, minus its head. He thinks.

"Thank you Officer McBride, you may step down." Anthony McBride looks again at the jury and grins.

Day Seven: Wednesday, January 22, 1986

McGill is wrapping up the Commonwealth's case this morning. His final witness is Officer Edward Jachimowicz, a police firearms examiner. Jachimowicz twiddles his thumbs and speaks in a low, heavy monotone. He has been a firearms examiner since December 1979, and since then has made some twenty-five to thirty thousand examinations. The old expert testimony—the MOVE members know the game. "Man I seen this on TV, an' all the mothafuckers do is go from room to room backin' up the cops is what. Shee-yit. Lyin' and lyin'. Mothafucker."

The establishment of Jachimowicz's expertise seems staged. But his apparent rehearsal is betrayed by his nervousness. There is a rumpled air about him. His dark hair is unruly, his beard is heavy, his voice thick with Philadelphia. And his fingers are constantly twiddling.

Jachimowicz is asked to identify the weapons found in 6221 Osage Avenue. Each weapon, or part thereof, is produced, held up to the jury by McGill, and then identified. The first, more or less whole but charred, is identified as the remains of a pump-action Model 500 Mossberg shotgun. Then, a "severely burned" Remington .22 rifle, with bolt-action feed. Fifteen bullets were found, unspent, in its tube. The barrel of a 12-gauge shotgun, along with its remaining action bar; a revolver, identified by Jachimowicz as a Model Military Police, Smith and Wesson, with a five-inch barrel; a Charter Arms .38 Special "Police Bulldog" revolver, its blue finish is gone, serial number remaining; a factory box containing the original parts for the Charter Arms revolver; a Winchester Model 1200 pump-action shotgun in mint condition. This last weapon was not found in the house. Rather, the Winchester is here for demonstration purposes, for it is similar to the two partly destroyed shotguns. Then, a color photograph of the Mossberg Model 500 shotgun with its pistol grip stock.

The Mossberg does look somewhat like the Winchester. With that in mind, McGill picks up the Winchester, points it at the ceiling, and fires five times rapidly. The gun is not loaded, but the impact is.

Click-pump-click-pump-click-pump-click-pump-click. Ramona is up, objecting. It hardly matters. The point has been made, all too effectively.

Questioning shifts to the Charter Arms revolver and the possibility that it might have been the weapon used in the shooting of Sergeant Connor. The revolver has been rebuilt at the Charter Arms factory in Connecticut, with only the barrel frame and firing pin remaining of the original weapon. Police tests have shown that the .38 special, unleaded bullet removed from Connor's flak jacket was probably fired from a Charter Arms revolver. But was this the weapon in question?

The bullet which struck Sergeant Connor was determined to have eight lands, eight grooves, and a right-hand twist. Seen under a microscope, these "characteristics" are as peculiar and as identifiable as a fingerprint, the jurors are told. For example, the Smith and Wesson .357s and .38s that Philadelphia police are equipped with have characteristics of five lands, five grooves, and a right-hand twist. Colt .38s, also standard Philadelphia police equipment, are characterized by six lands, six grooves, and a left-hand twist. Only Charter Arms and two other firms make weapons with the specific 8-8-right characteristics.

Standard police issue is a hollow point, 125-grain Peters .38 bullet. The bullet found in Sergeant Connor's vest is a solid-nosed .38 projectile made of uncoated lead. Its weight of 197.4 grains is, according to Officer Jachimowicz, "consistent with a 200-grain original."

The question, though, remains. Can it be determined "with certainty" that this Charter Arms weapon fired that bullet? "No, sir," Jachimowicz replies. The barrel of the reconstructed revolver is still slightly bent, and the bullet itself is badly flattened and marred. The evidence remains circumstantial, but not compelling.

With Officer Jachimowicz's testimony, the Commonwealth rests its case.

Wednesday afternoon, January 22, 1986

Following the lunch break, Ramona calls her first witness. She is Gloria Cheeks, a solidly built black woman in her fifties, with graying dreadlocks and levis rolled up at the ankles. Half-moons are formed by the very pronounced, but delicate, flare of her nostrils. She walks toward the witness box stridently, her feet striking the carpet with a thudding force.

Cheeks testifies that she has been familiar with the MOVE organization since 1978. She is not a member. "I'm a MOVE supporter," she says crisply. She has been a supporter since 1978. Ramona does not ask her to explain for the jury the difference between being a member and a supporter.

Throughout 1984–85, Cheeks visited the MOVE residence often. "I did shopping for Osage," she says. She was doing so on Mother's Day, 1984. "Yeah, 6221 had a meeting . . . with the neighbors because they stated it was Mother's Day, and that they had grievances with the system officials about the MOVE family that was in jail. . . . They wanted to give the information to the community that MOVE children's parents were in jail and it was Mother's Day, and everyone was celebrating; but MOVE had nothing to celebrate." The meeting, she says, was also held to let the neighbors know what MOVE's confrontation with the city was all about. "And they [MOVE] asked people if they had, you know, anything to say, they could step up and speak on whatever they had to say . . .

"MOVE was on the loudspeaker from '84—well a short period in '84, including putting out information. And they stopped sometime in, I think it was January of 1985."

Does she remember an incident in May 1984 in which a male MOVE member, his face covered by a black pullover, ran across neighboring rooftops, shotgun in hand? "Yes, I recall it, and all kinds of—well, the Police Department came out there, when whoever called the police. They came out to Osage, and there was no incident, you know."

The questioning shifts to that more menacing Mother's Day, 1985. Cheeks testifies that she was, as usual, doing the food shopping for 6221 Osage on Saturday, May 12. When she arrived on Osage Avenue a few minutes after 9:00 A.M., police barricades were already up. Cheeks was allowed to walk through the barricades, went up to the house, and spoke for a time with Theresa Brooks Africa. Then, with her "sister" Theresa Goodlowe, Cheeks drove off to get food for the MOVE animals. When they returned at 12:30, the police would not let her back in.

At sometime near 6:15 the next morning, Cheeks testifies, she found herself at Sixty-second and Pine Streets, "and was shot at." She was at Sixty-second and Pine because it was not possible to go any further with the police barricades.

Who was trying to shoot her? "The Police Department. They were trying to shoot my daughters, and the company that was with them and me. We ran and got in the car, and I sped off. And I remembered that I had to pick my grandchildren up that was at a friend's house in the 6100 block of . . . a small street off Larchwood."

How does she know she was shot at? "Because I know the sound of bullets, you know. And the helicopter was overhead. And the man was hanging out the helicopter with a gun—not a gun, but some type of an arm—and he shot five rounds down at me in the car. . . . [It] was an army-colored helicopter, olive-colored helicopter." It was now about 6:30 A.M. One of the helicopters belonged to a television station, she believes it was Channel 6. "The street was deserted. Wasn't nobody on the street. It was early in the morning. And I mean just the sound of hearing the helicopters, that many over your head, is enough to make you not want to come out." She did not return to the area after this.

Cheeks met Ramona in 1979. "You were outside City Hall, on the loudspeaker, giving people information, letting them know that it was a trial going on in City Hall, and that people should go up into the court-room so they could see the ongoing persecution of MOVE people, you know, in the courtroom." No, she has never seen any MOVE member initiate any kind of physical confrontation with anyone else. "MOVE did not initiate any confrontation. MOVE anticipated the confrontation . . ."

McGill begins. Had Mrs. Cheeks ever heard MOVE members on the loudspeaker before?

Yes, she has probably heard "all MOVE people that weren't in jail. I've heard them on the loudspeaker before." Yeah, that would have included Ramona, as well as Conrad Hampton Africa, Frank James Africa, and Theresa Brooks Africa. Yeah, she heard them in '84 and '85. Sure, she heard them on Mother's Day, 1984. No, she is not sure about hearing them in the summer of 1984, "because not long after [Mother's Day, 1984] they stopped on the loudspeaker. The only time MOVE got back on the loudspeaker was April twenty-ninth, when police went to the back of their house and the dogs started barking . . . and one of the MOVE members got on the loudspeaker then, you know, telling them that they were upsetting the dogs, you know, because they were in the back of the house."

Was that all MOVE said, that the police were upsetting the dogs? She does not remember the words "verbatim." No, she does not know why they were on the loudspeaker. She could only hear one person on the speaker; she does not know who. "I said MOVE got on the loudspeaker. I know somebody got on the loudspeaker and told the police that they were disturbing the life in the back of the house." She says she was there for about five minutes.

Why does she use the term "MOVE" like that, making no distinction between members? "That's the way we talk when we're speaking about anyone that's in the organization. That's the way we talk. We don't call a name, a particular name of a person. We'll say 'MOVE.' "

Is she saying that they are not individuals, but all one?

"That's not what I said . . . Look don't try—repeat your question again." She sounds defensive; McGill's strategy is working.

What does she mean by MOVE gets on the loudspeaker?

"That's the way we talk. We're a family, MOVE."

Why don't MOVE members identify themselves when speaking on the loudspeaker? She does not know; she is a supporter, and what's more she doesn't know what he's talking about. McGill's lips form a thin, tight smile.

In May and June of 1984, did Cheeks hear Ramona talk about the imprisoned MOVE members on the loudspeaker? "Yes." Her voice rises, and her body is stiff as she stares at McGill. Without further ado, she launches into a long, loud speech about the innocence of those MOVE members in prison, and then recites a history of Philadelphia policemen "beating MOVE men and women bloody, beating pregnant MOVE women, kicking them in their vaginas until they abort. Alberta Africa was pregnant in Rochester, and she was kicked in her vagina and she aborted in Rochester. But nobody has been taken to jail or locked up for all the crimes committed on MOVE. This city administration has been committing crimes on MOVE ever since MOVE's existence."

The jury members are nervous. They clearly do not want to hear what is being said.

How often and how long would MOVE be on the loudspeaker?

"According to the strategy. I wasn't there each time they got on the loudspeaker." She probably heard them on the loudspeaker four or five times during that summer. She does not know if Ramona was one of the people she heard. Yes, they all took turns on the loudspeaker.

McGill asks her about what she heard on the loudspeaker on May 13. "Well, see, the speaker wasn't that clear so I can't tell you who was, you know, really. It wasn't that clear from where I was." Could she recognize the voices on the loudspeaker? Her reply is slow, measuring, "Rad . . . Theresa . . ." There is a very long pause now. "And Mona." She says she heard them at about three o'clock in the morning.

Mrs. Cheeks says that she can recall nothing that Ramona said on the loudspeaker that morning, "because I was looking at what was going on with the police department."

McGill reads from the transcripts of MOVE's bullhorn activity the morning of May 13, " 'The first thing we want you to understand right now, if y'all come, if y'all come, y'all have to come fighting, shooting, so we ought to understand because we ain't gonna be another Grenada. See, we know how to fight.' " Did Cheeks hear Ramona say this?

No, because everybody sounds alike on the loudspeaker.

Would Cheeks say that someone who would say this would be in a "fighting frame of mind?"

Can McGill repeat the question?

"Did you ever hear her say, 'We'll drop you where you stand'?"

"That's not the question you just asked me. I asked you to repeat the question you just asked me."

Eventually, her answer comes, "If that talk was fighting language. You know, words don't—can't hurt nobody, you know. Words can't hurt nobody, so no, I can't say that . . . because MOVE been beat, shot, you know, murdered and now bombed. So—and they've never killed anybody. MOVE people ain't never killed nobody. You know, this system's police department, the cops, have beat, stomped, kicked MOVE babies out of women's stomachs, you know. They have burnt MOVE babies. They've tortured MOVE babies. And you know, you ask me about a word."

Yes, she has been inside 6221 Osage Avenue. No, she never saw any weapons there. Yes, MOVE talked about shooting, "MOVE said they wasn't taking no more beatings. . . . If the cops came at them, they'd have to come with it all. . . . Yeah, it's—self-defense is God-given. It's not man-given, and it's right."

McGill returns to the episode with the helicopter. Yeah, she was shot at five times. "I know what I heard." Yeah, someone was trying to kill her, "Well, I don't think he was playing."

So, she looked up and saw a man with a rifle inside a helicopter? No, there were three or four helicopters up there. Did they all have rifles, or just one? "The police department knows my car . . . I was constantly followed. And I'm constantly followed now, you know, people trying to intimidate me. But I cannot be intimidated by being followed by the police department. They know my license tag of my car. It's been in the newspapers and everything." Did she report this to the police? "No, I didn't. All the police were at 6221 Osage trying to do the same thing to MOVE that the man was trying to do to me from the helicopter."

Gloria Cheeks is excused from the stand, and the jury is dismissed for the day. The courtroom is cleared of witnesses, jury, and spectators. The press and the police remain as the otherwise empty courtroom begins to swell with lawyers.

At issue is a motion to quash the subpoenas which Ramona has sought for Mayor W. Wilson Goode, former Police Commissioner Gregore J. Sambor, and Fire Commissioner William Richmond; Lieutenant Frank W. Powell and Officer William Klein of the Bomb Squad; and Officers Richard Reed and Morris Demsko of the State Police. Klein made the bomb which was dropped from the helicopter; Powell dropped it. Reed and Demsko are helicopter pilots. The motion to quash is joined by the Commonwealth (for Demsko and Reed), the City Solicitor's Office (for Goode, Sambor, and Richmond), and lawyers Robert B. Mozenter and Patrick Artur (for the Fraternal Order of Police and Powell and Klein).

Assistant District Attorney Sarah Vanderbraak presents the case for the Commonwealth. Vanderbraak seems a peculiar choice for the assignment. She is inarticulate in a situation in which words are everything. Her argument comes down to this: Ramona Africa is engaging in a "fishing expedition." The expression on Stiles' face seems to indicate that he will rule against her. Vanderbraak must sense this too, for her presentation quickly grows even less convincing, more desperate: "She cannot turn this into the MOVE Commission hearings. I mean, she's party to the lawsuit. She will have ample opportunity to question the people involved there and go with what is extensive, intrusive civil litigation. But this is not the time or the place to engage in that kind of questioning, or putting people on trial concerning their decision to drop the bomb. And it's clear that she, at this point, has said, 'Oh, gee, let them be put on the stand. They were general eyewitnesses.' But that could be said about literally hindreds of people who were there. And those are not people that she's subpoenaed." Stiles says that he has heard enough to make his ruling. Vanderbraak pleads with him, "I would request that the testimony, then, be limited to what they saw that concerns the direct elements of the crime. Did they see shots fired at the officers who were the victims in this case? Those general—those types of issues. Not being able to go on and saying to Officer Klein, 'Oh, by the way, aren't you the one that dropped the bomb here?' . . ."

For the Fraternal Order of Police, attorney Patrick Artur argues that the subpoenas represent "an attempt to confuse the jury, obfuscate the issues, and to distract from the charges against Ms. Africa." But the losing has begun, and Artur makes his a short, pithy argument.

Carl Oxholm of the City Solicitor's Office is the last to speak. Young, mustachioed, with brown hair and a heavy beard, Oxholm, like Vanderbraak seems not up to the chore. He argues that city employees—from Mayor Goode to Officer Klein—are already defendants in civil litigation initiated by Miss Africa and should be protected from testifying at this time. "This jury," Stiles instructs Oxholm, "won't be privy to that civil suit." The burden, as Stiles reminds the many lawyers in the courtroom today, is not Ramona's to prove why she ought to be able to call a given witness. Rather, it is the Commonwealth's, the FOP's, and the City Solicitor's to show why she should not.

Robert B. Mozenter, Artur's partner, sits beside McGill in the jury box as Stiles denies motion after motion. Pursuing his lips, he curses, his teeth clenched.

Mozenter shakes his head, grinning now. McGill is twirling his mustache, tugging with one hand at his ear. He does not look too happy, but then again, he does not look surprised.

18

"Are You a Liar?"

Day Eight: Thursday, January 23, 1986

At 10:20 A.M. it all begins again. Ramona, dressed in a short-sleeved purple sweatshirt which exposes some of May 13's burn scars on her arms, calls Officer Marshall Freer to the stand. He is gray-suited, has a rugged blondeness, and a pierced ear. Freer testifies that he was given the assignment for the operation on Osage at Stakeout Headquarters on May 11. His supervisor, Lieutenant Marandola, assigned him to Sergeant Connor, who was responsible for Team B. He went to the Police Academy on Sunday morning to be briefed. He was then instructed to report to the Osage area at ten o'clock Sunday evening. Lieutenant Powell, Sergeant Connor, and Officer Tursi explained the plan of "what was to be accomplished" on Monday morning.

Freer recites the now often heard plan of action for his team, on which he was third in line. In the early stages of the operation, he could not see much because of the smoke. He testifies that he could at first hear only a male voice over the MOVE loudspeakers, then a couple of voices in the background. He could not hear Commissioner Sambor deliver his ultimatum, but was told by Sergeant Connor that he had done so.

Freer entered 6217 Osage through the east end (from Pine to Osage), climbed over a fence out of the view of those in 6221, and into the driveway. All told, Freer says that it took the members of his team less than two minutes to get inside 6217. MOVE was still on the loudspeaker.

Freer continues, talking of "securing places," and blowing holes in walls on that Sunday night. Through his testimony, Ramona makes it clear that there was no weighing of pros and cons in the team's strategy. If something did not work, they just tried something else. That was how it was done.

When he gets to the part about Connor's being wounded, Freer says that it was clear that MOVE was firing at them: Connor threw a flashbang through a hole in the retaining wall. After it went off, the team attempted to get back into 6217. Everyone made it back, except Connor, who was screaming, "I'm hit!" and was sliding down into the archway against the wall. Connor yelled "I'm hit!" three times. He fell forward on his knees, face down. There was heavy fire, which pinned Connor to the street side (6217) of the wall. Freer pulled him back. He thought he might have fired his Uzi into the MOVE house.

It was at this point that Connor told his men to go back because they were receiving heavy fire from 6221. Ramona asks Freer what he means by "heavy." Freer says that he could see the bullets hitting the eastern wall of the closet in 6217, while flashes were visible coming from the wall of 6221. He knew it was shotgun fire because of the loud booms. Pellets were striking the sliding doors. Eight, ten, twelve holes would appear at once. How long it lasted, he cannot say, but he thinks it was anywhere from thirty seconds to three minutes.

There is more of this kind of testimony from Freer. But despite his contention that the team was receiving heavy gunfire from the MOVE compound, Ramona has made her point. Little thought went into every action on May 13.

Maddie Thompson is an elderly lady, heavyset, slightly winded. She wears thick glasses and has a habit of jutting out her chin. Her hair is held by a red band, her sprawling body by a black dress with red trim.

Mrs. Thompson lives on Cobbs Creek Parkway, and MOVE adults and children passed her way daily between May 1984 and May 1985. If she had the time, she would play with the children for a few minutes. From where she lives, she could often hear MOVE on the loudspeaker.

She became aware of a plainclothed police presence in the neighborhood during the early part of the year. "I saw a lot of strange people around, and they said they were police or detectives and whatnot . . . When you see strangers and strange cars coming in, I began [sic] to notice and I understood they were police or individuals working in that capacity."

She was not at home on May 13, but rather "up to the church." The night before, the police had asked her to evacuate her home, and she had gone.

McGill has no questions for Mrs. Thompson, and she is dismissed.

Novella Williams is quite another matter. Short and stout, dressed in a blue blazer and a white silky turtleneck blouse, she rolls into the witness box. When asked to identify herself, she bellows, "NOVELLA WIL-LIAMS, MY TITLE IS PRESIDENT OF CITIZENS FOR PROG-RESS AND A COMMUNITY REPRESENTATIVE." What was she doing in the 6200 block of Osage Avenue on Sunday, May 12, 1985?

"In my own opinion, I—I believe, God brought me to that area. . . . I visited the area on Saturday, observed the tension and the activities of the people. I went to church on Sunday; and like a feather, when I came out of church I went to Sixty-second and Osage." The cadence of her words is strongly accented, with appropriate pauses to heighten the message. Williams arrived at Sixty-second and Osage "around the two o'clock hour" that afternoon. There, she "observed barricades all over the place." Initially denied access to the house by the police, she eventually found a Civil Affairs officer who let her pass through the barricades.

Sometime around 3:00 P.M. on May 12, Williams arrived at 6221 Osage Avenue. "I rang a bell that was there and waited for someone to come out. I was told by a gentleman standing in the street that I had better be careful. And I said, 'I'm just waiting for someone to come out.'" After some time, "A young lady did answer the door." This was Theresa Brooks Africa. "We talked. I said to Theresa that I was there to see what I could do to try and solve the problem and prevent anyone from getting hurt. Theresa told me that no one was going to get hurt as far as MOVE was concerned, because MOVE was not going to do anything."

"I asked her not to allow herself to be provoked. She said that she wasn't going to be provoked, because she knew what was about to happen. I asked her what the problem was. She said, 'We just want someone to begin to do something about our brothers and sisters who are incarcerated, in jail.'"

Ms. Williams says that Theresa asked that the press be admitted to observe the scene up close. She specifically asked for reporters from the black press because the police were "going to come here, and they're going to kill us; and if you're not here, they will come in the early hours of the morning, when nobody is around, and they [will] wipe us out."

Overhead, "the helicopters were swooping all over the house." There were three of them. Two MOVE children sat on the steps of 6221, another was seated near the door's threshhold. One of them started running up the block. Theresa shouted to the child not to be afraid; nothing was going to happen.

Williams quotes Theresa as saying, "They're coming for us. We know they're coming to kill us. They're going to drop something from up there, and they're going to come in the back door and they're going to kill us . . . Just tell them we just want our brothers and sisters out of jail . . . The reason you hear us talking [on the bullhorn] is that we've tried everything, and nobody is listening."

Williams then went to the police at the barricades and said that she needed to talk to someone in command, that she was afraid of what was going to happen. "I don't want them killed," she said. "And if you do what you're doing and contemplating doing, you're going to kill them."

Distressed by the lack of response to her pleas, she returned to the MOVE house and spoke once more with Theresa Africa, who told her to go talk to Gerald Ford Africa, one of MOVE's Ministers of Information.

Williams next proceeded to Sixty-second and Pine Streets, where she found again that no one would listen to her. She approached Captain James Shanahan of the Civil Affairs Unit and began to plead with him. Shanahan told her that he didn't have time to talk just now. As Williams saw it, "He brushed me off." Not knowing what else to do, she decided to return to the MOVE house.

On her way back to 6221, a police officer told her, "They're going to use water, they're going to use smoke." Sharing this information with those inside 6221, she warned that, "If the police come in here, you're going to be killed."

With another would-be negotiator, Williams tried to reach Mayor Goode from a telephone booth at Sixty-second and Pine Streets. Eventually, Goode returned their calls.

"I pleaded with him. . . . I asked him to call it off. . . . I said, 'Your Honor, you can't allow this to happen. If you allow the attack to be made on 6221 Osage, they will not come out alive.' "

The mayor told her "that he had the best experts in the country on this, and that something had to be done about the situation." Williams begged, "Just give us a little more time." The mayor replied, "What good would giving you more time do?" Goode was sure that, "Once the people have all of the facts, they will appreciate what I'm doing, and if I don't go in now, I will appear irresponsible."

Williams refused to give up, "And then I went on with my spiritual part. I said, 'I'm a Christian, and you [are] a Christian, and you can't kill those people. It will be wrong.' " The mayor hung up on her.

Williams ran back toward the house. An unidentified woman was behind the front door and would not open it completely. Williams told her not to be provoked, not to move first. The woman told her again that all MOVE wanted was the release of its imprisoned people. " 'There's nothing to negotiate . . . because that's all we want.' " Theresa then came to the door and said that she had a letter which she would like delivered to the governor and the mayor. Williams waited for an hour while Theresa worked on the letter. Then Theresa returned empty-handed, saying, "They're coming here to kill us anyway, so what's the use? Just forget it."

Darkness now cloaked the neighborhood. The police had "multiplied." By 10:00 P.M., the police had "just all kinds of artillery," "bomb trucks," "sandbag trucks," "the electric truck," "the gas truck . . ."

Williams heard "some of the guys . . . the young folks standing around there" say, "Going to blow these niggers away tonight."

Sometime before midnight, it started to rain. Her hopes dashed, Williams walked to Sixty-second and Pine, where she spent the night with her daughters Denise and Pamela. The next morning, the three of them were ushered out as the operation began in earnest.

It was in the early morning hours of that May 13 that Williams saw "an awful lot of police personnel; all kinds of policemen. It looked like an army. I can't characterize it. . . . I've seen such an incident, something that looked like it when I visited Europe. There was men with all kinds of artillery, big weapons. I mean large weapons, guns. . . . There was all kinds of ammunition. And I did see a truck that resembled the Bomb Squad truck parked on the corner. . . . There was [a Stakeout] officer . . . filling up these containers . . . in full view of everyone that was out there. . . . It was like a war. That's what it was like."

Williams was standing at Sixty-second and Pine at about 6:00 A.M., when, "I looked up . . . and I just . . . I said it was going to happen." The fire hoses were being turned on, the air was fogged with tear gas, and the shooting began.

Williams is really agitated now: "The bullets were zooming by my head, and I had to run . . . I mean really shooting. Dah, dah, dah, dah, dah, bing, bing, bing. I mean SHOOTING."

Near where she and a television reporter were standing, a policeman rode by on his horse. " 'Get out of the way! Get out of the way!' " he shouted at them. "And about that time, a bullet—ZING!"

The entire back row of the jury is laughing. No one disputes the seriousness of what Novella Williams has borne witness to, but her dramatics are overbearing. MOVE people are chanting, "Ah-ah-ah-Da-umn!" Most of the press are stifling giggles, as are many of the spectators. Williams read much the same script before the MOVE Commission. It is too bad; she has something to say but her delivery renders her words farcical.

Even Stiles is barely able to suppress a grin.

"And I ducked on the ground. And they were . . . shooting, shooting, shooting. . . . I mean really shooting, like something I have never heard and pray to God I never hear again."

McGill stares at the ceiling. Does Ms. Williams have political ambitions?

"Huh," she says, her voice a coy rumble. "WHO-oo would elect ME—ee?"

Had the witness ever been to 6221 Osage Avenue before Saturday, May 12? No. Had she ever spoken to the neighbors before May 12? No. What about her involvement with the neighborhood group? "I had not been invited . . . no, but I have friends on Sixty-second and Osage." She knew that the MOVE family resided in the neighborhood, and used to drive by there all the time. She was cognizant of the "activity" at Sixty-second and Osage, and, as President of Citizens for Progress, has been familiar with MOVE since 1978. Her frame of mind on that May 12 and 13 was simply, "I'm Novella Williams and I want to help."

Did she speak to Ramona on May 12 or 13? She's not sure, but she did speak to someone called "Maura" she thinks. Yes, it could have been "Mona." She mentions that that was her testimony before the Commission, and that is her testimony now. In what frame of mind did Theresa Africa appear to be in on May 13? "She was mellow." Was there any suggestion of surrender or of taking the children out? No, Williams explains, in an obvious attempt to justify MOVE's response, "I am a strong believer in the Constitution of the United States. . . . I would not want anyone to come to my house and ask me to leave. . . . I had no idea that there was an arrest warrant out for these individuals."

Williams did see another negotiator, Bennie Swans, but not while she was going back and forth to the MOVE compound. It was probably between 9:00 P.M. and 9:30 P.M. She knows it was not after 10:00 at night because the police would not let her past the barricades after that time. Yes, she saw Charles Burrus, who was also attempting to negotiate the confrontation. No, she did not see Judge Robert Williams. Was she aware of MOVE's request to bring Gerry Africa to the scene of the confrontation? She replies that she has heard testimony to this effect, but she was not aware of it at the time.

Day Nine: Friday, January 24, 1986

For the first time since the trial began, the spectator's line is packed at 7:30 A.M. W. Wilson Goode will be in the witness box today. The expectation is one of elevated and satisfying drama. Tension marks every face.

The television reporters are here with their crews this morning. They sit or stand against the wall opposite the line, talking among themselves, or watching the feed from their stations. The voice of Phil Donahue is heard loud and strong above the whisperings of the crowd. Here and there the intense glare of their camera lights gives short relief from the cold.

By 9:15 the line is long and disorderly. There is still only one line for press and public, and the late-coming reporters are beginning to push their way in. They have to. One of the last of the notepadded arrivals is forced to elbow her way into line—a line which is now reaching the end of the hall and about to turn the corner. "Excuse me, I had to go to the bathroom," she fibs. "Yeah," another reporter says, "I was saving her spot in line."

Some of the spectators are getting angry now. They are being pushed farther and farther back as more and more reporters arrive. A local hack writer wearing a tam-o-shanter begins to argue loudly with the late arrival. "Now," he says with cloying familiarity, "you *know* you weren't in line. I think you should do what's fair and go to the back of the line. *Right now!*" She is having none of it. "Look, I was here, and I'm not going to the back." Tam-o-shanter hollers at a deputy, "Sheriff! Sheriff! This line is supposed to be orderly. I want you to do something about it. Your lieutenant promised me yesterday . . ."

Suddenly the line begins to move. The door to the court's waiting room is thrown open. Tam-o-shanter leaves the line and pushes his way to the front. People, mostly MOVE sympathizers who have been here since 7:00 A.M., are yelling at him now. "Excuse me, I was here. This was my place," he lies. The MOVE family sees it for what it is: "He just creatin' a diversion, is all. Mothafucker."

Inside the courtroom, police and deputies line the walls, many sporting small earphones resembling hearing aids, all engaged in a constant scanning of the room. The front press rows are filled immediately, forcing many reporters to stand in the back of the courtroom. Front row seats are occupied for the most part by newspaper and television artists, the regular reporters on the case, a few local television "stars," and some local columnists who figure that this will be an easy write.

The laundry basket is rolled back into the courtroom and parked beside the jury box. The plywood facade stands out above the rest of the contents, charred badly at the edges, jagged like the missing parts of a jigsaw puzzle. The bullet holes are reminiscent of bull's-eyes in target shooting. The holes differ in size. Some are no more than small nitches, others gape, having been ripped wide by automatic fire. This is the Commonwealth's exhibit.

McGill paces not more than five feet from the basket. From time to time, he stares straight ahead at the empty witness box, as if lost in the task about to face him. It is a big day, a day which could be all Ramona's, a day during which God-knows-what could happen to the Commonwealth's case.

Mary Clare Leak is called to the stand. The crowd sighs with disappointment. Mrs. Leak is a chunky dyed blonde, in her late forties. A crucifix hangs from a chain around her neck. She is white. She is Theresa Brooks Africa's mother. When this becomes clear to the spectators and the jury, attention is paid. Black father, white mother, MOVE daughter.

Mrs. Leak says that she visited 6221 Osage Avenue many times. Was she present on Mother's Day, 1984? She was. What happened? MOVE, she testifies, "set up a forum between themselves and the neighbors . . . to sort out some of their differences." A bullhorn was used by MOVE speakers as well as the neighbors. Yes, there was some disagreement between MOVE and the neighbors. Some of the neighbors got out of hand. One took the microphone out of the hands of another. The day ended, she believes, in scuffling between MOVE and the neighbors. This is the only day she ever heard MOVE on the bullhorn.

When she arrived in the area on the morning of May 13, Mrs. Leak identified herself to a police officer, who told her, "You're too late. It's too late to be a mother." So she approached the barricades and identified herself to some of the journalists there, remaining with them until sometime in the afternoon, when Civil Affairs Officer George Draper led her through the barricades, enabling her to make an appeal over a bullhorn to the residents of the MOVE house. At the corner of Sixty-second and Osage, "I appealed to my daughter Theresa to come out. I also asked her to bring the children out. I also said, in between the appeals, to the officers on both sides of me, 'If they come out, you promise you will not fire on them?' That was my big concern, that that would happen." There was no response from 6221. Mrs. Leak is not certain that she was heard.

Draper told her not to be concerned, "because there was nothing going to happen that night; that they were not taking any action, and that they were going to wait it out overnight and it would be dealt with the following day, which would have been the fourteenth." Mrs. Leak remained in the area until "right before they dropped the bomb. . . . We were just getting into the car when we heard it."

During the year preceding the confrontation, Mrs. Leak was aware that something was going on on Osage Avenue, because she noticed "that there were police on the street. . . . Theresa would call me on the phone a lot, because I live in New Jersey; and the phone calls stopped, so I would go visit her. And she would say things like, 'It's getting more difficult for us to get around, because we're being watched all the time.'"

Detectives used to take down her license plate number when she would visit Theresa, and they would follow her until she passed the city limits.

Theresa would often discuss the topic of the imprisoned MOVE members with her mother. Theresa was "visibly upset" about the prison conditions endured by MOVE members, especially the female members. Ramona would often be a part of these discussions.

"But my daughter . . . would talk about a lot of the good things about being a MOVE member. She was a very loving girl. She became more loving when she joined MOVE." Mrs. Leak keeps swallowing. "She talked about a lot of the MOVE philosophy and the way they lived. And she lived clean. She was drug and alcohol free. She was a very honest and upright girl. And I found other MOVE members to be just the same. . . . I supported her fully as a MOVE member. I supported her convictions and her ideals. And that's what we talked about most of the time." In all of her conversations with Theresa, she was never given any indication that MOVE planned to initiate a confrontation with the city. She looks down as she say this. Her cheeks redden.

McGill has no small problem here. How in the world do you cross-examine a mother who lost her daughter on May 13?

A map of the Osage area is set up on a tripod and Mrs. Leak is asked to show the jury where she was when she made her plea. Mrs. Leak is somewhat confused as to her location. She knows that she was crouched, hidden in some bushes above a retainer wall. She was scared and had been kept relatively uninformed of the day's events and was ignorant of the various other attempts at negotiation: "I wasn't aware of any efforts on anybody's part to get anybody out, because I was isolated."

McGill poses a series of questions: When exactly did Mrs. Leak visit 6221 Osage Avenue? Did she speak to any of the other MOVE members? Was she aware of certain statements made by Gerry and Ramona Africa concerning the next police confrontation? Did she ever speak to John Africa? When she has had enough of this battering, Mrs. Leak replies, "Let me say something. . . . I went as a mother, okay? And I talked to my kid about how she was feeling, was she eating good, is she warm or is she cold?"

Yes, she was aware that a police officer had been killed in a previous confrontation with MOVE, but her response to this, in view of her daughter's membership in the group was, " 'Please don't get hurt.' I told her, I said, 'I support you in your convictions and I admire them,' I said, 'but you must promise me one thing; you will not get hurt.' And she said, 'I'll try not to, Mom.' " The effect of her words is plain, simple, and profoundly moving.

There is one stunning moment in Ramona's redirect examination, when she asks, "Did you notice the appearance of the house?" "Yes." "Were you informed as to the reason for its appearance?" "No." This is a little less than satisfying. Though Mrs. Leak testified that she never heard any MOVE member discuss the possibility of another confrontation, what else could the boarded-up windows and the bunker have spoken of to her? When Theresa told her that MOVE was being watched by the police, could Mrs. Leak have simply accepted her daughter's words at that?

Mrs. Leak is asked to step down from the witness stand. There is little time to absorb her testimony.

At approximately 12:15 P.M., W. Wilson Goode enters the courtroom through a side door. Clothed in a brown suit and blue shirt, he strolls past the jury on his right. Some half-dozen policemen and deputies are congregated near the witness box. Once on the stand, the mayor glances nervously at the jury, its two youngest black men pointedly looking up at the ceiling, away from him. Goode surveys the courtroom quickly. Rarely a man at ease, he is even more awkward today than usual.

The witness is sworn in: "Wilson Goode, G-O-O-D-E, Mayor of Philadelphia," he says in a voice constantly at war with a childhood speech impediment. "MURDERER!" shouts a MOVE adherent at the rear of the courtroom. The bodyguards can do nothing about words. Goode is at once taken aback and unnerved; the cry has stripped him of his position. He flinches and fiddles with his tie. He is still fiddling absentmindedly when Ramona Johnson Africa appears in front of him, a yellow legal pad in her hands. She sends a high hard fastball inside, as tight as they come. "My first question is: Are you a liar?"

Wilson Goode stares, waiting for the inevitable objection. The objection is of course, sustained, but the effect is keen. There is much murmuring, even some laughter. The MOVE people are all nodding their heads, and whispering about the "mothafuckin' lie-yah" up on the stand. Goode, meanwhile, is silent, hands in lap, his lips thin and closed, his eyes, though, still on Ramona.

The antagonism, the mutual distrust long hardened into loathing, almost physical, and surely palpable is manifest in every look exchanged between the two of them. Born poor and black, but ambitious for position, power, respectability, Wilson Goode has long since learned to control the expression of his emotions. But today, he has to try harder to contain his feelings and so remain W. Wilson Goode, Mayor of Philadelphia.

As a black man with pin-striped suits, he will always be a target for MOVE. He will forever be the man who fronted for THE MAN. He is what they—with their dreadlocks, odor of garlic, T-shirts, jeans, and workboots—have decided not to be, and moreover, cannot be.

There is, after all, an unspoken *quid pro quo* by which ambitious black men and women like Goode have been accepted and promoted within the urban political system: You keep your people reasonably happy and give us their votes so that we can run the business of this city profitably and without interruptions, and everything will remain swell between us. It is no accident that this overwhelmingly black administration—mayor, managing director, chief of staff, press secretary, two of three deputy mayors, city council president, heads of the City Solicitor's Office, Parking Authority, Redevelopment Board, Waterfront Development, and a goodly number of assistant managing directors—until May 13, at least, had been favored with the support of much of the Downtown white establishment. Goode and the rest of his coterie have everything to fear from MOVE.

Ramona is still contesting the ruling. "I'm asking that because this testimony is very important; and if a person has a problem with lies, then I need to know that, because that affects his testimony." Goode is trying, with minimal success to appear unruffled. Already, perspiration coats his forehead.

Over the next hour and three-quarters, the mayor is asked numerous questions about his role in the May 13 operation. This should be enlightening, but in fact, proves highly confusing. Ramona's questioning follows no strategic or logical pattern, skipping back and forth between the events of May 13 itself, the planning stages, and other seemingly unrelated incidents in the rancorous history of MOVE's relations with the city proper. Points are scored, then quickly lost in this idiosyncratic form of examination. For a jury which has professed to have precious little opinion of the events leading up to that thirteenth of May, the cumulative effect must be bewildering, and this is presumably compounded by the mayor's own imprecise dating of events in the planning stages.

Was Goode present during the May 13 confrontation? No. Did he speak that day with Sambor? No, he was only in touch with Leo Brooks, the managing director.

At what point did he first become aware of the exact date of the operation against 6221 Osage? "I became aware [of] the specific date on either the Wednesday or Thursday [May eighth or ninth] preceding May 13."

When was Goode first aware that there would be a police operation? "I became aware about a week preceding that . . . which would have been ten to twelve days prior to May thirteenth."

How did he become aware that there would be such an operation? Goode called a meeting "somewhere around May second and May third" with District Attorney Edward G. Rendell, Police Commissioner Sambor, and "various City officials" to "discuss whether there had been any violation of the law" at 6221 Osage Avenue. By the end of the meeting, it had been "concluded that perhaps there had been violations of the law and that warrants, in fact, would be gotten for certain arrests of persons in the house." No, the issuance of warrants is not a part of the mayor's job description.

Did Goode initiate the planning for the operation? "I initiated a meeting. Once I was told by the district attorney that there were five warrants that could be issued with four people involved, I initiated planning to ensure that there would be safety of the residents, of police officers, of fire fighters, and of people within the house, children in the house. And therefore, the plan which I initiated was to ensure there was proper planning that would ensure the safety of those persons, all of them."

Was the mayor aware of the possible presence of explosives in 6221? "We heard—I heard, I guess I should say—there might very well be explosives stored in Sixty-second and Osage, yes. To say I had any specific or precise information about anyone having seen explosives go in there, the answer is no. . . . It was certainly something that was on my mind. If you're asking whether or not others who planned took that into account, I can't respond to that."

On May thirteenth, the mayor spoke to Brooks "a dozen times" between 6:00 and 8:00 A.M. He spoke to Sambor on the eleventh, sometime around mid-afternoon, and on the twelfth, "perhaps one or two times, but only to make him aware of my location and to determine from him whether or not the plan he had outlined would proceed on schedule." The only "substantive" discussions he held on May thirteenth were those with Brooks.

The entire purpose of the operation was to make the arrests of the people named on the warrants. The police department had been instructed to "develop a plan which would enable us to make those arrests without causing harm" to anyone, should the wanted MOVE members fail to surrender. If they had surrendered, the Human Services Department would then have assumed custody of the children, and the Licenses and Inspections Department would have inspected the house. As to those MOVE members who were not named in the warrants, Goode says, they "were free to do what they wanted to do, I presume."

During the year and a half prior to the confrontation, Goode received most of his information concerning the Osage Avenue problem through the police department. He had no contact with Ramona or Gerry Africa during that time, but was contacted by Louise James and LaVerne Sims.

Goode was briefed by the police department in February 1984 to the effect that the house was occupied by MOVE members, that wooden slats had been put up in front of the windows, that the back alleyway had been partly blocked, and that there were complaints from the neighbors about sanitary conditions at 6221. Thereafter, Mayor Goode told his aides that he was to be informed only if the situation changed. He did not feel any need to monitor the situation from that point forward. "I had a managing director whose job it was to be aware of what was going on."

He was not aware, at that point, of any outstanding warrants for members of the MOVE organization in residence at 6221 Osage. Shouldn't he have been made aware of the warrants? "I would not regard that as unusual."

"I indicated, throughout the process, that it was not my job as mayor to make a judgment about how people lived; about, necessarily, words which they use; that it was my job simply to enforce the law. And therefore, the question which I always posed was, 'Is there any violation of the law?' And the person who would have to make that determination was the district attorney. And he would have to, in fact, bring the charges. And only if, in fact, he concluded that charges should be brought, and only if a judge signed off on that and said that these are valid charges would the mayor of the city have any role whatsoever to play."

As mayor or as managing director in the Green administration, was Goode aware of MOVE's longstanding complaints, concerning the "unjust imprisonment" of its members? "I recall having numerous meetings, dating back to 1980" with Gerald Ford Africa, Louise James, LaVerne Sims, and "others" whose names he cannot recall. Before the trial for the August eighth incident, Goode was approached about the possibility of, as managing director, his rebuilding the house in Powelton Village. "There was also discussion about the children, about food stamps and places for them to live, and we worked on all of those things with the organization over a period of three years." Discussion at those meetings always returned to the convictions stemming from the August 8, 1978 shootout at Powelton Village. "I frankly and candidly said to Gerald Ford Africa on a number of occasions that I cannot, as mayor, order the release of people who are in jail. . . . And I would point out that he was unhappy with my answer."

What prompted Mayor Goode to call a meeting with District Attorney Rendell in May of 1985? "I called the meeting primarily because I was concerned with the levels of concern expressed by neighbors and elected officials and others about the activity out there on Osage Avenue, and wanted to have an update, and find out whether or not things had changed from the year before. . . . I'm always concerned when neighbors are concerned and I think it's my responsibility to respond when there are concerns like that."

What about the concerns of the residents of 6221 Osage Avenue? "I believe that my action from 1980 through 1983 demonstrated a concern for all human beings. And I believe that if you had been inside of those planning meetings, that you, too, would know that I was concerned about all of the people. . . . Yes, I was concerned."

Was he also concerned about "innocent people being in prison for a hundred years?" "Whether or not a person is innocent or guilty is not something for me to determine."

Goode was asked early in 1984 by Gerald Ford Africa to set up a meeting with District Attorney Rendell for a review of the various convictions. Rendell refused to meet with Ford Africa. Ford Africa later told Goode that he had run into Rendell on the street and that Rendell had explained why he was unable to do what MOVE wanted. "That is the last time I recall contact with anyone" with regard to the situation involving the imprisoned MOVE members until the days preceding the confrontation.

Was it Goode's intention between May of 1984 and May of 1985 to avoid confrontation with MOVE? The mayor looks uneasily out of the corner of his eye at the jury, then towards the prosecution table where McGill has been joined by City Solicitor Handsel B. Minyard. Minyard, a thin, mostly bald, light-skinned black man, stares back impassively from behind his wire-rimmed glasses. The mayor chooses his words and replies, "It has always been my intention to avoid confrontations with anyone unless absolutely necessary."

When did he authorize the operation against 6221? He is not sure, but he believes it was between Tuesday, May 7 and Thursday, May 9. At the time, the mayor believed that there were "about ten" MOVE people, including children, in the house.

Goode testifies, incorrectly as it happens, that the police received court authorization to pick up and take into custody the MOVE children on Thursday or Friday evening (May 9 or 10). The arrest and search order was actually issued on Saturday, the 11th of May.

Was the mayor informed that Alphonso Robbins Africa, known as "Mo" Africa, had, that month, been involved in an altercation with Philadelphia police? "I was aware that there had been a confrontation between police officers and a man driving a truck." He was told that the driver, a MOVE member, came at the arresting officers with a tire iron. Did the mayor know that Mo Africa was brutally beaten by the same policemen? "That was not part of my briefing."

Did Mayor Goode, at any of his meetings with city officials during the planning stage, make mention of the presence or possibility of explosives in 6221? "My assumption was that it was general knowledge that there was a rumor about that." Was Commissioner Sambor present at meetings where there was talk of such explosives? "That is my recollection."

During Goode's conversations with Brooks on May 13, was he concerned about police actions in the face of the rumored possibility of explosives? No. What about when Brooks asked for authorization to drop the bomb? "If in fact, anyone said to me on that say, 'I'm going to drop a bomb on the house,' my response would have been, 'No.' In fact, what he said to me was that he wanted to use an entry device on the roof; and, in fact, the way he described it to me did not cause concern. . . . Leo Brooks understood full well my prime concern, which was, no injury to anyone."

Yes, he was also aware of the possibility that gasoline was on the roof of 6221 Osage, but nonetheless remained unconcerned because "no one said they were going to drop a bomb on the roof. . . . The overall philosophy that day was to protect the persons."

What details of the police department's plan was Goode aware of?

First of all, that Commissioner Sambor would read off the warrants, then give the MOVE people inside 6221 Osage Avenue fifteen minutes in which to vacate the house and surrender. At the end of the fifteen minute grace period, water cannons known as "squrt guns" would be turned on the house and tear gas would be shot at 6221. Next, under this cover of water and gas, police teams would occupy neighboring houses and put tear gas through the adjoining walls and into 6221. All along, police would be maintaining electronic surveillance of 6221 Osage Avenue.

Mayor Goode was aware of the police department's "ability to put holes on each side [of 6221] from the two adjoining houses," and that "some type of device" would be used to accomplish this. He asked if this would pose any danger to the children and was told that the method was safe.

As Ramona flips the pages of her yellow legal pad in search of new questions, Goode crumples up a chewing gum wrapper. Again, he looks quickly, nervously at the jurors.

Ramona continues. Was Mayor Goode aware of the presence of children in the house at 6221 Osage when the operation began? "Some, yes. . . . How many I did not know. . . . That's the reason for deciding to go to Court and get the warrants, and get an Order to take custody of the children."

Ramona, as she often does, responds by nodding her head, "Hmmh-hhum. Hmmm-hmmm."

What reasons did he have to be so concerned for the children that he believed obtaining an Order was necessary? Some of the neighbors had made reports of the children's abuse. He was concerned, citing a problem which arose after the 1978 confrontation, about where to place the children after their parents had been arrested. He also felt it was the City's responsibility to examine the welfare of the children.

When the operation began on the morning of May 13, did Brooks inform the mayor of the police department's use of explosives? No. And no, he received no information about the type of weaponry being employed by the department. It was his understanding that this was Sambor's concern, not his.

"Uhh-huh." There is no, "Thank you." Just "Uh-huh," the muttering as dark as a curse.

McGill springs to his feet. He has only a few questions for the mayor.

Was it clear to Mayor Goode that MOVE was uncompromising as to the demand that its imprisoned members be released from jail? "That was clear to me? Yes."

Goode has caught some of McGill's confidence. There won't be any problem here. He is facing the jury now, legs crossed, hands clasped.

After a very few perfunctory questions in which McGill stresses Goode's awareness of certain negotiation efforts, thus displaying the mayor's "concern," McGill is finished.

W. Wilson Goode is dismissed from this stand.

A bailiff's voice rings out, "Call to the stand Larry Howard." A door to the front right swings open, and a large, hulking black man, followed by two white sheriff's deputies, enters the courtroom. The image is striking. Police witnesses enter court through the large double doors at the rear, having spent their time in Room 251, lounging about a long table with other cops and deputies. Their day is spent in company of coffee, cigarettes, and newspapers. For them, there is group support. Wilson Goode, and later, former Police Commissioner Gregore Sambor, are in turn accompanied by bodyguards and lawyers. They enter court through the side door behind the jury, the same passage the jury makes. MOVE witnesses here and tomorrow, enter through the ominous door with the meshed wire glass window at the right—Ramona's door. The right side of the courtroom hosts MOVE supporters, the defense table, and more deputies than the left side of the courtroom. Group support of a very different sort.

His skin the fine color of coffee and milk, Larry Howard is swathed in prison fatigues. Dull purplish brown, both pants and shirt are made of the same dismal stuff. A man of considerable physical strength, he is bulk layered on bulk. There is a beard, not heavy. He looks as though he would be most at home playing for the Oakland Raiders football team. A red plastic band on his right wrist tells the real story: Prisoner of the Commonwealth of Pennsylvania. In a loud, firm voice, Larry Howard announces himself, "I'm a revolutionary supporter of the MOVE organization." He takes great pride in the announcement.

So, tell us about Mother's Day in 1984. "The MOVE organization, we called a meeting with the neighbors in the Osage area." What happened? MOVE put forth its position, gave the neighbors some background on MOVE: "the history, the beatings, the . . . illegal arrests of

MOVE [members]." They asked the neighbors how they felt about MOVE and MOVE's position. There were about two hundred people there.

Did he speak on the loudspeaker after the Mother's Day meeting? Yes. What did he say? "During that whole period of time, the information was solely based on the fact that we had nine MOVE members in jail." MOVE had exhausted every legal channel available to them in seeking the release of their fellow members, who at this point, had been imprisoned for six years. MOVE told the neighbors it had no problems with them, that the confrontation "was solely directed at the City Administration and Mayor Goode." It was the city, who "slammed the door on us. They spit on us."

Was there any change in MOVE activity from May of 1984 until August of that same year? No. "I was on the loudspeaker on a regular basis . . . normally three of four times a week. . . . The loudspeaker was solely to get out our message. We were trying to draw attention to our situation."

Howard, who testifies that he has been associated with the MOVE organization since 1979, says, "We never initiated any confrontation with the officials." Instead, MOVE was the constant victim of official harassment. "We've been jailed innumerable times—I can't count it."

Numbered among those countless arrests, Howard continues, was his own in early August 1984. Howard and Ramona had been arrested in March of 1984 on a disorderly conduct charge. Released on his own recognizance, Howard failed to appear in court, hence the bench warrant which was served on him in August. Raymond Foster Africa had been with him when he was arrested. This was the last time Howard was anywhere near his home at 6221 Osage Avenue.

The question now concerns Alphonso Robbins Africa and his arrest on June 10, 1984. As Howard tells it, Mo Africa was innocently driving his tow truck when he was pulled aside by police who immediately drew their guns. There were MOVE children in the tow truck. Mo was going food shopping; this was his assigned activity. There was no reason for the tow truck's being stopped. As usual, MOVE was just being harassed.

Mo Africa told the police he had not done anything, had not bothered anyone. So one of the policemen took out his gun and threatened to shoot him, and Mo did what he had to do, he "defended hisself. And as a result, he was charged with assault and battery and given some twenty thousand dollars bail."

"The MOVE organization's position has always been a defensive position. Any incident that's been publicly made, we've always took the defensive. We've never took the offensive against police or city officials, or whatever. We've never took that position. It's always been defensive. May thirteenth speaks to that. August eighth speaks to that."

Were city officials, as well as the Osage Avenue residents aware of what MOVE wanted? "Definitely. No question about it."

On cross-examination, McGill has quite another message to impart. MR. HOWARD CAN YOU HEAR ME ALL RIGHT? "Yeah, I hear you." What is a revolutionary supporter of MOVE? Howard is patient with the pagan. "When we speak of revolution, we simply mean change, changing that which is wrong to that which is right. It doesn't necessarily mean violent change." Could it, at times, mean violent change? "It could come to that, yes. . . . MOVE, we don't advocate violence. We're not into that. We defend ourselves as a family, as an organization, just like all families. John Africa teaches us that if a snake—if you walk into a forest and you step into a snake's lair, in his home, then the snake—a rattlesnake will hiss at you to give you warning that you intrude in on his home and his privacy, and that warning means that next time, you'll be bitten; and from that bite, you'll become poisoned."

What if MOVE is attacked or provoked? "We would defend ourselves." This is what McGill has been waiting for. Would that mean shoot? "If shot upon." Only if shot upon? "Exactly." When you shoot would that mean shoot to kill? "We would do whatever is necessary to get the intruder off of us." Was shooting involved in 1978 and 1985? "I wasn't there. . . . I believe, yes, shooting was involved." Shooting by MOVE members? "From what I understand, yes." Bingo.

If the police attempt to serve arrest warrants on MOVE members which the organization feels are invalid, MOVE would not allow the police in their house and would act in a defensive manner, is that right? "Exactly."

Is M-1 an organization comprised of men ready to defend MOVE? "I can't speak of that any more."

Is it true that the majority of arrests of MOVE members have been illegal? "More than half, definitely." The other half are legal? "I can't speak on that."

Howard hates the police, doesn't he? No. Wasn't he arrested and convicted of shooting a policeman in the face in 1972? "Definitely." And isn't he in jail now because of a parole violation stemming from that shooting, and Howard's subsequent absconding? Yes. "You're not there because of any disorderly conduct charge, are you?" McGill is in high gear now, speaking rapidly, tersely. A certain violence is borne by his demeanor.

"Officer Thomas Parson was just sitting in his car wasn't he; and are you going to tell me you took a defensive position in shooting him?"

Howard tries to backtrack. "At that time I wasn't associated with the MOVE organization." No, he wasn't associated with the Black Panthers then either. Was he a member of the Black Liberation Army? Didn't Howard become involved with MOVE in Holmesburg Prison? And didn't he take part in a MOVE-sponsored riot there? No, no. And weren't some seventeen guards injured during that riot? Maybe. Was that defensive on you part? Yes.

Stiles, losing patience with McGill, whose manner is decidedly furious, repeatedly tells him to slow down. It matters little, for the hammer is striking the chords.

Wasn't Howard instrumental in the fortification of the MOVE house at 6221 Osage Avenue? Howard says the barricades went up on Christmas day, 1983. Yeah, he helped put the boards on the windows. No, he didn't help bring any sandbags in. No, he had nothing to do with constructing the bunker. No, he didn't help in any rebuilding inside the house. No, he had nothing to do with the selection of the row house as the new MOVE headquarters. Yes, he made some comments on the loudspeaker about killing the police, putting a bullet in Wilson Goode's head, though he cannot remember the exact words.

McGill stretches, then tiptoes forward and pushes his chair slightly towards the tabletop. Slowly at first, then more and more animatedly, he rocks the chair, pumping constantly up and down off the balls of his feet. His head with its fine, immaculately combed silver hair, is angled back. He pushes his tongue out toward the left cheek, moves his eyes from the floor to the jury. *These* are his fans, his audience. But he will never know if they are truly fans of his—or fans of this one moment in time.

Ramona attempts to restore some kind of credibility to her witness. Yes, he remembers how he and Ramona used to jog between the MOVE houses at Fifty-sixth and Chester and Osage Avenue during the summer of 1984. Does he have any hostility for police? "Yeah, certainly I have. I've had it. But I don't walk around with a chip on my shoulder about police." No, his attitude hasn't changed about police. "I know how they are." But "I've never heard of a MOVE member attacking the police . . . a sheriff . . . a guard." Quite the opposite. "I've been victimized by guards attacking us. It was nothing for us to be walking down the street, and you were with me, on occasions where police would ride up and make obscene gestures to us, call us niggers, talk about our hair."

What was Howard like before joining MOVE? "There probably wasn't anything I didn't do, unlike anybody else. I drank, I smoked, I shot drugs, I stole, I lied, I robbed. Upon coming into MOVE, upon following the teachings of John Africa, I gradually moved away from those things to the point where most of them things, I don't even do any more. . . . I did everything prior to MOVE."

Have the MOVE people he has been acquainted with ever expressed a desire to kill police? "Defensively speaking, yeah."

A young black juror with orange tinted hair is fast asleep, her hand barely steadying her jaw. For her, as for everyone else in this courtroom it has been a long, long day.

"That will be all for today, thank you," Stiles says. The words are spoken—and heard—with relief.

19

"Birdie, We Love You!"

Day Ten: Monday, January 27, 1986

One of the bit players in this immense drama is a radio talkshow host named Irving Homer. Heavyset, squat, bespectacled, he is middle-aged, wears his gray hair cut short, and has the look of a high school science teacher. Known to his radio audience as "Irv Homer," he seems an unlikely member of this cast.

Homer has known various MOVE people since "approximately the year 1978, '79." Over the past eight years, he has received "letters and communication almost weekly" from MOVE members and their sympathizers and supporters. Many of the letters arrive marked with prison return addresses.

Among Homer's MOVE correspondents was Ramona Johnson Africa. Homer says that he has received four or five letters from Ramona, all "signed by your name, and I believe 'Director of Communication.' And some of them were 'Minister of Information.' No, Homer never discussed the letters with city officials or with the police. Yes, he still receives correspondence from imprisoned MOVE members.

Ramona's point here, insignificant as it may seem, is that: 1) MOVE members are not only nonconfrontational, but 2) constantly willing to engage in some form of dialogue. Scores of others—mostly newspaper editors and broadcasters—receive those same letters.

McGill's questioning is brief and touches on the same points. Was Mr. Homer aware of what was said on the loudspeaker on the morning of May 13? No, Homer has not read the full transcript of "the dialogue."

Dialogue? Homer must be less familiar with those words than he would seem. The ease with which such small phrases constantly transform history is the greatest obstacle of this trial. "Words don't never hurt nobody," Gloria Cheeks had said.

A courtroom spectator has, meanwhile, fallen sound asleep. When the bailiff comes over to wake him, the man stirs at the touch of the hand on his shoulder. "No sleeping in the courtroom," the bailiff says gently. "You'll have to leave if you're gonna take a nap." The man is fully awake now. "I was just meditat'n. Are you say'n I can't meditate?" The MOVE people chortle appreciatively. Even the bailiff laughs. McGill turns and eyes this latest little affront to his own, well-developed sense of decorum, his irritation plain. Stiles covers his smile with a broad palm.

A recess is called as a blonde-haired young black woman on the jury pales. It is a quarter of noon.

Few leave the building for lunch; most return to their places of waiting. Paper bags, hoagie wrappers, and styrofoam cups litter the halls. Still smoldering cigarette butts die beneath winter's shoes. Reporters and spectators alike are more anxious than usual today. All anticipate the arrival in court of Birdie Africa.

"Birdie, we love you!" "Ona MOVE!" voices suddenly shout in strident chorus. Heads swivel. Birdie's father Andino Ward and his lawyer David Shrager lay hands on the small back and turn away with him—anywhere but down this hallway.

MOVE women continue their shouting. Cameramen chase down the corridor. Everything is fast now, mostly emotion. Female reporters choke. Small tears are halfway down some cheeks. Heads go down, to the side, shake back and forth.

Some of the press seem shocked by what it is all about. Birdie, now known as Michael Moses Ward, was walking down that hall. It was expected that he would be led into the courtroom through the back door, so that he would not be subjected to this crowd, and its possibilities. But here he was.

There is some recovery, little exchange or reaction, and a great lot of self-conscious talk of "necessary evils" from members of the press. Nothing, of course, justifies what we have witnessed. And then, when heads are up, it happens again. The lawyer, the child, the father walk unsteadily towards the same sea, the same violent waves. "We love you Birdie!" "Birdie!" Birdie!" "Ona MOVE, Birdie!" Camera sounds, pushing, shamed silence. Some reporters will not even look as the boy and the men walk near them and into Courtroom 253. A television reporter turns his head and mutters, "Fucked-up. Fucked-up. All fucked-up."

Room 253 will be, for this one afternoon only, reserved for the players themselves—judge, jury, attorneys, cops, Ramona, and Birdie. The others —reporters, MOVE members, and the usual idle and curious spectators —will witness the afternoon's testimony on closed circuit television.

Accordingly, press and spectators file into a courtroom across the hall. Deputies fiddle with the television monitors while the room fills. The sketch artists sit in the front row, some already drawing, though not even a shadow of the child is to be seen. Two young reporters, one from UPI, another for a suburban paper are trapped by a veteran wire service man who looks around the room while he talks at them. There has been warning of a great snowstorm, and there are frequent and somewhat furtive looks toward the window on the right.

There is a blip on the monitors. A reporter runs out of the room, but as soon as she is gone, a picture appears. The camera moves first to the flag, then the defense table and the prosecution table—both empty.

Soon Stiles's face and voice come out of the box. He explains to the jury that the courtroom is empty of spectators because the testimony presented will be that of Michael Moses Ward. He has decided to present Birdie's testimony this way, with spectators in an adjacent room watching on television monitors, he tells them, out of concern for Birdie's youth, "and because of the just general difficulty of testifying in a courtroom crowded with strangers."

Stiles asks that Birdie be brought into the room.

Ramona protests the number of people in the courtroom, whom she lists as policemen and sheriffs. These people were not in the room during other testimony, she says, when there were spectators in the courtroom. Why are they here, she asks, if not for the sole purpose of being spectators? Those to whom she is referring cannot be seen on the monitor, and so at the moment, there is no way of assessing her claim.

Another of the many, seemingly endless sidebars is called. Stiles, McGill, Stevenson, and Ramona quietly huddle together alongside the far wall of the courtroom, well away from the jury box. The courtroom reporter silently types the record while decisions are made as to who may stay, who must leave.

Michael Moses Ward is sworn in. It is not romantic to describe this child's beauty as hypnotic; even without knowledge of the event, and whatever characteristics are heaped on him as a result, his affect would be such. On May 13, a photographer saw him naked and burned in a police vehicle. The photograph he made that night is the visual record of the last day of Birdie Africa's life in MOVE. Michael Moses Ward is here now, dressed in tiny man's clothes, a little suit, a little tie, little loafers. His hair is combed and barbered. His scars, unlike Ramona's, are not exposed.

The lives and faces of the other children remain unknown; it is only the manner of their death which has been of concern. But even out of that day of death, in Michael Moses Ward, came the future.

Stiles introduces himself to Birdie, tells him to speak into the microphone. Birdie nods his head, says yes. His voice is quiet, hesitant, lonely.

Ramona says, "I know you're nervous. Just relax, okay?"

This does not have the sound of someone trying to make someone else at ease. It has nothing of the sound of a woman soothing a child, nothing of the sound of intimacy.

She asks him about the day. Yes, he remembers the whole day. No, he never saw her with a gun or any kind of weapon on that day. Yes, he remembers where he spent most of that day, in the garage. No, Ramona never left him, she was with him in there all day. Yes, there were other people in the garage with them.

Does he remember Ramona's saying anything when they left the garage?

"No. You was just telling me to climb up—up the fence." Yes, he remembers exactly when they went outside. Yes, there were other people trying to come outside. "Um, we was trying—all trying to come out . . . Um, first we was yelling, saying we wanted to come out; and—and then Rad opened the thing up and then, uhm, we was trying—all trying to come out." Not everyone came out then. Birdie says he does not remember what happened.

There were two times that he can remember the people in the garage attempting to leave it. Does he remember anyone saying anything while they were all still inside the garage? "Um, I remember what—when Rad came downstairs and told my mom that they got some big bombs."

Birdie was asleep in the hallway upstairs before he went down into the garage. He stayed up there for a while before he went downstairs, with everybody else.

Does he remember MOVE talking about the police coming out to Osage Avenue?

"No. But we—when we had to take watch, the cops was sneaking around the alley." About "take watch"—"You know. Make sure the cops didn't try to come in." Why? "So they don't get us."

"Now when you were watching for the cops, do you remember the day before all this stuff happened that you're talking about now?" He does not. He does remember seeing the police at the barricades at the corner, on the day, he says, when they had to take watch.

"Was that a long time before the day of the bombing, or do you remember?"

"It was just yesterday from it."

"Now, were you and other children going outside, going to the Park and going to other places up to the day that you called yesterday before the bombing?" No. Ramona tries again, needing his answer to be different. "Did you go to other places, like other MOVE houses, or walk out on the street with other MOVE supporters?" Yes. "And was that up to the yesterday before the bombing?" Yes, he remembers that.

Yes, he remembers when both he and Ramona were outside the house, after the bombing. No, he did not see Ramona hit or kick or do anything to anybody.

Was there anyone else outside the house with him and Ramona?

"Yeah. When we was out there, Tree and Phil was out—Tree and Phil was out there." He did not see Tree and Phil go back onto the house.

After being told to leave the garage, "We started all going out." He remembers their trying to tell people that they were coming out. "We were screaming. . . . We were saying, 'We want to come out.' " Birdie and the other kids repeated this "a lot of times."

Were he and the others trying to protect themselves from anything? "Shooting. And they were shooting tear gas in. . . . They was shooting, and shooting tear gas in and water."

Did he think someone was trying to hurt him? Though Birdie's face has been expressionless throughout his testimony, he lifts his eyebrows. His voice, often barely audible, sounds now as strong as his questioner's, "Yeah."

He remembers other MOVE people talking about August 8, 1978, about how the police tried to kill them. And he remembers something happening with Mo. "They was questioning his car and stuff, um, and they shot him and was always stopping him and beat him up." He did not just hear about this, he says, he saw Mo.

He did see police in the neighborhood, when he was going to other houses or had been sent on MOVE activities, but does not know whether they tried to take him away before the bombing. He has been taken away from MOVE by the police before, "a real long time ago."

When he came out of the house on May 13, the first thing Birdie saw was fire. He did not see any people and did not see any police until he had made it almost all of the way down to the end of the alley. The police told him to come to them.

He has never seen MOVE people attack a policeman.

There is a short recess. One of the MOVE members walks over and stands behind one of the courtroom artists and scrutinizes her depiction of Birdie. The artist looks up at him, expecting, if not approval, some words, a gesture from the stranger, but he simply walks back to his seat.

The chance of the district attorney's office's obtaining an assault conviction from the jury has almost certainly been eliminated. McGill is armed, though, with a witness who, while leaving 6221 Osage, had no knowledge of time, and was easy prey for the effects of tear gas, smoke, explosives, fire, an empty stomach, and absolute terror. Here, too, he is easy prey for the linguistic calculations of McGill and Ramona. The prospect of Birdie's imminent interrogation by McGill is unsettling.

The presence of Birdie's lawyer David Shrager, along with the lawsuits he will be pursuing against the city for Birdie, make it certain that no professional assessment of Birdie's state of mind will be revealed to this jury.

"Hi, Michael. I'll ask you some questions now, okay?" McGill begins.

"All right, yeah."

"You said no?"

"I said yeah."

"I'm sorry. I can't hear very well." It is difficult to understand how McGill could be unaware of the effect of his phrasing.

How old is Birdie? Fourteen. Had he attended school before May 13, "the day of the fire"? No. No, he did not know how to read and write before May 13. Yes, the man beside him is his father.

"Before May thirteenth, were you ever permitted to see your father?"

Stiles asks to see McGill at sidebar.

Stiles asks McGill to substantiate the relevance of his questioning. This is his reply: "Your Honor, the time period that the defendant has questioned this individual, Michael, covered a period of years, saying for many, many years you have been with MOVE; and the different things about going to the park, selling watermelons and talking to people when you do this, making it seem like a nice little family, which it was not."

Ramona remarks that she doesn't "have to make it seem."

"And I think that I have the right to a few questions only, about three or so more, to show this jury that maybe it wasn't a nice little family."

Stiles disagrees and so sustains Ramona's objection, instructing McGill that the "MOVE lifestyle" is not the issue here.

While they go back and forth in sidebar, the frailty of the spectators' reactions is disturbing. The distress that comes with the notion of a child's forced submission into a group like this should put everyone in agreement with McGill. But many in the audience seem to be as alienated by his methods as by Ramona's, a fickleness that mimics what is condemned in the attitude of the city towards MOVE.

McGill asks which "big people" were there on "the day of the fire." Birdie names Conrad (Hampton), Nick (Frank James), Ramona, Rhonda (Ward), Theresa (Brooks), CP (Raymond Foster), Ball (John Africa, Vincent Leaphart).

Nobody was the boss, Birdie says. Yes, there were activities given out. An activity is "like when you would be working or something." Nick and Ball would give out the activities. There would be meetings, which anyone could call. There was no one who would speak more than anyone else at these meetings

There was someone whom everybody, as McGill says, "looked up to, especially." That was Ball.

Birdie says he never heard the phrase "minister of defense." He did hear the word "headquarters," which meant "down Powelton Village . . . the house that they tore down."

He did hear the word "confrontation." That meant "that the cops coming." Everyone talked about confrontation. He heard the word "coordinator," that meant Ball. He heard the word "pervert"; that meant "people that wasn't in MOVE." People who were not in MOVE were not allowed inside the house at 6221 Osage Avenue. "Bunker" means "like a wooden bunker that be on the roof."

Rad and CP and Mo built the bunker, using wood, "like beams and stuff." There were holes in the bunker, there were holes in the steel. He says he does not know what they were for. Yes, he remembers talking to a person on television at another time. Yes, he remembers that he said that the holes and the windows were shooting holes.

Shooting holes, Birdie answers, are like, "When you shoot out of them. You shoot." Yes, you could move the bunker on the roof forward, toward the edge of the roof, "so they could see when cops and stuff coming." He did not take watch in the bunker; he watched from the back yard. Ball and Nick gave him this activity.

Conrad "tore the tents and stuff down, and all; and brought some of the wood, the wood that was up there" before the confrontation.

There was another bunker in the hallway of 6221 Osage, with "tree bark all on it," and railroad wood and windows. It was smaller than the bunker on the roof, but could also be moved toward the front of the house.

In addition to the garage there was a cellar room. And there were steps going from the basement to the first floor. And there was something to put on top of the steps, "there was like a door. . . . You just slide it up into the steps." Something could be put across that kind of door, "so they can't get down the cellar." Yeah, he means the cops. Yeah, there was wood on the cellar windows, but "we didn't put the wood on the cellar window." Railroad wood was used to keep the door in the back of the garage closed. There were spikes and nails too.

Was there a room that he and the other children were not allowed to go into? "No, only a closet." What did they think was in the closet? "I don't remember." Did he and the other children ever think, or tell anyone, that they thought there were guns in the closet? "Yeah."

"Did you ever try to sneak cooked food?"

"Yeah."

"And were you disciplined for that?"

No response.

"You don't know the word?" No response.

"Did you have to go to a meeting for that?"

"Yeah."

The microphone woke him up that morning. Mona was on the microphone. He "heard her say, um, 'We got,' um, 'gas on these roofs.'" He remembers her saying something about glass breaking. He does not remember anything else she said. A "pervert" was on the police loudspeaker before Mona, "Commissioner Sambor. . . . He was telling them to come out."

Did Ramona answer that they weren't coming out and that if a cop came in, he would be killed? "Yeah." Did that scare him? No. Did he want to go out then? No.

Did he ever want to leave MOVE? Once.

Does he remember that there was a generator at his house? Yes. A water pump? Yes. The water pump was on the roof; the generator, in the garage. The water pump was there to drain the water out of the house, the water, "that the cops was putting in."

Yes, he remembers before May 13 that there was someone on the roof with a rifle. It was Nick. He does not know why Nick did this. But yes, he does remember telling someone that Nick was up there to show the cops that MOVE had guns.

Down in the basement, they covered their heads with blankets, but they didn't keep them on all the time. It was dark in the basement; none of the windows could be seen through, because of the boards. Phil was under the blanket with Birdie. He knew there was a fire. The garage door was nailed shut. There were times when he was scared.

The grownups told the children that when they got scared, they should say, "Long Live John Africa." He was still scared when he finally went outside. He believed he was going to cycle.

"And cycle means what?"

"Dead."

He was confused, scared, and dizzy while he was running down the alley. He was dizzy even before he left, while he was in the basement. He wondered where he was. He just ran anywhere to get away from the heat. He remembers fainting. He does not remember falling into water.

"Do you now know that a policeman saved your life?"

"I got up on my own, and I started running."

"And when you ran, did you fall into the water?"

"No. They grabbed me under here"—meaning under his arms—"and was dragging me."

In redirect, Birdie says that it was Ramona's voice on the speaker that woke him up that morning. It was not long after he was awake that he heard Commissioner Sambor. It was still dark outside when he woke up. He heard glass breaking on the roof while she was on the speaker.

Ramona was in the bedroom while she was on the speaker. Birdie does not remember where she was when he heard Commissioner Sambor's voice.

He does not remember Sambor saying that, in Ramona's words, "he wasn't able to arrest anybody because there was nothing done wrong, there was no crime." He does not remember anyone on the loudspeaker but Ramona.

Does he remember telling people that he hadn't seen John Africa since he was little? Yes. "Now, when you say 'John Africa,' do you—do you see John Africa as a person, or do you see John Africa as life?"

"Hum?"

"Do you see John Africa as a person, or do you see John Africa as life?"

"Life."

"And when you say 'life,' do you mean all life, like the rain and the sun, all life?"

"Hum? Um-mm. No."

"Can you tell me what you mean?"

"Um . . . um, like life."

"Like he's life?"

"Yeah."

Was the person called "Ball" better than everyone else? "Yeah. . . . I mean he, um, he knew more about MOVE and stuff."

Ramona tries to undo some of the damage done by McGill. Yes, Birdie remembers saying that he would sometimes sneak cooked food and meat. Yes, he was told at meetings that cooked food makes him weak and raw food makes him strong. Yes, he was told that MOVE people want their children to be stronger than they are. And yes, he remembers their telling the children that because they had been eating cooked food for so long that they could not stop. The reason for the children's denied access to the closet, Birdie now says, was, "That you would shut somebody's hand in it, or shut . . . or slam a kitten, or the cats in it."

Everyone is finished with Birdie. Heads turn toward the high, old windows. The snow is heavy and wet. No amount of money that his lawyer may be able to secure for him, no abundance of warm clothing and food, no eventual impression of his wellness could remove what he has, and will probably continue, to suffer at the hands of adults.

20

The Commissioner

T he shoulders are strong, and the chest is wide. The face is square
and colorless; the mouth a thin line firmly clamped into place;
the blue eyes behind the glasses utterly devoid of expression.
These are unsurprising trappings for a former police commissioner, but
they are not all that mark him. Transformed by television cameras, he
seems a bulky metaphor for machismo. Through human eyes, an odd
quality of the priestly is apparent, as well as the weary air of his nature;
as though having heard too many sordid confessions, "Father" Gregore
Sambor is prepared to hear yet another.

"Did you come out there to arrest me or to drop a bomb on me and
my family?" Ramona begins the assault.

"I came out there to make an arrest," Sambor replies, calmly, slowly,
eyes unblinking behind tinted glasses.

Her surprise attack a dismal failure, she tries again. "When you came
out there, did you come out there to arrest MOVE people, or did you
come out there to kill MOVE babies?"

The slow, even reply comes again. "I came out there to make an
arrest."

Did Commissioner Sambor know what the charges against MOVE
people that day were?

"I do not. . . . I was out there to serve legally issued warrants issued
by a judge of the Commonwealth of Pennsylvania."

Ramona then asks several questions which revolve around the length of time it took him to plan to "kill MOVE people" to which several objections are sustained. The usual kind of squabbling breaks out between McGill and Ramona, who contends that she is, "not interested in this Court. I follow the dictates of MOVE law, what's right. . . . I just want to point out on the record that Mr. McGill, or nobody else in this courtroom, is going to intimidate me at all. You know, I'm doing what I have to do. I'm fighting for my freedom. I'm—I'm putting the truth out; and if that's contrary to what the rulings of this Court is, then the rules of this Court is wrong, not me. . . . Do Court rules sanction the murder and bombing of innocent people? Is that what the Court rules dictate? . . . I abide by the rules of God."

Stiles's customary mediation restores a kind of order. An aspirin bottle now stands prominently on his desk, where, in other courtrooms, a gavel might rest.

Did frustration enter into the police state of mind on May 13?

"That did not enter into my decision to utilize the explosive device," Sambor replies.

Does he feel that he and the rest of the department were not able to handle the MOVE situation in the way he believed it should have been handled?

"There is no particular way that I felt that MOVE should be dealt with."

Ramona: "Except dropping a bomb.

"When you had that bomb dropped on 6221 Osage on innocent MOVE women, babies, men and animals, were you concerned about the children inside?"

He was. Was it that concern which provoked him into dropping a bomb on the people inside 6221?

No. His concern "was for their safety and to use the minimum amount of force that was required; and that is exactly what was recommended."

"So the minimum amount of force, as you see it, was dropping a bomb?"

The question has been asked so many times; the answer heard just as often: Sambor's reply, expressed with barely audible voice, so measured that a metronome's tick could not yield more precision. "It was using an explosive device for the purpose of placing a hole in the roof to put tear gas in there to force the evacuation of the occupants, and also to, hopefully, dislodge the fortification, now known as a bunker."

Why were the children not picked up before the confrontation was allowed to begin in earnest?

"You kept them inside."

Why couldn't he wait until the children had been removed before bombing them?

Sambor bristles. "I didn't decide to bomb you until, as *you* put it, until later on in the day."

Wasn't he concerned about the children?

"I was concerned about them. And what I am simply stating is that, according to your past track record, you would never have allowed the children out as long as there was a police presence there. You have done it in the past, where you have put up the children and used them as decoys and shields, and you did it again that day."

On what basis does he claim this?

Sambor's jaw is jutting out. "If you're asking me how you used them, in 1978 and on other occasions, any time there was an imminent police confrontation, you pulled the children inside and you used them for protection. . . . In 1978, you held them up in front of you when you came out of the house on Pearl Street."

In 1978, Ramona Johnson was a student at Temple. She was not a member of MOVE, nor was she present at the confrontation in Powelton Village. For Sambor, as well as for the MOVE organization, all MOVE members are one, whatever is to be shared of MOVE's sordid history is to be shared by all of its members.

How can Sambor say that babies represented any kind of shield for the adults?

Self-confident in this subject, a calmer Sambor responds, "I've already answered that."

Ramona continues in her usual confrontational questioning, while Sambor answers with his usual measured style, Ramona suggesting intentional killing and Sambor reiterating the intent not to harm life.

Was Sambor aware that the whole front of 6221 Osage had been blown away by an explosion on the morning of May 13? No, he was not. "I saw the front of the house that was damaged, but I did not know that it was blown off, as you put it." When did he find out that this had happened? Sometime during the late morning or early afternoon. What was he told? Just that the front of the house had been damaged, "I do not know, to this date, how it was damaged."

And he had no problem ordering that a bomb be dropped onto the roof of 6221? "We did not." Did he believe there was a possibility of fire? No, he had been told that there was no possibility of fire. Was he in-

structed to put the fire out? Yes, he was. When he was given this instruction, did he follow it? "I did not, because I was not the fire commissioner."
Was the fire extinguished? No.

What reason did you have for dropping a bomb . . . ?

"I dropped a bomb on the house," Sambor says, with strong emphasis
on the last three words, as though, with its occupants, the house was a
single, inanimate object.

When did he become aware that the bomb dropped by Powell and
constructed by Klein contained something other than Tovex?

An internal investigation was launched, and testing was conducted at
the Philadelphia Police Academy involving like amounts of Tovex exploded next to gasoline cans. After studying the videotapes made of the
tests, Sambor concluded that C-4 had indeed been added to the Tovex.

Has disciplinary action been taken against Officer Klein?

"Not to this time."

McGill rises and approaches the former commissioner with an excessive, almost condescending politeness, as if he could thus mollify the
possible damage that Sambor's manner could do to the Commonwealth.

Would Commissioner Sambor please describe the steps that were
taken on the morning of May 13 to insure that justice was properly
executed?

First, Sambor checked "via handy-talkie" with the various fire posts
to make sure that the people in 6221 could hear his announcement of the
search and arrest warrants. They could.

The announcement itself was written on what Sambor describes as a
"foolscap yellow tablet paper on which I had written a message which was
delivered by me personally to the members of the MOVE family at 6221
Osage at approximately 5:35 A.M. on thirteenth May 1985."

Would the Commissioner read that message?

This is the Police Commissioner. We have warrants for the arrest of Frank
James Africa, Ramona Johnson Africa, Theresa Brooks Africa, and Conrad
Hampton Africa for various violations of the criminal statutes of Pennsylvania.
We do not wish to harm anyone. All occupants have fifteen minutes to peaceably
evacuate the premises and surrender. This is your only notice. The fifteen min-
utes start now.

Yes, Sambor recalls the words he heard on the MOVE loudspeaker
on the morning of May 13. MOVE members inside claimed, "that they
would kill police officers, that our wives would be celebrating and spending
our insurance money that evening. . . . They stated that they would

destroy the neighborhood. They stated that they would make America sit up and take notice. . . . Therefore I had to be ready for whatever they did."

(But America only sat up and took notice when MOVE had at last provoked its enemies into doing something. Before Gregore Sambor and Wilson Goode and five hundred policemen, MOVE, to America, was nothing. Absolutely nothing.)

When did Commissioner Sambor discover that the bunker was reinforced with steel plates? When was he notified of the presence of the "log cabin" on the first floor of 6221?

Only later in the day.

Would the commissioner please describe Tovex for the Court?

Tovex was described to him, by the "experts," "as a very safe form of explosive material, which gave little or no potential for a resulting incendiary blaze, was very safe to handle."

Would the police department's plan have been any different if the bunker had not existed? "Yes, sir. There would have been no need to employ that device . . ."

Most of what follows, if not all of what follows, is a recapitulation of old, old history: Sambor's by now oft-heard version of what happened on May 13, along with McGill's detailing of August 8, 1978, enhanced by Sambor's accounting of the injuries suffered by policemen and firemen at the hands of MOVE that day. The precious little that the jurors professed to know of such a well-chronicled story seems increasingly bewildering.

The floor is given back to Ramona. Was Sambor aware that Delbert Africa was "beat almost to death when he surrendered with nothing but his hands up on August 8, 1978?"

"It was reported in the newspapers, yes."

Is it Sambor's belief that MOVE deliberately selected 6221 Osage Avenue as "a place or position for confrontation."

"I do," Sambor replies without the least pause.

Did MOVE have the power to order the police to come to Osage Avenue and "shoot at us, tear gas us, bomb us and burn us up alive?"

"We did not do any of those, nor did we come to 6221 Osage to do any of those."

Had there been no bunker, would there have been cause to drop a bomb on the roof?

With no hesitation, Sambor replies that he "would probably have deployed the device" in order to "employ the use of tear gas."

McGill's face reveals no dismay, in spite of Sambor's changed answer that before linked the existence of the bomb to the bunker.

And if the bomb had not been effective in moving the bunker, or if the bomb had never been dropped, what would the city have done?

There would have been a meeting the next morning to determine how to deliver tear gas into the house at 6221 Osage.

The jury sits impassively through the testimony, but among the press, there is the shaking of some very surprised heads, the blinking of eyes, a single word formed on the many lips: WHAT? No one has ever said anything about any conference to have been held the next day. This is a revelation. Ramona does nothing with it.

She begins instead to form questions about the use of silencers on May 13. When asked about the "license" for her line of questioning, she turns defiantly towards McGill. *"My* license, sir." In another time, under different circumstances, Ramona's defiance might have been deemed "pluck." But the diatribe that follows, spoils the effect. "Was the Holocaust legal? Were both the Holocaust and slavery upheld by legal process?"

It is the same, old, wearisome litany, the discourse that every MOVE member has been taught to recite by rote. This is the only note that Ramona Johnson Africa strikes.

The prisoner's door opens, and Alphonso Robbins Africa, known as "Mo," comes through it. Tall, skeletally thin, with scraggly beard and bones all seemingly out of joint, his attire the usual dull prison purple, his eyes skate the courtroom as he shouts, "Onamove! Long Live John Africa!" Then the grin, more nearly a leer, reveals a wide gap at the front of his teeth. The long, long, boney hands sway to and fro as he marches to the stand.

He has been "a dedicated, loyal, and committed" member of the MOVE organization for thirteen years, since about 1973. "The teachings of John Africa is opposed to violence," Mo says. "Everything John Africa teach us, teach us to stay away from violence."

Self-defense, on the other hand, "ain't judge-given. It ah—ain't police-given. . . . Self-defense is God-given. . . .

"Because, see, the system will teach you that when a cop point a gun at somebody, it's in defense of the police. But when the people point guns at the police, it's in defense of nothing. . . .

"Right now, what happened to MOVE is—all MOVE has ever done is defend ourselves."

As an instance of the latter, Mo is asked by Ramona to impart what happened to him in the summer of 1983 and fall of 1984.

"You know, and the interesting thing about this, too, is that the police claim they had a hands-off policy on MOVE people. Yet, I was beat three times, brutally, by police."

On the night of June 5 or 6, 1984—he can't remember which—at approximately 10 P.M., Mo Africa drove away from the house at 6221 Osage in his white tow truck. He was bound for the MOVE house in Chester.

According to his recounting, he was stopped at Sixty-second and Essington Avenue in Southwest Philadelphia. His tow truck, converged upon by as many as ten police cars, was pulled over. Their guns already drawn, "using all kind of foul language," the cops hollered, " 'Get the fuck out of the truck!' " This was all "set up" by Officer George Draper.

Mo Africa testifies that he was pulled out of his truck, blackjacked, and cursed repeatedly. "They called me all kinds of racial names. Nigger this, nigger that, and so forth." He quotes the police as saying, "The next time we see your ass, you ain't gonna be in the MOVE organization because you're gonna be too scared to go back to MOVE.' " Mo says that the cops hurled the food sacks he was transporting into the middle of the road. Then, they dragged him down the highway and into a police van where they began "whacking me on the top of the head with this black-jack."

In the early afternoon of Saturday, June 10, 1984, Mo and the white tow truck containing MOVE children were headed toward Chester, when, at Sixty-third and Osage Avenue, he stopped to let a car pass. A police vehicle suddenly rushed in front of the tow truck and slammed on the brakes. "I jumps out of my car, and the first thing I think of is, you know, here's the cops again. . . . I say, 'Well, here goes another, you know, one of those things.' "

"The cop rushes over to me, drawing his gun on me . . . And I told him, I said . . . 'You gonna shoot me, you better be prepared to put all six of them bullets in me, because if one of them bullets hit me and it don't take my breath, I'm going to fight you to the last—to the last drop of breath in my body. . . .

"Then he started—he tried, with his Mace, he tried to spray his Mace in my face, and I ducked. And at the same time, because the tire iron was right in the door [of the white tow truck] and handy to grab, just immediately when he started making his move towards me, I grabbed the tire iron and hit him over his head. And when I had—when I hit him over his head, what he did was it knocked—as he was coming up with his gun, when I hit him in the head, it knocked his aim off me, because he had his gun levelling at me, at about the level—at my chest." Mo received a slight, surface wound from the stray bullet.

Police backup units arrived, the confrontation now wholly one-sided: "They just started raining blackjacks off my head. They beat me so bad that I wasn't able to walk for six months. They broke my ankle. They busted my hand. They busted me in the temple. My eyes was all swollen up. My face was swollen up too."

The saga of Mo Africa continues in the usual vein: Courtroom appearances, police beatings, God-appointed self-defense as the only recourse. On May 7, 1985, Alphonso Robbins Africa was finally sent away to prison.

He continues to speak after Ramona has finished questioning him. "All MOVE is doing is what's natural. We're doing the same thing that —that anything else natural will do. Like a snake. When you a snake— when you running across a snake in a field, if you get close to a rattlesnake in the field, the snake hear you coming, it's gonna rattle a warning to you."

There is more of the same. The lion's roar, the upfront first line of defense. Now a new analogy: Defense Secretary Caspar Weinberger and the Libyans: "When—when Libya—when the Secretary of Defense feels like he's threatened by Libya, he's going to issue a threat. . . ."

Mo Africa talks animatedly, breathlessly, analogy following analogy, the whole connected: *Anda-anda-anda-anda-anda.*

McGill finally gets a word in. What does Mr. Africa mean by swearing to the principles of John Africa?

"What I mean is that I will not hallucinate, speculate or fantasize about my belief; and neither will I allow you to do so. . . ."

Is he aware that he has on occasion been in violation of various of the Commonwealth's laws?

Mo answers, "You higher courts have validated the shipping of black slaves to prison."

So Mr. Africa objects to the entire legal system? Emphatically, Mo Africa replies, "EXACTLY!" What he is talking about, Mo says is, "God's law." And God's law is MOVE's law.

What about M-1, the so-called MOVE Underground?

"Yes, M-1 exists." John Africa himself went underground from 1984 on, and M-1 was formed a long time before that time. "The above-ground chapter don't have no contact with the underground," so Mo knows nothing of the specifics of the M-1's actual organization.

But he does know that, "M-1 is to MOVE as the sheriff is to the city."

Has Mr. Africa ever seen MOVE people armed?

"I never seen any MOVE people with weapons."

Ramona is on her feet, denouncing McGill as an "actor" and object-ing to his line of questioning. What does M-1 have to do with anything?

Stiles chews on his pen, his cheeks reddening with anticipation.

Ramona goes on and on, "And right now, you know, they have that White House fortified. Are you calling the White House criminals?"

The court adjourns as the words of Alphonso Robbins Africa echo through the room: "Anybody who thinks he has the right to do wrong is confused about the principle they're trying to distort."

21

Uncivil Affairs

Day Twelve: Wednesday, January 29, 1986

Draper again. Brown suit, purple tie, cream-colored shirt. He is Ramona's witness this time. He tells her that he has been familiar with MOVE since the early nineteen seventies. Yes, he has arrested MOVE people since that time, usually during demonstrations. Yes, he remembers that some of those demonstrations were at the zoo and some at a pet store called Puppy Palace.

As those demonstrations escalated and the arrests became more frequent, weren't MOVE people also beaten when arrested? "They sustained injuries," Draper replies, slowly, matter-of-factly.

Does Draper agree that May 20, 1977, the "Guns on the Porch Day," was a "crystalization" of the confrontation? "It's a possibility." What were the issues as far as MOVE was concerned? He can't remember.

Officer Draper was regularly assigned to Sixty-second and Osage between May 1984 and May 1985? Right. Did he receive complaints from Osage residents about the residents of 6221 Osage during that time? Yes. Could he resolve those complaints? "Maybe one or two of them. But the majority of them had to do with the people at 6221."

Did Draper take any action concerning the issues which he was unable to resolve? "No, I did not."

Does he remember what happened on June 5, 1984? Yes, Alphonso Robbins Africa was arrested. "I believe he was stopped at Sixty-first and Essington. Mo Robins would not identify himself. He had no driver's license. He had no ownership papers. He had no insurance. He was taken into the Twelfth District for investigation." Was Mo Africa beaten? "No."

Was Draper aware of any hands-off policy with regard to the MOVE organization? Not at that time. What about later? No, he was not aware of such a policy.

Did Draper ever hear threats over the MOVE loudspeaker? Yes. Could he recognize MOVE people's voices on that loudspeaker? Yes. Did he arrest anyone for making terroristic threats? No. Why? "Because later . . . they were at 6221, inside the house." Stiles is drumming his fingers over a plastic clipboard.

"Most of these threats came over the loudspeaker. They were duly noted, made into a report, and turned in." Taking advantage of the casualness of Draper's reply, Ramona sounds off. Her "freedom is at stake," and she wants Draper to "talk straight." McGill objects, arguing that Ramona's speech is "typical" of "them." The predictable murmuring from MOVE's chorus rises, then dies.

Is it department policy for an officer to write a report when he sees a crime being committed? "My understanding, if you see a crime being committed in your presence, a physical crime, you make an arrest. What she's talking about, and what I'm saying is that the threats came over the loudspeaker. It was duly noted. A report was made up and turned in . . . I was told to make a report every time the loudspeaker went on, tape it, and turn it in to headquarters."

Yes, he was told not to arrest MOVE members. Yes, in early 1984, he saw Ramona and Conrad in Cobbs Creek Park. No, he didn't arrest them. Why? Because they weren't making threats. Why didn't he arrest MOVE people, whose voices he has said he recognized, after they made their speeches on the loudspeaker? "Because they were inside the house."

Is Draper aware that they would sometimes walk to the phone at Sixty-second and Pine to make telephone calls? Yes, he saw Ramona and Theresa using that phone. Why didn't he arrest them then? "Because at the time, the threats were being investigated by other persons, and there was no talk of an arrest made at that time."

No, to his knowledge, despite the tapes and his reports, no one endeavored to arrest MOVE members.

Draper testifies that he was told to take the MOVE children into custody on either the eleventh or twelfth of May. Does he remember seeing them after that? Yes, on May twelfth he saw some of the children on the porch of 6221 Osage. Yes, he saw those children in a blue Chevy driven by Gloria Cheeks on that morning. Why didn't he take them into custody? "Because I didn't believe that they were the same ones that were at 6221." He only saw the tops of their heads, he says. What caused him to believe these weren't the children who lived in 6221? Well, the car was just coming into the area, and, "I didn't know." No, he didn't make any attempt to find out.

Well, didn't he see it as important to take these children into custody? "These particular MOVE children, it was my belief that they were not to be taken."

"If you didn't know if these were the MOVE children that you were supposed to take into custody, why didn't you find out?" Ramona continues to needle.

Draper's reply is slow and exasperated. "The reason being is that it were a number of MOVE people that was around. I didn't want to start a confrontation at that time. There was no reason for me to start an incident. There were a number of teenagers and other children that were on the corner when this particular car came by. There was no need for me to start an incident at that time."

"Would you rather see these children killed in a house?

"Would you rather see these kids burned up alive?" Objections are sustained to both questions.

"Isn't it true that you didn't make any attempt to find out if these were the MOVE children because you didn't care? Don't wait for no objection." No, Draper says, that isn't true.

How did Draper plan to pick up the children if he couldn't recognize them? "I recognized some of the children . . . It would be obvious that if you didn't recognize them, you weren't familiar with them, so you wouldn't bother." Did he try to find out if there were police pictures of them or any other kind of identification? "The children that I recognized that were—that was in 6221 are the same ones who I seen on different occasions leaving or entering that particular house. Now I know of no pictures that were taken of them at that time . . . I keep stating to you, I was familiar with them." Yes, he also told her there were some he was not familiar with.

Who told him about picking up the children? Lieutenant Connelly. Did Draper explain to Connelly that he was not familiar with all of the MOVE children? No. Why? "Because as I stated before, I was familiar with a number of the children . . . There was no need . . . Because I wasn't asked that question."

Does Draper have any personal grudges against the MOVE organization? "None whatsoever."

"You don't have any problem with MOVE people exposing the fact that your son is accused of setting a man on fire and murdering him?

. . . It doesn't cause you to have a grudge against MOVE people by constantly putting out about your son, constantly telling people about your son?" The point is no doubt lost on the jurors. But with another young man, Draper's son stands accused of burning a man to death. The younger Draper will soon turn Commonwealth's evidence and his partner will be sentenced to death. George Draper blanches.

Does Draper remember riding by MOVE women, sitting on the porch with their children, and cocking his finger like a gun at them?

MOVE's chorus is at it again: "Liar. You lyin motherfucker. With a murderer for a son. Where you think he get it from?"

Ramona returns to her seat, and McGill begins.

Is it not true that in the case of an indirect threat, a police officer must obtain a warrant from a judge, via the District Attorney's office? Yes, that is correct, Draper replies. And is it not true, "that when you saw Conrad Africa in the park and Ramona Africa on the telephone, that neither one of them threatened you?" Yes, this is true.

And was Officer Draper present at the site of the so-called "Guns on the Porch Day," on May 20, 1977? He was not, but he was aware that MOVE's weapons were much in evidence then.

McGill tries to introduce as Commonwealth's evidence some pictures of the MOVE members on that porch that day. Ramona protests, and Stiles sustains her objection.

Whose voice did Draper hear on the MOVE loudspeaker on the morning of May 13, 1985 from 1:15 to 1:35 A.M.? Ramona Africa's. He was on duty that day from noon until midnight, but had to wait until 2:00 A.M. on May 13 for someone to relieve him. He was there to transcribe what was heard on the loudspeaker, and he did so.

Thank you Officer Draper. And now would you tell us about the June 5 arrest of Alphonso Africa? "We thought he was acting suspicious at the house, and that it was—it was dark. He gave an indication to me at that time that he was trying to hide something, whatever . . . in the boxes." Did Draper at any time strike Alphonso Africa? No. Did he see anyone strike Alphonso Africa? No.

McGill smiles wanly and announces that he is done with the witness. Thank you, Officer Draper.

Ramona returns, asks a few more cursory questions. Then she too is finished.

The foot-soldier is dismissed from the stand.

Day Thirteen: Thursday, January 30, 1986

Theodore Vaughan, a police officer in the Civil Affairs Unit, takes the stand. He is so tall that the tops of his knees can be seen from behind the witness stand. The hard blackness of his skin is enhanced by gold-rimmed glasses. His hair is short, well kept atop a very large head. Everything about him speaks of meticulousness. Despite his size, he seems more like someone's grandfather than someone who carries a gun.

He has been familiar with the MOVE organization since before the confrontation in 1978, and was involved in the arrest of MOVE women in Virginia that year. He too was present at the August 8, 1978 confrontation.

Between May of 1984 and May of 1985, he was often assigned to monitor MOVE activities at 6221 Osage Avenue as well as other MOVE residences. He could identify many of the people living at 6221 Osage, but could not "really" identify the children living there, "because I didn't see them all the time . . . There were few children that I could see all the time."

He was not given orders to remove the children between May 1984 and May 1985. But in "that time" of 1985, "it was mentioned, not by supervisor, but by word of mouth, if you see any of the children, pick them up . . . I was to stop the children and notify who would then say where the children would be placed, or what would be done with them." He received that information "close to May thirteenth."

Vaughan did not see any of the children after receiving those instructions. Yes, he saw the issue as important. Did he believe the lives of the children were at stake? "I took those instructions as orders given to me by a supervisory person. For what reason, they had their reasons; and I just followed the orders that were given to me . . . Anything that's told to me by my commanding officer, I consider it important."

He did not inform his supervisors that he was unable to identify all of the children, "because there were other personnel on the scene that could identify all the children." These men were "other persons in the Civil Affairs Unit that were stationed at that time at the barricades, which I wasn't; and I—I really don't remember the names of the people, but I know they were there at the barricades."

Yes, he was in the area on May 13, and yes, to his knowledge, none of the children were taken into custody.

Vaughan knew that Frank James should be taken into custody for parole violation, and in the late summer of 1984, he saw a bench warrant with Ramona's name on it. No one instructed him to take her into custody.

Having been aware of the necessity of arresting Frank James and Ramona since August of 1984, Vaughan was nonetheless unable to do so because the MOVE members whom he saw after that time were, "Just one or two. I saw Janet, Mike. That was part of the group. Raymond Foster. I saw Theresa Brooks."

The policy from May of 1984 and May of 1985 concerning the arrest of the MOVE members who resided at 6221 was, according to Officer Vaughan, "If there was a crime being committed by a MOVE person in my presence, I would put them under arrest. Other than that, anything else that was not a felony would be considered—to take the information down and turn it over to the DA's office to find out if criminal charges would be placed." He would file a report, and turn it into his commanding officer, Captain Shanahan.

Did he witness any criminal activity? "Criminal activity as far as what I previously stated, no. Misdemeanor, harrassment or something like that, would come under a city violation that would have to be interpreted by the DA's office. Those are what I turned in . . . I said felony charges in front of a police officer, you would be arrested. Other complaints that would come under that statute of a misdemeanor, or whatever, would be turned in and determined by the DA's office as to what action should be taken."

So he would not arrest a MOVE member if he saw one committing a misdemeanor? "Not if it came under the Code, where I would have to be told what Criminal Code it came under so that I would be aware of it. I don't know every misdemeanor crime that's committed."

"So if you saw a MOVE person committing a crime, then you would have to find out, I guess through some person that would know, if that crime fell into a certain category before you could make an arrest?"

"If it was not a felony. If I didn't see the store—holding it up, shooting somebody on the street or whatever, a felony and a misdemeanor, if I'm not familiar with it, then I would call in and get information."

He does remember submitting a report in May of 1984 which stated that MOVE was "going to put a bullet in Wilson Goode's head." Yes, he considered it a threat, a threat to the mayor.

Why didn't he make an arrest? "It was a threat to the mayor, and that would be getting information as far as from the DA's office to what charges would be placed on threatening a person in political office."

In any case, Vaughan is uncertain as to who made the threat. Had

Ramona personally "threatened me, then I would have arrested her for threatening me."

He did not receive any "feedback" from his superiors on that report.

Did he think police action might be taken against MOVE after he had received the orders to pick up the children? "If I thought there was going to be action taken? Possibly yes; possibly no. I don't know. It never entered my mind one way or the other."

Was Ramona, to Vaughan's personal knowledge, involved in the events of April 29? "I really don't remember. I don't recall."

Yes, he was instrumental in the drawing of the warrant issued for Ramona for the events of April 29. "The warrants were compiled with information from April 29th, which I was not present or that I saw and that I read as to what took place on that date. Then there were other complaints from the neighborhood which, in some cases, involved residents of 6221. Somewhere in that scope of getting the information together, your name appeared in there. Now I don't recall right offhand whether it was April 29th or May 5th, but your name was in with the group, and that's why a warrant was issued."

The warrants were signed May 11. Vaughan says it was the day after this that he received the order to detain the children. He was in the area on May 12, he was looking out for the children, he did not see them. How did he expect to be able to carry out this order if he could not identify the children? "I said I did not recognize all of them; and if I saw two that I didn't know, or if I saw children that I felt as though were MOVE children, then I would detain them until such time as they were identified. If they weren't MOVE children, just people in the neighborhood that looked like MOVE, they would have continued on their way. If not, then I would have followed my instructions as to what to do with the MOVE children." He did not check to see if there was any police information which would enable him to identify the children.

His assignment on May 13 was to make certain that all of the residents in the surrounding area were removed from their homes. Yes, he saw this assignment as important. He did not explain to them why they were being asked to leave; no one asked him why. Yes, he was aware of the warrants for certain MOVE people while he was evacuating the neighbors; to him this meant that "possibly" some police action would be taken.

He did not make it known to his superiors that he had not taken any of the children into custody and he did not ask if anyone else had. The thought never came into his mind.

22

Saturn's Rings

Day Thirteen: Thursday, January 30, 1986

Through the prisoner's door, its ugly little window wired and cloudy with dust, Janine Phillips Africa steps into the courtroom. Her body is taut and lean save for the stretch of hips. A man's jacket and pants contain her in a kind of blue that is so deadened it is hardly a color. Her nostrils are flared, lips protuberant; it is difficult to tell whether these are anatomical features or the results of something within. Her eyes are black and round. Anger defines her, surrounds her like Saturn's rings. She is the person you instinctively step aside for on city streets, her world something other than what you might know or want to know.

The MOVE people greet her hungrily. "Long Live John Africa!" they shout. "Onamove, Janine!" "Onamove, ya'll!" she replies. The cries fly back and forth from the witness and her devotees. MOVE women exchange admiring remarks with one another: *"Don't* she look good!" "Yeah, she got *good* color." A MOVE woman cups her hands and hollers, "You look'n GOOD, Janine!" The witness grins.

She will tell the truth as John Africa teaches all MOVE people. The questioning starts.

Can she define for the jury the difference between a MOVE member and a MOVE supporter? A MOVE member is committed to John Africa. A MOVE supporter is working to become as committed as MOVE members. Janine has been a MOVE member for over ten years.

She had never been arrested before joining the MOVE organization.

Does she remember "a crystalized confrontation" between MOVE and the city in 1977? "By 'crystalized' I mean something that was identified as a confrontation, as opposed to an ongoing confrontation," Ramona explains.

Janine says that MOVE members had a peaceful demonstration in front of their Powelton Village home in reaction to persecution from police officers and City officials. What does she mean by "persecution"? "What I'm referring to," Janine answers, "is the beatings and the unjust jailings of MOVE members stemming from as early as '72, '73, and on up to the miscarriages that MOVE women have suffered from being beaten while in the custody of police, and on up to March twenty-eighth, '76, when my baby—three-week old baby was killed by police in front of our house, and Rhonda Africa's baby that was killed after being beat up here in City Hall holding cell by sheriffs. . . .

"Up until '76, when the babies were killed, we were contacting officials, judges, appealing court cases, filing for investigations, trying to go through all of the legal channels to deal with this persecution . . . that the police were doing to MOVE members, but nothing was done about it. . . .

"The last straw was when our babies was killed. And that's when MOVE people stopped talking and said we had to bring attention to this persecution, because nobody else would do it."

This, she contends, was why MOVE had taken "such a drastic, such a strong confrontation stand" on May 20, 1977.

Ramona asks for the photographs of May 20, 1977, the photographs she would not allow McGill to introduce as Commonwealth evidence. Photographs which could do more damage to her case than anything we can imagine. Photographs which will add a whole new dimension to MOVE's incantations of "truth" and "fact."

McGill's cheeks puff in and out, and his eyes circle the ceiling. He twirls his moustache, obviously gloating. What luck.

Ramona shows Janine the first photograph and asks her to describe it.

"The picture is supposed to be depicting MOVE people taking a stand on May twentieth '77. In the background is what resembles our house, and that's my sister, and she has a deterrent in her hand. This is a deterrent that we used on May twentieth '77."

(So this is supposed to be the "resemblance" of something, not the thing itself. A resemblance of a house, not the house. But that is her sister, why is this not a "resemblance" of her sister? Or why isn't the deterrent a sawed-off shotgun?)

Stiles asks her what it is that the sister has in her hands.

"A deterrent."

"Deterrent?" He repeats, his eyebrows stretched, his voice expressive of absolute dismay.

"Yes."

Ramona continues. "Now, when you say—when you label that a deterrent—I *know* MOVE people don't play word games—can you explain to me what you mean?"

Janine answers. "I and all MOVE people call these—what you say is a gun, as deterrents, because they were inoperable; and the only reason why we had these that could be seen was because the police believe in guns, okay? And for years, we had been being beaten bloody and our babies killed, and we were, as you say, unarmed. We didn't have anything that you would call a gun or a stick, or any type of what you would label as weapons to defend ourselves. And we were beaten for it.

"When we took that stand on May twentieth, we brought out these inoperable guns; and I say 'deterrents,' because it was inoperable. It's not a gun. But we brought it out so that the police would see that. And when they saw that, they did not know they were inoperable. All they saw was us having—having a gun, and they having a gun. When they saw the situation as balanced, as they see it, they were not quick to come up on the platform as they have done repeatedly in the past. And the deterrent were used just for that reason, to have those cops not come in that house and attack MOVE people and beat MOVE people like they did in the past. And that's why I call it a deterrent, because it was inoperable. It was not a gun."

Another photograph is handed to the witness. "That's the same area of Powelton Avenue where our house used to be, and it's the same confrontation in '77; and there's MOVE men and women up on the platform, and it looks like—all right, that's a plainclothes policeman right here . . . directly in front of the platform; and the platform and the fence was right in front of the house, like where most people would have a yard. The platform was over the yard area of our house."

Was it common for plainclothed policemen to stand so near the platform? "The police would come that close and closer. There has been times where they would stand up on this ledge. And there's a tree stump there that used to be in front of our house. They would stand on there, and they would talk to MOVE members for hours, a lot of times, discussing why we was taking that stand; and a lot of them just talking to hear

MOVE law, the teaching of John Africa, because they had been out there —these police that were surrounding our house, some of them had been around MOVE people ever since the above-ground chapter of MOVE surfaced in Philadelphia, and they were familiar with MOVE people. And a lot of them would come and talk to MOVE people, because a lot of them had witnessed the beatings, you know, and they knew what was really happening. They knew that MOVE people had been beat by the police and sheriffs. . . .

"I saw a lot of policemen out there that day that I had witnessed at different beatings and stuff, that would come and talk to us, all right? And I knew them from seeing them at different demonstrations, or whatever. And they would talk to us about the confrontation and about MOVE."

Was anyone shot or hurt by MOVE people on May 20?

"No one was shot. No one was assaulted, or anything like that. MOVE members never came into contact with anybody physically. . . . Our position was that, you know, we were tired of being beat. We were tired of being unjustly jailed, and we were tired of the murders of our babies being ignored, and that we wanted somebody to do something about it because we were not going to tolerate it any more. And we was tired of having our families evicted because they were MOVE members, because at that time, they there were still MOVE members who did not live at our headquarters at Powelton Avenue, and they were just being evicted because they were MOVE members. And we were protesting all of that.

"And we was protesting [that] our brothers and our sisters was unjustly jailed and given time in jail because they were MOVE members, and we was demanding their release."

Did the May 20 demonstration end peacefully?

"Yeah," Janine says, nodding her head. MOVE handed over all its deterrents to the police, and its people were released from jail. "The city had made an agreement to end the situation. . . .

"There was a whole process done. . . . Before we came off the platform, the police came in the house. We allowed them to come in to search all through the house. And before they came in to search, they had two police standing in front of the house while the blockades were still up, and the deterrents was handed down to them by MOVE members; and as each one was handed down to them, it was looked over, checked and labelled, tagged and stated the condition of the deterrent. And this was all done in May, early May."

What does she mean by the "condition of the deterrents"?

"The police looked at . . . what they say they thought was a gun, to see what type it was, and whether it was operable. And when they looked at it, they labelled what they called it, and then they would say if it was operable or not. And every one they would say was inoperable, and they would say why it was inoperable."

Could Janine explain the "process" which ended with an agreement between MOVE and the City of Philadelphia?

"Yeah," Janine says emphatically. City officials made "a lot of promises." They agreed, for example, "to stop persecuting us" and to let MOVE's imprisoned people go free on their own recognizance.

MOVE members, in turn, agreed to have attorney Oscar Gaskins represent their interests in court. "The city did not want MOVE members to come in court again, *ever.*"

MOVE members had never objected to appearing in court. "As a matter of fact, that was MOVE's position," Janine explains. "And it was our activity to go into the courtroom and put out the truth about this system, put out the teaching of John Africa . . ."

Did MOVE's position about going to court ever change?

Yes, but "only because after years of giving this system the opportunity to do what was right and after going into courtrooms and being beat, being beat right in front of the judges while in the courtroom, we stopped going to the courtroom because, you know, it was like walking into the lion's den. You know, nobody would expect the Christians to walk into the lion's den or the Jews to walk into the gas ovens for Hitler. . . .

"One of our brothers was beat so bad his eyes was almost knocked out, you know; and Rhonda was beat up by the sheriffs, and she was pregnant and her baby was born and died a few hours after being born. And. . . ." It goes on and on.

What was MOVE's position about coming to court in August of 1978? "August first, the city came and said that we had to appear in Court for a civil action against MOVE and we refused to go. . . . They [the city] started backing off and they started trying to demand of us things that was not in that agreement. Like they stated that we had to kill all of the animals in our house, which was not part of the agreement. And anybody knows that MOVE, because of John Africa, they know we love all of life and how we loved those animals . . . and they tried to tell us we had to kill all those animals. They told us that the people who came home from prison, who were released from prison, could not come into their own house. In that situation, Sue Africa, whose child was in the house, couldn't even come and get her baby because the police told her if she came into the house she was going to be arrested. This was not part of the agreement . . . All of these things here was being done. And this is why . . . we refused to go, because we knew the intention that they had if we were going in that courtroom, we was not coming back out . . ."

Did the city, as a result, take action against MOVE?

"On August eighth, the city attacked MOVE's house for warrants they said coming from . . . a civil case, all right? . . . It was some civil action happening back in '75, '76 . . . and it had nothing to do with the charges that the city put on me during that May confrontation, all right?. . . . And when they came out, they just moved on the house. They just attacked the house, saying for these warrants, you know. They knocked the house down, fence down, knocked on the windows, poured in thousands of gallons of water, tear gas, shot at us; all they say, for serving those warrants on a civil matter. . . ."

Has it been MOVE's position to kill any policeman who attempted to arrest them? "No, MOVE's position was a position of defense. It was made very clear from the day of May twentieth, '77, when we took that stand, it was made very clear that, you know, the deterrents that we had was only to protect ourselves. As long as those police did not attack us, then it would be no physical confrontation, all right? We made it clear that if they came at us with their hands, we would come back at them with our hands. If they came at us with sticks, we would defend ourselves with sticks. If they came at us with guns, we would defend ourselves with guns. The position was made very clear that MOVE was not out there to kill cops. . . ."

There are more, too many more, of the usual questions and answers concerning MOVE's feelings about policemen. Listening is hardly necessary. There is no such thing as the personal response of a MOVE member. There are, instead, only endless recitations of the same rehearsed lines.

Janine is talking up the results of the August eighth confrontation. "I was convicted of third-degree murder, and given thirty to a hundred years in prison for the shooting of this cop they say was killed. . . .

"You know, I was given thirty to a hundred years in prison for shooting one cop, and I was not given any weapons charges and I wasn't given conspiracy. . . . And, you know, how can you shoot someone without weapons charges? And they're saying weapons was on the scene, okay? And this cops was shot . . . from the back, and the bullet traveled down; when I was in the house, in the basement."

Ramona again travels the, by now, all too familiar path: the history of the MOVE Nine, of the organization's work on behalf of the imprisoned brothers and sisters, of the innocence of those same members.

"Does the teaching of John Africa speak to defense, self-defense, as well as what violence is?" Ramona asks.

"John Africa has pointed out to me about violence and self-defense, and how violence is wrong and that self-defense is a God-given right; and that everybody has the right to self-defense, but nobody has the right to violence." There is nothing hesitant about Janine's answer. It is obviously rehearsed.

After a short recess, it becomes McGill's turn. He begins at once to needle her. "Ms. Africa, if there's any time that you cannot hear me, please stop me and ask me to repeat. *Okay?*" She does not respond.

The witness was convicted of third-degree murder, as well as seven counts of aggravated assault, and conspiracy. Was she not? "That's right."

The charges were based on the death of one policeman, the injury of three others, and the injury of four firemen. Isn't that so? "That's what the charge was for."

On August 8, 1978, Ms. Africa was in the basement when she was arrested. Correct? "That's right." And prior to that date, she had willingly handed over several weapons. Is that so? "We turned over several deterrents before August 8." After all the killing and injury was done on that day, eleven operable weapons and two thousand rounds of ammunition were found in the basement of MOVE Headquarters. Isn't that so? "I wouldn't know. That's what they say was recovered. I never saw those things while I was in the house." That's right, she repeats, she lived in that house every day from May 1977 until August 8, 1978, and she never saw so much as one of those weapons.

Didn't she then wonder where the weapons so prominently displayed on the platform in front of MOVE Headquarters on May 20, 1977 disappeared to? "I had no reason to question what happened to any deterrents. As far as I'm concerned, all deterrents was handed over to the police in May of '77."

Yes, she follows the teachings of John Africa, including his vision of self-defense. Nonetheless, she had no weapons with which to defend herself from May 1977 to August 1978, "because as far as the city was concerned, I had no reason for self-defense because they claimed that they were not going to persecute the MOVE organization any longer. . . . Let me explain it to you this way: that MOVE people were not under any false illusions [as to] the honesty of this system. We experienced the dishonesty of this city's system, okay? The reason why MOVE people made that agreement with the City of Philadelphia was not because we believed them, but so that people would get a crystallized example when they wrote that agreement and attacked MOVE people; and that's what we had to let everybody see, because everybody thought that MOVE started that confrontation and that MOVE did not want no peaceful resolution to the confrontation. . . .

"What I'm trying to tell you is that after turning over the deterrents in May, those deterrents were no longer part of the strategy for the May '77 confrontation."

Well, then, what would MOVE members use in their God-given right to self-defense?

"I'm going to tell you something right now. You're telling me to hallucinate. John Africa teaches me not to hallucinate, right? You go on about 'what if, what if.' We don't deal with that, all right? . . . You're asking me to hallucinate, and I'm not going to do that."

No, says McGill, he doesn't want Ms. Africa to hallucinate, he simply wants her to answer his questions. And isn't it true that, according to John Africa's teachings, "Nonviolence really means nonviolence to MOVE members and not to non-MOVE members, because they are not to be considered since they are outside of the proper lifestyle?"

"No, John Africa did not teach that. Matter of fact, the fight that John Africa is doing is for all life. The fight that we're making against this system is the fight so that you can have clean air to breathe, clean water to drink, and fertile soil for your food to be strong so you be healthy. Because when MOVE fights against the oppression and injustice of the system, you benefit just as much as me. You have to be, just as me.

"The industry that's poisoning your air is poisoning mine. You benefit from that, all right? And when you talk about nonviolence, okay, and violence, the whole point and the whole purpose of the MOVE organization is to stop the violence of this system."

If John Africa's law were to conflict with the law of the Commonwealth, then Ms. Africa would follow John Africa's law?

"I follow God's law. And your law, as you call it, does conflict with John Africa's teaching because your laws is the industry that poison the air. Your laws are the makers of jails. And John Africa's teaching, the law of God, is for pure air, as God intended, and freedom for all subjects, as God intended. So you see, you do conflict with us, and that is the whole point of the above-ground confrontation units of MOVE. That was our whole thing from the very beginning, to confront the system, because it has been conflicting with John Africa's teaching ever since the inception of this reformed world's system. . . .

"Your laws had me taking drugs. John Africa's law took me off drugs. Your laws make guns, all right? And they blow people away and kill people, makes wars, and John Africa's fight [is] to stop that. So you see, I am, I am trying the best as I can not to follow your training, as you call it, your law, because your training messed me up all my life, which is why I came to MOVE, all right?"

McGill hammers away. "Ms. Africa, if one of the things that society does, which is wrong, is to create guns and use them, why would you use them in what you call self-defense?"

"All right. Let me explain something to you right now. If a person has a whip they use to whip somebody, that is a weapon. But if a person is drowning and another person comes along, who don't believe in murder and killing, takes that whip and throw it out to the drowning person, are you telling me that the whip is a weapon—or is it being used to save life? . . . I would agree to anything to defend myself."

Is it all right to kill in exercising God-given self-defense?

"You are twisting things up. First of all, killing is a waste of life. It has no purpose, and it causes destruction."

Well, then, why did Ms. Africa become involved with weapons and ammunition and kill an unarmed policeman? Was *that* self-defense?

The usual arguments for MOVE's innocence in the death of Officer Ramp, their lack of arms on August eighth, the police department's murderous intentions, all ensue. The Jews and Hitler, the Christians and the Romans, the same old analogies are each in turn invoked in MOVE's defense.

McGill continues to hammer away. What about strategies for use in the courtroom? Aren't John Africa's followers taught specifically how to respond in court?

"No. What is happening with MOVE people is we are taught to tell the truth, all right? And in a situation with MOVE, the MOVE organization is very misunderstood. A lot of people do not understand what MOVE stands for, and why we do what we do. And when we come in court, because people have been trained by your system to believe that whatever you do is right and anybody else that don't go along with what you do is wrong, MOVE has to explain thoroughly why we do things so people will understand it. . . .

"We don't make speeches. We put out information. We put out the truth. If you want to call the truth a speech, then that's on you. But the truth is just that. The truth is fact."

After more of the truth, the jury hears more about the evils of the system, more about "inoperable deterrents," more about innocence and about dead babies and brutal cops.

McGill asks Janine about the alleged death of her own child at the hands of Philadelphia police on March 28, 1976. Did she speak to the District Attorney about it?

"We tried to get all kinds of charges pressed against the police. We filed for federal investigation and filed a suit in Federal Court about investigating that situation and getting those cops who was involved in that, responsible, arrested and put in jail for what they did, but nothing was done about it."

Did Ms. Africa cooperate with the Medical Examiner when he volunteered his help? "No Medical Examiner came out to talk to me." If McGill were to tell her that the Medical Examiner, who at the time was Marvin Aaronson, has said that MOVE members refused to cooperate with him, refused even to let him see the child, what would she say?

"That embalming and dissecting and doing those probes on a person's body is against our belief. We would never put our children or any MOVE members in the hands of somebody to violate their body like that, all right? And second of all, the baby—the body of the baby was viewed by several officials in the City—Lucien Blackwell, Councilman Coleman. News media and preachers, reverends, all viewed the body of my child— all right?—after the cops said that I wasn't even pregnant and never had a baby."

Ramona, too long out of the limelight, now erupts: "The city ain't never tried to investigate no brutality heaped on MOVE people. Over six MOVE babies been killed. MOVE women—my sister Alberta Africa ain't no bigger than me, and she was held down on the floor at Eighth and Race [the Police Administration Building] and kicked in her vagina until she miscarried. This man gonna sit up here and talk about MOVE not allowing the police to investigate? The police was right there, and they did nothing. Did we stop the police from investigating that, when they was the ones that kicked the baby out of Alberta Africa's stomach? Are you investigating the deaths of MOVE babies on May thirteenth?" The old argument goes on and on, with Janine putting in a word or two from time to time.

When it nears five o'clock, Janine announces that she has to go to the bathroom. After the passage of some ten minutes, Stiles calls an end to this day of court.

Through the darkened windows there are glimmerings of light, reds and greens, tungsten hard; flourescent and vapor-lit street lamps; the winking of traffic signals; the streaking glares of car lights. But darkness carpets the night sky and defines the hour, becomes metaphor for this day, this trial.

Day Fourteen: Friday, January 31, 1986

Williams Phillips, "Phil" Africa, succeeds his wife Janine in the stand. The litany begins.

Innocent MOVE people and villainous cops, God-given law and Judge-given law, the snake's rattle and the lion's roar, the Romans and the Christians, Hitler and the Jews.

At some point, August 8, 1978 is discussed. "Delbert was . . . brutally beaten, brutally, in front of the whole world to see. . . .

"My brother Edward [Goodman Africa] was taken down to Powelton Avenue, in front of the drycleaners, his pants pulled down to his ankles, and beaten, in his testicles until they was as big as grapefruits, and then carted off to jail."

"I was dragged behind a sand truck by my hair, handcuffs put on my hands and feet, and stomped on by police until Police Commissioner O'Neill told them, 'Don't do it, because they're witness,' because the . . . news reporters had filmed the beating of Delbert. So they grabbed me by my hair, cross my stomach, crossed the cement . . . took me down to Eighth and Race [the Police Administration Building], through the basement.

". . . . After I got to Eighth and Race—we was taken out to a van. . . . There was nothing but police there. I could hear them telling us, 'Get out. Get out.' They closed the door. I was beaten from the time I was taken out the wagon, grabbed by the hair, with a million witnesses. They didn't care. A million. Sitting in the tank down there . . . they had a tank where you wait to get arraigned at. They drags me all the way around to the back where the holding cells is. They threw us in there. From there we were stripped of all our clothing. We was given hospital gowns to wear. And we asked for clothes. They told us, 'Well, you ain't nothing but monkeys, anyway. You don't need clothes.' "

Later, with wobbly voice, Phil explains, "Our children, next to our belief, is the most precious thing we have in our lives. We protect them children with our lives." A bony hand covers the face, another slaps the microphone aside. The echo of his sobs is returned by the MOVE presence in the courtroom. A recess is called.

McGill's strategy on redirect is predictable, but he scores, nonetheless.

More photographs, more deterrents. Shotguns, carbines, MOVE. Brother Edward with deterrent. Brother Delbert with deterrent. Brother Phil with deterrent. "Look like me," Phil says, grinning idiotically.

More photographs, still more deterrents, more MOVE members. Janet Africa, sawed-off carbine. Alberta Africa, sawed-off shotgun.

McGill and Phil Africa parry and thrust. "We trust our belief," Phil tells him, "But I wouldn't trust you." There is much snickering from the MOVE benches. A sneer crosses McGill's face and disappears.

Some of the jurors pale before the photographs, which they pass among themselves. Juror Thirteen has assumed Number One's seat. A thin young white man with a beard has vanished, replaced by a white woman who looks to be in her early sixties. She has a large cameo at her throat, glasses resting on her nose, and short gray hair tinted blonde. She breathes heavily, and clutches constantly at her throat. "What," she may well be wondering, "am I doing here?"

23

"Eat'n This Joint Up!"

Day Fifteen: Monday, February 3, 1986

The first the courtroom crowd sees of him comes by way of the yawning iron door at the right. A red bandana of a headband pushes back scraggly dreadlocks. Delbert Orr Africa struts into Room 253. The walk is not unlike John Travolta's opening swagger in *Saturday Night Fever,* and there is an aura of ready physical force. His voice, a match for his build, sounds, "Onamove!"

In response to the echoing cries of "Long Live John Africa!," "Onamove," and the like, Delbert glances around the courtroom at his assembled audience. "Ya'll look'n *mighty* strong!"

He is dressed in a tight white pullover and the usual prison pants. He fidgets in the box, rubs his hands together, pushes the dreadlocks out of his face, strokes his semblance of a beard. "Eat'n this joint up!" he says and then whistles into the microphone. Across his left wrist is the red plastic band which identifies him as a prisoner of the Commonwealth.

The usual small drama then unfolds. No one is surprised when the witness is sworn in as, "Delbert Africa, Minister of Defense for the MOVE organization . . . On the MOVE! Long Live John Africa! Down with this rotten ass system!" No one is surprised to hear McGill object, "I ask that the witness be properly sworn." No one is surprised to hear Stiles say, "Thank you, Mr. McGill. The witness has been sworn. Proceed, Miss Africa."

Ramona asks if Delbert is a deeply committed MOVE member.

"A deeply committed MOVE member," he replies. "The way I've

been taught, the only commitment a person can make is . . . to life, and that commitment must be serious all the way, one-way revolution. To do otherwise is to play schizophrenic games, mind-hopping schizophrenia, like frustrated college students. And we're—MOVE are not frustrated college students, not excitement-seeking hippies, not deranged cultists. We're a deeply committed serious family of revolutionaries dedicated to ridding life of the stigma of this lifestyle, the lifestyle that has continually, historically, polluted life, filthed life, raped life."

How long has he been a member of MOVE? "I've been in the MOVE organization all my life, for I have been taught that once entering the flow of life, from the inception of so-called birth, you can only flow with life. And that is what MOVE is all about, life, all right? The awakening to that flow, the overcoming of them blockages that this system puts in front of that flow. Flowing with life wasn't overcome until I met John Africa, until I encountered the MOVE organization, which happened back in 1971.

"Before that time, I was just as lost as people in this system are lost today, thinking that the system was going to do something for me and ignoring the ass-kickings I was getting by the system repeatedly, the raping of my mind, the beating of my body. The oppression of this system has gone on, and will continue to go on until the crystalization of John Africa's strategy overcomes and wipes out this putrid mess."

Delbert is asked to describe the procedures used by the MOVE organization in the handling of its problems with the police and the court system.

"We went to city officials. We went to state officials, particularly Governor Shapp. We went to Lucien Blackwell, City Councilman. We went to any and everybody. We went to lawyers. We went to everybody to tell them about the oppression that the city was putting on us, to tell them about the attempts of corrupt cops to steal money from our car wash that we had going to support this organization, to tell them about the beating and killings that was going on, to tell them about the abortions that the city forced on our—on our MOVE women, miscarriages from kicking them in the belly, when they were pregnant, down at the round-house."

McGill objects. Delbert continues, "We told the city time and time again . . ."

Stiles sustains the objection and instructs Ramona to ask another question. Delbert tells Stiles, "I was answering the question when he interrupted me. . . . What the MOVE organization—what efforts the MOVE organization took to let the city know about our grievance. That's what I was going into. The man shouldn't be objecting to the truth, unless he got something to hide. I got nothing to hide. Like you asked me when I first came here, I told you, I live truth. I affirm truth, I ain't got nothing to hide. I can put it all out here. I don't have to hide behind no Fifth Amendment, no constitutional rights, nothing. Because what I stand on is a firm foundation built by John Africa, never toppled by this system."

The prison-issue pants, the red band, and the big armed cop seated behind Delbert tell another story.

MOVE members, Delbert says, made repeated visits to newspaper offices. Their goal, as always, was to let the truth be known.

August 9, 1978. Larry McMullen, a *Daily News* columnist, recalls the history of MOVE: "Members of the movement appeared periodically at newspaper offices. They begged for coverage. They got it only on very slow days when a writer needed desperately to fill a space. The coverage was more than MOVE deserved. . . . Reporters hid when they saw MOVE members come into their office. The media could use only slight doses of the weird hairdos, the dirt-encrusted bodies, and the outright silliness of a back-to-nature philosophy that offered as one of its centerpieces the nurturing of rats. . . . The media paid attention only when MOVE changed its act to include guns and threats of violence and a siege at 33rd and Pearl . . . MOVE owed its existence to the media. Until very recently, it was nothing more than a clown show that the media found unfunny. . . . With guns, bullets, and even talk of adding an atom bomb to its arsenal, MOVE suddenly became a story the media could sell. . . . God help us all."

Delbert Africa resumes his testimony. MOVE members appeared on radio and television shows to express, "the urgency of the situation to stop this oppression of MOVE, because our founder, John Africa, saw it coming to a head. We saw it. We felt it." They went to Harrisburg and met with a representative of the Governor. They met with federal representatives in Washington, D.C. They worked with "people" in New York, "in hopes that their political pimps would get together and call off the pressure they was putting on MOVE." Chicago, Detroit, Virginia; they tracked a lot of miles. They even met with Philadelphia police officers, giving them the message that MOVE was not interested in a confrontation with the city.

MOVE called for a debate between themselves and Mayor Rizzo. "We said, 'Make your position plain. Put it before the public. We'll be there. And we can put our position before the public.' He refused to do it."

August 1, 1978. Mayor Frank Rizzo, at a news conference, addressing the MOVE situation: "There will be no more talks or agreements or barricades. No more negotiations. It's been a circus long enough. We've been tolerant. If they resist, sufficient force will be used to get them out. They name the game. Whatever force they use, we'll use more."

MOVE held demonstrations, Delbert testifies, wherever Rizzo went during his reelection campaign. MOVE's purpose was to "tell this maniac 'Leave us alone!' "

May 1, 1977. Mayor Rizzo, at ceremonies honoring the 127th anniversary of the Philadelphia Police Department: "We have many people who would like to get a piece of us, but can't. The police will never be pushed around so long as Frank Rizzo is around."

Ramona enters into evidence a letter which is addressed to U.S. Representative Parren J. Mitchell, a Maryland Democrat, the then Chair of the Congressional Black Caucus. The letter is dated July 17, 1978 and is signed by Sue Africa and Robert Africa.

Delbert says that this letter, and others similar to it were sent, "to people all across the nation." MOVE even went to the United Nations and pleaded for help.

"The Philadelphia authorities always put out that MOVE was irrational and that we didn't have—that they didn't have any recourse but to beat us, but it was always us that was making the effort to cool things out."

August 4, 1978. Chuckie Sims Africa, addressing cameramen in Powelton Village, after first hurling rocks at them. "We want you motherfuckers to go to your own neighborhoods and put lights on your mother's house or your own house and see your wife in bed with your best friend."

Stiles instructs the witness on the topic of hearsay and inadvertently gives Delbert another rallying point. "The whole case with MOVE has been based on hearsay. I understand what you're saying. But I want to point out, because I'm not just here for—testifying for my sister—but I'm here to put out information, as I've been taught; and this man sitting right here is opening up his case on hearsay, what the cop told him, what Brad Richman [an assistant district attorney seated next to McGill] is telling him. Everything he's based on is hearsay [sic]. He don't know me. He don't know my sister. He don't know any MOVE people out here. Everything he know about MOVE is based on hearsay. He ain't never been in my house. Everything the Commonwealth has ever did to MOVE was based on hearsay.

"You got the media, talking that trash about MOVE being unhealthy. That was hearsay. You—you got the broad right there, Kitty Caparella [a *Daily News* reporter], talking about what's going on in MOVE house, ain't never been in MOVE house. She put out lies about bomb in MOVE house, and she had the nerve to put arrows where they was at based on hearsay because one of her pimp boyfriends told her where it was at. This is what we talking about. Y'all been biting us, stomping us for years on hearsay. When we speak about hearsay, you tell me that's against the rules of the Court. You know, I understand what you're saying; but I want to point out, legality ain't got nothing to do with right. What's right and what's legal is two different things, especially in this corrupt system."

Stiles replies that regardless of Delbert's personal motives, he must respond to the Court's rulings.

"Okay. But I spoke to you and put out information as a whole, because you also are a representative of this system. You are a representative of the very people who we approached. We say y'all the judges. Y'all, you know, can throw something on a piece of paper, order somebody to do this, order somebody going, all that. That's why I'm speaking to you, so that you know what's right and what's wrong, so the jury will know what's right and what's wrong, despite all the legal things, because we in MOVE have been taught that this system have came up with this system of legalities not to simplify things, but to complicate things, because law is simple. Law is one.

"If you, with your robe and everything, go out there and stand in the rain with me, you going to get wet just like me. You can't put no Contempt of Court order on the rain. That's law."

Stiles' cheeks are flushed. He swivels away from Delbert and looks out a window at his left.

"If you are standing in the way of a truck, you can't say, 'Hold up, I'm the judge.' That's law. You going to get run over just like I would. That's law.

"We, in MOVE, practice law. We practice equality. We practice justice. Right now, you got my sister down there. The whole Commonwealth of Pennsylvania versus Ramona Africa. Now is that justice? That's what her citation read. The whole Commonwealth of Pennsylvania. Ain't nothing right about this. That's what we saying. We understand what you saying. We saying it ain't right and it needs to be changed, and you the ones who are in a position to change it, need to be the first to change it. You got to quit misleading people, quit telling me this thing is right."

Stiles tells him that whether or not he thinks it is right, he will have to answer the questions without commentary, or forsake his right to testify.

Delbert says, "I understand that. You let me ask you. Do you think it's right?" Stiles tells Ramona to ask another question. She asks Delbert to read the letter and describe its circumstances.

The letter, dated July 17, 1978 and addressed to Representative Mitchell was composed, Delbert says, after a meeting between MOVE members and Parren Mitchell.

"It read, 'Dear Chairman Mitchell: As a result of our earlier meeting with you, we came back to see if there was any action initiated by you in regards to the harassment of the MOVE organization by Philadelphia cops and City officials. We were told today (July 17, 1978) by Mr. Rotan Lee, that to his knowledge, nothing had been done.

" 'We realize that you do not and cannot regard this situation with the same urgency as we do, yet we feel that since our lives are on the line in Philly, and since you and the members of the Caucus have publicly stated an interest in the problems of black people, poor people, oppressed people, you could at least schedule a meeting between MOVE members and members of the Caucus. We would like to meet with as many members of the Caucus as possible, as soon as possible.

" 'Please do not take this situation lightly. At some point, people who did not respond to this situation are going to be asked why they didn't. Hoping to hear from you soon. On the MOVE, Robert Africa, Sue Africa (Disciples of John Africa).

" 'In natural law we trust. All praises to the order of life. The power of truth is final. Long live MOVE. Long live revolution. Long Live John Africa.' "

Ramona asks if Delbert was sought out to negotiate a peaceful solution to the confrontation which began in May of 1977.

"In regards to the confrontation that started May twentieth, 1977, when MOVE people mounted a platform in front of our house to protest the city's continued oppression of us, and to show people worldwide that they did not have to give in to this corrupt system, I was approached a number of times as to what they—by 'they' I mean the city—could do to end this demonstration, this confrontation that was being mounted in May '77.

"I was approached by people that were looking for MOVE's welfare, and approached by city officials who wanted to get that pressure that John Africa had on them off of them, because the pressure that John Africa had on them was waking people up all up and down the east coast, all across America . . ." The police, the district attorney's office, and the mayor's office all sent representatives to MOVE headquarters in Powelton Village. Then Mayor Rizzo started talking to the newspaper about how he was going to "crush MOVE."

May 23, 1978. Mayor Frank Rizzo: "We'll just stand by. Nobody's been hurt. We don't want anybody hurt, not even MOVE . . . Our concern is the loss of life and we're not going to precipitate this . . . I don't want anybody hurt, anybody killed. If there's violence, they'll start it, and we'll finish it."

May 24, 1977. The Philadelphia *Daily News:* "MOVE members yesterday exchanged the guns they had brandished outside their headquarters for red baseball bats and said, 'If anyone comes through this door, they're not leaving.' . . . SEPTA [the regional transit authority] yesterday changed its Route 31 bus route, which normally passes MOVE headquarters, 'to keep away from people with guns.' 'We had reports of shotguns being leveled at the window level of our buses,' said a SEPTA spokesperson."

Delbert testifies that, "I was contacted by Rizzo's representatives straight up. They called up on the phone. Called up and said, 'Look, what can we do to end it?' "

August 2, 1977. Delbert Africa: "There's no deadline on MOVE. . . . We are not going to honor that agreement because that agreement has no honor. We are going to stand up to Frank Rizzo. Stand up to his gestapoism."

Delbert continues, "They sent [Police Inspector] George Fencl out there with his red-face self talking about, 'Look Delbert,' like he know me. We told him what would end it. We told him, said, 'Send our people home. Get up off our back. Leave us alone.' Because unlike what the City tried to portray, that confrontation May twentieth '77 was not about the house. It was not about dogs. It was not about neighbors' complaints. It was mounted to bring our people home, to bring attention to the fact that MOVE was tired of getting beat, seeing our women being caused to have miscarriage. We was tired of getting our babies killed. And I was contacted by the City about that many a time to like, say, what could they do to end it? But they didn't want to send our people straight home, because they didn't want the . . ."

Stiles sustains McGill's objection and tells Delbert, "That means you stop."

McGill adds to Delbert's instruction, "When it's sustained—*Listen to the Judge!*—that means *you* stop."

Delbert asks McGill if he is conducting law classes. Stiles again sustains the objection. Delbert addresses him, "I'm saying you the Judge; he's the DA. He ain't supposed to be telling me what to do, is that right?"

Stiles tells Ramona to ask another question.

But it is Delbert's voice, "I'm saying if you allow—oh, I know what's going on. He's coming up with this intimidation, attempted intimidation, the taunting and all that. And I ain't going to lie. When you said 'sustained' I stopped. Then he started coming on with, like, telling me what I'm supposed to do."

Stiles sustains McGill's objection. Delbert says, "Okay. Let's get it on."

What charges were brought against Delbert after the May 1977 demonstration?

Charges of terroristic threats, riot, disorderly conduct, and resisting arrest were levied against Delbert and all of the MOVE members the police could identify on May 24.

Who was the complainant on the arrest warrants?

"We were never told nor shown or no one was identified as who was the complainant as to the riot we was allegedly engaged in, as to the terroristic threats, as to the disorderly conduct or the resisting arrest. We were never given any weapons charges which they used at first."

Was Delbert approached to be a negotiator in 1984 or 1985?

"The city never contacted us about the impending May 13—by 'us' I mean myself and my brothers up at prison. Up at Dallas Prison, I'm speaking on. We were never contacted, unlike they did May 20, when they turned on the phone and they had some of them call in and say, 'Why don't you all cut it out?' . . . In May of '85, they never contacted us one time as to members of MOVE to say, "Could you talk to your brothers and sisters on Osage Avenue?' or anything, because their aim, obviously, was to eliminate MOVE . . . They didn't want to have any contact or negotiation."

Is it true that Delbert was approached by city officials after May 13?

"I was approached by city officials three times after May 13. They sent a representative of the medical examiner's office to my cell in the dungeon of Dallas Prison, where myself and my brother Carlos Africa were housed for the last two years, down in the basement. And this medical examiner came to me and told me . . . he wanted my help."

Delbert waves at the MOVE people. Someone holds a small child up for him to see. Visibly moved by the sight of these people, he strokes his goatee and smiles.

A representative of the medical examiner's office visited Delbert in August of 1985. He was next visited by a counselor at Dallas Prison. "Each time they came, each of the persons that came, they came for the task, they said, of wanting me to help them identify some remains; and each time I told them, 'Get the hell out of my face. Ain't no way I'm—in the world I'm going to help the same people who murdered my family do any damn thing.'

"And when they came up the third time, at that point—excuse me. This was the second time. The second time the medical examiner got— came up, and I told him if he ever approached me again on that subject, like, we do him some grievous bad body harm if I ever got to him, and leave me the hell alone, because they obviously not concerned about my welfare after leaving me two years down in the dungeon of a prison, after notifying me of the murder of my family by way of sending eight baton-wielding helmeted guards into the exercise yard where I was at, because they said, quote . . . 'You're a dangerous person.' "

Did any city officials try to enlist Delbert's efforts in negotiation before May 13?

"No, they never did. Prior to May 13 . . . they were acting like they didn't have any idea that we were in prison."

Did any of the city officials who eventually visited him speak of any problems they encountered in getting in touch with him?

"No. They walked right in. . . .

"Even after I told the prison that I didn't want to see them, they sent some nuts in there time after time after time until I told them the next one I get hold of, I'm going to make them pay. Then they stopped coming."

Ramona shifts back to 1978 and asks about the agreement between the city and MOVE stemming from the May 20 incident.

"Yeah. Beginning in March of '78, the city first approached us. Not first approached us, but like on a face-to-face basis, approached us in March of '78 that—what could they do about ending this confrontation. Rizzo had tried everything he could. The blockade. Rizzo made the statement about not even a fly would get in." Various negotiators, some from the district attorney's office, some federal agents, and some community activists came to the MOVE house to see what they could do to help. "And once again, we stated our demands to bring our people home, the five people who we listed that we wanted home; said, 'Leave us alone,' and so forth."

The agreement which was finally drawn up consisted of a "public" and an "unpublic" part, according to Delbert. This was an indication to MOVE that the city was trying to hide something.

Delbert says that the "unpublicized" part of the agreement, which he helped negotiate, stipulated that four imprisoned MOVE members, and one imprisoned MOVE supporter, would be allowed to come home. MOVE would be given enough time to leave their residence, and then move to houses in North Philadelphia as well as to places in New Jersey and elsewhere that the city would make available.

August 4, 1978. The Philadelphia *Daily News:* "At least one of the five North Philadelphia houses offered to MOVE for 'token rentals' of $1 a year has been declared 'unfit for human habitation' according to housing activist Milton Street. 'You've seen the place the city's demanding that MOVE vacate . . . Tell me, in all honesty, how does that place compare with this?' . . . Then why did MOVE leaders Delbert Orr Africa and Phil Smith Africa sign five-year leases on the condemned house along with four other rundown properties [in North Philadelphia]? . . . The properties MOVE leased are owned by Arab A. Ali . . . One source described Ali as a 'slumlord.'

"He 'has at least 100 homes scattered in the marginal areas of West and North Philadelphia.'. . .'The ludicrous thing is that the city is trying to drive the MOVE people out of their present property on the claim that it's unfit for human habitation. But the same administration obviously would be very happy to see them move into a situation up here that's far worse.' [said Street] . . . Noting, arguably, that the radical back-to-nature group is now housed in a 'mostly white' area, the North Philadelphia Councilman [Cecil B. Moore] declared, 'We're not going to be another cesspool and dumping ground for filth. What ain't good enough for white folks ain't good enough for me . . .' "

Delbert again: As part of the agreement, MOVE would be left alone by the city and the police department. All of this would occur if MOVE kept its part of the "public" agreement.

This was, Delbert continues, a civil, not a criminal matter. "The whole thing was a civil case where MOVE was saying that we had the right to maintain our house, which was a private dwelling. There were no complaints from any inhabitants of our house, yet the housing inspectors came up with a housing violation and a complaint about the inside of the house, when nobody inside the house had ever complained. And they, as a civil matter, demanded the right to come inside our house. MOVE made the stand that it was our house. We wasn't complaining about it, and anything inside our house was our business. Anything outside the house, on the sidewalk, was they business. They could have that. Inside, leave us alone."

MOVE went from the housing inspecting authority to Common Pleas Court to the Supreme Court in an attempt to prevent the housing inspectors from gaining entrance to their home. And then, Judge G. Fred DiBona revoked the bail of those MOVE members who were imprisoned after the May 20 demonstration.

August 3, 1978. According to the *Daily News*, "Judge DiBona yesterday issued arrest warrants for 21 MOVErs who'd been arrested during confrontations with police at the Powelton Village site on May 20 and June 7. Most of the 21 are still believed to be in the house, but there was no indication when and if the police would serve the warrants. Judge DiBona said he wanted the 21 brought in 'within 10 days. . . . We'll try to convince you of something that everybody in the world is convinced about [said DiBona]. They [MOVE] are not immune from this court. They are not going to be treated any differently from herein than any other citizen . . . I find they are in violation of that [May 3, 1978] agreement. I now revoke all [parole] and set bail for $50,000.' The May 3 agreement . . . said MOVE members would be released on their own recognizance if they would leave their headquarters within 90 days. That period expired at 12:01 A.M. yesterday [August 2, 1978]."

Ramona asks Delbert to identify the document she hands him, which she says "was gotten from civil court."

"It's a Rule to Show Cause that was issued by G. Fred DiBona, the Judge, and is the basis of August 8, 1978, in which the police of

Philadelphia rushed out, because in his Rule to Show Cause, Judge G.
Fred DiBona stated that these people listed, which were certified to him,
Janet Africa, Consuella Africa, Janine Africa, Charles Africa, Edward
Africa, and pencilled in here, 'and others as attached hereto,' which is a
list of people who they associated with MOVE, and MOVE members,
that those people should show cause why a civil contempt of court for
failing to vacate the premises in compliance with paragraph nine of the
order of May 3, 1978, should not be issued. And I want to emphasize,
that's all it says, a civil contempt. Wasn't nothing said about bringing six
hundred cops out there and trying to kill us. Wasn't nothing said about
bringing tanks out there. Wasn't nothing said about bringing the Uzis and
submachine guns."

(The number of police and firemen assigned to Powelton Village on
August 8, 1978 has been estimated to be three hundred.)

"It states that, 'The Philadelphia Police Department is hereby authorized and is deputized to act as sheriffs for the City and County of
Philadelphia." Delbert contends that it is the county sheriff who usually
takes care of eviction matters, and that DiBona assigned the police department to the task because, "he was looking for a confrontation. He was
looking to kill MOVE members."

Stiles instructs Delbert to read from the document.

"All right. Do that. It says further, 'to serve the Attachments issued
by this court and to enter the premises and take MOVE members occupy-
ing or residing at the premises 307–309 North Thirty-third Street, and
any other Africa members, parties to agreement and subject to the order
of May 3, 1978, wherever situated.' In other words, wherever you find
MOVE members, in Los Angeles, Hawaii, Virginia, wherever you find
them, he was telling the Philadelphia Police to arrest them. He sent
people . . ."

Over objections which Stiles sustains, Delbert continues.

"That is what is says, 'wherever situated,' the . . . police just did what
the order said. Said wherever MOVE members were situated. They went
and got them. Richmond, Virginia . . . It says 'wherever situated,' take
those MOVE members 'into custody and bring them before this Court
for hearings within ten days of the date of this Order.' "

DiBona signed the order on August 2, 1978. It further states that,
"Members of the MOVE group who continue to occupy or reside at
premises 307–309 North Thirty-third Street are in violation . . . of the
Order of this Court." But, Delbert contends, "Obviously, the MOVE
members that wasn't residing there wasn't in violation . . . the only people
—MOVE members he wanted arrested were the ones that were still at

307–309 North Thirty-third Street . . . G. Fred DiBona took it upon himself to order all MOVE members wherever situated, according to this.

" 'Members of the MOVE group have not vacated premises 307–309 North Thirty-third Street and continue to occupy or reside at the premises to the present time', which was August 2. . . . And it states George Fencl attested to five people being at the house; yet the City of Philadelphia went all over the nation hunting down MOVE members.

"G. Fred DiBona was a Common Pleas Judge handling civil matters, in particular, the case of *City of Philadelphia* versus *Donald Glassey.* And his ruling from the original September term, 1975, indicates—allowed him to keep issuing orders, warrants and so forth on things that didn't even have anything to do with the case. But he's the main person . . . that can be held accountable for August 8, 1978."

August 2, 1978. Chuckie Africa: "This is a cause we'd die for. If police take us away from our home, we'll fight with the strategy of John Africa. I ain't gonna tell you the details."

Did the police confiscate all of MOVE's weapons?

"Right. It was approximately about May 8 we got all weapons, so-called firearms, all material as they said, whatever, and any arms, gunpowder, explosives, and we brought them to the front of our platform in our house, in the presence of Police Inspector Fencl, the Alcohol, Tobacco and Firearms agent Walt Waslyk, Assistant D.A. Straub. . . . Everybody was there. Firearms experts and all that. Along with a police videotape machine team that videotaped the whole proceedings.

"And then we proceeded to give them all that they asked for. We gave them a can of Ajax that was wrapped up in black tape, that they and Kitty Caparella [the *Daily News* reporter] was talking about was high explosives.

"We gave them the stock that they claim was a firearm in a picture that Sue Africa was holding, which they have her fourteen years for holding it, and come to find out it wasn't but a piece of wood with nothing but empty metal in it, or nothing at all.

"We gave them—we gave them all that they asked for in this agreement. We gave them the sticks of dynamite that the—that they thought were dynamite; and as it turned out, to be railroad fuses.

"We turned over the revolver that didn't have a cylinder in it. We turned over the plastic Luger, which turned out to be a water pistol." This was all they had.

"We then allowed them to enter the house, which they searched for six hours with the metal detectors, a team of five policemen, and they went through both houses, 307–309 for six hours with the metal detector. They searched each and every MOVE member. They even checked the dogs out. They did everything that they said in the agreement would guarantee that we wouldn't have any weapons on the property.

"And we turned over what we had to them that day, approximately May 8. . . . And as I handed it to [the police firearms examiner], I would tell him, 'here's one piece of stock with no trigger, no piece of metal. Here's one authentic water pistol, Luger.' And I would say, 'Here, six wrapped-up cans of an Ajax cleanser with store fuse in it. Here are ten bundles of railroad fuses,' that them idiots thought was dynamite.

"I turned over the one blockaded pistol with the barrel blockaded, and the cylinder fell out as I turned it over to them. The whole bit. I gave it the whole thing. And the city never publicized all that, because they didn't want to know that MOVE had once again made fools of them."

Was the police presence maintained after May 8?

Yes, Delbert says, because part of the Order read, " 'During that period—it is agreed by and between the parties hereto that there will be a police presence maintained in the neighborhood, and the civil rights of both the neighbors and MOVE protected and maintained.'

"The only thing they did in terms of civil rights, obviously, was to keep a police presence. . . .

"On Pearl Street, adjacent to the side of the house, the police were there, and they were continually walking the neighborhood. Inspector Fencl, who was head of Civil Affairs, he came out there periodically . . . all the big shots would come out there. And a police presence was kept there twenty-four hours a day from—it never stopped. People were still being harassed, even after the barricades had came down by the police that were there until we complained about that. . . . Many times, as people would come to the platform, the wife of a MOVE member or friends of MOVE members would bring us—were bringing us food, vegetables, the police were stopping them and [going] through their bags."

Stiles asks Delbert if there remains anything he has not told the jury about the Order.

"The point that MOVE, number six, 'MOVE will immediately proceed to dismantle the platform in front of 307–309 North Thirty-third Street.' That was an add—add in. I don't know if y'all can see it. That was something that they added in and pencilled in later on that—we didn't have to do that. They just wrote that in there. Somebody didn't want the platform there, and wrote it in there. But later on, that was cancelled during the ongoing talks we was having with the city. All during this so-called agreement, this Order was in effect.

"Number ten, 'MOVE will permit and hereby agree that Oscar Gaskins, Esquire, does and will represent them in court, and MOVE waives their personal presence in courtroom proceedings in order to avoid further confrontations.' This paragraph we wanted in there in, and the city agreed that was in there. We wanted it in there for the purpose of, as it says, to avoid further confrontations. But then when we didn't come to court, like it says on August second, didn't Judge DiBona put warrants on us?

"And it specifically states in the Order that he signed that we didn't have to come to court. It's right here, on paragraph ten, MOVE will not come to court. All right? This is what the city said. But they turned on around and said because we didn't come to court August 2, we have warrants on the whole organization. This is the things the city keep trying to hide from the public for years, the fact that they push the thing for August 8 to occur. MOVE was, in good faith, trying to get out of the neighborhood, out of the city, and they kept on pushing there.

"They act like it was ninety days," Delbert sneers. (MOVE was given more than ninety days to vacate its headquarters in Powelton Village.)

Stiles tells Delbert again to read what is before him and tells Ramona to ask another question. Delbert turns toward Stiles and asks what his objection is, saying, "You and him, you know, both of y'all work together or what? You and the District Attorney?"

Did Gaskins go to court on behalf of MOVE from May 3 to August 2?

"Yeah, Oscar Gaskins went up there to and including August 2 as it said, so that we wouldn't have to, to avoid any confrontation. Plus, it was part of the agreement, the unwritten agreement, unpublicized agreement that we made which is written. I've been saying unwritten, but it is unpublicized. It's written. Oscar Gaskins got a copy of it. We wouldn't come to court not only to avoid confrontation, but because the city had an agreement that the charges against us would be dropped in four to six weeks, that there wouldn't be any charges against us, that the District Attorney Rendell said that it was a meatball case, you know. Wasn't nothing to it, and we could work it on out."

August 2, 1978. The Philadelphia *Daily News:* "Oscar Gaskins . . . announced he'd been dismissed because . . . the radical, back-to-earth group has a 'religious belief' that no non-member can speak for them."

August 5, 1978. An editorial in the *Daily News:* "Oscar Gaskins fought the good fight for MOVE. His intervention . . . helped win that band of costumed woo-woos treatment that most citizens simply would not have gotten. . . ."

The police, Delbert testifies, not only came to Powelton Village to serve the warrants, they went as far as Richmond, Virginia, where Birdie, his mother Rhonda, and a number of other MOVE women and children were housed at "The Seed of Wisdom." "August eighth, the police came out to our house early that morning and announced, 'You're under arrest. We got warrants for you', and so forth, and 'We are here to bring you before Judge G. Fred DiBona.' And there was a lot of other of other things that I don't remember clearly that they said.

In effect, they was telling us to come on out of the house before we got hurt, and all this and that. And they attempted to, I guess, implement this illegal warrant that G. Fred DiBona—illegal and wrong warrant."

Delbert was inside the house, "the whole day, all throughout the whole attack on our house . . . Then after coming out othe house on the side of Pearl Street, I sustained other injuries when D'Ulisse, Mulvihill, Zagame and guys—members of the Philadelphia Police . . . began jumping up and down on my head, kicking me in my groin, swelling up my testicles, broke some ribs on my right side, broke the occipital bone around my eye, broke my jaw, and knocked out a tooth, and I think—believe it —it was some broken left wrist or fractured left wrist, or something like that. Them the injuries I received after surrendering, after surrendering to the Philadelphia Police unarmed, no shirt on, hands spread. They claimed that they had to do that."

Delbert testifies that he was not in possession of any weapons while leaving the house, nor did he have any while inside the house.

August 9, 1978. An eyewitness account in the *Daily News:* "An officer swings a helmet, hitting Delbert in the head. (I find out later that Delbert was armed with a knife stuck in the small of his back and a clip of bullets before he was knocked with the helmet) . . ."

Did any children came out of the house with him?

No, everyone else had already left the house through the front entrance. "The policeman at the side of the house where I was at was looking through the window with a gun pointed at my head, ordering me to go out the side. . . . I was trying to make my way up front when, you know, he told me, 'Come here, nigger.' I said, 'I'm going on out the front.' He said, 'I'll blow your damn head off. Come on out here.' When I'm climbing out the back of the house, with the policeman with the gun at my head; and at which point I came out, stood up, there were no children around, as everybody was up front. And the policemen on the side of Pearl Street, the guys I name, that's when they proceeded to, you know, kick in my head. . . .

"They charged me with the murder of Ramp. They charged me with the the the assault of various policemen and firemen. They charged me with resisting arrest. They charged me with everything but weapons charges, yet charged me with the murder of Ramp. And these charges came as a result of August eighth, '78, charges in which they attempted to put everybody in MOVE organization that was at the house that day under wraps for keeps."

August 9, 1978. The Philadelphia *Daily News* reports that, following the confrontation in Powelton Village, Stakeout officers removed 1600 fired and unfired cartridges and 11 rifles and semi-automatic weapons" from the basement of MOVE Headquarters.

The arrested MOVE members, now "barefooted, handcuffed, and dressed in hospital garb," were arraigned the same day before Judge Louis Hill who "read the charges of murder, conspiracy, and eight counts each of aggravated assault, recklessly endangering another, and *weapons offenses* against them."

Ramona says, "I have a newspaper photograph here, and I want you to tell me if this accurately . . ."

McGill is on his feet. "Objection, Your Honor, particularly to her effort to expose it to the jury. Objection."

Ramona faces McGill, and erupts. "I am trying to expose the truth to the jury. He testified about being beat—almost killed on August 8."

McGill will not look at her. "Objection. Objection. Every trial they do it, Judge; and I object, once again."

"Yeah, we tell the truth at every trial."

Stiles overrules McGill's objection. The photograph is marked.

"Yeah, at the point when them cops were beating me. That's Zagame pulling on my hair. That guy's a cop whose wife shot him dead, kicking me in my nuts . . . Zagame is in the picture, pulling on my hair . . . Guys is in the picture kicking me in my groin . . . I'm in the picture getting brutalized by these cops, unarmed. Unarmed. All right? The same cops who talk about, you know, all that honor, serve, and protect, all that . . . No cop has ever gone to prison for any attacks against MOVE."

The policemen in the photograph "wasn't even given a chance to be acquitted. The Judge . . . Stanley Kubacki said, I quote, 'I'm taking it upon myself to be the lightning rod for any further . . . violence. If there be any, let it come down on me,' and took it out of the hands of the jury, and let the three cops that were on trial for beating me, let them go before they even got the chance to get to the jury. Because he said, as I said, that he's taking it upon hisself . . . No, they wasn't acquitted. They was just let go.

"And my pockets was emptied, at which time I had some of the organization's money in it. One cop was going to take it. . . . At that point, I was taken to a wagon that was on the street, put into a wagon and— matter of fact, I received another injury there when a plainclothes cops got into the wagon as I was sitting there handcuffed . . . the cop got in and slapped me across the face, as I was bent over, then I reared back and kicked him, you know, to show him that I wasn't dead yet; and his partners pull—pulled him out of the wagon."

He was taken to the hospital where a shotgun pellet was taken out of his chest, and was then taken to the Police Administration Building. Charges were filed against him about two hours afterwards, he says.

On cross-examination, McGill gets right to it. Has Mr. Africa ever seen a photograph of the dead body of Police Officer James Ramp.

"I seen several photographs of Ramp laying out after his cops—fellow cops shot him dead."

No, he hasn't ever seen photographs of the injuries sustained by the four firemen and three policemen who were also wounded by gunshots.

"You're still walking around, aren't you, Mr. Africa?"

"Yeah. Yeah. Strong as hell." The MOVE women in the audience repeat Delbert's answer admiringly: "You bet your mothafuckin ass, he strong as ever!"

"I'm sure of that, sir," McGill replies, barely containing himself.

"You better believe it. Ain't nothing you gonna do gonna put me down. Come up with all the brutality you want. I ain't never gonna back up. You ain't gonna make me weak."

"Wouldn't want to do that, Mr. Africa. You've always felt like that, haven't you sir?"

"No, I haven't; not until I came in contact with the teachings of John Africa from the MOVE organization."

"Is that when you became like that?"

"Understand what I'm saying. Before that, I was as weak as other people were, misled by this city's system; people who are tricked into anything, like coke is hip, something to get into while they stand there killing theirself. People who think the disco is hip, until like it catches fire and burns down around them. People who think, like, the space shuttle is hip until it blows up in their damn face. I was as dumb as anybody else is dumb in the system.

"Just like you big-ass scientist go be teaching you that everything is perfect; that [the] sun is perfect. The sun will burn out today, ain't nothing you can do to stop it. You mix that whiskey with that water all the time like it's important, but you, what you gonna do about the water to mix the whiskey with? The wisdom of John Africa is about cleaning up the evilness of this system, the things that allow you, as prosecutor, persecutor, peer, to sit up here and mess with my sister; this system that don't work for you; this system that got you to force on people; this system that got you to impose on people. Don't nobody like this stuff. You force it on them.

"The first time your lungs ever tasted cigarette smoke, they reject it. The first time a baby ever come into this world, they don't want this system the way you do it, and you got to beat it into—into awareness, spank it upside down, its ass, make you think it's okay. MOVE children are born peacefully into the world, smoothly. This is the difference that John Africa gave me, that's why I won't let you pull me back into your corruptness, your foulness. I ain't gonna sit up there and stuff no coke down my nose. I ain't gonna sit up there . . ."

Stiles tells him to limit his response to a direct answer.

"Whenever he, you know, said he don't want no more, I'll turn it off and we can start again."

"I'm going to have to do that," Stiles answers. "But rather than"—Delbert is scanning the courtroom, grinning, seemingly paying no attention whatsoever to what Stiles is saying—"*Listen* to me. Rather than interrupting you, do your best to limit your responses to what is necessary to answer. All right?"

"Hey, I understand what you're saying. I'm saying I want to give it all. I got years of pent-up stuff that I want to tell. I understand this guy here. I understand he called for me. He said, bring me down . . . so I'm going to give him all he can stand."

Stiles tells Delbert that he'll "have to stop a little short of that."

"I'll do that, I'll do that. Everything I'm going to do, I'm going to speak directly to what he's coming from. If ever it gets too much for him or yourself, all you got to do is tell me. We'll stop, and start with another question."

Stiles recesses court. It is lunchtime.

Court resumes. Delbert has a gym bag now. It is red, and in white letters it says, "LIFE." Someone yells, "Where'd you get that bag from?"

Delbert says, "Hey, you know. Life—see what it says?"

McGill is sitting with his arms crossed tightly. He asks Delbert if he has any trouble hearing him when he speaks. No, Delbert tells him—Go ahead.

Does Mr. Africa remember saying in open court, before Ramona began her questions, "We are filling this joint up; the system is about ready to fail; you can feel it."

"That sounds about like what I said. It's the same, in the general direction of what's going on right now. Saying when you see the problems that you, as a purveyor of the system, is having, you can see that what John Africa has written is true. The system is faulty.

"People ain't satisfied with your rule. That's why they revolt against you now. That's—your sons is revolting against man trying to be homos. That's why your daughters is out on the street using dope, because they is revolting against the system. But John Africa has given MOVE the direction to revolt against that which is revolting in the same way. Not to replace one problem with another diversionary problem, but to get rid of the problem, to dwell in solution rather than problematical framework."

Is total revolution the method for achieving John Africa's goals?

"Total revolution must be engaged with in order for there to be any revolution at all. When cancer struck your putrid body, you're not going to cut a little bit of the cancer out. When you get gangrene in your leg, you going to amputate the whole thing. You understand what revolution means?

". . . Total revolution means doing it all away, or it won't get done.

". . . We are against violence. You understand that? . . .

"Every time this system comes at us and we protect ourself, they want to call us terrorists. But we didn't come out to their house with antitank weapons, .50-caliber guns, Uzis, M-16s. We didn't fire ten thousand rounds of ammunition at their house. We didn't throw no C-4 explosive at their house. You did this to us; you, as a representative of the system.

. . . We told you a long time ago, we won't be stopped. You can hurt us, but we won't be stopped. We'll keep coming at you, because you're wrong."

Did Mr. Africa, in 1974, say something like "there was no need for a police force because the laws of the country are illegal and the Police Department is enforcing illegal laws"?

"In general, it sounds like something I might have said. But I usually make a point of, as a representative of MOVE, when speaking to the police, city officials, whatever, so that I don't get misunderstood, to explain it fully. In other words, Police Force is hired by the rich from the ranks of the poor to keep the other poor oppressed, because don't nobody who is rich want to be no policeman, no guard, no sheriff.

". . . . Although MOVE ain't taught to hate cops, we know what the cops doing. If one cop's standing there talking about being a good cop because he ain't beating me while he watching his fellow cop bust me in the head, he's the same as the cop doing the beating. Be the same if you watch your wife getting rape, and can't do nothing about it. Talk about you ain't . . ."

McGill cuts him off. Did Mr. Africa make remarks such as, "This country and its government are corrupt and will be overthrown, and that MOVE has no respect for the Police Department and can take care of itself"?

"That sounds like *The Guidelines* as taught to us by John Africa, because we have been taught that we do not respect that which is disrespectful. I'm saying I don't respect somebody that has shown themselves to be corrupt. I mean right to this day, you got the Philadelphia Police force is the laughing stock all over the world. They're known as corrupt people, graft-takers. The police in Philadelphia got a reputation for kicking ass and shooting people in the back. That go back years. MOVE ain't the only ones suffered this oppression. . . ."

Does he remember saying that, "We are deeply committed in our religious beliefs, and I will kill our children rather than have them put in foster homes as a result of any inspection"?

"No, I never said that. I know for a fact I never said that. That statement was put out by the media as having been stated, right?. . . . MOVE would never kill our kids anyway. Understand this. We deeply love our kids. Always protect our children as John Africa has taught us. And if that statement was made by a MOVE member, it was only made for the protection of the children to keep . . . the cops off us as a lie."

"It would be the same thing if your daughter, or somebody was to intercept a rapist about to rape, and she tell him, 'Don't come in here.

I got a gun.' I would not condemn her for being a liar long as it kept the rapist off her. Would you? Would you? . . . Maybe YOU would . . ."

Did Mr. Africa keep any of the weapons he allegedly surrendered in 1977–78 or obtain new weapons before August 8, 1978?

"No. We gave everything that we told the city we had, we gave them to the police. They the ones for them asked for them. We don't worship weapons. We don't collect guns, explosives and all that. The police do."

"We tell people continually—at the beginning of the confrontation that you're speaking of, we told the police, say, 'You worship these guns.' Said, 'Y'all love them. We don't have any need of them.' MOVE had no need for weapons on August 8 when the police arrived with arrest warrants. . . . We had no need to have any firearms on August 8 because we were armed with the truth of John Africa. We were armed with the protection of John Africa. That's what kept the cops off us. That's what's keeping them back today. That's—whether you can see it or not, it's gonna eliminate this damn system forever."

Yes, he was there on May 20. A letter "was given to me to pass on to George Fencl. The letter, I believe, was signed the 'Black Guard' or 'Smoke on the Black Guard,' and was signed with a chemical quotation, chemical formula."

The letter is marked as a Commonwealth exhibit. McGill asks Delbert to read it.

" 'This is a message to the Mayor of Philadelphia from the Black Guard Western Europe, French, German, English and Polish militias. Don't attempt to enter MOVE headquarters or hurt MOVE people unless you want an international incident.

" 'We are prepared to hit reservoirs, empty hotels and apartment houses, close factories and tie up traffic in the major cities of Europe. We have occupants in two major hotels and two apartments houses in each city the Guard is situated in.

" 'We want Robert Africa, Gerald Africa, and Conrad Africa released from Gratersford Prison and flown by helicopter and taken to MOVE headquarters immediately. We also want Robert Bethel Africa released from Huntington State Correctional Institution and flown to MOVE headquarters by helicopter immediately.

" 'We are not going to negotiate with you. If you don't release our people, we are going to hit the Russian Embassies, the French Embassies, German Embassies and Polish Embassies in all major western European countries and that's just a start. Get this message to the Mayor of Philadelphia immediately and to the person or persons in charge of the confrontation in front of MOVE headquarters.

" 'If you think this is some kind of joke, you better get in touch with the Prime Minister of England.

" 'We have not notified the news media because we are not looking for publicity or a confrontation. That will come out of the situation, should you force us to go through with it. All we want is your cooperation and the whole incident can be settled quietly which is to your advantage.

" 'We know you don't want this information to get to the news media and fall into the hands of other organizations that will eagerly adopt this strategy and use it.

" 'Any attempt to trace messages called in from any western European militias and the message you have just received will automatically go into effect in all major western European countries as well as America. You better be certain that nothing goes wrong because if we lose contact with any of our members in any western European country or America, they are instructed to start the operation and continue until contact is restored. We are well equipped, well trained, and experts in guerilla tactics. We will make no compromises, concessions, or allowances of any kind.

" 'This is our position. Either we get what we want or we move. We are not in this for the excitement. We are not a bunch of excitement-seekers. We are not a bunch of frustrated middle-class college students, irrational radicals, or confused terrorists. We are a deeply religious organization, totally committed to the principle of our belief as taught to us by our founder, John Africa. We are not lookin' for trouble. We are just lookin' to be left alone.'

"And it's signed, 'CH3C6H2 (NO2).' "

Delbert says that he does not know what that formula represents. If McGill were to say "nitroglycerin," would this refresh Delbert's memory? No, "Ain't nothing to refresh as far as that go. . . . I'm saying when you refer to this nitroglycerin and stuff, that's your reference anyway. See, you believe in it . . . If you say it's nitroglycerin, fine. Y'all known to have a lot of that."

McGill hands Delbert a photograph, and asks him about the weapon, or object, in Delbert's hand.

"Talking about the microphone?"

"That certainly is an object. How about the other hand?"

"In the other hand is another object."

"Yeah. What is that object?"

"It appears to be—looks like a—some kind of gun, or replica of a gun, or something similar to a gun."

Where did he get it?

"I acquired it. I really don't remember where. . . . I just don't remember where I acquired it, you know. Understand this. You make the big point about guns and what appeared to be guns . . . If you have an objection to guns, tell Smith and Wesson to quit making them. Tell Colt to quit making them. I didn't manufacture it."

Delbert says he doesn't know how the guns were acquired; he just handed them out. "I told . . . different members, said, you know, 'Pick up that piece of wood; you get that one; you get that one,' and that was it."

All of the guns were obtained from Donald Glassey, Delbert says. "Donald Glassey, the same man who is on the street now because the Feds let him go, gave him a new identity and all that, long as he can turn MOVE. Yeah, Donald Glassey gave him this gun, just like Donald Glassey had all the guns they had accused . . . MOVE members of having. Donald Glassey always had all the weapons. The only operable weapon ever to come out of May 20 was—was Donald Glassey's goddamn weapon. Yet Donald Glassey is still on the street. But you got MOVE people in jail right now, like Sue Africa, holding this piece of wood right here, which was turned in May 8, that did not have any firing pin and all that. She doing time for having this inoperable piece of wood. But Donald Glassey had all kinds of explosives caught on him. . . ."

"You certainly believe in self-defense, don't you?" McGill needles.

"Self-defense is the first law of nature. Saying right now, if I was to come over there to you, you wouldn't write no petition, no complaint. You'd try to defend yourself as best you could; all right? All this thing about calling on somebody else for defense is foolishness concocted by this system. You're supposed to defend yourself.

"If you snap your finger at a baby, a child, an infant, it will blink his eyes in defense; all right? This is God's law, nature's law. This what John Africa has shown us. I believe deep . . . I believe other than self-defense is to be a masochist.

"If you come at me with your fists, I'm going to bust you upside the head with my fist."

The MOVE men and women in the audience chant their agreement loudly, "Got that straight." "Ain't that some shit."

"Would it include a gun?"

"If you come at me with a gun, I'd be foolish to wave a feather at you, wouldn't I?"

More photographs of more guns. Are the photographs representative of the weapons recovered from the Powelton Village headquarters after the August confrontation?

"See, now you play games. . . . Yeah, I disagree with it. . . . Whatever it is, they undoubtedly made thousands of them. You the one that's claiming you got it out of my house, when everybody knows that the police were the only ones ever seen taking any weapons into the house. Your former Police Commissioner O'Neill, right there on his own, you seen passing weapons in the house."

So, O'Neill passed all of the weapons into the house?

"As many videotapes as they got, they don't have one videotape of any policeman bringing anything out of our house."

Delbert claims in answer to McGill's question that he is not certain whom he heard on August 8, 1978, when various people were pleading with MOVE to come out. He did hear Walt Palmer, the civil rights activist and negotiator that day.

"I heard Walt Palmer saying several things. One, Walt Palmer said, 'They got it in for you Delbert. Come on out, Delbert.' He called Phil. 'Come on. Come on out. Man, they gonna hurt you if you don't come out. They gonna hurt you.'"

Did Palmer also agree to come in and walk out with Delbert?

"He might have. I don't know. See, you haven't been there. Even though you be in the situation, if you look out your window, see cops, special cops, SWAT teams, CIA, FBI, bunch of power-hungry . . ."

Why wouldn't Mr. Africa listen?

"All them people laying around your house. You ain't been in there, You ain't seen them lined up. All talking about, 'Yeah, come on,' working the guns. You ain't felt all of that, all right? All of that would not have MOVE coming out into they arms. Talking about 'Come on out. We ain't gone hurt you,' when we had a history of them cops beating us, shooting us.

"In the first place, what was five hundred cops, six hundred cops doing at our house anyway? We didn't come out to their house. You be putting up this front about you concerned about August 8, about Ramp. Everybody in this courtroom know you don't care nothing about Ramp. Ramp don't even travel in your social circles. If you was to see Ramp right now, and Ramp was to try to join your country club or your gentlemen club, you would say, 'No, we don't want that poor white trash there.' You consider Ramp and the rest of them cops just frontline fodder to get rid of. Now you try and front some concern about Ramp, like you care about Ramp, like you concerned about what happened August 8."

Does Delbert feel that Officer Ramp deserved to die?

"I feel Ramp got what his belief called for. Ramp—I didn't go to Ramp's house. Ramp came to my house. Understand that. Ramp left his desk at Stakeout Headquarters to come there. He wasn't even assigned there. He came out looking for trouble, looking for excitement, looking to kill some black folks."

August 2, 1978. The Philadelphia *Daily News* reports that all white and Puerto Rican members of MOVE have been ordered to leave the Powelton Village headquarters, so that any ensuing confrontation will be translated as a racial incident. Chuckie Sims Africa is quoted in the same account: "There's no white membership in our house tonight. Won't Rizzo's stormtroopers like that? They can come in here and kill black men, black women, and black babies."

Delbert is still going on about Officer Ramp: "He came out there. I didn't go to his crib. When he came out there, and the rest of them cops got to shooting at each other, he got his belief. I didn't carry no gun up to his house. That's something you people got to deal with. That's something the jury got to deal with.

"You done put the blame on ten innocent MOVE people, instead of putting the blame where it belongs, right on Rizzo, right on the city, right on the cops. Everybody know that's why the city tore down our house two hours after we was arrested, so that they couldn't show the trajectory of no bullets. That's the only time anybody ever heard about a murder scene being destroyed that damn fast.

"Everybody know that your own Police Commissioner O'Neill testified Ramp was shot in the back, and that side wound was an exit wound. Then come three days later, turn around, they done flip-flopped the whole thing. Now it's an entry wound, and that's an exit wound. Man, look here, we know—them people know that that was a set-up. August 8 was a set-up to get rid of MOVE."

"That's a set-up? So what happened was that, I guess, the police then carried in all the weapons. The police shot their own people, and then . . ." McGill is shouting; his cheeks are scarlet.

"I don't know."

Is Mr. Africa claiming that "policemen must have shot themselves, injured themselves, injured the firemen, killed Ramp, no weapons and ammunition in your place whatsoever? All shooting done by police and you didn't do anything at all. Is *that* what you're saying?"

"I didn't have any weapons. Ain't any MOVE members have any weapons there, as witness the fact wasn't no weapons ever found with our fingerprints on the. . . .

"The first time the public hear about the weapons, when Frank Rizzo sat his catastrophic ass out there, says. 'This is the weapon come from MOVE.' They sitting up there all bright and shiny. Not one of them with mud on them. How do you account for it? It wasn't MOVE."

Does Mr. Africa recall mentioning at his own trial that the weapon which is alleged to have been responsible for Ramp's death was purchased by William Phillips Africa?

"No, that was never testified. That's right. You want to get into this, this so-called murder weapon. And the public can dig on this. The so-called murder weapon was never identified in terms of 'This is a murder weapon.' The only thing your police ballistics expert and firearms expert said was that it was a .223 bullet that killed Ramp and wounded the others, and the police had .223 weapons out there. This is why they ain't never bothered about going deep into it, because they know they ain't never been able to identify no single MOVE member."

August 7, 1978: "The *Daily News* has learned that MOVE allegedly acquired .38 caliber police guns with snub-nosed bullets. MOVE members allegedly have a suicide pact where 'they are going to blow their own people away' when police attempt to arrest them.

"If a bullet hits and travels through a body, and the projectile is not recovered, you cannot prove ballistically it came from a specific gun,' the source said. The tipster did not see any guns, but was 'scared to death.' 'If indeed they have the guns, then those sons-of-bitches are setting you up. If you are going to be had, how do you protect yourself?' "

Delbert continues to harangue McGill: "And you, as a representative of this city, DA Department, long-time political stooge in that office, you know what's going on. . . ."

Has Mr. Africa been instructed to give a speech in answer to a question instead of responding directly?

"I'm telling you. I've been taught that to overcome the callousness on the brains of people in this system, that's been imposed upon people in this system, that you must be clear, concise and put out total statements. And that is why I answer the thing fully, to overcome any of them hints, any of them innuendos or whatever that you be attempting to put out. Cause, see, you here playing a game. . . ."

"We're not talking about a game."

"You playing a game man. You sitting up here, Perry Mason, like you gone on TV or something."

This remark is greatly appreciated by the MOVE supporters, who repeat "Perry Mason, yeah, motherfucker" over and over again. They are loud and jazzed.

Does Mr. Africa recall testimony that not only the murder weapon, but three .22-.223 Ruger Mini-14s were also purchased by William Phillips Africa, and recovered after the August 8 confrontation, despite MOVE's allegedly having turned over all their weapons?

No, he does not.

Well, then does he remember only what he wants to remember?

"I'm going to tell you what I want to remember. I want to keep in my mind all the bullshit you and those like you done did to my family. I'm going to keep the murder that you done committed on this family. I want to keep all the kickings, the beatings, all the trauma that you done did. I want to keep the fact that you done separated me from my children, my sisters, my brothers, my wife for eight—coming on eight years because of something that I didn't do; because of something you did and your belief did. That's what I want to keep in mind. You understand that?"

Does it bother Mr. Africa that he, "literally separated from life a police officer who also had a family?"

"I'll tell you straight up, I didn't kill Ramp."

How did two thousand rounds of ammunition get into MOVE headquarters?

"I have no knowledge of two thousand rounds of ammunition, none of that. Ask Smith and Wesson."

On August 8, 1978, did Mr. Africa say, "You've been wanting to come in all this time, but before you do, you better call home and make sure your insurance policy is paid up"?

Yes, he said that. "I said that when the—when the cops were first pulling up the bulldozers in front of our house, and bringing up a crane in front of our house; and I said that. I told them, 'Get on out of here; leave us alone.' I said, 'Take your ass back up to the Northeast where you belong.' Said, 'You don't live in Powelton Village. This ain't your house.'

"I said, numerous times, to get on out the neighborhood. I said a lot of things like that to keep them from invading our house, to keep them from killing our kids, to keep them from smashing in our heads with their water hoses, all the rest of that. I tell somebody anything to get them away from killing my family. Understand that. I wasn't at their house. That's what you can't get around. You call us terrorists, but they the ones had all the tanks. They the ones that came to Osage Avenue with the antitank weapons, with this plastic explosive. You want to label us terrorists, like we violent, when you . . ."

So MOVE had no weapons on August 8, 1978?

"That's what I'm saying. Exactly my point. You lied, the city lie, the media lied . . . Excuse me one moment." Delbert turns toward Stiles. "Hey, Judge, like I said earlier, he called me. He called me out. He wanted to get off on an ego trip, on a challenge thing. Why don't you take the wraps off? Let's get down and dirty about it.

"I'm not about no challenge, okay? Challenge is for them insecure people that ain't aware of what they is and want to prove it. John Africa done taught us if it's in doubt, that's when you got to prove it. When you know you're a man . . ."

Stiles asks for Delbert's attention. He tells him that this is not a forum for discussion, or for Delbert to address questions to him.

"You right. I don't want to ask what you call a question. I just put that out for clarity, because, you know, you a judge. You got experience. You know he's playing a game. He trying to taunt me before the jury, with the public in all this; and I'm saying come on with his belief and I'll come on with my belief, and we'll see what's going on."

Does M-1 supply MOVE with weapons?

"M-1 does what M-1 has to do to defend the above-ground chapter of MOVE, which is M-1's job. M-1 does not supply us with anything other than that protection, other than looking out for us, you know. They do all of that."

McGill's refers to Larry Howard's contention that M-1 is like the Sherrif's Department, without naming Howard, and asks Delbert if this is an appropriate analogy.

"They're not brutal. They're not sadistic like the sheriff—like some of the sheriffs, you know. If the analogy is to like protection that the city has in the form of sheriffs, police or so forth like that, that analogy could be done, except that M-1 is not violent. M-1 is not sadistic. M-1 does not go out looking for somebody just on somebody else's word, you know, just because somebody else say something. Go lock him up and go lock her up. Go put cuffs on—M-1 doesn't assume somebody is guilty because someone else says so, and then proceed to sanction them with a nightstick upside the head."

Has MOVE developed certain procedures of confronting the police?

"Yeah, we have procedures to confront police. We're not just out there for excitement. We're not just out there playing games."

What about MOVE procedures for confrontation in the courtroom?

"We've been taught by our founder, John Africa, how to deal with all those situations. See, we're a deeply committed, serious organization. We know our founder, John Africa, knew that we would not—would be confronting situations in court, and our founder strategized things that would make it not only easier for us, but easier for the jurors, witnesses, judges, and so forth that you mentioned, to understand what we had to say. And when it became necessary, we would raise our tone, lower the tone, do whatever we could."

Does Mr. Africa remember saying to Judge Malmed, "We are going to put your bald-ass head on a rack and hang it on the wall, Mr. Motherfucker. We ain't coming to court, motherfucker, tomorrow. Do you understand that? Everyone of you better come up here and understand that. You are going to have to show your heart, motherfucker. That's right. All your motherfucker sheriffs, guards, judges, cops, all you motherfuckers, you might as well start it right now. That's right. You hear what is being said right fucking now? We ain't giving up. We ain't never compromise. You are a coward, Malmed. You, your God, your sheriffs, all you fucking Gestapo acts, you are going to be the first motherfucking hunted dead"?

"That sounds like something I would say."

Did he also say to Judge Malmed, "You are going to have to get right or back up. That is what is happening. This organization refuses to compromise with you. Do you understand that?"

"That sounds like something that I would say; and the same thing I said today, as a matter of fact. You got to get right, not me. You got to get going. Saying I'm on the path of revolution. I don't want to be the way I was in this system. I like being strong, the way John Africa is made. I like having my children healthy, the way John Africa has helped us make them."

Item Five from the "Motion to Quash and for a Protective Order on Behalf of Michael Moses Ward," filed by David S. Shrager, the attorney for Ward, formerly known as Birdie Africa: "For a period of about ten or more years, until May 13, 1985, Michael was with the exception of an approximate one year period [when he was in a foster home in Richmond, Virginia] in the custody and control of an organization or cult known as 'MOVE,' which group included his natural mother, Rhonda Cheryl Harris Ward (who had assumed the name 'Rhonda Africa'). During this period of time, Michael was not permitted to attend school and thus at present is largely illiterate; was not permitted to enjoy or receive a normal diet, thus suffering from what has been diagnosed as protein deficiency; was largely deprived of a normal cultural environment, thus suffering from what has been diagnosed as cognitive deprivation; was forced to live in a social environment based upon interpersonal and familial relationships largely alien to accepted values, being instructed at 'meetings' and otherwise, inter alia, that his 'family' was MOVE, his 'father' was John Africa and he was not to associate with outside culture or society."

Delbert: "I don't want to be like your system, where your kids get raped in nursery school; or where your wife is told one day to enjoy sex with everybody, then you start crying when she come home with the herpes. See, I don't want my sons going out there to be homosexuals with AIDS. I don't want all that."

August 9, 1978. According to the *Daily News,* "Eleven children, ranging in age from 16 months to 8 years, yesterday became wards of the city Welfare Department . . . after the children were removed from the demolished compound [in Powelton Village] . . . Bathing was nearly nonexistent and the daily diet was a nutritional disaster. [A doctor at the Stenton Child Care Center said of the MOVE children] 'They're drinking orange juice like it was going out of style. And they're eating all our raw food. Raw eggs, garlic, apples, raw potatoes, and uncooked rice . . . For many of them it was their first true bath. They were afraid of soap and water.' . . . Before being taken to the Stenton Center, they were taken to Hahnemann Hospital . . . to destroy body and head lice . . . In accordance with MOVE philosophy, the children had lived naked and barefoot at MOVE headquarters . . ."

"Yeah, I told Malmed that he got to get right. He got to understand that the things he inflicted on us in that courtroom were wrong, Malmed and all those other judges, who sit in them elevated positions so you can look up at them, like they—they playing a game. . . .

"So you, the prosecutor, supposed to be looking for justice, and you sitting up here prosecuting my sister. How come Mayor Goode, who said he's responsible for May 13, ain't in this courtroom, instead of my sister? He sat up in public and said he take full responsibility. Bring his, his legal peeing ass up here. Burn him to the stake, while you got Mona up there. You say you want justice, then give out justice. What's just about you trying her?"

Does Mr. Africa remember saying, "You're going to have to realize this organization ain't never backing down. We know we right. This country is putrid. It's wrong, and you know that. You speak about law. What you're really about is money. What you're really about is finances. You're about them Cadillacs, about having them flunkeys come up here to address you as Your Honor when you know you're a dishonorable bastard. MOVE is going to trample all over your ass"?

"Yeah. I recall saying that and more, and telling the judge about how they buy them judgeships, about how they profiteer when they get them judgeships, how the cops come up to them and they let them go with probation. They get a cop shooting a kid in the hip, and they assign him probation at a teen center, or something like that. I also told Malmed about all them Cadillacs. And the whole system is founded on nothing but money. If Malmed, them sheriffs, them guards, them cops wasn't paid money, they wouldn't be doing what they're doing. All they is is modern day gunslingers, paid bounty hunters to come in, strap on the heat. . . ."

"Mr. Africa, I have one more question. See if you recall saying this to Judge Malmed. 'When are you going to stop that? I'm telling you that we ain't gonna take your goddamn game plan. Understand that shit. Because you know, we ain't giving up. We ain't gonna answer your damn questions and, you know, it serves no purpose to bring us down in doing that. And because we have shown our purpose, because we done showing we wasn't backing off your ass, there come a time when you are going to have to face confrontation. You are going to have to make a decision whether you are going to be an executioner. It ain't gonna be MOVE blood, motherfucker. We are telling you we are prepared to put blows back on off yours. Ain't gonna be no motherfucker man. You are going to have to shoot us or be done with it, motherfucker.' Did you say that?"

"That is a mistake by the stenographer. What I told the Judge—you right up to that part. The stenographer is right up to the part where it said the 'MOVE blood.' What—what I told him was, 'It won't be only MOVE blood that is spilled in this courtroom, motherfucker. If you come at us with them sticks, we gonna bust you upside your head and take them away from you. We gonna make you come to blows with us' or either draw them damn guns, or something like that. It was to that effect at that time. And that was put out to explain to the Judge that we wasn't gonna take no intimidation from them sheriffs no more.

"The reason it was put like that—people talk about profanity in the courtroom, but, you know, we really explain in the courtroom and explain to Malmed. Said, 'Ain't nothing more profane than them billy clubs. Ain't no four-letter word that swelled up my groin up to the size of pineapples the day them cops was kicking me. Wasn't no four-letter words that bust my head up at Holmesburg Prison. That was all the works of the night-sticks, billy clubs and all of that.' To speak of a four-letter word and ignore what's causing the word to come out is the same prejudicial treatment the media has given us. They will have words about 'MOVE explodes in a Burst of Profanity in the Courtroom,' but they never say what push it. They never say what topped it."

Delbert is back in Ramona's hands.

Did Judge Malmed ask MOVE members if they would promise to behave themselves in his courtroom?

"He said, 'What I want to know, yes or no, will you behave?' We told him, said—gave him examples that the Germans thought they were behaving when they threw Jews into the gas ovens. That was legal, according to them, to get rid of the Jews. How Malmed['s] slave-ridden ancestors legalize and thought they were behaving, and it was proper conduct, as they saw it, to bring blacks from Africa. So that's just what we told him. Say 'We can't just answer "Will you behave, yes or no?"' We told him we do godly. He's so decrepit and so nasty he couldn't even put up with that statement.

"We told him we was going to act godly. Objected to that. He wanted us to act legal. Legal, as we all know, is a front for—anything this system want to do to you, they make legal. They say they want you to knock on the door. Breaking and entering is against the law, if I do it. They can come up with no knock, walk in your house, and gun you down. It's okay when they do it. That's legal.

"What we in MOVE say, we don't accept them compromises. We don't accept that jive coming from the system. This is what we told Malmed each time he brought us down, until such time as we got tired of coming down; and told him, say, 'This is it. We ain't coming down no more. You and all the stooges that you sent to bring us down here gonna have to pay the price.'"

Can Delbert describe what he means by court procedures and strategy so that he will not be misinterpreted?

"Yeah. Regardless of what the DA was trying to put out there, when we say procedures, we mean how we handle ourselves. The same way he'll sit up there and attempt to talk about with his staff there, how they gonna handle the case. And that's what MOVE mean, how—how we're gonna handle the case, how we're gonna, like, present the best foot forward to the jury. Cause when the jury or people in the courtroom—cause when we come into court, we come in there to make a statement. Cause we ain't never gonna get no justice from this system. So all we know, we can get them into court, spread the word, spread the truth so it can be picked up like it's being picked up right now, today, you know . . ."

What does he mean by procedures for confronting police?

"Say like at a demonstration, when we would form up to go to a demonstration, our procedure would always be to have certain people carrying picket signs, certain people doing the speaking, certain people who were assigned that if anything—if anybody was attacked by the cops, if anything came down, that they would, you know, get the children and get out. Certain people were told not to get arrested. All of us were always cautioned, all the time, not to give in to the taunting of police."

Conrad Hampton Africa, shouting into the loudspeakers at 6221 Osage Avenue, early in the morning of May 13, 1985: "See, Goode, Wilson Goode that big head, black wide-nose motherfucker, he sent you white cops out here to get killed. You know why he sent you motherfuckers out here, see he know that you motherfuckers is itching to get a hold of some black lady. He know that you white racist motherfuckers is itching to kill some black boy in the street, and he know, Wilson Goode know that you white racist motherfuckin cops can't stand his motherfuckin ass and he know it, that's why he sent the motherfuckin guy in to get killed, that's what you don't know. See all that. Motherfuck that plaque you got down in City Hall, you know that plaque they got down the Center City Hall there. Well your motherfuckin name is written down there too. The next time you have that thrill show motherfucker it's gonna be for you and your mother, your kids, and your mother's boyfriend is gonna have thrills spending that motherfuckin money, they're gonna have thrills spending that motherfuckin pension that you worked so hard to get. See we know you motherfuckin cops ain't willing to do a goddamn thing, you motherfuckers all you care about is that motherfuckin dollar, but don't worry about it, the motherfuckin man that gonna be fuckin your wife and in the same time fuckin your daughter is gonna appreciate that money, cause he helped spend that money, he gonna be spending your share, he gonna lay in your motherfuckin bed and he gonna lay in your daughter's bed. See, cause that's what them motherfuckers get. See cause that's what the fuck you believe in. All you motherfuckers is filthy . . ."

Delbert: "For instance, they would have police at them demonstrations, and they'd be coming up with the usual lockerroom stuff, 'Go on, nigger. Go on back to Africa.' Laughing, taunting us, trying to get us going. Because they—they would have the excuse to like wade on in and start beating us up. . . . And the procedure was . . . to ignore them and keep putting out the information that we had to give out, because we knew that the spoken word was hurting them worse than any whack upside the head could."

Frank James Africa on the loudspeaker at 6221 Osage Avenue, late on the night of May 12, 1985: "We got something in this house for all you motherfuckin freaks. That's right. We got something in this house for all you motherfuckin freaks. So bring your motherfuckin macho asses the fuck on down here right now and get what the fuck y'all got coming. All you sick motherfuckin slimy ass motherfuckin freaks. Motherfuckers fucking around with them goddamn on your hip trying to intimidate some motherfuckin body, flying all over our house all hours of the goddamn night and day with a motherfuckin helicopter like that's suppose to do something. Y'all motherfuckers is sick. I'm just going to ignore you motherfuckers. All you got is a bunch of motherfuckin bully tactics intimidation tactics and a bunch of motherfuckin plans but see we got something for your motherfuckin plans. We got something for your goddamn tactics too, and that so-called strategy y'all think you're prepared with. We gonna give you motherfuckers what the fuck y'all asking for. See, we gonna end you motherfuckers, that's right, we gonna end you motherfuckers, we gonna finalize you motherfuckers. . . .

"Come on you motherfuckin SWAT magicians and we gonna swat you motherfuckers down. That's what the fuck we gonna do. We gonna treat you motherfuckers like SWAT. We gonna swat you motherfuckers down where you stand. We gonna drop you motherfuckers and let you swim in your own motherfuckin blood . . ."

What is MOVE's strategy concerning its children?

"The strategy held at all times to keep the children as close, as protected as possible, to definitely not send them away, because this system has shown that there's no such thing as a safe house when it comes to MOVE. We've had houses that wasn't involved in confrontation . . . that the police raided."

Ramona asks if Delbert has ever used a child as a shield or protection in a confrontation with the police. "Never. . . . The police just use that as more propaganda, some more lies because we know full well, the police don't care nothing about our children, and that using a child as a shield would never do any good."

Delbert turns toward the bench. "You know, at this point, your rulings could be to let my sister go. That should be your only ruling. If you really care about justice, you should just . . . let her go. Stop the proceeding right here, and let her go. . . . Talk about doing what's right. Then do what's right."

McGill is objecting all the while that Delbert speaks.

Stiles asks if Delbert will please just respond to the questions asked of him.

"I intend to give out answers, not play no games. You done killed our children. You murderers gave us a hundred years in jail, and you still act like this is just a party, just something to do. Talk about procedure."

Ramona asks if it is MOVE's intention to overthrow the system violently?

"They want to try and eliminate nature, God, and we intend to eliminate this system. They will attempt to put blockages between the wind and you, between food and you, and we intend to eliminate them dams, them blockages. We intend wholeheartedly to eliminate it. But never was it said that we are going to violently overthrow nothing. It has always been MOVE's stated purpose that the violence is coming from the system; that we will not perpetuate the violence. It has always been MOVE's intention to eliminate this system that we see is wrong; because it ain't life that's causing these problems, it's just lifestyle, man's death style, and it needs to be eliminated.

"All the problems that anybody in this courtroom, in this world complain about, they don't come from MOVE, they come from this system. People be talking about the headache they got. They be talking about heart attacks, ulcers, and all the rest of that. . . . That's your lifestyle that bring it on."

Can Delbert explain what MOVE means by the police's enforcement of illegal laws?

"We tell people we will do what's right. . . . So we don't follow the dictates of a bunch of hemorrhoid-ridden old men in Harrisburg or Washington, D.C. We do what is right. Can't nobody externally control you. You were put here by God to control your own self. If they think they had control over you, they could control your bowel movement, sexual drive, and all that."

Delbert testifies that when the imprisoned MOVE members heard about May 13, "it did hurt us. And we had told people before, because this system teach people about being macho or not showing any feelings. That's the robotism that they—the system teaches, and we're against that. John Africa has carved away that callous on us. People that used to be cold, unfeeling, in the system, we got them feelings. We very close to all our family members, all those that are close to life, and we feel that.

And we told them, 'Y'all hurt us May 13, but you ain't gonna stop us. You never will stop us.' May 13 . . . was felt deeply by all MOVE members . . . whether they MOVE members or not." Ramona says she is finished. McGill has no more questions.

Stiles thanks Delbert for his testimony and tells him he may step down. Delbert picks up the gym bag and faces the bench, "On the MOVE! Long Live John Africa! Down with this rotten-ass system!"

Then he addresses Stiles, "You got your part to do, and anybody else that claims to be concerned about what's happening. Got to get it right sooner or later, man. You know it's wrong to have my sister on trial right now.

"This guy"—McGill—"done brought up May 20, done brought up '77, '78. What about May?" Stiles calls for a short recess and sends the jury out. As the jurors leave the room, Delbert stands up and walks across the courtroom and towards the prisoner's door. He carries with him the bag labelled "LIFE."

In twenty minutes it will be five o'clock.

24

The Circus Comes to Town

Day Sixteen: Tuesday, February 4, 1986

Alberta Wicker Africa enters the courtroom. She is shorter even than Ramona, but delineated by the same childlike chunkiness. Altogether cloaked in a strange masculinity.

The greeting she receives from the MOVE family seems strained, forced, anemic. Her seeming lethargy, the lack of any impression of physical or mental strength distinguishes her quite profoundly from the other MOVE members who have been on the witness stand.

There is the usual swearing in in accordance with John Africa's laws, the usual recitation of passionate commitment to MOVE, attention called to harassment and imprisonment because of belief. The litany, spoken in a low monotone, is by now provocative of nothing but boredom in the faces of the jury.

Ramona's voice drifts in and out, "The media has portrayed MOVE people as a bunch of uneducated people, crime-oriented dregs of society, and I'm trying to establish the credibility of my witnesses as far as being an educated, articulate person."

Stiles permits Ramona to ask Alberta to establish how far she went in school.

And so Alberta alludes to an education laced with religious training: eight years at St. Agatha's Catholic School, four years at West Catholic Girls High, another two at community college. Between McGill's objections, she manages to assert that she was never in trouble with the law before joining the MOVE organization. Somewhere along the line, she checked out of the church and into the fold of John Africa. How this came about is not made clear. For fourteen years she has been "in MOVE."

Did she participate in demonstrations which concerned the incarceration of her brothers and sisters? "Yes, I did." She has more, much more to say, but Stiles heads her off before the inevitable take-off, saying that she has answered the question.

"Will you let me speak?" Alberta asks in her monotone. She stares, her eyes depthless, at the jury. She wants only to add that she was arrested for the first time in her life as a result of participating in these demonstrations.

Alberta has been incarcerated at Muncy state prison since December of 1982, as a result of her conviction on riot and other charges she cannot remember following the May 20, 1977 demonstration. Her sentence is twenty-two months to seven years. The demonstration, she says, ". . . came about as a result of my sister Janine Africa's baby being killed by the cops." She has not been paroled, because, "Every time I'm ready to see the Parole Board, I get set up for write-ups that stop me from seeing the Parole Board. You know, I can, I can give you examples. My sister Sue . . ."

Ramona begins to delve into Alberta's alleged problems with the Parole Board. Stiles forbids this, and sets her off. Such questions are important, she contends, because, "People need to know why MOVE was demanding the release of our innocent brothers and sisters; and the information as to why we're doing that stems directly from information that MOVE people got from people like my sister Alberta and, you know, other MOVE members in the state prisons."

Stiles disagrees.

"Well, what you're saying is that you're trying to stifle the truth, because people can't get the truth from a one-sided picture or a limited picture."

"There's been no one-sided or limited picture here, Miss Africa."

"It's been limited as far as people knowing that we demanded the release of our brothers and sisters, and not knowing why." Stiles directs her to ask another question.

Ramona's mouth is puckered with temporary defeat.

Is Alberta aware of MOVE members ever stating that they would kill a policeman?

Alberta, her voice loud for a change, addresses the jury. "Well, during the May 20 confrontation and just prior to the confrontation, before we sent our children to Virginia to a safe house, we did tell the children that if the cops tried to kill them, that in order to prevent a cop from killing our children, that we would kill a cop; and we did it to protect the children, to let them know that we would, no matter what, that we would defend them, even if it cost our life, because our children need to know that, because some day they are going to be parents themselves."

Were MOVE children exposed to abuse or harassment from officials in the period leading up to the May 20 demonstration?

"Well, the children that were in that house were babies, and—but they weren't so young that they couldn't comprehend; and they were very frightened. They were terrified. Every day they saw police surround the house, with guns pointed at us . . . On the day of May 20, hundreds of cops came out and stood in front of our home and positioned themselves on the roofs of houses that were around, and were around the house; and they had guns, and all type of ammunition, and it was all aimed at us, pointing at us. The children were out on the platform. They were crying. They were afraid. We had no choice but to have the children there, because they were all breast-feeding babies. The older children we sent away so that they would be protected, but that didn't work because the cops went there and drug them out of the house. . . . They drug them out of a house in Virginia, and put them in a home."

What did adult MOVE members tell the children to alleviate their fear on May 20?

"Well, nothing was said to us as far as you know, from John Africa. We, as individuals, as parents, as mothers, you know, told our children that if, you know, the cops were out there with the guns aimed at us, and the babies, if they tried to kill them, that we would kill them. And you know, our children, they believed us . . ."

Did Alberta write any letters descriptive of her conditions at Muncy or explanatory of MOVE's demand that she and others be released from prison?

Yes, she wrote hundreds of letters to Ramona, as, "It was her activity to handle letters from the prisons, and describing the conditions that, you know, we were being forced to live under, the way we were being tortured. We have been locked in isolation for three years."

MOVE members wrote in vain to city councilmen, local politicians, the Governor, and even to President Reagan.

"Nobody wanted to do anything to resolve the situation peacefully. In the meantime we were—suffered very bad." The imprisoned MOVE members lost their health, their teeth; their hair fell out.

They warned the politicians they wrote to of their belief that something would happen if actions were not taken to bring about their freedom. They filed petitions for appeals.

"Our appeals were mysteriously, you know, just overlooked, and there was nothing done about that. And everybody that, you know, always, all these judges that were contacted, they just . . . turned a blind eye to the situation, even though they know MOVE people are innocent."

McGill has no questions.

From the MOVE spectators: "Well ain't he a slimy motherfucker." Stiles thanks Alberta.

More rumblings: "He didn't want to ask her no questions. They don't WANT that shit to get out."

Alberta Africa is smiling faintly as she leaves the witness stand. She pats Ramona on the head as she moves behind the defense table and waves to the MOVE people. No one shouts "Long Live John Africa!" No one says goodbye. And Alberta vanishes into the oblivion of the imprisoned.

Sue Levino Africa, her face framed by long straight hair of indeterminant color parted in the middle, enters the courtroom. Her skin is drawn so tightly over her cheekbones that her skull is more than an imaginative possibility. Her eyes are heavily lidded. Her mouth is full and long, a great slash revelatory of missing teeth. The physical affect is one of a cadaver; the intuitive response is one of danger and great imbalance.

She is a white woman in a nearly all black family. She is also the mother of one the the children who could not escape on May 13.

"John Africa teach MOVE people to tell the truth," Sue says, "and I intend to tell the truth." It begins.

Sue Africa, in response to Ramona's efforts to establish her credibility, says that she attended a religious college, Wesley Junior College in Dover, Delaware for one year, spent some time at Indiana University (in Pennsylvania), and "was getting ready to go to Temple University" for her last two years. She never did. Instead, she "came into the MOVE organization." She has been a member of MOVE for thirteen years.

Did Sue come from a middle-class background?

Stiles sustains McGill's objection.

Is her father a professional scientist?

McGill objects. Sue answers, "Yes he is. He worked for the government thirty-five years."

Stiles sustains McGill's objection.

It is Sue's voice, "Judge Stiles . . ."

Stiles says, please, but she continues, "May I ask you something?"

"No, I'm sorry, you cannot, Ms. Africa."

"You know there's a lot of prejuduce . . ."

McGill objects. Sue keeps it up: ". . . because they try to paint us as dregs of society. My background would have a lot of . . ."

McGill objects.

From Stiles, "Just a moment."

". . . into dispelling that prejudice."

"Ms. Africa, you cannot, as a witness, rule on objections or overrule my rulings."

"I was asking to ask you a question."

"I know that you heard me say you cannot. I wish to allow you to testify, but you have to abide by the rulings that I make, and I'm going to sustain the objection to the last question, and ask you to ask another question."

McGill is speaking. "My objection, Your Honor, goes to both witnesses, as well as Ms. Africa, who will constantly use, as they do in every trial, that they have in MOVE, opportunities to argue, to sum up."

Ramona baits the old tormentor, "He's sitting there putting out misinformation. He's talking about every trial. I want to know how many trials has he participated in or sat in on? Are you talking about hearsay that y'all always talking about?"

Stiles tells her not to interrupt.

"Why are you afraid to let MOVE speak the truth in this courtroom? What are you people trying to hide?" Sue shouts, and simultaneously stretches her arms towards the opposite corners of the witness box like a kind of animal sacrifice.

Stiles does his best, reprimanding her most gently. He tells Ramona to ask another question.

Was Sue ever in trouble with the law before joining MOVE?

Over McGill's objection, she answers. No, she had never been arrested before becoming a MOVE member.

Has Sue considered leaving MOVE since May 13?

Stiles sustains McGills objection.

"No, I haven't."

Has her membership in the organization been difficult because she is white?

Stiles sustains McGills objection.

"From the system, yes."

Stiles sustains the objection again. His head hangs downward, his chin cupped in his left hand.

McGill does not resist articulating the obvious, pointing out that Sue is responding in defiance of the Court's ruling.

Stiles again sustains the objection. He is not looking at any of the people before him.

"This information speaks directly to the character of the MOVE organization, and . . ."

With downcast eyes, Stiles interrupts. "The character of the MOVE organization is not what's on trial. You are on trial." His voice is growing louder.

"Oh, yes, it is. Yes, it is."

"I disagree. The objection is sustained."

"I'm saying that the Commonwealth has presented evidence to give people the impression that MOVE are a bunch of terrorists . . ."

Sue gets back in: "And racists."

Ramona continues, "I didn't present police witnesses to give people the impression that MOVE is terrorists. All I'm saying is this is a MOVE member who is not being allowed to speak to the character of the—of the MOVE organization. I'm saying I'm being put on trial here because I'm a MOVE member, all right? I'm saying it has been testified, over and over again, how people have been involved in the same situation with MOVE people, but yet only committed MOVE members ended up being prosecuted and going to prison. . . . See I don't understand that. People are allowed to have character witnesses to testify specifically about their character."

McGill objects. Stiles acquiesces and tells Ramona that he will permit Sue to respond to "typical" character questions.

Has Ramona treated Sue any differently from any other MOVE member?

Sue answers over McGill's objection, "There is no racism in MOVE."

Stiles tells Ramona that since Sue has answered the question, he will allow it, but that he will sustain character questions which are not presented in admissable form. Ramona strikes back. The issue before them all, she says, is the murder of her family.

Sue begins to sway in the witness box.

The voice is Ramona's: "All that protocol and procedure—I'm interested in getting the truth out here. All this issue about procedure and protocol, I'm saying, you know, that means nothing when my freedom is at stake, when I know my family was killed because of court procedure, because of police procedure and protocol.

"I'm saying, you know, protocol and procedure have never been limited as far as putting MOVE people in prison, beating MOVE people, killing MOVE people; but when I get into this courtroom, then all of a sudden, you know, you and any other judge that's heard MOVE cases wants to stifle me. You want to stifle the truth, and try to limit MOVE people to some type of protocol and procedure. What kind of protocol and procedure was used May 13? What kind of protocol and procedure was used when a baby was kicked out of Alberta's stomach, that just walked out of here? Was that protocol and procedure?"

Sue's head moves in a kind of somnambulistic nod.

Stiles tells her that she may ask another question.

"You don't have no comment on that?"

"You're correct." He looks away from her.

Is Sue imprisoned now?

Yes, she has been at Muncy State Prison for five years, three of which have been spent in solitary confinement. Since May 13, she has not been allowed out of her cell for exercise or for fresh air.

Yes, she is imprisoned as a result of her conviction on charges based on the May 20, 1977 demonstration.

"Now, were you the only MOVE person to go on trial as a result of those charges, or did you go on trial with other MOVE people or . . ."

Sue is ready. She interrupts Ramona's question. The only thing the City of Philadelphia is interested in is ". . . locking MOVE people up. . . . It's not an issue of guilt of innocence. I'm in jail now." She was sentenced to twelve years with fifteen years probation "because I'm a white MOVE member." If she had denounced her affiliation with MOVE, like some other former members, she says, she would be free.

Did she pursue further court action in her case?

Yes, a lawyer filed an appeal for her, but nothing has been done about it for five years, because, "The Commonwealth of Pennsylvania refuses to give court-appointed attorneys my transcripts. At first, they said they lost my transcripts, it's—as incredible as it sounds. . . . Now they just out and out refuse to give a lawyer my transcripts."

She has been speaking over McGill's objections. McGill asks Stiles to instruct Sue to follow the Court's orders.

But it is Sue who speaks. "How can I answer so people will understand the truth and the extent of the persecution with this organization unless you speak . . ."

McGill repeats his request.

Stiles tells her to respond directly. Isn't her answer that she has attempted to reverse her conviction but there has been no resolution for five years?

"No, it's not. There's been no decision. He can't even file my appeal, because he won't be given the transcript. I could sit in jail another twenty-five years, and they could say that they've lost the transcript or refused . . ."

McGill objects and asks Stiles to request an end to the "speeches."

"Objection sustained." Then louder, "Objection sustained. Ask another question, please."

Is Sue aware of attempts to resolve the May 20, 1977 demonstration peacefully?

"There was no attempts made at negotiation May 13, because the city's intention was to kill all MOVE people, to kill our babies."

After a question from Stiles, Sue apologizes for misunderstanding the question. Yes, she was one of the participants in the negotiations on May 20, though she was in prison at the time.

"I was—I was brought to a courtroom."

Stiles asks Sue if it is her testimony that she was in custody before May 20, 1977.

"No, not prior, see . . . I was at the house May 20. I had the same charges on me that all the people had from May 20." But she was arrested three weeks after the incident, as she was leaving the house. While in prison, she was brought into Judge G. Fred DiBona's courtroom to discuss and help negotiate the agreement made between MOVE and the city, which eventually led to the August 8, 1978 confrontation.

Was she sought out as a negotiator in the May 13 confrontation?

No, but she was available and the city knew how to get in contact with her. If the city had had any interest in resolving the matter, she and other imprisoned MOVE members would have been contacted, but, "The fact is, they wanted to kill MOVE people and they wanted to kill our babies."

Stiles sustains McGill's objection, but it doesn't stop her.

"They wanted to kill our babies, because they know how strong our babies are and they want to kill our babies."

It is close to happening. Stiles reminds Sue that the objection was sustained.

Ramona gets back to work. So Sue was not contacted in any way concerning negotiations for May 13?

"It's possible that they might have tried through the mail, because

Muncy is always tampering with our mail, but I received nothing. We're not allowed phone calls up there, but the city could have arranged to contact me and my sisters at any time. We was never contacted, because they never wanted to settle this thing peacefully."

Was she contacted after May 13?

"We were told nothing until they told us our babies were dead. Then they sent a guard up, and he said, 'Your son is dead.' " She is shaking now, but her tremors seem bogus and robotic.

Was the approach made to her as a negotiator in the '78 confrontation initiated by the city?

"Yes they did, yes they did. They knew that MOVE wanted our people out of jail in 1977, just like they did again on May 13, and because I was in prison and three of my brothers were in prison, they contacted us and worked through us . . . because Rizzo was in office, public opinion was high about . . . the things he did."

Stiles sustains McGill's objection. "Ms. Africa . . ."

"But this time you had a black mayor, and everybody could be convinced it wasn't a racist issue, because he was a black mayor."

As Stiles begins to address her, she breaks in, "Isn't everybody accepting it?"

She is screaming.

"Ms. Africa . . ."

"I had a baby that I was told was killed. This is not a clinical discussion for me here."

McGill asks for a brief recess.

"I'm personally involved in this situation."

Stiles denies McGill's request.

"I am controlling myself as much as I can, but anybody that expects me to get up here and clinically discuss my son . . . while you got the murderer that did this still leading the city—I love my child. You understand that? MOVE people are very close to our children."

"Ms. Africa, I know this is a difficult thing for you, but you have to understand that when I rule on an objection, if I sustain an objection, you're not going to be permitted . . ."

"You—you are asking me to cut off my emotions on and off like a running faucet. My feelings for my child are not like that. I'm not a piece of technology that can be turned on and off. I am trying the best I can."

There is much sniffling coming from the MOVE women. Sue is striking powerful chords among the faithful.

Stiles tells Ramona to ask another question.

Between 1983 and 1985, was Sue able to speak to any of the residents of 6221 Osage Avenue?

"Yes, I had a few opportunities to talk about the torture and the persecution that was being inflicted on us."

"Did you say you had an opportunity to talk to MOVE people?"

"I talked to my child on the phone one time.

If her rights had not been violated, *vis-à-vis* her imprisonment, wouldn't Sue have been home with her child on May 13?

Stiles sustains McGill's objection.

Sue answers, undaunted. "MOVE people don't leave our children. We've been snatched away from our children by cops and sheriffs and judges."

Stiles instructs her for what seems the thousandth time.

When Sue spoke to her child, did he give her any indication that he was being mistreated?

"No, when I talked to my son, he—he was happy . . . When he talked on the phone to me, he was always telling me how strong he was, how he was going swimming, and running, and how strong he was getting; and telling me—giving me attention. I'm his mother. Telling me, 'You stay strong, Rea.' That's what he call me, Rea. 'You stay strong. You do your work, and that make you strong. I do my work, and that makes me strong. When you come home, I'm gonna be so strong, I'm gonna pick you up.' He was so secure and protected, and full of confidence."

(Boo was two when his mother was imprisoned, nine when he died.)

"If he had been held hostage or mistreated in any way, he wouldn't have been free and full of life, and happy like that on the phone. He was telling me to stay strong, that John Africa was bringing all MOVE people home because we innocent, we right. He was telling me to do my work so I could come home strong, and we could be together and run together and swim together.

"My son and I are very, very close. I delivered him myself, without a doctor, a midwife, even my husband there. We don't even leave our babies when they're real little. They stay right on our breasts for months and months. We don't even go out to a store and . . ."

She does not mention having bitten off the umbilical cord with her teeth. That part is turned off for the jury.

Ramona continues: "Now when you say you talked to your son on the phone, do you remember the last thing he said to you on the phone?"

Stiles sustains McGill's objection.

"Do you remember the last thing he said to you?"

Stiles sustains McGill's objection.

"He loved me, and he loved all MOVE people. And I want to know why the cops . . ."

There is little exhaling. It is like watching a pencil creep toward the edge of a desk, knowing it will hit the floor.

Stiles attempts to address the witness. He fails—utterly.

"The cops that made the bomb don't even have to come into a courtroom."

It is happening.

McGill objects twice.

"They don't even have to come into this courtroom and testify, and my sister is on trial?"

"Ms. Africa . . ."

"My family is dead!" She wails. "The city told me that my son is dead and the cops that dropped the bomb, made the bomb, don't even have to come into a courtroom of law." McGill is on his feet.

Stiles sustains McGill's objection. Twice. Then he announces a recess.

The court officer dismisses the jury. It is 11:35 A.M.

A sidebar is called. Standing as they always do in sidebar—alongside the far wall near the bar, the length of the courtroom separating them from the jury—Stiles, McGill, Stevenson, and Ramona confer in whispered tones among themselves.

Yes, Ramona tells Stiles, she has more questions for Sue. Well, then, she will have to abide by the court's rulings, Stiles replies.

No rules were abided by on May 13, when a bomb was dropped on her family, Ramona retorts.

"This is not May 13. This is not at Sixty-second and Osage."

"The same thing is going on. You're not dropping a crystalized bomb on me, but I'm saying you're keeping me from presenting an adequate defense. What my sister said is exactly right. Powell and Klein are not being forced to come in here and testify.

"On May 13, I was told that a document was issued that ordered me to come to court and present a defense. What my sister is saying is right. Powell and Klein was issued a paper to come in here to speak to the issue of May 13, but they're not being forced to come in here. When I refused to submit a paper, a court process to come to court because I know what those cops was standing out there ready to do to me, and in fact they did do when they shot people back into that house on May 13, a bomb was dropped on my house. You're not making no cops come . . ."

McGill asks her to keep her voice down.

". . . in and say that they wasn't going to testify. But when MOVE people are accused of thumbing our nose at the law, of not going along with the law, a bomb is dropped on us; and that's the inconsistency that my sister is seeking. You know, that subpoena, that order that told us to come in here and present testimony is no different than the . . ."

McGill objects.

". . . the cops. But when people refuse to go along with that piece of paper, the document, knowing that we ain't gonna get no justice in these courtrooms, knowing exactly what's happening now and what happened May 13 was going to happen, a bomb was dropped on us, allegedly because we refused to submit to a piece of paper telling us we had to come to court, we had to submit to court process. What's happening to Powell and Klein? That's inconsistency that nobody can explain. Nobody."

Stiles stands with his hands clasped behind his robe, staring at the floor, sometimes quickly looking up at the ceiling and going back down. It is obvious that Ramona is doing most of the talking but she looks at none of the men gathered about her as she speaks. Both her's and McGill's agitation is plain, and McGill, too, looks at no one. From time to time, he runs his eyes over the courtroom. At other times, he strokes his chin or his perfect mustache, tipping back and forth on his feet.

The sidebar ends, and the judge, defendant, and prosecutor move slowly back to their spaces. McGill requests that the witness be removed.

Ramona responds before Stiles. "Based on what? Because she told the truth?"

Stiles begins to say that he is going to question the witness. Sue directs a remark to McGill. "He's not concerned about law and order. . . . I can't sit here and listen to that. That's what the Jews were told . . . that they have to go along with the law. Told to walk into the gas ovens. That's what you're telling MOVE people, that we have to go along with this. That's what blacks were told when they were enslaved, that that was the law."

"Just a moment, Ms. Africa."

"If your child was in that house, could you sit here all academic and controlled? Would you be able to do it? You're telling me to sit up here like a robot and conform to rules and regulations. I got feelings. Despite what the news media portrays about MOVE people, MOVE people are very close to our children; very, very close. My son was everything to me. You hear me? Everything to me. And you talk about his life like I'm supposed to sit up here like a scientist dissecting a frog."

Stiles says that he understands the intensity of her feelings.

"No, you don't understand. You don't understand. Unless your child had been in that house, there's no way that you could understand."

"I'm not suggesting to you that I can understand your feelings. I understand feelings are very strong. The question I have for you is whether you'll abide by my rulings, and not answer questions after I sustain objections? Will you do that?"

"You're telling me to just cut off my emotions. I did not come into this courtroom to disrupt this courtroom, I keep telling you. The feelings and emotions and love cannot be put into—categorized and put into—in a box, and that's what you're telling me to do."

Will she abide by Stiles's rulings?

"Listen, you're trying to give . . ."

"Can you answer that?"

Ramona interrupts, "Before my sister answers, I want to put something on the record."

Sue interrupts whomever might speak next. "MOVE people are taught to be honest. I cannot sit in this courtroom with the callousness and the prejudice and the coldness against MOVE, while you show tolerance for Powell and Klein and Goode, and not express my feelings for that. I am not a whole robot. I cannot do that. I cannot—cannot express my love for my child. I cannot confine my—my grief for my child, or my love. I can't do that. I can't do that. I can't do that."

Ramona gets back to the record. "Well, listen. I just want to point out for the record, though, that when this prosecutor was examining, questioning cops and trying to make a point about August 8 of '78, when a cop was killed, I'm saying it was acting. I know he's not sincere about it. But he got very theatrical about a cop being killed. 'Why did you kill that cop? Isn't it true that you were involved in shooting a cop in the face?' When he questioned Larry Howard, did you tell him not to be emotional? Did you tell him to calm down, and abide by the rules of Court? But, see, when my sister talks about her son, and you know, being told that her son was killed on May 13, murdered by a bomb being dropped on our house, you telling her not to display any emotion; you know, to sit there and calmly ask questions about something that ain't no MOVE people calm about.

"You see, you sit up there trying to—trying to give people the impression that you're trying to be fair, you're trying to handle this thing, trying to give me a fair trial. If you was trying to be fair, I wouldn't even be sitting in this courtroom. You have petitions been put before you stating clearly that this—the charges ain't valid, and you dropped half of them. You know the charges stemming from what the cops said they was coming out there for, you dismissed them; which negates the whole thing. But you wouldn't dismiss the May 13 charges. You dismissed the charges coming before that, coming from April 29, the excuse that the cops used to come out there and kill us . . .

"You know, you trying to give people the impression that you're trying to conduct a fair trial here, but you're not. You know, and I can't sit back here and allow you to sit up there, so-called soft-spoken, and like you're trying to placate somebody; you know, like you're trying to be fair. I'm saying if you was trying to be fair. I'm saying if you was trying to be fair, I wouldn't even be in this courtroom. The whole world knows I'm innocent. The whole world knows what the city did to MOVE people on May 13. And you gonna sit up there and act like you know. You don't know that. There is no way, with the authority that, you know, people see you as having, the authority that you have as a judge, to do what you know is right—you know I'm innocent. You know that. And you have the opportunity to demonstrate your fairness. You had the opportunity to demonstrate your fairness. You had the opportunity to show yourself as a righteous person and do what's right, and you didn't do it. So it's no way you can lie up there soft-spoken, like you know, giving people the impression that you're trying to be fair about this thing. There's no way. There is no way.

"When Powell and Klein came in here, you knew as well as I knew the significance of, you know, their testimony, that they should be allowed to testify, should be forced to testify . . ."

McGills objects.

". . . but you sat up there, let them come in the back room and say they were going to take the Fifth. So what? So what? You know, I don't care what they do. But they got to be made—and you know it—that people ought to know, you know, what they're trying to do. All right?

"On May 13, my brother, Mo Africa, was in jail. All right. But now the city is talking about how he's got to defend himself in court, that he's being held responsible for May 13. Now Mo Africa was not even at Sixty-second and Osage. He was in jail.

"But when them cops who was out there, who dropped a bomb on MOVE people, you know, who are responsible for the scars you see on my arms and the scars you can't see on my leg, you're telling me that they can just say, 'Well, I'm not going to testify'? That's what MOVE people was saying May 13; that we're not going to submit to the court process. But when we said it, it was justified, because we were seeing our babies killed as a result of a gang of cops coming out there, saying that they had a piece of paper for us to go to court, to be submitted to the court process, when they made it clear that they wasn't going to testify, you know, no way they was going to take the Fifth, because they're under investigation, you know, you just sat back and allowed them to go on like it was nothing to it.

"You know, I'm being investigated now, you know, in this trial. This is nothing but a criminal investigation. But I'm being put in a position of having to defend myself, and fight the whole Commonwealth of Pennsylvania. But when them cops who dropped a bomb on MOVE people on May 13 came in here and said, 'Well, you know, I don't care about this piece of paper, we're not testifying. We'll you know, put a catch phrase on it, we're taking the Fifth,' there was no problem with that.

"The point I'm making is when MOVE people took the same position that we're not submitting to the court process, a bomb was dropped on us. And you don't see no inconsistency with that? You see that as fair, right?

"See, I understand. I'm not on trial here. You are. You're on trial. The whole City of Philadelphia is on trial, and the whole world is watching. They are watching. See MOVE people been telling people since MOVE that it ain't no justice in these courtrooms. It's even been said that you have to drop a bomb on people to wake them up. Well, the bomb was dropped May 13. When are you going to wake up and take a position, and utilize the authority that you have as a judge to do what's right, instead of covering up, you know, for the filth of this system, for the murder of this system?

"These cops, the whole City of Philadelphia is trying to wash the blood of MOVE people off their hands you know, through this trial; and they're trying to use you as the water. They're trying to use you to justify what they did. They're trying to use you to say that, you know, what they did, they had no choice of doing. It was all right. And you're going along with it. You are going along with it.

"This ain't been no fair trial, you know. And I sat here for weeks and weeks seeing just how far you would go, seeing just what would go on in this courtroom. See, my point was, I didn't have to make no points in this courtroom. My point was made May 13. That's what everybody is seeing. You know, whether I'm acquitted or convicted by this jury, that's not the issue. That's not the issue. Any time people can see a bomb dropped on people, know that innocent young children were shot at by cops, shot back into a house, you know, as testified to by a young child, a young child who was obviously telling the truth. And this child goes on—and you tell my sister that she—she has to abide by the legal law that sanctioned that? You're telling my sister that the city can legally murder her child, and then

she has to submit to the legal process. that she has to conduct herself in
—you telling her she has to kill her child, that she has to sanction that,
that she has to go along with that? That's insane."

Stiles tells her that the issue is whether or not Sue will respond to the
court's rulings.

Sue answers. "It's not a matter that I can't abide by your rulings."

"Well, then, choosing not to. The question is when you have . . ."

"You know, I can't—I can't . . ."

"Just a moment."

"I can't pidgeonhole my emotions. That's what you're telling me to
do. You make it sound like I'm sitting up here saying 'The hell with this
courtroom. I'm not doing anything you tell me.' It's not a matter of that."

"Ms. Africa, right now!" Stiles shouts. "I'm talking to Ramona Africa,
who is the defendant here, and I'd ask you to allow me to do that. It's
been characterized that I'm asking her to hold her emotions in check. I'm
not doing that. Other MOVE members, other people have strong emotions as well. They have abided by my rulings. This witness, who may be
the last MOVE member to testify, has said that she's not able to. I'm
asking you . . ."

Sue is talking willy-nilly to herself, the judge, the press, Ramona, the
long-empty jurors' chairs.

His voice now reduced to a whisper, Stiles asks Ramona if she has any
further argument.

"Well, the only thing to say about that issue is the truth. That's what
my sister needed to tell. All right? Now to sit up there and say that if she
indicates to you that she cannot abide by the rulings of this court, are the
rulings of this court in conflict with the truth? Is that what you're telling
me? Are you accusing my sister of not telling the truth?

"See, all those legal words, and words about ruling and courts, that
means nothing to me. John Africa has taught people to see things simply
and clearly. My sister is here to tell the truth, all right? That's what she's
done. Unless you're accusing her of lying, then you're acknowledging that
as far as you know, her testimony is the truth.

"Now if you're telling me that any court procedure that you're bound
by is in conflict with the truth, then you got the problem; not my sister.
All right? The problem is that court proceeding, protocol, procedures are
in conflict with the truth, and that is the issue."

Sue butts in, "I'm not saying I flagrantly refuse to obey the rules of
this court. I'm not saying that. I want that to be clear, Judge Stiles. I am
not saying that. You asked me a question. I told you that we tell the truth.
I cannot sit here and promise that if you ask me a question, that my

emotions might—I can't promise that. I'm not sitting here saying, 'The hell with this courtroom. I'm going to turn it out.' I am not saying that to you."

"Ms. Africa, I'm asking you to do your best . . ."

"I told you before that I would do my best."

"You told me that you could not."

"You asked me could I control myself. I said I can't control my emotions."

No, he did not ask her to control herself. He is telling her, though, that if she persists in speaking after he has sustained an objection, her testimony will be stricken and she will be prevented from testifying further.

While McGill requests that Sue be dismissed, Ramona says she has no more questions. McGill certainly does not have any.

Sue Africa leaves the stand, walking behind Ramona and embracing her.

"The power of truth is thine," Sue proclaims, "is thine."

"For ever and ever," the chorus of MOVE spectators mutters.

25

Walkout

Day Sixteen: Tuesday afternoon, February 4, 1986

The waiting has gone on for something more than an hour now. Bailiffs and deputies have been sent out to search for a videotape machine. The court reporter sits, her blonde head resting on the tiny desk. Her name is Helene and her hair contains all the light that her namesake commanded. When she lifts her head her face is blank and expressionless.

Stevenson emerges from Stiles's chambers. He moves to the row behind us. Mrs. Johnson, on the end of the row puts her Bible down and greets him with hushed voice. The female MOVE supporters seated next to her tell Stevenson they have a message for him to give to Ramona. Mrs. Johnson opens her Bible.

A profile in yesterday's *Daily News* was entitled, "He Defends Ramona on the Side." The article was accompanied by a picture of Stevenson, hamming for the camera in a leather trenchcoat. There was mention of how he would have handled the case if his client had been so willing, and no small implication that he believes his doing so would have been more beneficial to Ramona than the path she has chosen.

The message from the MOVE women in his hands, Stevenson walks to the defense table. As soon as he is out of earshot, one of the women says, "All he do is sit on his ass and collect his paycheck." Another: "Yeah, and boo-sheet, muthafucker." "He just like McGill. Just a actor."

At four o'clock, the television monitor rolls into the courtroom. Officer John Sigmann, a twelve-year veteran of the police force, eight years with audio-visual, is on the stand. Reporters know from the MOVE Commission proceedings that Sigmann plus monitor equals "Motherfucker Tape." The remark the jury is about to hear—more than the antitank gun, the Uzis, the BARs—speaks of war.

Sigmann took the videotape while stationed on the second floor, front, of Post One, 6218 Osage Avenue. He remembers that Lieutenant Marandola was there at the time, he did not see Commissioner Sambor, nor was he familiar with any of the other members of the department gathered near him. The film was made at about 6:30 P.M. on the thirteenth of May.

The film is shown.

In response to a question from Ramona, Sigmann says he saw no civilians there. During the time he was filming, he was not aware of the remark which was made. He did, however, hear the laughter after remark. He repeats for Stiles that he was not aware of the remark until he reviewed his work. Ramona asks that the jury be shown the tape once more.

Afterwards, Sigmann says that after arriving at Sixty-second and Osage at 3:35 P.M., he spent about sixteen hours there. He began filming at 6:30. What has just been shown, and what was assigned to him to make, is the official police videotape of the events of the day.

McGill has no questions.

It is little over an hour now since 5:27, when the helicopter loosed its parcel. Flames swallow the bunker and the house.

A man's voice is heard over this visual background: "That's the last time they'll call the police Commissioner a motherfucker." Then, the nervous laughter of men.

Day Seventeen: Wednesday, February 5, 1986

It is 11:00 A.M. Stiles recesses court until 1:15 as there is no available witness. As the room empties, a sheriff's van arrives. Two men wearing dreadlocks sit in the rear hold of the vehicle.

Upon returning to 253, a man is leaning over the rail speaking to Ramona. He is Charles "Charlie Boo" Burrus, one of the city's "negotiators" on May 13. He works for the Mayor's Office of Community Servies now, he is also president of the Inter-City Organizing Network, Inc. (ICON), a "community action" housing group, working under contract to the city. What most do not know is that Charles Burrus is under investigation by the district attorney's office for alleged financial improprieties, mounting perhaps into the hundreds of thousands of dollars. Some of the allegations concern MOVE. That, for example, Gerald Ford

Africa was on ICON's payroll, and that through ICON, City of Philadelphia money may have gone directly to MOVE in the days before May 13.

Burrus is dressed in a black shawl-collared sweater, white shirt, tie, and gray pants. Above the sweater is a black head of short gnarled hair, a goatee of similar texture. The eyes are small and deep set. The body is small and wiry.

Having taken the stand, Burrus says that he has known some MOVE members all of his life. Because of this, he was asked by Robert Hamilton, the husband of Goode's Chief of Staff, and Fareed Ahmed, who is known as a "community activist," if he would serve as a mediator in the Osage problem. Burrus does not mention Hamilton's connection to the Goode administration—his wife Shirley, considered by many the *eminence grise* of Goode's administration.

Burrus explains what was asked of him. "Very briefly, what I was told —asked to do—was to try to have, to convince the members of the MOVE organization to remove themselves from the property at 6221 Osage Avenue before a confrontation would develop. You know, in other words, to be a preventative person, if possible, and try to convince the MOVE organization to move out of 6221."

Ramona asks if during these discussions there was any mention of MOVE's complaint concerning the innocence of MOVE members in prison, or any investigation of this issue. Burrus says that this was not a concern of the city's, but had been brought up by Gerald Ford Africa who showed Burrus documents revelatory of Ford Africa's work on behalf of these people. (Ford Africa and Burrus are neighbors. They have also been friends since childhood, but Burrus does not mention this now.)

In May, Burrus met with Hamilton, Ahmed, and Ford Africa at Burrus's home in order to come up with a plan to prevent any confrontation on Osage Avenue. Ford Africa said that he would do everything he could to help "alleviate the problem at Osage Avenue" if MOVE could simply sit down with someone from the city administration to see if there were any way that those MOVE members in jail for Ramp's murder could be granted a new trial.

Ford Africa's main concern was "that some type of action start . . . no specific action. But if they would just start something, something."

Hamilton, Ahmed, and Burrus met with the mayor on the Thursday before the confrontation. Burrus is not certain of the date. They expressed Ford Africa's hope that the city make some gesture towards the imprisoned MOVE members, and emphasized their common fear of the possibility of a confrontation on Osage Avenue. Ford Africa would make no concessions, according to Burrus. Ford Africa's position was "if this happens, this will happen. But he was only explaining what was wrong and how to right the wrong . . ."

Burrus also met with the mayor on Friday, May 10. "And at that meeting, again, the three of us that were mediating were trying to set up another meeting, because at this time we felt that things were getting very hostile . . . So we met with the mayor to ask him if he would convene a meeting, or meet directly with Mr. Ford, who was acting as a spokesman for MOVE at that point."

There was no meeting after that Friday. Burrus had telephone conversations with Goode on Sunday, the twelfth. There was no contact between Burrus and any city official on Saturday, the eleventh. During those conversations on May 12, however, Burrus was not informed that warrants had been issued for some of the residents of 6221 Osage. Ford Africa similarly was deprived of this knowledge, according to Burrus. To Ramona, he says, "We, if you recall, I had a conversation with you on the stoop of the house [on Sunday], and . . . I had asked where was Gerry; and one of the civil affairs officers told me he was locked up.

"The first thing that I did was to call the mayor and ask him why was he locked up? And we were trying to resolve a confrontation, and their spokesperson was in jail. The mayor informed me that Mr. Africa was not locked up." Burrus had this conversation with Goode around 4:00 or 5:30 on Sunday afternoon.

Ramona asks Burrus to describe what he did at Sixty-second and Osage on Sunday, May 12. Burrus was there all day, and, "Basically my activities on May 12, 1985 was going back and forth, communicating with MOVE members that were in the house and trying to contact various city officials to alleviate the confrontation." He spoke with Goode "four, five, [or] six" times on the telephone, and had conversations with the people in 6221 Ossage "four or five times."

He was not there, Burrus says, as an employee of the city. "I was acting as a concerned person, because those were friends of mine that I grew up with, and I was concerned about—about their safety."

In Burrus's conversations with Goode, "Basically, our main topic is that lives should be preserved, and no one, no matter how long it took, should be hurt behind this incident. Because to us, it was just a civil complaint. . . . It was a civil matter, and we didn't want to see anyone get hurt. And we made numerous efforts to convince not only the City of Philadelphia, but the members of MOVE to try to do this, just eliminate the confrontation." Goode never mentioned the warrants.

Burrus pleaded with Goode. "If they were going to have a confrontation, why weren't the children going to be removed or arrested? . . . The mayor had told us that the whole time while we were talking, his main concern was to save life, and that's what he kept pushing to us, that that was his main concern. But on May 12, you know, I—I saw four hundred police, so that's how you form people's own judgment."

Goode revealed no plan for dealing with the children in the house to Burrus, nor did he indicate that the confrontation would be delayed until the children were removed. Burrus's last conversation with the mayor was held at about 9:00 P.M. Sunday night. Before this last conversation with Goode, Burrus was told that Gerry Africa "was acting as spokesperson at that time, that being on the twelfth, and if any other negotiations or mediations, or whatever terminology you want to use, was to take place, it had to be done with him."

Goode never mentioned to Burrus turning on the phone in 6221 Osage, as a means of communication with its residents, a method of negotiation which was employed during the 1978 confrontation in Powelton Village.

Burrus remained near Sixty-second and Osage until about 8:00 the next night, May 13. He spoke with Goode again around 7:30 or 8:00 on that morning, ". . . and I asked him what the hell was going on, because all hell had just broke loose."

Because of Burrus's ignorance of the issued warrants, he believed the police were there for, ". . . an eviction of MOVE from the neighborhood because they had upset the neighbors. That's the only thing that was put out there . . . to remove you [MOVE] from the house."

There were other people making varied attempts at negotiation along with Burrus. "There was Ms. [Novella] Williams . . . Robert Perkins and Nelson Robinson from my organization that were there all day long. And there were various other people trying to bring about some type of peaceful solution."

It is McGill's turn. He asks Burrus how long he has been acquainted with various MOVE members. Of Gerry Africa, "We're both thirty-seven years old, so I would say thirty-seven years . . ." He has known Ramona for ten years, knew Conrad all his life. He knew Theresa for a couple years, and did not know Frank James Africa.

When he was speaking to the residents during the days immediately preceding the confrontation, he spoke to them from the steps, outside. He spoke only to the aforementioned MOVE members.

McGill mentions Maude Roberts, whom he describes as a civil rights leader who was also present and attempting to negotiate. Burrus saw her there, but exchanged no more than a hello. McGill asks many questions about exactly when Burrus might have seen her there, which in Burrus's recollection was infrequently, and insinuates that because, as he claims, Ms. Roberts was there from Thursday on, then Burrus could not have been as frequently on-the-scene as his testimony indicated.

McGill mentions Bennie Swans, who heads the Philadelphia Crisis Intervention Network and asks if Burrus had dealings with him. Burrus did not speak to him, he says, but did speak to someone from the network. McGill badgers Burrus about when and where he might have seen Swans, and whether he had the opportunity to find out if Swans was having any success in his negotiations. "Sir, I did not question anyone's motives or alternatives to be in there. I knew that people were there to—the same as I was. We were concerned about the situation. And we didn't question each other why we were there. We were there because I think we all cared about what was—was happening."

McGill's response to this is, "I'm sure you were, sir."

He asks Burrus if he had a chance to speak to the Honorable Robert Williams, a Common Pleas judge. No, he did not, though he knows the judge. He and Williams testified together before the MOVE Commission, and McGill asks if he remembers the judge's testimony that, "he made special efforts with Gerald Africa in order to set up an arrangement where he, on May the 13, 1985, could be in a position with the loud-speaker to seek out the individuals in there before the confrontation concluded, sometime on May 13, 1985, the latter part of the morning, early afternoon?"

Yes, he remembers.

Does he remember Williams's testimony that Gerry Africa refused the terms of that agreement, namely, that Ford Africa would be tied up with a rope so that there would be no danger of his running into the house? Yes, he remembers.

Does he remember that Williams testified that he pleaded with Ford Africa to consider the children, to plead for their release, and that Ford Africa replied that, "If they died, the children [would] die with them"? No, Burrus does not remember that.

Certainly, Burrus was present for the duration of Williams's testimony, "I was sitting right next to him. If I may, it was a very tense time for me, and I had trouble understanding my own testimony to make sure I told the truth and gave out exact—I was not paying any attention to anybody else's testimony."

McGill spars with Burrus about the nature of Gerry Africa's expressed demands. He claims that Burrus testified that "Mr. Africa stated his very much and specific concern that the individuals who were incarcerated must be released." Burrus says that Gerry Africa "did not use the term that his people must be released. He said some type of judicial action to bring about a new trial, or something like that. . . . That's what he relayed to me. Three hour's worth."

Was there, in Burrus's conversations with Ford Africa, Hamilton, and Goode, any mention that if the residents of 6221 did not leave within forty-eight hours, there would probably be some arrests?

Burrus replies that Goode informed him of this possibility on Friday, May 10.

Isn't it also true that when Ford Africa was informed of this, that MOVE would have to leave the house within forty-eight hours, that he said he would not take it back to his people?

"To quote him, he said, 'I don't think my people will go for that,' " Burrus replies.

Burrus mentions that Goode and Ford Africa never met with each other, in his presence, at least.

But, McGill persists. Burrus knew that the two of them had spoken with one another and that Ford Africa had turned down the negotiation arrangement proposed to him, so did that not indicate the imminence of arrest to Burrus?

"What happened is that they said—the mayor said that if they would remove themselves from the premises within forty-eight hours, they could go and no one would try to apprehend them."

Burrus turns toward Stiles. "I don't know if this is in order or not, Your Honor. But if he—how come Judge Williams is not here answering all these questions in reference to Judge Williams?"

Stiles, smiling, says that he cannot answer Burrus's question.

"I don't know if I'm out of order or not. I try to stay out of these kind of spots."

McGill, with snide conviviality, quips, "I can appreciate that, Mr. Burrus." Exactly what time was Burrus taken to Sixty-second and Osage to make a final plea for the release of the children? Burrus says that he was too tired to know what time it was.

Well, then, does he at least remember pleading, over a bullhorn, that the children be released? Burrus replies that no, "I requested, if anyone was alive, and at that point I had doubts whether people were alive or not after all those bullets and all that water that went into that property during the day, and I had doubts if anyone was alive—if they would come out. Yes, I did."

After more irritating questions about precisely when Burrus was there, all the while repeating, "Again, I'm not trying to pinpoint out . . ." McGill finishes.

Ramona's asks Burrus if his perception was that the mission of the day was the removal of the MOVE members, ". . . rather than apply the law?"

"All I knew, that it was to get them out of the house so that they could be out of the neighborhood, which would solve the civil dispute. As I testified earlier, I thought it was a civil dispute between neighbors and the MOVE organization, and they were just trying to eliminate that."

Burrus, dismissed, takes a seat in the rear of the courtroom. During the quiet of yet another sidebar, his voice can be heard, not loud, but not soft either: "Bobby Williams, Bobby Williams? He go, 'Yump, yump, yump.' Ain't nobody can understand that nigger. Who the fuck can understand Bobby Williams?"

As the jury files out of the courtroom, the grating sound of handcuffs being fastened is heard. They are being placed round Ramona's wrists. She is putting out some information, sounding very much like a spoiled brat who hasn't gotten her way at the playground. "I want y'all to know I'm not participating in this trial anymore," she hollers at the jury.

Halfway through the prisoner's door, she turns around. "Y'all let me know how well *Stiles* does for me." Then she is gone.

No one hollers, "Long live John Africa!" Yet the courtroom is swollen with whispers and mumblings. The sound is not unlike the roaring of bees.

Mrs. Johnson is talking with a reporter. "I'm sorry she did that," Mrs. Johnson says softly. The MOVE women next to her look away. Mrs. Johnson does not speak for them.

One of the male MOVE members is standing, addressing the rest of the entourage. "Better start mak'n bail, y'all," he says.

An elderly black man is talking up the injustice of it all. "I'm *still* try'n to figure this shit out. I know this nigger didn't get justice."

McGill leans on the bar, keeping some gum busy. He surveys the courtroom, glancing slowly from left to right.

Stevenson has moved into a seat next to Mrs. Johnson. The usual frivolous blarney is gone. There is large desperation in his voice. "You mean to tell me she isn't gonna close? Isn't she gonna close?" It's as if Stevenson, who should be immensely familiar by now with the workings both of his client and her people, still can't believe what is happening.

One of the MOVE women has a favor to ask. "Can you get a note to her upstairs? It's very important."

He takes the note, then appeals again to the MOVE women. He tells them that if Ramona continues with her walkout, then he may well have to argue the case for her. "I'll have to if the Court orders me to. It's too late."

Protecting himself, he adds, "It's her case."

"If the Court HAVE TO," one of the women mocks, after Stevenson has left. *"HAVE TO!"* She spits out her words contemptuously. Another vigorously nods her head up and down. "Motherfucker." "He wanna do it is all. Been waitin to get up there with that other actor. Been waitin to perform, motherfucker."

Another theorizes about John Africa and how *he* would have handled this.

It is some seven minutes past three o'clock when District Attorney Edward Rendell unexpectedly enters court in the company of Brad Richman. Despite Brooks' Brothers' best, Rendell projects a street toughness.

He was Joe McGill's boss, and was once Michael Stiles's. And he is the man who had the warrants drawn up against the people in 6221 Osage.

Rendell's is a face that deserves some attention. There is nothing pretty about it. Craggy, slightly tanned even in winter, the face is that of a youthful looking man of early middle-age. The dark hair is receding, the facial whiskers, though closely shaven, are darker still. It is a face that should belong either to a movie actor or to a gangster, or to an actor playing a gangster.

Rendell, together with Richmond, leans against the far left wall of the courtroom. Like the good Philadelphia pol that he is, he holds court. Cronies and hangers-on, assistant DAs, fellow attorneys, and cops alike walk up to him, shake hands, and have a word or two with The Man. The MOVE women murmur among themselves. "That's Ed Ren—DELL," one says scornfully. "You know what he's doi'n here. Try'n to cam—*paign.*" "He put our ass in jail." Then, laughter.

A young MOVE woman cradles a baby in her lap while she discusses the situation with an older woman. "Motherfucker been motherfuck'n MOVE all these years." "Look at them," another says of Rendell and McGill, "in their red ties. Color of blood. Blood ties. MOVE blood."

Stevenson is back, standing in the aisle, leaning over and trying to persuade the MOVE women to help him with Ramona. "Do you folks want her to close?" You can tell from his voice that Stevenson isn't sure about anything.

One of the women gives him yet another note for "Mona." The

woman tells him that it's all Judge Stiles's fault. "She not bail'n out. He *pushed* her out."

Another agrees. "She was *pushed* out."

Yeah, he says, "But she also pushed me in."

"Pushed him in? Nobody done pushed his fat white ass but hisself." The women talk among themselves. "Mona's doin what she has to do." As for Rendell, "They think they goi'n to Harrisburg." The prospect of Rendell in the governor's mansion provokes great laughter and the usual obscenities. "He look like Castille," one says of Rendell and his former assistant Ron Castille, the successful Republican candidate for Philadelphia district attorney.

Naw, naw, another sister says, "You can tell Castille. He ain't got but one leg." Castille lost his leg in Vietnam. More laughter.

Burrus's voice drifts over the buzz of many others, "I was talk'n to Wilson," he says of the mayor, "and he says, 'If you take it past Friday, it's gonna be outta my hands.'"

Stevenson is back, yet again. "I don't think it's in Ramona's best interest," he says of her walkout.

"Did Mona tell you, *'Don't!'?*" the MOVE women ask. What they want to know is did Ramona forbid Stevenson to try the case in court.

"No."

The MOVE women don't act like they believe what Stevenson just said.

"Are you folks gonna see her tonight?"

They say they don't know. But they do have another letter for her.

He takes the letter, shakes his head, and hurries off to Chambers. When he emerges sometime close to four o'clock, he heads again for the cluster of MOVE women. He is wrapped in confusion and damaged ego. In forcing his hand, Ramona has made it clear that he does not serve her in any way; he serves himself. He can talk all he wants to about the "good rapport" between the two of them, but he is an alien in her world. "You hear from her," he tells the women, "you let her know that unless she comes down, it's me."

Day Eighteen: Thursday afternoon, February 6, 1986

Former District Attorney Rendell is at last called to the stand. Ramona is no where in sight.

Rendell explains that from January 1978 until January 1986, he served as the elected District Attorney of Philadelphia County. "As District Attorney, I was both unwilling, and more than that, legally unable to do any negotiating." Rendell says of his reluctance to deal with MOVE's demands. "I neither had the legal power nor the desire to negotiate over those convictions." Under no circumstances would he have considered releasing the nine imprisoned MOVE members or reducing their sentences, even if he had the power to do so. There was an established guilty verdict, and a formal appeal. "To be honest, I certainly, after weighing everything, did not feel that we were in a position to even begin to open up negotiations about that trial and those convictions."

McGill is finished. Stevenson has no questions, citing Ramona's direction.

Detective Nathan A. "Nate" Banner is in the witness box. Late middle-aged, heavy, his face pasty, his thinning hair brushed back, Banner testifies that in mid-June 1984, he was ordered to go to Channel 17 to pick up a videotape of an April 31, 1984 television interview with Ramona and Gerald Ford Africa.

A portable videotape machine and television are set up in front of the witness stand and just to one side of the jury. Neither press nor gallery can see the picture on the screen.

"M-1, MOVE's underground organization's going to do the bulk of the fighting," Ramona is saying.

A snarl grows on Banner's face as he listens. He watches the set intently.

Only a tiny amount of tape is heard, after which Banner is dismissed from the stand.

Officer John Cresci of the Civil Affairs Unit follows Banner to the stand. Short, stocky, swarthy, Cresci has a black moustache and wears a brown suit and a purple tie. He testifies that it was his job to videotape a November 21, 1985 television interview with Ramona. This time the interview was seen nationally on ABC's *20/20*. The reporter was Geraldo Rivera, and the interview consisted of three questions and three answers, after which Ramona angrily refused to answer any more.

The videotape has been carefully timed so that the jury will hear only a portion of the interview. Stiles, McGill, Stevenson, Cresci, and some others worked on the timing while the jury was out earlier.

When it comes time to play the tape, though, McGill manages to run it for an extra few seconds, just enough for the jury to hear Ramona screech how, "They're in-*sane. . . .*" *They,* of course, are the police, the courts, the officials of the System.

Stiles's face flushes to the bone. McGill didn't make any friends at the bench today.

Cresci then reads from the transcript of the interview.

Rivera asks, "Would you do it that way again, given the terrible cost?"

Ramona answers, "I would do whatever is necessary to protect my belief, to protect what I know is right. I will do what is right."

"Eleven of your brothers and sisters died. Was it worth it?"

"There is no measure of what righteousness is worth." Simple. "How much is it worth to you to be right?"

"I don't know if it would be worth my son's life."

"Well, to MOVE, being right is all there is."

This is it. The whole history in a nutshell.

A sidebar begins as soon as Cresci has left the stand. Soon, Stevenson hurries out of the courtroom. Everybody knows where he is going. Some twenty minutes later, Stevenson comes through the double doors of the courtroom. Grinning a little too broadly, he gives a thumbs-up salute. He is off the hook. Ramona will be giving her own closing arguments.

Stiles turns to address the jury. "You will begin your deliberations on this matter tomorrow."

Day Nineteen: Friday, February 7, 1986

Morning is dim with the fall of February snow.

The passageways inside City Hall harbor neither warmth nor light. The floors are obscured by water and mud. But it all goes on. Coffee moves in and out of the press room. The MOVE people press against the wooden barriers that block the entrance to 253. The idle and curious are no less up for the grand finale.

Through the door to the anteroom of 253, past the metal detectors and the searches, the reporters file one by one into the courtroom, as heavy doubledoors silently close behind.

A single plastic red rose sits on the court reporter, Helene Christian's table. The tip of the rose barely reaches the top of the bench. To her right lies the large laundry basket, now filthy with use and dust. McGill sits nervously leafing through photographs, stacks of police reports, old court transcripts. He fingers Sergeant Connor's flakjacket again and again, without touching the bullet hole.

Ramona's jacket is draped over her chair at the defense table. Her face in smiles, her arms bare, she leans on the bar, in conversation with the faithful.

Ramona pleads her case first. It is approximately 11 A.M. as she strides over and places her hands on the jurybox. She stands facing the jurors on her far right, Numbers Three and Four. She doesn't want to be here any more than they do, she tells them. But they know they will be going home afterward, she will not.

She is only here because she is a MOVE member, not because she committed any crime. She is here because she is committed to the truth, John Africa's truth. The prosecutor has been intent on prejudicing the jury against her; that is why he brought up all the stuff about MOVE's confrontations with the city in 1977 and 1978 when she was not even a member. "You see, throughout the history of the MOVE organization, city officials, state officials, and even federal officials have created a blatant hysteria against MOVE." They have depicted MOVE as terrorists, "as people that are simply out to provoke a confrontation and kill police." She is certain, however, that the jury has a different notion of what MOVE is, that there are now "some holes put in the image that you have been presented of the MOVE organization prior to this trial."

MOVE adopts its uncompromising position because it is right. They don't do it for any paycheck. She and her brothers and sisters did not "witness babies being kicked out of my sister's stomach and continue to stay in the MOVE organization because of money." The prosecutor, though, is doing a job; his is to convince them that she is guilty, at all costs.

Take a look at the truth, she asks them. (Not one member of the jury is looking at her.)

They have heard the testimony, and they should realize that if the Philadelphia police department was simply intent on serving four warrants, they had plenty of opportunity to do that. "The reason I was not arrested . . . is because it was not advantageous." That's not what the police department had in mind for MOVE people.

She is not asking them to determine the innocence of her imprisoned brothers and sisters. But they should understand MOVE's position, that they had exhausted all the legal remedies, and that was not enough. Hence the loudspeaker. They were convicted, and they were innocent. "I'm saying Jesus Christ had his day in court, and Jesus Christ was sentenced to be crucified on the cross." Conviction does not equal guilt. If this were so, "I'm saying you are telling me that Jesus Christ is guilty. You are telling me that blacks that resisted slavery, even though it was legal, even though they may have been convicted as fugitives, were wrong." Think about it, she says. MOVE people submit to what is right, not to legality. "You know, millions of Jews and others were put in gas ovens, were tortured unbearably, legally. Hitler's government was legal. Christians were fed to lions legally. . . . Millions of Africans were put into slavery and tortured legally."

MOVE will never accept what is wrong.

There is no evidence that she assaulted anyone. The police, on the other hand, dropped a bomb on MOVE people. No weapons charges have been placed against her, yet she is supposed to have assaulted someone. The police were the ones with the big guns.

And why didn't the city wait until the children were removed, if they just wanted to serve those warrants? It is no accident that MOVE children were killed. MOVE's kids are even stronger than its adults; they have never been influenced by the system. That's why the cops kicked Alberta Africa's baby out of her vagina.

It is a myth that MOVE considers itself above the law. MOVE members have been in these courtrooms thousands of times. They told the truth, only to be told to shut up. They were beaten in front of the judges. Their babies were taken from their mothers, "and held upside down by police."

The subpoena which was delivered to Officers Powell and Klein was a legal document, just like the warrants that the police served on May 13. But Klein and Powell, who are men sworn to uphold the law, did not submit to the legal process. The only difference between what they have done and what MOVE did May 13 is that they are officials. That's the double standard that MOVE will never accept.

If MOVE is so dangerous, how come so many people testified to having conversations with MOVE members? Why, if some of the cops, before May 13, walked right up to MOVE members and spoke to them, did they have to bring all those weapons out to Osage Avenue on May 13?

"How much were the Christians expected to take before they rebelled and resisted being fed to the lions? How much were Jews expected to take before they rebelled and resisted the Holocaust? You know, at some point after people have suffered for so much, they say, 'No more!' "

MOVE has constantly been asked, was May 13 worth it? "All I can say to you is it is never worth it to do wrong, to submit to wrong. If I am doing what is right, standing up for my belief in right, then there is nothing else. What else can I do; submit to wrong? You know, what purpose would I have for living at the point that I submit to wrong?"

The only thing she is guilty of, Ramona says, is taking a stand against injustice.

If the jury has any doubt about the intentions of the police department on May 13, all they have to do is think about why the cops were shooting at MOVE people at the back of the house. "Nobody was supposed to survive May 13."

"You see, it's no accident that world leaders all over, numbers of them, spoke out about May 13, and Reagan didn't. He didn't. And it's not an accident. He didn't hesitate to speak out against the unfortunate deaths of people in that satellite that went up, because he saw that as a tragedy. But you see, because of prejudice against MOVE, people don't see the death of MOVE people as a tragedy. . . . People see it as, well, MOVE people got what we deserved.

"You see, the same prejudice that will allow people to see a deer or a possum run over on the highway, splattered all over the ground, and just ride on it and just look at it and keep driving, is the same prejudice that will allow the people to feel nothing about MOVE people being killed."

If MOVE's intent was just to kill police officers, well, they've had their addresses, as well as those of city officials, for years. They could have done it. And they know about people who were willing to do it for them, but MOVE doesn't want that.

She is certain that whatever prejudice the jury might have about MOVE has not been completely dispelled. But even with that prejudice, it should be clear that nothing, nothing can justify May 13.

None of the charges against her has been proven. That's why the prosecutor is relying on the conspiracy charge. But, "I don't have the authority or the power to summon police officers out to my house on a particular day, and arrange to shoot them. I don't have the authority to do that."

"If police officers ever try to give you the impression that they felt threatened by MOVE because of statements that may be made, I'm saying you've got the full explanation of why we say and do, you know, certain things; out of protection. But I'm saying you have crystalized examples of what the police did. All right? And that was not out of any protection at all. It is not out of protection when you come out to my house, armed with all types of military explosives and high-powered weapons, allegedly to make an arrest. . . . All right."

She can't tell the jury whether the weapons that the prosecutor made such a big deal out of were really taken from 6221 Osage. But even if they were, just compare them to the weapons the police brought out there that day. There is no comparison.

"Now I know you're not familiar with MOVE belief, the way MOVE lives; and for you to try to interpret it would be like a person wearing sunglasses trying to interpret how light or dark it is outside. It's impossible. But you can look at facts, and keep in mind that you are dealing with a very serious issue here and make yourselves determine not to allow any prejudice to enter into your decision, into, you know, the conclusion that you come to.

"As I say, I'm innocent. Your verdict will either affirm it or deny it, but it can't change it. It cannot change my innocence any more than condemning Jesus Christ and putting him on a crucifix could change Jesus Christ's innocence. I am not concerned with whether or not I am sentenced to prison or whether, you know, it ends up with me going back on the street, because John Africa has cleared up any confusion in my mind as to the difference between a street block and a prison block. You see, my freedom is in the ability to do right. That's it. You know, and I will do right in any situation that I'm in."

Do something for yourselves, Ramona tells the jurors. Affirm your own righteousness. Leave clean, with a clear conscience, like MOVE. Okay, so you might be thinking about the children. "They were in a very deadly situation and they did not want to leave us because they feared the cops more than us." MOVE children saw Delbert beaten. They saw their mothers and fathers taken away by the police. MOVE didn't have to give them any anti-police attitude.

"John Africa has taught us, over and over that when your reference is right, you don't have to run from it, hide from it, make excuses for it . . . true law stands on its own . . . and any time that you compromise right, then you are no longer right." There are different levels of wrong, and only one level of right. MOVE knows that its position is right.

"To quote John Africa, 'The lie only starts the entrance to the mind. The truth erases the lie, and plants itself in your mind forever. . . . Long Live John Africa!'"

This is the last chance that McGill will have to address the jury. He would like to thank them; it's been such a long trial. Time away from things dear to them. He understands being sequestered. And he is grateful for their acceptance of their responsibility.

The jury is looking at McGill. Some of the women are smiling.

We live in a society that is governed by laws. That's why everybody's here. It's important to remember three words: responsibility, common sense, and courage. (Reporters look at one another and grin wanly. MOVE women mutter.)

Responsibility. Voting. In an election or here, your vote will make something happen. The sentence is not your responsibility; that is out of your hands.

This is a Philadelphia event. That's why we have a Philadelphia jury. Philadelphia has been imposed upon. Not just some of the people who testified. Community people. People who work hard. People who provide for their families. Buy their own homes. Love their community. People like you. This event involves you. (Smirks are exchanged on the press row. Dark mutterings continue to emanate from MOVE people, "Philadelphia Ee-vent, my ass. Boo-sheet, muthafucker." "Mmm-mmm-hmmm.")

Recognize the distinction "between the charges that are concerned with an incident and events, and alleged actions of this defendant and co-conspirators at certain portions of the day. . . . The latter part of the day, that aspect dealing with what has been called a bomb . . . and the admittedly tragic results . . . involve an incident that occurred twelve hours after the initial action started, ten to twelve hours." We aren't concerned about those actions. They are being taken care of somewhere else.

The police have to do their job. If they have to serve arrest warrants and are fired on and something happens later, those are two separate events. One doesn't have anything to do with the other.

Common sense, McGill continues. "Something that all of you have. A very wonderful way to have a jury trial." You can make judgments about witnesses, sense their credibility. Sift through the evidence.

Courage, courage to act. Reach a verdict based on the evidence, not sympathy to either side. Not based on fear or anxiety. Do not feel intimidated. Have the courage to state your verdict in open court.

It is clear, as Gerry Africa said, that MOVE's goal is total revolution. It is clear that to them legal does not mean right. It is clear that MOVE acts as one; didn't those witnesses reveal that to you?

Why weren't the children picked up? You heard them say they would kill rather than surrender the children to the system. Well, there isn't anything wrong with having intense beliefs. But it's how you impose your beliefs on others, your methods, the legality of the results of those beliefs.

To MOVE, what is legal does not matter. What is right matters. And they know they are right. That is what you are dealing with.

You can find the defendant guilty of riot. There was an intent to prevent or coerce an official action, with others.

No matter how much sympathy you have about what happened that day, none of us can resist the legal process of arrest. To do so is to ask for chaos. Those warrants were legal and proper. And we live under the laws of this city and the Commonwealth of Pennsylvania. This city and this state are not governed by MOVE laws.

I'll try not to put you to sleep. I know you're hungry. Stay with me.

They said they were going to be more prepared than they were in 1978. In 1978 twelve weapons were recovered. The police don't usually go out armed like that. There was a reason for it. They didn't know.

It's a logical assumption that if these people say they are going to die for their beliefs that they are willing to do that. And it would be stupid for the police to go out there unarmed when those people say it's going to be ten times worse than in 1978. They didn't have the bunkers in 1978.

People will talk about MOVE's puny arsenal compared to what the police had. But this is no puny weapon. This is a Mossberg shotgun. It kills.

Ramona interrupts. Would McGill please point out to the jury that the weapon he holds in his hands was not taken from MOVE's house? Stiles overrules her, but points out to the jury that the shotgun was not recovered from 6221 Osage Avenue.

McGill has arranged a "show 'n tell" presentation for the jury. There is nothing subtle about it. Sergeant Connor's blue stakeout unit jacket occupies a prominent place on the Commonwealth's table. The single word "POLICE" at the very top of the jacket shows clearly. Beneath the jacket sits the bulletproof vest with the bullet hole neatly exposed.

(All this is no doubt effective, but there is something positively old maidish about the way McGill has gone about this business. First, the civics class lecture, now the show'n tell. The intellectual level in the courtroom is absmally low.)

McGill continues. Let me make that very clear. This gun was a demonstration model. Something that looked like this was found at 6221.

Remember cult mentality, particularly on the West Coast in the late sixties? Some of you may have been a little young. Individuals who have the commitment to total revolution are the most dangerous to deal with.

You saw them here. You can tell by their faces, their stares, their looks, their expressions that they shout resistance and hostility and hate and danger. With that cult mentality they can be and are, extremely dangerous.

Remember what Gerry Africa said: "We go through these legal things because we know they're not going to work. None of them work. We want to expose this system because we are right. We're going to show you when we go through it."

Listen to these people.

As McGill reads from the words of Frank James Africa's words, Louise James screams, "My son! My son! Frank!" The MOVE women mutter, "Goddamn she phoney." "She scared."

"Booo-sheeet."

"She really is."

Mrs. Johnson is looking at Ramona, both of them smiling. Civil Affairs officers swoop down on Louise James. The Temple students sitting in front of her are quite out of their minds with fear. The police carry the still screaming James, in a sacrificial lamb hold, out the back doors of the room. The MOVE women are laughing. Stiles calls for a recess.

Afterward, the jury having eaten, McGill says he'll only be another half hour. He talks about conspiracy, resistance, and riot. He reads more MOVE speeches. He talks about the fortification of the house. He talks about MOVE keeping the children in the house, exposing them to danger. He talks about the policemen's injuries. A MOVE woman whispers, "Mmmmm, he a sick bastard."

He quotes Ramona, "Well, to MOVE, being right is all there is.' Ladies and gentlemen that's why we're here. That's why May 13 is there. That's why 1978 was there."

Stiles opens a huge law book. Don't worry, he tells the jury. They laugh. He reads silently. Soon the crier says that no one will be permitted to leave or enter the courtroom during the judge's address to the jury. There is dead silence. Stiles turns toward the jury and gives them their task.

While Stiles is explaining self-defense, two of the jurors stroke their chins. One woman leans deeply forward; her fingers and mouth form a triangle. There are murmurings from the gallery while Stiles makes his way through the charges. All of a sudden, a young white man shoots up in the back of the courtroom. He has been coming here for some time now; to look at him is to know that he will do something like this. "I wanta read the jurors their real rights," he announces to all. He is hustled out, and later announces to a television camera that he is "John Hughes. Consultant at Large."

"Son of a bitch. He didn't do noth'n," the MOVE women mutter.

"Son of a bitch." "That guy didn't do *noth'n.*" "They all paranoid." "They gonna take him out and beat him up."

The jury is ushered out of sight and into a conference room where it will begin its deliberations. The case of *Commonwealth* versus *Ramona Johnson Africa* is, at long last, up to them.

26

Verdict

Day Twenty: Saturday, February 8, 1986

The hallways and corridors are almost empty this morning. No more than a handful of MOVE people are here, and even fewer of the hangers-on. The routine of so many days is disrupted. The stage is the same, but the minor actors who crowd it are gone.

Every day, for more than two months, there has been a regular pattern to everyone's behavior. The same people line up in the same places, surround themselves with the same people, even depart together for the same rest rooms. But there are other faces here today, different sets of hands in the washbasins, and vigorous definition of territory between the press and the spectators. Most worrisome is the palpable contempt wafting from the MOVE camp towards members of the press, a contempt which was heretofore little more than an undertone.

It is only a little past ten, but most of the usual print and television reporters are already present. Newspapers are spread out on the floor, to be read, then sat upon. There is a bet sheet being passed around among the reporters and the camera crews. Not will she or won't she be found guilty, but rather what time will the jury come in with the verdict. Bets are a dollar a shot. The pot never builds up to more than fifteen dollars. It is just something to do, some way to relieve the tedium of waiting. Most of the crossword puzzles are finished.

The few chairs that there are in the hallways have all been commandeered. MOVE women with their babies sit in a couple of these. The rest belong to the television crews, with their bulky lights and cameras. Four clusters of chairs, people, and equipment line the opposite side of the hallway. At the center of each group is a small television monitor. Each group sits apart from the others, yet apart also from the daily press. The TV crews talk among themselves or else watch television, mostly Saturday's cartoons. Occasionally a MOVE person will wander over and look at cartoons too.

A young blonde sheriff's deputy tells of confiscating Ninja stars, the razor-bladed discs made famous by their use in Kung-Fu movies, from the bags carried by MOVE people into court. "Ever seen what a Ninja star can do to a man?" he asks, quite excited by the prospect. He goes on about how the deputies have been cautioned by their lieutenant to respond calmly to any disturbance. "Good thing," he says. "I'd have busted a couple of those sonsabitches by now." For all his talk though, the young deputy is invariably polite in dealing with the crowds.

The few MOVE kids here today sit in their mother's laps or else run around the halls. One boy of about ten or eleven works out with a MOVE sympathizer. First, the pushups. Dozens of pushups. Then, stretches of all sorts. The kid lines up in front of the adult, who grabs him by the arms and pulls him off the ground. Giggling, the boy is held tightly, his feet just above the man's feet. The man is laughing too. "Right there," he says. "Kick real hard. Right there, see." The kid is going, "Uh-huh," and he is giggling some more. "Kick real hard right there, and you'll break his damn ankle sure. Cop know to let you alone then."

Past the man and the child, past the ladies' room, down the hall and across from the mayor's office is the press room. The desks are cluttered with yellowed newspapers, stacks of papers and letters of all sorts, legal pads, legal directories, a *Who's Who* of city hall, and ancient typewriters. There is also a semi-functioning black and white TV that makes tinny, nearly unrecognizable sounds, a water cooler, a soft drink machine, and bulletin boards. Tacked to one of the bulletin boards is a reminder that this used to be a three newspaper town. An old *Bulletin* front page is posted there, dog-eared, crumbling, but still hanging on.

A television reporter wanders in presently. He begins a rambling observation of issues far and wide: the Black Panthers as he remembers them in his Chicago days, Philadelphia drug dealers, the cops, MOVE.

Another reporter becomes visibly agitated as he goes on. "Were you there? Were you there?" she spits at him. "Well, I was. I *saw* Ramp get shot. And he got shot from the front. *They* shot him. How do I know? I was there! I saw it," she says. Then she gets up and demonstrates what she saw, the impact of the bullet hitting Officer Ramp, the way he fell back, the way he hit the ground. "That's *exactly* what I saw."

The day winds down from there. The chill becomes unbearable. Reporters prowl the hallways for the sheer sake of movement.

Day Twenty-One: Sunday, February 9, 1986

The new day begins as the old one ended. The same cold, the same dank ill-lit corridors. Worn down, stomachs filled with coffee and greasy doughnuts, remains of old newspapers, used as seats as everyone hunches in little groups against one side of the wall or another.

By early afternoon, the waiters and watchers begin to think the same thought: We could be here for days to come. The jury went to church this morning. Then they had lunch. Now there is a chance they will be given the afternoon off.

But then someone yells, "They're coming in! The jury's coming in! They've reached a verdict!"

The race is on to get down the hall as fast as possible. In front of Room 253, the MOVE group has readied itself for the cameras. They have stretched out a computer printout and taped it onto the wall across the way: "FREE RAMONA AFRICA!" For a group that so loathes the modern technological society, this seems a strange expression.

The time is approximately 4:30.

Stiles looks about the courtroom, then speaks, "Ladies and gentlemen, as you probably have surmised, we have a verdict. We, of course, have no idea what that verdict is." He thanks one and all for the manner of their conduct during the trial and says that this must continue; there will be no outbursts.

The jury re-enters the courtroom. None of them even sneaks a look at Ramona.

Have they reached a verdict?

The jurors respond together, "WE HAVE."

"Do all twelve agree?"

"Yes."

"Would the jury foreperson please stand?

"To this Bill of Information 830, July Session, 1985, charging Ramona Africa with criminal conspiracy; how say you, guilty or not guilty?"

After looking at her handheld notes, she replies in a ringing voice, "Guilty." There are no gasps, no words, no mumblings. Nothing at all is heard from the gallery.

"To this Bill of Information 832, July Session, 1985, charging aggravated assault; victim being Sergeant Connor, how say you?"

The foreperson looks again at her notes before replying, "Not guilty." There is a distinct pause between the two words.

Neither McGill nor Richman show emotion. They sit, stone-faced, at the prosecution table. Seated next to them is Officer Michael Tursi, co-planner of "Operation MOVE," sharpshooter at Command Post One that day, and one of the many more or less independent actors in the rear alleyway during the hour between seven and eight P.M.

Ramona is found guilty on two counts (criminal conspiracy and riot) and not guilty on ten other counts (simple and aggravated assault against the persons of Sergeant Connor, Officer LaCon, and Officer Young; reckless endangering of Lieutenant Marandola, Officer Young, Officer Mitchell, Officer Freer, Officer Draft, Sergeant Connor, Officer LaCon).

Stiles, sniffling rather noticeably from the effects of a cold, asks the jurors to leave the courtroom.

The jury files out, and the judge lists for Ramona the legal remedies that are available to her. Post-trial motions, Stiles tells her, must be filed within ten days or she will forfeit the possibility of appeal.

"Whatever motions need to be filed," Ramona replies, "I'll file them." There is anger in her voice and the merest touch of a sniffle.

"Thank you."

"There is something I'd like to raise now," Ramona says.

"Yes."

Ramona asks that her bail be reduced to ROR, "released on own recognizance." In open court, the point is disputed by McGill. In the end, Stiles reduces the bail to a total of two hundred thousand dollars. Ramona is not going anywhere, except to the women's detention center.

Stiles announces that sentencing will be held on April 14, at 3:30, once again in Room 253, and adjourns court.

"Down with this rotten-ass system!" Ramona hollers. These are her last public words in this courtroom. Shortly afterwards, she is led out through the prisoner's doorway. The MOVE people are being unusually quiet.

Court officially adjourned, the jury is led back into 253. Stiles has one last task to perform.

"Understand," Stiles tells the jurors, "that my comments are not meant to reflect any opinion about your verdict. I would tell you these things regardless of what your verdict was. I never express an opinion on the verdict. I tell the jury, as you've heard me say, it's your opinion that counts. . . ."

He thanks the jury, compliments McGill and Stevenson, and pays tribute to Miss Christian the court reporter, the gallery for displaying such "good manners," the court officers, policemen and sheriff's deputies assigned to the trial.

His final words, however, are reserved for the jury again. "You've heard enough talking from judges, lawyers, and everybody else. I would like an opportunity to thank you privately. . . .

"You have our thanks, and you are excused."

Then Stiles stands, nods to the gallery and to the jurors, and quickly walks back into chambers. The jury members are ushered in after him.

As the courtroom empties, the MOVE people are quietly busy, taking down their banner. Bright lights glare in the hallways, as the television reporters and their camera crews swarm about McGill and Stevenson. The beat reporters make do as best they can, shoving their cassette recorders up as close as the TV crews with their cameras will allow.

While McGill basks in the lights, the MOVE people walk together down the hall, past the press room, past the mayor's office. They carry their banner with them. The computer paper banner drags along the floor. They do not seem defeated. In just this way, they leave City Hall, still very much a family. Kenneth, with the beautiful features and the sweet voice, walks with them, the cap gone, the dreadlocks revealed.

Some few minutes later, Ramona is led out the opposite side of the old building, through the prisoner's entrance. With no fanfare and with few reporters or photographers present to watch, she is hustled quickly into a waiting sheriff's van. The door to the ugly, brown-colored wagon is fastened closed. The deputies in their ugly brown uniforms hop in, the engine starts up, and they are off. The last seen of her is an image of the dreadlocks, the head turned, and the big men with their upraised shotguns melding into the distance.

The afternoon air is drizzly cold and the dampness penetrates to the core. A large wooden sign in the courtyard of City Hall stands guard over a construction project. "PHILADELPHIA IS ON THE MOVE," it says. "W. WILSON GOODE, MAYOR."

27

Sentencing

April 14, 1986

O utside City Hall, a white kid with hair shorter that a Marine's and a T-shirt which has "Urban Guerilla" written on it solemnly paces the edges of a small gathering. He wields a papier-mâché facsimile of Ramona's head attached to a long broomsticklike pole. It is a freakish and menacing sight.

This is a "Free Ramona" rally. MOVE members and sympathizers, many of whom never attended the trial, take turns with a bullhorn shouting disconnected and often incomprehensible histories of their's and Ramona's plight in the city of Philadelphia.

Before them is a folding table on which rest stacks of xeroxed leaflets which ennumerate crimes committed against the MOVE organization. The leaflets are passed out to a continuously gathering and dispersing crowd. It is near noon, and people leaving City Hall for lunch or passing through its courtyard cannot help but stop and watch. Most move on quickly.

The bullhorn can be heard for four blocks.

An out-of-town reporter, here for the first time, has a miniature tape recorder in front of the mouth of a black man in his late forties. He tells her repeatedly, insistently, excitedly that it is not Wilson Goode who is the villain in this story. It is not Ramona Africa, or the MOVE organization, or even Gregore Sambor. It is Robert Hurst, president of the FOP, the Fraternal Order of Police. His language is coarse, his argument nonsensical. She listens to him, asks questions, keeps the tape recorder going.

She listens to him in the way that some white people listen to black people, with earnestness all over her face, patronization in her questions.

Outside Room 253, a MOVE member stands at the fore of the "spectators'" line. He has a bullhorn and is reading a letter from Ramona. The letter is about setting her free. Other MOVE members and friends to the cause surround him. Earlier this year, it was discovered that Wilson Goode had used "taxpayer's money" to pay for speech lessons to enhance his image. He remains one of the poorest speakers ever to stand behind a microphone. The man on the bullhorn speaks well, and there are jokes about how he should have been the person hired to give the speech lessons.

There are too many people here. Maybe one-tenth of them will gain entrance to 253. A great deal of pushing goes on, coupled with unintelligible shouting. Small fights break out on the spectator side. A couple of reporters try to work their way through other reporters to get to the other side but, reaching it, don't stay long. There is no word on how many seats will be allotted the press. No one wants to lose a place.

There is no small element of fear. The unspoken sentiment is that something will happen.

There is a general consensus among the press that Ramona should be set free today. To evaluate the genuineness of this opinion, however, is difficult. The acknowledgment of holding another point of view would win no prizes and would most certainly prevent the possibility of certain longed-for post-sentencing interviews.

Finally one of the sherriff's deputies gives a nod to the first reporter in the press line. As he goes through the door, some people in the spectators line start pressing hard, yelling about how the trial is supposed to be open to the public and how the reporters are going to take up all the seats. Plainclothed policemen all too calmly reply that reporters won't take up all the seats, that everyone will just have to be patient and wait. The angry ones just seem to grow in stature dwarfing the policemen like the Blob moving over the diner.

There are so many press people that Civil Affairs officers put an additional row of chairs in front of the rail of justice and allow those who still remain without seats within earshot to fill the jurybox seats.

Stevenson stands behind the rail. His briefcase is on the windowsill at the end of the press row, and he is taking out folders, rifling through them, and putting them back inside. Brad Richman, who has taken the case now that McGill has left the district attorney's office, huddles with fellow prosecutors, reporters lean into one another, court personnel joke with one another, deputy sheriffs confer.

Richman sits where McGill had sat during the trial. He is small, blonde, chubby, and bearded and looks more like one expects an accountant to look than a lawyer. McGill is standing towards the back of the courtroom, where there is a heavy concentration of plainclothed policemen.

Stiles enters the room. All but the MOVE people stand.

Stevenson reads a letter from Ramona's mother into the record.

"I'm asking all people who express their concern at the outcome of the trial of Ramona Johnson to sign this petition. This is to inform Judge Michael R. Stiles that Ramona should be released, taking into consideration time already served, the fact that she should not have been on trial in the first place and the fact that Ramona was not a threat or danger to to the community. Ramona should be released. This petition will be used only for this said purpose. . . . It will be submitted to Judge Michael R. Stiles at sentencing. . . ." There are over a thousand signatures on the petition.

Ramona, standing, addresses Stiles. The conspiracy charge has not been specified, she says. She does not know what she has been convicted of conspiring to do. She cannot accept this. Furthermore, the jurors' remarks to the press, which indicated that the verdict was based on their desire to make a statement about May 13, invalidates that verdict. It is her understanding that a jury is limited to a consideration of the evidence and the testimony presented to them, as well as to the charges themselves in determining their verdict. Statements made by some jury members that they had decided beforehand that there would be no hung jury is revelatory of prejudice, and it is her understanding that this is illegal. It also indicates that some jurors may have acquiesced to a verdict which they were in disagreement with.

It is obvious to everyone, Ramona says, that her conviction should be overturned. It is obvious to everyone that there is no evidence that she rioted or conspired to riot.

There is more that she would like to say, should Stiles deny her post-trial motions.

Stiles says that he has received her post-trial motions, noting that they were handwritten.

There had been other handwritten notes from Ramona:

"Anybody who thinks they gonna jump on MOVE, wipe us out and leave an example of a well-organized plan is out they god damn mind. When you come in here, it ain't gonna be swift and clean it's gone be a *mess*. If MOVE go down, not only will everybody in this block go down, the knee joints of America will break and the body of America will soom fall and we mean it.

"Before we let you mutha fuckas make an example of us we will burn this mutha fuckin house down and burn you up with us."

Stiles remarks that Miss Africa had raised other issues, as well.

Yes, she says, in her post-trial motions she pointed out that the conspiracy and riot charges should be merged, as conspiracy is included in the definition of riot.

She would like to make it clear that, "Because of some devious acts on the part of the district attorney's office, my back-up counsel at that time and also the medical staff at Giuffre Hospital," the date of her preliminary hearing was postponed without her consent or her knowledge. The trial could have begun sooner except for this and Stiles's calendar. That she was not tried within 180 days, in defiance of Rule 1100, is clearly illegal and reflective of the truth that when a policy becomes inconvenient, it is the victim who suffers, and she is the victim here.

"To tell me that my rights to be tried within 180 days comes secondary to the availability of a calendar date, of a date, you know, that a judge can begin trial, that's secondary to Rule 1100 . . . is a major reason why MOVE people do not respect this legal law, because the officials that demand that MOVE people and unofficial people abide by it don't believe in it themselves . . ."

Richman counters that the case was postponed legitimately and reads a letter from Dr. Giuffre to the court.

This will certify that RAMONA JOHNSON (aka AFRICA) is currently hospitalized at the James C. Giuffre Medical Center and under my care for the treatment of 1st and 2nd degree burns of her left arm and forearm, left hand, right arm and right forearm, left flank and left leg.

She underwent a split thickness skin graft with debridement to her left leg, left arm, left buttock and left posterior buttock on Thursday, May 30, 1985. Treatment post-operatively consists of daily dressing changes under strict sterile conditions and complete bedrest.

It is therefore imperative that she remain at bedrest without mobilization for at least three weeks post-operatively, at which time the condition of her burns will be reevaluated. June 5, 1985. James C. Giuffre, M.D.

Richman continues. The delay which followed as a result of this was proper, in the face of the information received, and was relatively brief.

The case was tried within about seven months of the event. Miss Africa's rights were not violated.

Furthermore, Richman argues, had the case come before any other common pleas judge, the case certainly would not have come to trial as early as it did. What Miss Africa has done is to say, "Judge Stiles, I'm Ramona Africa, drop everything else on your calendar and try me first . . ." and no defendant should be serviced at the expense of other defendants.

Richman then poses a long argument, asking that Ramona be sentenced separately on the conspiracy and riot charges. Stiles maintains his position that he would be sentencing her twice for the same conduct, which he will not do. He asks Ramona to address herself to the sentencing.

"Well, one of the first things that I want to state about this so-called sentencing is that because of the teaching of John Africa, the powerful wisdom of John Africa, I'm not hallucinating, that I'm being sentenced to death. I was sentenced on May 13 and there's no question about that in my mind. Any time hundreds of cops come out to my house with the type of artillery that they had on May 13, I was sentenced then. I was sentenced to have the skin burned off my body and leave me scarred for life. I was sentenced to have ten thousand rounds of bullets shot at me and my family in less than ninety minutes according to police records. I was sentenced to have thousands of pounds of water, you know, forced on me, the force of a deluge on May 13. I was forced to see my family burnt up, shot down in the alley on May 13. I was sentenced to that on May 13 and there is nothing, nothing at all that you can do today that will even begin to compare with what I was sentenced to on May 13.

"This is nothing but a formality. That's all it is. You see, John Africa is very clear and has taught MOVE people to be very clear on the fact that any time I am taken into custody, denied my freedom, any time I'm denied the love and sensitivity of my family because they are murdered, I was sentenced. You know, anything about waiting until a later point, waiting for a trial is ridiculous. I was tried, convicted, and sentenced on May 13. This is nothing but a formality. I want everybody to understand that I'm here simply because I'm a MOVE member, because I survived. . . .

"Not one single cop, not one single official has been brought into a courtroom, tried, convicted, or acquitted of anything. They are still walking the streets . . ."

Ramona claims that she is here only because she and her family will not endure the prison sentences of innocent MOVE members. She is not here because she committed a crime. She simply refused to tolerate injustice, "including the murder of our babies, unjust prison sentence, being beaten in front of the judges right here in City Hall . . ."

What would you want your family to do if you were put in prison for a crime you did not commit? Would you want them to accept this, or would you want them to fight for you? "And in case you're wondering, that's not a question, because the answer is clear. It's not a rhetorical question either. The answer is implicit in the question and anybody that tries to say that they would not want their family to take a strong uncompromising stand for them is a liar . . ."

MOVE will never tolerate injustice, she says defiantly. MOVE will always confront a wrong. And a system that consciously sends innocent people to prison is wrong. No one who confronts wrong can be wrong. We should all be clear on this.

What do you want from me anyway? Ramona asks. "Do you want me to go out and party, to smoke cigarettes, to smoke reefer, to pop pills, to be a punk rocker, to come in here with my hair dyed purple, green, to have safety pins in my ear? Do you want me to dress fashionable in Calvin Klein jeans or Gucci dresses? You want me to put some curls in my hair? I'm sorry, I'm not going to do that. Would you like me to be an actor? Would that be acceptable to you? Would it be acceptable to you for me to be a female Rock Hudson with AIDS, you know, with all types of perversions? Would that be more acceptable to you? You probably respected Rock Hudson and looked up to him. A lot of people do, but if that's what you want from me, you will never get it."

She is close to screaming at Stiles.

"Would you prefer me, would it be more acceptable to you if I was an industrialist in this system that takes drugs, pops pills to wake up, pop pills to go to sleep, pop pills to lose weight, pop pills to gain weight, pop pills to make your heart beat fast, pop pills to make your heart beat slower, become an alchoholic because I can't deal with the pressures that industry puts on me? Would that be more acceptable to you? It's not to me and you will never get it from me. You see, you want me to live your way, the system's way, instead of John Africa's way, God's way. . . . You want me to become a so-called model citizen, to become an indication of what this system represents and I will not do it."

She will not forsake the godliness given to her by John Africa for the wickedness this system embraces. That would be insane, she says. That would be wrong.

She has placed her faith in what is consistent. "I'm talking about the law of the sun that is consistent, that if there was ever a break in the sun's consistency, we would not be here, no life would be here. I put my faith in the faithfulness of the air we must breathe, that we do breath without question consistently. It never changes. I put my faith in the movement of the water and the consistency of the water that we can't live without . . ."

She will not allow this court to hallucinate that MOVE is to blame for May 13. What happened that day can never be justified. This court should realize that it is perpetuating the "cycle of confrontation" by putting another innocent MOVE member in prison.

It is probably easy for Stiles, in the face of political pressure, to think things will die down after he sentences her, but every other official involved over the years has felt the same way and has been proven wrong. The only easy thing for him to do is the right thing.

"Confrontations, resistance is inevitable. As long as you try to impose wrong on people, confrontation is inevitable. Now you can interpret that any way that you want to. I'm not threatening anything. I'm not predicting anything. I'm simply telling you as a matter of fact that as surely as you will be burned if you put your hand in fire, when you impose wrong on people, you will force them to resist. It is as simple as that.

"Now the rest is on you. You got to do what you feel like you got to do today and just have to remember that you are the one that will have to answer for everything that goes on in this courtroom. Long live John Africa! Power of truth is final!"

Stiles thanks her and turns to Richman.

Richman calls a witness. Milton Williams takes the stand.

Prior to May 13, he lived at 6237 Osage Avenue. Yes, he recognizes Ramona Africa. He thinks she lived on the block for a least a year. Richman asks what it was like to live near Ramona Africa for a year.

"Well, just living hell." What makes him say that? "Constant harassment, threats, ten, twelve hours of the bullhorn constantly day and night, weekends." What kind of statements were made over the bullhorn? "Verbal and derogatory vulgar statements." Yes, some were directed at him. "Well, I was referred to as—I happened to be walking by one day and Conrad made the statement that he would . . ."

Ramona objects: "I'm sick of the whole MOVE organization being put on trial. Richman says he would like to be allowed to question his witness. Ramona continues, "All I'm saying is when a Ku Klux Klan member goes on trial, do the whole Ku Klux Klan go on trial? When a alcoholic goes on trial, do every alchoholic go on trial? . . . I'm saying that for this man to get up here and talk about what Conrad did, what somebody else did, I mean, shucks, may as well name the whole MOVE organization."

Richman contends that insofar as she has been convicted of conspiracy, then Stiles may consider the effect her actions as a co-conspirator had on the neighbors. Ramona and Richman begin to squabble.

Suddenly, loud noises are heard coming from the hallway. It sounds like people pushing against the door. The sound of this physical force combined with the strength of the hatred in the front of the room brings a shared tension toward the edge. There is fear on some faces as detectives in the room move out toward the thudding noises. The MOVE people curse Richman loudly, obscenely.

Stiles threatens to clear the courtroom if there are any more outbursts.

Richman argues that Conrad Hampton was a co-conspirator, when Ramona, raging, interrupts, "Where is Conrad at right now? Where is he at right now? Where is he at?"

Richman continues with his questions of the witness. Yes, Milton Williams says, the incident and the period before the incident had an effect on his children; he has a seven-year-old boy who is undergoing psychological treatment. The child has been in counselling for almost a year. Williams says counselling was made available to the residents right after the confrontation. The boy, according to his teacher, from time to time "babbles" about May 13. He, "acts strange, talks about the fire. . . . He screams sometimes."

Williams has not moved into his new home yet. He fervently hopes that Ramona does not move back into her old home.

It is Ramona's turn to question the witness. Did the strangeness exhibited by Williams's children manifest itself before May thirteenth?

"No, ma'am."

What is he saying?

"I am saying that due to your harassment and the threats that we received on a daily basis affected my children that we had to bring them inside, indoors, to keep them from hearing what you and your people had to say and the effect of it affected them psychologically."

"Who was responsible for that? Was it me, was it my brothers and sisters?"

"You were there. As far as I'm concerned, you're part of the problem."

"What about Wilson Goode? Was he part of the . . ."

Richman objects.

"Was this system that encourages racism in your children, that encourages your son to be a homo, your daughter to be a drug addict and a whore, is that conspiracy?"

"Miss Africa, I'll say one thing, if you weren't here, I wouldn't be here."

"If Wilson Goode hadn't burned down that whole neighborhood, I wouldn't be here. You would be in your house."

"You threatened to burn my house down."

"Who did? Are you telling me that words bothered you more than your house being burned down?"

Richman asks if the witness may step down. Ramona has no more questions. Milton Williams leaves the stand.

"Yeah. I want to know why you hate MOVE. Is it because MOVE showed you how weak . . . and systematic you are? Is that why you hate MOVE so much, because you ain't strong enough to do for your family what MOVE does for our family?"

Richman asks if Williams can step down. Ramona has no more questions, and Milton Williams leaves.

Ramona faces Richman, "You know, if you was in South Africa right now, them blacks would put a bullet in your head. You couldn't be in South Africa right now." Stiles tells her to allow Richman to make his arguments.

There are certain things which the judge should take into account, Richman argues, these being the causes and disastrous results of Miss Africa's actions. There are others to whom some blame might be apportioned; those are matters being considered before other bodies. But the relevant issue here is Miss Africa's role in the events and consequences of May 13, 1985; and that role was a great one.

"In 1978 a police officer was murdered by nine members of the MOVE organization."

"By cops, you mean," Ramona interjects. "Don't put that on my family. MOVE people ain't never killed a cop, never." Stiles asks her not to interrupt. "He's got to be permitted to tell lies?" Stiles says no, but he must be allowed to finish his argument, just as she was.

"I'm talking about lies. You say arguments. I'm talking about lies. That man know just like Malmed and everybody involved in that trial know good and well that my family didn't kill Ramp, they know it, they know it . . ." She has explained that Jesus Christ was hung on the cross, but that did not make him guilty. Richman knows MOVE didn't kill Ramp. He stands up there talking about the tragedy of May 13, but he has no compassion for MOVE people. She won't let him stand up and display a "sympathetic attitude" about how awful it was that MOVE people were killed. He wouldn't care if every one of them had died on Osage Avenue.

Richman ignores the baiting. What Miss Africa and those who conspired with her did was to hold the city hostage in order to obtain the release of murderers whose sentences had been reviewed and appealed. Those same people deliberately created an impression that they were heavily armed and ready to shed the blood of Philadelphia policemen. There is no other way to interpret the statement Miss Africa released before May 13, in which she claimed, "This is going to be ten times worse that Powelton Village. We have more now than we did then." Miss Africa and her co-conspirators coerced the city into some kind of action.

"Yeah, we forced y'all to drop a bomb. We forced you to, we made you do it, we demanded that you do it." Ramona is practically shouting, the sarcasm dripping in her voice.

Richman continues. MOVE made living on Osage Avenue unbearable for its residents, ". . . people who have kept that neighborhood with pride, who have worked and built homes and family only to see their children have to go to psychotherapy sessions, only to see that they can't sit outside of their homes on holidays and on other days because of the constant barrage of threats and of violence, threats of violence, obscenities . . ."

Not only those residents but the entire City of Philadelphia has suffered "much too much and long enough."

The Commonwealth, Richman says, harbors no illusion that rehabilitation is an issue or a possibility here. It is clear that Miss Africa does not believe that she is in need of it. There is no question here concerning the possible return of the defendant to the kind of activity that brought her to this room. The defendant has said that if she is convicted, she will work from prison. Work, that is, for the release of those convicted MOVE members.

Miss Africa has shown no remorse, not even for the deaths of other MOVE members. On national television she has maintained that there is no price attached to being right.

Ramona tells Richman that he sounds like "an idiot." Does he have a problem with being right? Does her want her to be wrong? Long Live John Africa!

If Miss Africa is released from prison, Richman claims, there will be another Osage Avenue. There will be another generation of children traumatized because of her actions and those of other MOVE members.

Ramona interrupts. "What about the generation of MOVE children who are denied access to their family because you got them locked up in jail? What about the sisters and brothers and mothers and fathers of MOVE people that you got locked up in jail right now for a total of nine hundred years? You worried about future generations, you got concern for children? You talk about what Osage residents were made to endure.

What about what MOVE was made to endure? What about the beatings, the baby killing, the unjust sentences? What about that? MOVE should endure that?"

"Judge, this defendant has told you that confrontation and resistance is inevitable."

"As long as you're wrong," Ramona snaps back. "As long as you try to impose wrong on us, that's right. Every time you get something caught in your eye it waters, every time. Every time you get something caught in your throat, you choke."

The court has a responsibility, Richman says, to protect Philadelphians. He requests the maximum sentence of five to seven years incarceration so that for at least three and one half years Miss Africa will not be enabled to make life in another neighborhood intolerable, and ". . . to reek the type of havoc with the lives of these people that brought about this entire very . . ."

Ramona continues to interrupt at will: "You talk about we make havoc with people's lives and I condone it. You sanctioned the bombing and burning to death of innocent babies, men, women, animals, and talk about reeking havoc."

With little more ado, Richman concludes his stolid yeoman's performance.

Michael Stiles speaks. "Miss Africa, I've considered the arguments that have been presented here today. I've reviewed the pre-sentence report and psychiatric report. In essence, those reports support what I already know, that you are an intelligent woman completely committed to MOVE and its philosophy.

"I've ruled that the conspiracy merges with the riot for sentencing purposes since it is my belief that those two crimes cover the same conduct and the law does not allow me to sentence you twice for the same conduct.

"Riot is a felony of the third degree which is the least serious grade of felony. It has a maximum sentence of three and a half to seven years. That is the crime for which I must sentence you today. It's important to note that you are not being sentenced for the more serious crimes which were charged involving serious assaults to police officers. If you had been convicted of those crimes, the sentence would be different here, considerably different, but you were not and that can play no role in the sentencing.

"The jury convicted you of riot, that you participated with two or more persons in the course of the disorderly conduct with the intent to coerce official action.

". . . In deciding what sentence to impose today I recognize that for most of May 13 you were huddled in a blanket shielding the children in your basement. I think the jury recognized that as well but the jury also decided in their verdict that you were guilty of conduct which initiated this entire catastrophe. It was your conduct along with co-conspirators which set into motion the confrontation with the awful consequences that it had and that must be considered. I note that those consequences had a drastic impact on you as well as on this community, and contrary to the Commonwealth's memorandum, I believe I must consider the harm that you have suffered as well as considering the harm of the community in determining your sentence.

"In considering your responsibility for this crime and the magnitude of the entire matter I believe that to sentence you to anything less than the aggravated range of these guidelines would be inappropriate and would diminish the seriousness of your crime, but considering what happened to you and the adults and children with whom you lived on May 13 as well as the fact that this jury chose to convict you of the least serious felony and acquit of other serious crimes, I believe that the sentence in excess of these guidelines would also be inappropriate under the law.

"For the reason that I've stated, on Bill of Information No. 842 of July term 1986, I impose the sentence of not less than sixteen months nor more than seven years to be served in a state correctional institution.

"You have ten days from today's date to petition this court for reconsideration of your sentence. You have thirty days from this date to appeal to the Superior Court of Pennsylvania. If you cannot afford counsel, counsel will be appointed for you for those purposes, if you choose.

"This court is adjourned."

Stiles leaves quickly. Ramona is taken out quickly. It used to be dark through this window in this room at this time. Now, with the calendar, light lingers. Television reporters scurry into the hall, toward the big lights. It is 5:30 and there is an hour remaining on each of the local news broadcasts.

McGill and Stevenson stand in front of their tables, each surrounded by reporters. McGill is soon dragged out into the hall to face the cameras. Stevenson remains, and a couple of reporters have their pencils moving, but no one really has much to ask, and no one has much to say. He too, leaves for the lights.

And so it ends.

Epilogue

Mayor Goode promised publicly after the May 13 confrontation that the Osage neighborhood would be rebuilt by Christmas 1985. The homeless neighbors would be taken care of in the meantime and housed at city expense, the mayor said. Most were placed in townhouses and apartments in International City, near the Philadelphia International Airport.

The task of rebuilding sixty-one houses in the Osage neighborhood was first awarded by the Goode administration to a firm controlled by black Philadelphia contractor Ernest A. Edwards, Jr. The $6.74 million contract signed by Edwards in August of 1985, called for completion of the project by December 30. A performance bond of $6.2 million was required of the developer, Edwards & Harper, as part of the agreement. On September 9, the deadline for posting the bond, Edwards announced that he had been unable to raise sufficient funds.

A Norfolk, Virginia construction firm, G & V General Contractors, Inc., posted the bond on that date and so became the general contractor for the Osage renovation. Meanwhile, Edwards, through his Premier Construction Company, was subcontracted to carry out the carpentry, drywall and brickwork repairs. In February 1986, Edwards told workers that he could no longer guarantee their salaries and walked off the job. The burden for carrying out the work now fell squarely on G & V, one whose owners, George McCadden, later claimed that Mayor Goode promised him that, "I would not get hurt." "I'm a black man," McCadden said. "I know how hard it was for [Mayor Goode] to get to where he is in life, and I know how hard it was for me to get to where I could put up a six million dollar bond. . . . Now one job and I'm destroyed." How could it be, G & V said, that a black mayor would lie about such things to a black family-owned firm?

In March of 1986, the city announced that the cost of the Osage reconstruction had risen close to $8.5 million. In August, the first few families began to move into their new homes, which featured oak floors, three bedrooms, a den, and a utility room. Most of the remaining families had by Christmas 1986 returned to Osage, where the cost of individual homes now averaged more than $138,000.

The Philadelphia Special Investigation Commission, referred to by almost everyone as the MOVE Commission, had been formed by Mayor Goode on May 22, 1985 to act as a "board of inquiry." Seven full-time special investigators were soon hired to work under the direction of former FBI Agent Neil P. Shanahan. During the summer and fall of 1985, more than nine hundred interviews were carried out by Commission investigators. The major participants—and a host of minor ones—from May 13 were interviewed and their words transcribed.

Open hearings began on October 8, 1985 in the heavily guarded studios of public television and radio station WHYY in Philadelphia. Over the next five weeks some ninety witnesses provided over one hundred forty-four hours of testimony, almost all of it broadcast live. The parade of witnesses before the commissioners and their counsel included Louise James and LaVerne Sims, Osage residents, city functionaries (housing inspectors, assistant managing directors, and the like), firemen, cops, outside expert witnesses, and politicians.

The police officers were practically all represented by the Fraternal Order of Police firm, Mozenter, Molloy & Durst, and these officers were advised by counsel to preface their testimony by reading a prepared protest. The record, the FOP counsel said, should show that the officers were coerced into testifying by order of Mayor Goode.

Public questioning was carried out by the Commission's counsel—former Assistant U.S. Attorney William B. Lytton and his deputy, former Assistant District Attorney H. Graham McDonald, along with Special Counsel Carl Singley, the then-dean of Temple University's Law School —and by the individual Commission members themselves, most notably Chairman William H. Brown III, former FBI Assistant Director Neil Welch, and former Watergate Special Prosecutor Henry S. Ruth, Jr. Welch in the course of the hearings distinguished himself for the doggedness of his questioning, Brown for his intelligence, Ruth for his eloquence and humaneness. Witnesses before the MOVE Commission, including the mayor of Philadelphia, all too often found tha they were in for a gruelling ordeal.

In the course of testimony, there were many muffled—and some not so muffled—asides to the police witnesses, along with strenous, sometimes violent, objections to the Commission's line of questioning by FOP attorneys Robert B. Mozenter and Patrick Artur. A few officers seemed largely to ignore the advice of counsel; Sergeant Albert Revel, for one, was cited by Commission members for his cooperation. Detective William Stephenson, the man who kept the police log on May 13, was represented by separate counsel. Most officers testified, but some did not.

Among those interviewed by Commission investigators but unwilling to testify publicly were Lt. Frank Powell and Officer William C. Klein, both of whom claimed the Fifth Amendment against self-incrimination. In such cases, transcriptions of staff interviews (the so-called "302s") with the missing officers were read into the record instead.

By late October, members of both the press and the Downtown establishment had concluded, after listening to the testimony before the MOVE Commission, that city government was simply not working in Philadelphia. MOVE Commission member M. Todd Cooke, the head of the city's largest banking institution, the Philadelphia Saving Fund Society (PSFS), pointedly lectured the mayor as to the utter incompetence of his administration during the course of one of the hearings. The *Inquirer*, meanwhile, ran a lead editorial praising the MOVE Commission for having shed light on the inadequacies of Philadelphia's city government.

Pete Dexter, the *Daily News* columnist, took a different tack, advising his readers to "forget Wilson Goode and Leo Brooks and Gregore Sambor for a minute. Study the parade of middle-management bureaucrats from L & I [Licenses and Inspections] and I don't know how many other departments that testified in the earlier phases of the hearings, and you will be struck by an absolute indifference to the well-being of the city."

In another column, Dexter recalled how he had sat in the studio of WHYY, "listening to some city drone tell the MOVE Commission that a bunker built on top of a house in a residential neighborhood did not appear to be in violation of any building codes. And I remember exactly what I thought then. That this city punishes the helpless and feeds on the weak. That some huge, cowardly force was at work in the structure of City Hall, and it took a shootout and a fire and a bunch of crazy people to put any public light on it at all."

Mayor Goode, former Managing Director Brooks, and Commissioners

Richmond and Sambor appeared both individually and as a group before the MOVE Commission—"The Four Stooges," a *Daily News* editorial called them, following a performance which was marked by much contradictory testimony, by Commissioner Richmond's teary account of his role in Operation MOVE, and by Mayor Goode's apology to MOVE Commission member Henry S. Ruth, Jr. for what had happened on May 13: "I don't kow what else I can say except, Mr. Ruth, I'm sorry."

After Mayor Goode's apology, Chuck Stone, the influential black senior editor and columnist for the *Daily News,* acidly commented on the mayor's words:

"Sorry?

"Sorry when he boasted he would have done it again.

"Sorry when he showed absolutely no remorse at the horrid deaths of five black kids.

"Sorry when he failed to resolve the blatant contradictions of his actions by all of his top officials.

"Sorry when he reportedly declared to a group within hours after the hearings ended that Philadelphians would forget the MOVE trauma by next year and judge him by how he collected the trash.

"Sorry when he reportedly told this same group that he could give any senatorial candidate a run for his money.

"Sorry?

"He's sorry, all right. The sorriest black mayor in America."

By the end of 1985, Mayor Goode was still claiming success on many fronts. In interviews with the *Daily News* and *Inquirer* conducted in late December, Goode noted how business trends were up in the city. Construction was booming. There had been a net gain of 17,000 jobs in Philadelphia during the two-years of his administration. City government was more effective than ever. He had created a city inspector general's office to weed out "corruption, fraud and mismanagement." Already in the past year alone some 550 complaints had been acted upon.

There was still much for him as a leader to accomplish, Goode told reporters: the funding and construction of a new convention center, the coming of cable television of Philadelphia, the building of a new solid-waste disposal system (this would become the much debated proposal for a trash-to-steam plant in South Philadelphia). He was excited at the prospects. He would put the MOVE disaster behind him. It was time for Philadelphia to go forward: "We're on course in terms of improving the city's image. I think that our program, 'Philadelphia Get to Know Us!;

that overall public program is working very, very well; that [in] all of the polls that I've seen, people do in fact feel better about the city than they felt two years ago."

On March 6, 1986, the MOVE Commission released its final report, *The Findings, Conclusions, and Recommendations of the Philadelphia Special Investigation Commission.* The report concluded that MOVE by the early 1980s had become "an authoritarian, violence-threatening cult," but that Mayor Goode's policy in response to MOVE "was one of appeasement, non-confrontation, and avoidance."

The Commission's findings were scathing. Former Managing Director Leo Brooks and former Commissioner of Police Gregore Sambor were singled out for their "grossly negligent" conduct in the planning and carrying out of Operation MOVE. Among the most important of the Commission's findings were the following:

[The mayor's] failure to call a halt to the operation of May 12 when he knew that children were in the house was grossly negligent and clearly risked the lives of those children.

The mayor failed to perform his responsibility as the city's chief executive by not actively participating in the preparation, review and oversight of [Operation MOVE].

Explosives were used against the MOVE house on the morning of May 13, 1985, which were excessive and life-threatening.

The plan to bomb the MOVE house was reckless, ill-conceived and hastily approved. Dropping a bomb on an occupied row house was unconscionable and should have been rejected out of hand by the mayor, the managing director, the police commissioner, and the fire commissioner.

With only a single dissent, that of former Pennsylvania State Supreme Court Justice Bruce W. Kauffman, the Commission also concluded that, "Police gunfire prevented some occupants of 6221 Osage Ave. from escaping from the burning house to the rear alley."

The deaths of the five MOVE children, the Commission said, "appeared to be unjustified homicides which should be investigated by a grand jury."

Another of the Commission's members, attorney Charles W. Bowser, went further than that. In a separate concurring opinion, Bowser made it clear that he believed that some of the escaping members had actually been shot by police gunfire in the alley.

The MOVE Commission's March 6 report fell short of recommending the resignations of city officials involved in Operation MOVE. Chairman William H. Brown III, however, told the *CBS Morning News* that he believed that Fire Commissioner William Richmond ought to resign at once.

That same day (March 7) Mayor Goode was the featured guest on a local call-in show. He reaffirmed his support for Commissioner Richmond, then told the radio audience that, "The real me hurts, hurts—and I'm very, very sad and sorry" about what happened on May 13.

On Sunday night, March 9, Mayor Goode went on live television to give a formal response to the MOVE Commission's report. "Tonight," the mayor began, "I come to have a heart-to-heart talk with you." The past ten months, Goode said, "have been difficult for all of us. I apologize for all that this city has suffered as a result of May 13." As for the MOVE children who died, the Mayor said that, "I weep for them and for their families. A part of me died with those children. And to their families and to all of you, I say I'm sorry."

At a City Hall press conference the next day, the mayor was expected to make specific reponses to the Commission's findings. Instead, Goode told reporters, many of them representatives of the national print and broadcast media, that, "I do not feel that I will be indicted. I do not feel there's a reason to do so." He conceded, however, that he had displayed some "instances of poor judgment" in his handling of Operation MOVE.

Following a brief question-and-answer session, Mayor Goode turned the conference over to his new managing director, James Stanley White, while his press secretary and her assistants handed out bulky informational packets. Inside the slick, embossed ("PHILADELPHIA, Get to Know Us!—W. Wilson Goode, Mayor") packets were dozens of "fact sheets" detailing the progress made by city government since May 13, 1985 in the matter of "Crisis Management/Emergency Preparedness." This would constitute the mayor's response to the MOVE Commission findings and recommendations.

One fact sheet bore the title, "Commissioner's Table Top Exercise." Yet another noted that, "Unfortunately, crisis management is being sharpened by real life crises, too." Among the numerous city bureaucrats listed as participating in these "table top exercises" were General Leo Brooks's former aide Clarence Mosely (now Assistant Commissioner of Licenses & Inspections) and May 13 negotiator Bennie J. Swans, whose city-contracted business, the Crisis Intervention Network, was assigned the task of operating "a 24-hour rumor control hotline" during a potentially explosive "Situation in Southwest Philadelphia."

Mayor Goode was not the only major actor in Operation MOVE to pronounce himself a changed man. Former Police Commissioner Sambor found himself the featured speaker at "Ordnance Expo '86," a two-day convention in Orlando, Florida, organized by arms manufacturers and attended by law enforcement officers.

Sambor's talk was billed as, "The Philadelphia Confrontation!" and a convention schedule proclaimed that, "No one in Law Enforcement can afford to miss this seminar." Tickets were priced at fifty dollars each, and more than a hundred fifty takers paid to hear the former police commissioner speak.

Sambor now believed, he told the crowd, that "there were people in the [city] administration and possibly the police department that were passing information to [MOVE] during those last two years about everything we were going to do."

He was convinced, Sambor said, that the bomb dropped by Lt. Powell from the helicopter had not started the fire at 6221. Sambor claimed, moreover, to have a photograph showing MOVE men on the roof of 6221 sometime after the dropping of the bomb. At least "two civilians and a police officer," Sambor said, had seen what they had at first believed to be water being poured by the MOVE men onto the fire. Yet, as the "water" fell onto the roof, the fire "flared up."

May 13, the former police commissioner concluded, had been "a terrific experience," but he added that "all in all," it had been "one of the most regretful days in my life."

MOVE Commission counsel and staff director William B. Lytton told reporters that Sambor's talk had obviously been an attempt to "reinvent history."

On April 11, 1986, inspectors from the city's department of Licenses & Inspections were turned back from a home on South Fifty-sixth Street in Philadelphia. The home belonged to Mary Robbins Africa, wife of Alphonso "Mo" Robbins Africa. Other occupants of the house included MOVE sympathizers Beverly Williams, Theresa Goodlowe, Denise Garner, and approximately six children.

The first anniversary of the May 13 confrontation passed peacefully. MOVE members and sympathizers held a vigil in a West Philadelphia park. The local newspapers ran supplemental sections commemorating the event. The burned-out Osage residents, most of them, were still waiting to come home.

Despite the hype of Mayor Goode's "Philadelphia Get to Know Us!"

campaign, many of the city's business leaders had not forgotten May 13 either. Ralph Widner, the executive director of the influential Greater Philadelphia First Corporation, explained to a reporter that, "Essentially, [the Philadelphia business community was] on an upbeat curve before the MOVE incident. There was a feeling that the [local] economy was on the move, that we could solve problems. The MOVE incident stopped that in its tracks. The MOVE Commission showed that we have a Stone Age city government."

On May 14, 1986, the newly elected Republican district attorney, Ronald D. Castille, petitioned Common Pleas Court President Judge Edward J. Bradley for a special county investigating grand jury "because of the existence of alleged criminal activities" in connection with Operation MOVE. Castille argued that he had information already in his possession which would justify such a probe. "The events of May 13, 1985," he wrote Judge Bradley, "can best be investigated using one or more of the following tools of the grand jury: The power to compel the attendance of witnesses; the power to compel the production of documents and other evidence; the power to compel testimony under oath; the power to compel immunized testimony; the power to initiate contempt proceedings." Yet another investigation, this time on the part of federal authorities, had been launched in the early fall of 1985 by U.S. Attorney Edward S.G. Dennis, Jr., then on December 6, 1985, transferred to the Criminal Section of the Civil Rights Division of the Justice Department in Washington.

To the obvious question of how a group like MOVE came to own real estate and was able to buy food and weapons, automobiles and gasoline, there was by the late summer of 1986 finally an answer, or at least a partial answer.

On August 1, the *Inquirer's* William K. Marimow broke the story. A front page banner read, "City Money Went to MOVE." May 13 negotiator Charles Lee "Boo" Burrus had in the months before the confrontation paid several thousand dollars in city housing funds to his boyhood friend Gerald Ford Africa, MOVE's minister of information. Using money that his Inner City Organizing Network (ICON) had obtained from its lucrative contract with the city, Burrus wrote checks totaling $2,460 payable to Ford Africa, ostensibly for the purchase of tools, for electrical work performed by Ford Africa, and for the lease of a beeper service to Burrus. The first check was written January 17, 1983.

Ford Africa told the *Inquirer* that the monies had gone to his Commu-

nity Action Movement (CAM), a group whose June 10, 1976 incorpora-
tors included Donald Glassey, Janine Phillips, Mary Robbins, and Cassandra Goodman, all of them at one time or other active in MOVE. CAM,
Ford Africa said, had merely acted as a purchasing agent for Burrus's
ICON.

Assistant District Attorney Hugh Colihan, the *Inquirer* reported, had
written a July 29, 1985 memorandum to Deputy District Attorney Eric
B. Henson that the transactions strongly inferred "that city housing
money was passed through the MOVE [via Gerald Ford Africa] during
the period in which the Osage house/bunker were undergoing siege
preparation."

An audit of ICON's contract with the city was prepared on May 28,
1985—fifteen days after the confrontation—and showed the disposition
by checks totalling $527,524.12 in funds provided by the Philadelphia
Housing Development Corporation and the Housing Association of Delaware Valley. The contract between ICON and the City of Philadelphia's
housing authority was terminated in June 1985.

Charles Burrus was subsequently hired on November 20, 1985 as a
$17,000 a year direct services coordinator in the mayor's Office of Com-
munity Services. Burrus later found employment with fellow May 13
negotiator Bennie Swans's Crisis Intervention Network, a "nonprofit
agency that specializes in preventing youth violence," as the *Inquirer*
styled it.

Possible criminal actions involving Charles Burrus and ICON and as
well as those concerning Ernest Edwards, Jr., and the reconstruction of
the Osage neighborhood have been referred to the regular, standing
Philadelphia County grand jury by District Attorney Castille.

On October 6, the *Daily News* reported that Stakeout Officer James
Berghaier, the man who rescued Birdie Africa on the evening of May 13,
had been transferred to the police department's personnel section. Berghaier intended, he said, to take early retirement after seventeen years
service. The memory of May 13, the officer said, "never goes away." In
order to survive as a policeman, Berghaier said, "you have to detach
yourself from what you have to do, and I never have been able to do that."
On May 13, "we didn't know how many kids were in [6221] and then
when the report comes that there were X amount of kids, how can you
feel? . . . I'm constantly reminded of the way that kid [Birdie] looked at
me, but it's not something other people can understand. I don't know.
It destroyed me."

Birdie Africa, now known as Michael Moses Ward, lives in seclusion with his father, Andino R. Ward, somewhere in the metropolitan Philadelphia area. The exact whereabouts of the boy are closely guarded —both from MOVE and from the press.

The City Comptroller's Office announced in mid-November that the May 13 confrontation had cost the city some $17,737,664, with funds provided mainly by the city's redevelopment authority.

Common Pleas Court Judge Juanita Kidd Stout had been named to oversee the special county grand jury investigating possible criminal charges stemming from the May 13 confrontation. On November 4, 1986, Judge Stout ordered that separate attorneys be provided for all police officers called before the special grand jury. The exclusive use of the FOP firm, Mozenter, Molloy & Durst, would, she wrote, constitute possible conflict of interest in the case.

"Seldom, if ever, in the annals of American jurisprudence," Judge Stout wrote in her *Final Finding of Fact*, "has there been a grand jury investigation in which the public has a greater right to every man's evidence than this one which inquires into criminal liability of those responsible for the killing of 11 citizens, five of whom were children, by bombing, fire, and gunshot, and the destruction of 60 homes by those who are charged with the guardianship of life and safety.

"Of all the officers involved in Operation MOVE, the members of the bomb squad were and are unanimous, and the most persistent in their efforts to resist cooperation with [the MOVE Commission] and the county investigating grand jury."

Judge Stout therefore disqualified the Mozenter firm from acting as sole legal counsel for police officers summoned before the grand jury: "That investigation must not be thwarted by the concrete silence of many represented by a single attorney."

In the same *Finding of Fact*, Stout restated her own conclusion that, "The police operation [of May 13] resulted in the deaths of 11 persons, some from fire caused by a bomb . . . and others from gunshot as they tried to go to the alley to escape the fire."

As expected, the Mozenter firm and the FOP appealed Judge Stout's decision before the Commonwealth Supreme Court. Attorney Anthony Molloy carried their argument further. The MOVE Commission, Molloy argued, had been set up illegally and had had no right to compel testimony. As such, the interviews and testimony given to the MOVE Commission and its staff ought to be considered tainted evidence, invalid in the course of any subsequent criminal actions against the police witnesses.

Commonwealth Supreme Court on December 12 unanimously upheld Judge Stout's ruling—along with the validity of the MOVE Commission and the admissibility in court of the testimony gathered by the Commission and its investigators.

At last count, twenty-three policemen involved in the May 13 operation had been subpoenaed to appear before Judge Stout and the special county grand jury, whose operations are, as is the case with grand juries, conducted behind closed doors. Five of those subpoenaed—all members of the Bomb Squad—were said to have invoked the Fifth Amendment. A grant of limited immunity from prosecution, meanwhile, was made to former Sgt. Edward Connor, who in turn did testify.

The special county grand jury is expected to conclude its work and make known its findings sometime in early spring of 1987.

At year's end, Wilson Goode knew that he would face a difficult reelection campaign, his opponent in the May 19 Democratic primary being former District Attorney Edward G. Rendell.

In February Frank Rizzo received the endorsement of the Republican party hierarchy. A theme he would sound often throughout his campaign for mayor, Rizzo said, was the single word "MOVE." The prospects are for a tough, if not positively dirty, mayoral election in the months to come.

On December 18, 1986, Alphonso "Mo" Robbins Africa was convicted and placed on two years probation for assaulting Police Sergeant James McDonnell on June 10, 1984. Trial and sentencing took place, as usual, in a courtroom at Philadelphia City Hall.

Later that month, Ramona Africa petitioned the Pennsylvania Board of Probation and Parole for parole. The Board announced its decision on December 30, 1986: Her request had been denied.

Ramona Johnson Africa will not be eligible again for parole until October 1987.

We are left to ponder the meaning of May 13 and the appeal of John Africa to the poor and the disaffected. Was Philadelphia's tragedy unique or was it a metaphor for a larger American tragedy? On the eve of the confrontation, Ramona Africa warned that "the knee-joints of America will break." Perhaps she was right.

Given the typical urban American setting in which men and women of different colors and classes do not, and seemingly cannot, meet in what William Penn, the Quaker founder of Pennsylvania, called "the broad pathway of good faith and good will," is it any wonder that John Africa could attract a tiny coalition of the most depressed, alienated, and poor and turn them into devout believers? Given the deep-seated indifference of both elected officials and bureaucrats to the plight of ordinary citizens in our cities, should anyone be shocked that little or nothing was done to stop the tragedy from happening? Given the macho atmosphere of the day, is it surprising that the official response to terrorism ultimately manifested itself in terror? Or that innocent children bled and died for a cause that was not their own?

Ralph Ellison was not wrong when, in *Invisible Man,* he warned of white America's blindness to the conditions regularly endured by blacks in the United States. "Someday that kind of foolishness will cause us tragic trouble." Ellison hastened to add that "all dreamers and sleepwalkers must pay the price and even the invisible victim is responsible for the fate of all." Even the John Africas have their own responsibility to the world as a whole, and not only to their own faith or vision.

The burden for the tragic failure of May 13 is abundantly shared. Some part of that burden, whether accepted or not, belongs to us all.

Index